HIROSHIGE

AF711278

Matthi Forrer

HIROSHIGE

Prints and Drawings

with essays by
Suzuki Jūzō and Henry D. Smith II

Prestel
Munich · London · New York

First published on the occasion of the exhibition 'Hiroshige'
Royal Academy of Arts, London, 3 July – 28 September 1997

Exhibition made possible by The Nippon Foundation

Exhibition Curator: Matthi Forrer
Exhibition Organiser and Curatorial Assistant: Emeline Max
Exhibition Assistant: Sam Oakley

Editor: Michael Foster
Additional editing by Lucinda Collinge
Editorial Coordinator: Sophie Lawrence
Photographic and Copyright Coordinator: Miranda Bennion

All texts by Matthi Forrer translated from the Dutch by Peter Mason
Essay by Suzuki Jūzō translated from the Japanese by Joe Earle
Maps by Martin Lubikowski at ML Design

Cover illustration: *Poling a Raft on a River, c.* 1834 (cat. 52)

© 2001, Royal Academy of Arts, London, and
Prestel Verlag, Munich · London · New York
(Hardcover edition 1997)

Prestel Verlag
Mandlstrasse 26 · 80802 Munich
Tel. (089) 381709-0, Fax (089) 381709-35;
16 West 22nd Street · New York, NY 10010
Tel. (212) 627-8199, Fax (212) 627-9866;
4 Bloomsbury Place · London WC1A 2QA
Tel. (0171) 323 5004, Fax (0171) 636 8004

Prestel books are available worldwide.
Please contact your nearest bookseller
or one of the above Prestel offices for
details concerning your local distributor.

Die Deutsche Bibliothek – CIP-Einheitsaufnahme and
Library of Congress Cataloging-in-Publication data is
available

Designed by WIGEL, Munich
Color separations by Reproline, Munich
Printed by Pera Druck Matthias GmbH, Munich
Bound by R. Oldenbourg GmbH, Munich

Printed in Germany on acid-free paper

ISBN: 3-7913-2594-9

Contents

Foreword

The Royal Academy's connection with Japan began in 1982 with the 'Great Japan Exhibition', a celebration of the art of the Edo period. In that vast survey of all the arts it was possible to show only a representative selection of colour woodblock prints. In London we have been fortunate in having the opportunity to study this most refined art more closely, first at the Academy's exhibition of the work of Katsushika Hokusai in 1991, then at the British Museum's show of Kitagawa Utamaro in 1995 and now again with our exhibition of prints and drawings by Utagawa Hiroshige.

The Hokusai exhibition, curated by Matthi Forrer and held in the year of the British Japan Festival, was a revelation to connoisseurs and public alike, showing as it did the finest impressions of Hokusai's prints from throughout the world. Now we are delighted to be able to honour his contemporary Hiroshige in the year of the bicentenary of his birth. Once again we extend our warmest thanks to the exhibition's curator, Matthi Forrer, who has travelled the world in search of the best impressions of prints by the master just as he did for the Hokusai exhibition.

Quality of impressions is crucial to a full appreciation of the subtlety of Hiroshige's art. Through the most delicate of adjustments of line and colour Hiroshige was able to convey every nuance of the passing seasons: of mist, of snow, of rain, of early spring light or of fireworks over water on a sultry summer night. Like Hokusai, Hiroshige made numerous series of prints, and his *Fifty-three Stations of the Tōkaidō Road*, the highway that runs from Edo to the Imperial capital, Kyoto, proved to be immensely popular. Indeed, some of his landscapes were in such demand that editions of thirty or forty thousand were printed. Hence the importance of showing only the best impressions in perfect condition.

We are deeply indebted to all those who have generously lent to this exhibition. We also extend our warmest thanks to The Nippon Foundation, whose support has made this exhibition possible. Suzuki Jūzō, the world's foremost scholar on Hiroshige, and the distinguished historian Henry D. Smith II contributed essays to the catalogue. We are confident that this exhibition of Hiroshige's work will provide as much pleasure as that of Hokusai.

Sir Philip Dowson CBE
President, Royal Academy of Arts

Acknowledgements

I would like to thank all those who have been so unfailingly helpful during the preparation of this exhibition and the publication that accompanies it. I owe a particular dept of gratitude to those who allowed me to study their collections: their readiness to interrupt busy schedules and to help me carry out my work efficiently were heart-warming. Unfortunately, there is not space enough to name all who ought to be mentioned, but that certainly does not mean that I have forgotten those who carried box after box of material to my desk or continued searching for prints and drawings that were at first difficult to locate. Besides the directors, trustees and registrars who granted permission for the works in their care to be loaned for the exhibition and reproduced in the catalogue, I would like to mention:

Peter Schatborn, Director, and Ger Luyten, Curator, of the Rijksprentenkabinet, Rijksmuseum, Amsterdam; Amy G. Poster, Curator of Asian Art at The Brooklyn Museum, Brooklyn, NY; Stephen Little, Pritzker Curator of Asian Art, Bernd Jesse, Curator, and his assistant, Betty Siffert, of The Art Institute of Chicago; Gerhard Pulverer, Cologne; Jan Buhl; Michael Ryan, Director, and Yoshiko Ushioda, Curator, of The Chester Beatty Library and Gallery of Oriental Art, Dublin; Frank Dunand, Curator of The Baur Collection, Geneva; H. George Mann, Highland Park, IL; Julia M. White, Curator of Asian Art, and her assistant, Susan Thomas, of the Honolulu Academy of Arts, Honolulu; Victor Harris, Acting Head of the Department of Oriental Antiquities, and Timothy Clark, Curator, The British Museum, London; Rupert Faulkner, Deputy Curator of the Far Eastern Department at the Victoria and Albert Museum, London; Yu-ying Brown, Keeper of the Japanese Department of The British Library, London; Valrae Reynolds, Curator, Asian Collections, The Newark Museum, Newark, NJ; Arthur and Charlotte Vershbow, Newton, MA; Barbara B. Ford, Curator of the Japanese Department, The Metropolitan Museum of Art, New York; Huguette Berès and Annisabelle Berès; Giselle Lambert of the Département des Estampes and Kosugi Keiko of the Division orientale, Département des Manuscrits de la Bibliothèque Nationale de France, Paris; Jean-François Jarrige, Director, and Hélène Bayou, Curator, of the Musée National des Arts Asiatiques Guimet, Paris; Deborah Del Gais Muller, Curator of Asian Art, The Museum of Art, Rhode Island School of Design, Providence.

In addition, I would like to thank the following for their advice and assistance: Peter Dailey, New York; Israel Goldman, London; Wilt Idema, Leiden University; Suzuki Jūzō, Tokyo; Roger S. Keyes, Woodacre; Ellen Landis, Curator of Art, The Albuquerque Museum, Albuquerque, NM; Minami Kazuo and Komazawa Daigaku, Tokyo; Peter Poldervaart, Rijksprentenkabinet, Rijksmuseum, Amsterdam; Edythe Polster, Deming, NM; Anders G. Rikardson, Tokyo; Henry D. Smith II of the East Asian Institute of Columbia University, New York; and Christiaan Uhlenbeck, Leiden.

It has again been a particular pleasure working with the staff of the Royal Academy of Arts. Among those to whom I owe a special debt of gratitude are Norman Rosenthal, who, once more, has shown the greatest confidence in me, and Emeline Max, whose efficiency and ceaseless enthusiasm have contributed so much to the realisation of this project.

Matthi Forrer

Author's Note

The items in the catalogue are arranged according to subject-matter and, within each thematic group, chronologically. Prints of birds and flowers (cat. 1-5) and a selection of views of Edo (cat. 6-16) are followed by series devoted to Japan's chief roads, the Tōkaidō and the Kisokaidō (cat. 17-49). These are followed, in turn, by views in the various provinces of Japan (cat. 50-92), interrupted by a group of still-lifes (cat. 81-5), and by a selection from the artist's last great series, *One Hundred Famous Views in Edo* (cat. 93-106). Preceded by images in which mist, rain, snow and moonlight play a particularly important part (cat. 107-26), the final section contains a number of drawings and other items relating to the genesis of individual prints (cat. 127-40).

The catalogue entries are arranged as follows:

Titles. Each entry has a descriptive title against the catalogue number. Where this is followed by a further title, this title is a translation of the Japanese that follows it in parentheses, which, in turn, is the title as it appears on the print. Where applicable, the series title as it appears on the print is given in translation and, in parentheses, in Japanese. Here, and throughout this volume, Japanese written characters are transliterated according to the Hepburn system of romanisation, with the usual modifications.

Publishers and dates. The name of each publisher is followed in parentheses by that of his firm where this also appears on the print. Dates given are those of the first publication of a print or series of prints, which can often be derived from the seals (see below). These dates sometimes depart from those customary in the literature on Hiroshige; the reasons for this are explained in the essay on pp. 11-27 of the present volume.

Signatures. Signatures are transcribed as they appear on the prints. The words *ga* and *hitsu* following the artist's name mean 'drawn by' and 'brush of' respectively and are a convention in Japanese art comparable to *pinxit* and *delineavit* in the West.

Seals. Apart from the artist's and publisher's seals that frequently appear on a print, the censorship seals may be of particular importance in establishing the date of a print (see Glossary). These dates appear in the form of the zodiacal sign for the year; the month given is that according to the lunar calendar in use in Japan until 1872. Throughout the present volume the zodiacal sign is translated into the equivalent year in the Gregorian calendar and the month is given in Roman numerals; where applicable, the day has been added in Arabic numerals. Thus '1858/X/9' refers to the Ninth Day of the Tenth Month in the Year of the Horse.

Block-cutters. Block-cutters are named wherever possible, with the full name followed in parentheses by the abbreviated form as it appears on the print.

Dimensions. Most prints and books were issued in Japan in standard formats. These are cited here by their indigenous names (*aiban*, etc.), which are explained in the Glossary, and followed by the exact dimensions of the sheet, in millimetres, height before width.

Owners. Where known, the names of former owners of works, preceded by 'ex-', are given in parentheses following the name of the present owner.

References. In the text of an entry '(a)', '(b)', etc. denote the various impressions and states of a print. These designations are used again, in square brackets, in the references at the end of the entry, which are mainly intended to direct the reader to additional reproductions. The literature in the references is cited in abbreviated form; full details are to be found in the Select Bibliography.

Terms that are used regularly throughout the volume are explained in the Glossary.

All verse translations from the Japanese and the Chinese are by the present author.

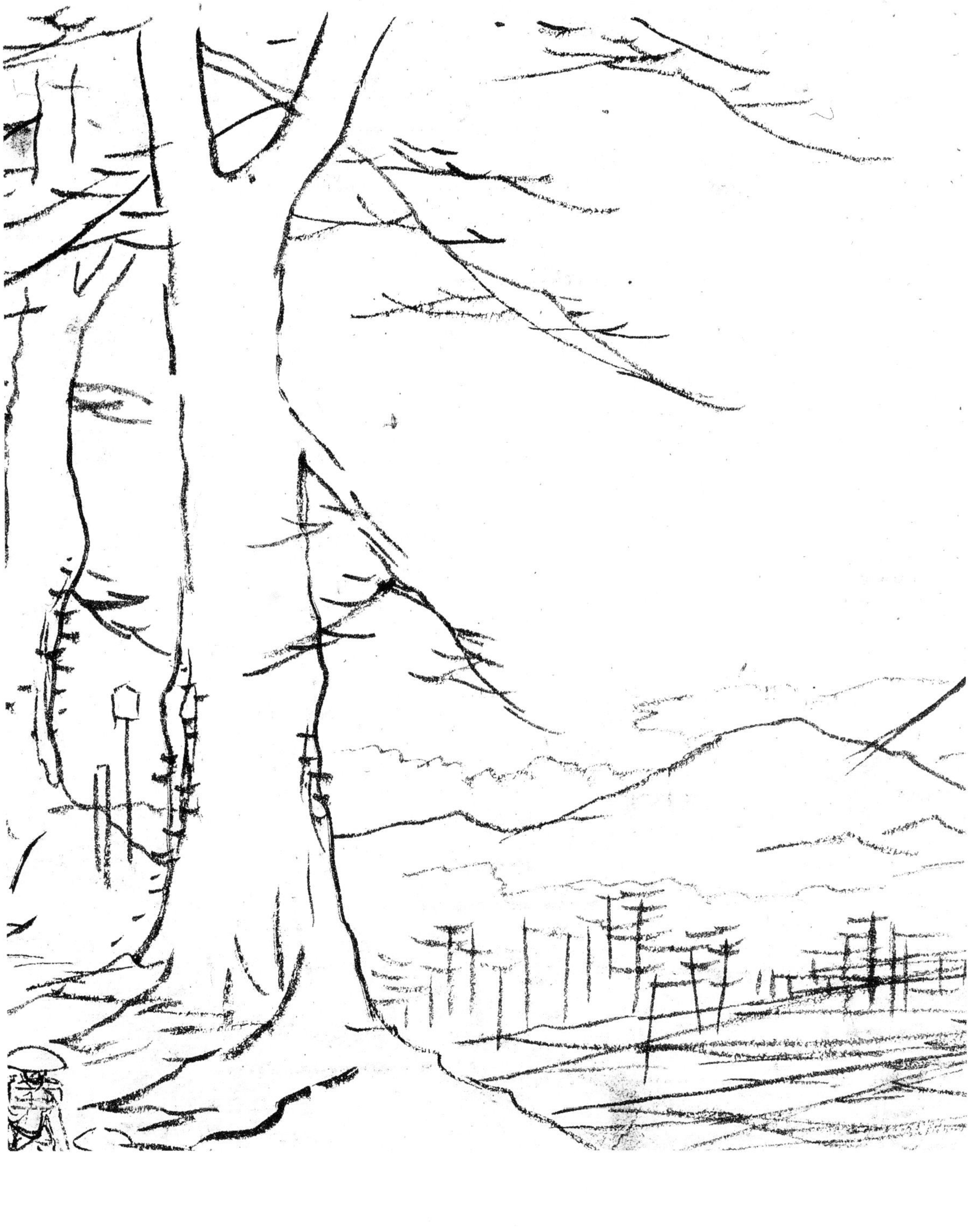

Travellers on a Sloping Road (cat. 129), detail

The Art of Hiroshige

MATTHI FORRER

Hiroshige and Hokusai are generally regarded as the two leading landscape artists in Japanese printmaking. Any list of the 'Big Six' Japanese masters of the woodblock print, in which Utamaro would naturally figure as the specialist in portraits of beautiful women and Sharaku as the specialist in portraying kabuki actors, could justifiably include Hiroshige as the foremost specialist in landscape. Choice of the two artists to complete the list—Harunobu with Kiyonaga, Moronobu or Toyokuni—would vary according to taste, but Hiroshige's place in this company is assured.

Landscapes undoubtedly constitute the most important and constant factor in Hiroshige's oeuvre, and they therefore dominate the present selection of his prints. Yet he by no means concentrated exclusively on landscape. During his early period he focused on prints of beautiful women, actors and historical figures. This was followed by a long period in which he produced landscapes and prints of birds and flowers, and, in turn, by a period of yet more landscapes, this time with fashionably clad women in the foreground, as well as several series on historical and time-honoured, 'classical' themes. Later still, he concentrated on prints with a humorous content. Nor should we forget that, like all print designers, Hiroshige also created designs for more practical purposes, not only fan prints and envelopes, but also advertising prints and boards for the game of goose. Moreover, throughout his career, he designed illustrations for countless books, many of them in more than one volume. Space precludes discussion of all these aspects of Hiroshige's career here. The present essay will therefore focus on certain features of his life and art, notably his work of the 1830s.

YOUTH AND EARLY CAREER

Utagawa Hiroshige was born in the Yaesugashi district of the Japanese capital, Edo (present-day Tokyo). The generally accepted year of his birth is 1797, though this is based solely on the memorial portrait of him by Utagawa Kunisada, which states that Hiroshige died in 1858 at the age of sixty-two. From 1758 on, his father, Andō Genemon, occupied an official position as fireman in Yaesugashi, in the present-day ward of Marunouchi in the Chiyoda district of Edo. A family document drawn up around 1866 states that Hiroshige's first name as a boy was Tokutarō. Later, he also bore the names Jūemon and Tokubei. He is supposed to have assumed the name Jūemon himself at the age of thirteen, shortly after he had lost both his parents and taken on the responsibility of caring for his family. Hiroshige inherited his father's position, and the regular income thus accruing to him may have encouraged him to embark on the precarious career of a print designer and may also help to explain why that career was so slow in getting off the ground.

Information on Hiroshige's early career is fragmentary and derives mainly from posthumous sources; however plausible, it cannot be confirmed by other evidence. For instance, a source dating from Hiroshige's lifetime reports that, at the age of ten, he made a painting of a delegation of the king of the Ryūkyū Islands to the shogun. Although a painting does exist that matches the description (*Kobijutsu*, 1983, no. 1), it is hardly possible to draw any conclusions from it. Even if an authentic work by the young Hiroshige—and the position of the signature is highly unusual—its extremely amateurish drawing bears no relation to later, better documented work by the artist. Another early work by Hiroshige is of more importance: a New Year's print showing a still-life that consists of a hat used in nō dances and a small drum (*Kobijutsu*, 1983, no. 2). The print was dated to 1813 by Uchida Minoru, but must have been designed for the New Year of 1819. The signature, 'Ichiyūsai Hiroshige', is probably the first datable use of this name on a print and corroborates information given in other sources, namely that Hiroshige received his training as a print designer from Utagawa Toyohiro (1763?–1828). The earliest mention of this was made in 1833 by Hiroshige's fellow artist Keisai Eisen (1791–1848) in *Miscellaneous Writings by the Old Anonymous* (*Mumei-ō zuihitsu*), a biographical work on print designers. Another source states that, as a child, Hiroshige had already received lessons in the traditional Kanō painting style, from Okajima Rinsai, an amateur painter and fireman who lived in the same ward. This would certainly not have been an unusual step. It is also conceivable that Hiroshige, as mentioned in yet another source, tried to obtain tuition at the age of fourteen or fifteen from the most successful designer of portraits of kabuki actors of his day, Utagawa Toyokuni (1769–1825). However, Toyokuni supposedly rejected him as a pupil, and he turned instead to Toyohiro. This would have been in 1810 or 1811, when Hiroshige was thirteen or fourteen, the usual age to begin learning a profession; but the claim, made in the first serious attempt at a biography, Iijima Kyōshin's of 1894, that he received the artname Utagawa Hiroshige from Toyohiro as early as 1812 seems improbable. By this time Toyohiro was producing no more than illustrations for one or two popular novels by Santō Kyōzan every year, and Hiroshige's alleged initial choice of teacher is wholly understandable: not only was Toyokuni highly productive, illustrating almost ten popular novels a year in addition to designing a large number of prints; he also seems to have ensured that his pupils received commissions. Toyohiro does not appear to have had this to offer: the designs for book illustrations that Hiroshige, like most aspiring print designers, created in order to make a name for himself can only have been isolated commissions that were obtained with difficulty. This goes some way towards explaining the paucity of biographical details on Hiroshige's early career.

It is difficult to assess what Hiroshige owed to Toyohiro. Some writers have attempted to demonstrate, none too convincingly, that similarities exist between city views by the two artists. These are, however, highly standardised images and, in fact, Hiroshige's earliest known prints display much closer similarities to those of the successful designers Utagawa Kunisada (1786–1865) and Keisai Eisen. These early works depict kabuki actors (1818), beautiful women (probably *c.* 1825–9, although usually dated slightly earlier) and famous heroes of the past like those found in the prints of such contemporaries as Kunisada and Utagawa Kuniyoshi (1797–1861). However, they are little more than curiosities, Hiroshige failing to match the quality of his models. The publisher Iwatoya Kisaburō seems to have been virtually the only person to have recognised talent in Hiroshige's designs and it is therefore hardly surprising that none of the early biographical sources mentions these early prints. What *is* surprising is that Hiroshige's role as an illustrator of popular novels was also marginal in the 1820s. His main contributions to this field were illustrations for two novels by Tōri Sannin (1790–1858), *Ongyoku nasake no itomichi* (4 vols., 1820) and *Dehōdai mucharon*, Part 2 (6 vols., 1822). Hiroshige also wrote and illustrated a few small works himself, such as *Shirai Gonpachi* (1 vol., 1824) and *Yoshitsune senbonzakura* (2 vols., 1824). He seems to have achieved a measure of success in 1827, when he illustrated a number of novellas, but this vanished completely during the following years. Illustration does not appear to have been where his future lay, and indeed, it was not until well into the 1830s that he started to receive commissions for illustrations for the annual de luxe poetry albums issued by clubs of amateur poets (cat. 41–8, 91, 92).

EARLY VIEWS OF EDO

After the death of the publisher Iwatoya Kisaburō around 1830, Hiroshige visited the well-known writer Takizawa Bakin (1767–1848), who introduced him to the up and coming publisher Chōjiya Heibei (Bunkeidō). There are no signs of a collaboration between Hiroshige and Chōjiya, who was chiefly a publisher of books and therefore not the person to help promote, as Iwatoya had done, Hiroshige's activity as a designer of prints of beautiful women.

Hiroshige's search for regular cooperation with a publisher may well have guided him to the new subjects that appear in his work from the early 1830s on: views in Edo and birds and flowers. Both genres had a place in the tradition of Japanese printmaking, though very different ones. Views of easily identifiable places in Edo first occur as a regular theme in prints dating from the end of the eighteenth century, notably those by Torii Kiyonaga and Katsukawa Shunchō in the then fashionable triptych format. In these the city functions primarily as a foil for fashionably dressed women as they walk through Edo, visit temples, cruise on the Sumida River, picnic during the cherry blossom season or frequent tea-houses in the Shiba and Takanawa wards along the Bay of Edo to the south of the city. As we shall see, the genre was to become a vehicle of Japanese experiments in Western-style perspective.

From 1800 on, the residents of Edo became increasingly aware of what their city had to offer and, probably as a result of growing prosperity among the urban population, many people found opportunities to visit temples, tea-houses and restaurants or, in the summer, to go on trips to the coast or to drift on the Sumida River and explore the quiet stretches on its eastern bank. The first record of this phenomenon can be found in de luxe poetry albums. Amateur poets, mainly drawn from the class of well-to-do citizens, wrote poems on famous places in the capital, usually illustrated by Hokusai. Individual prints depicting famous places in Edo are exceptional, the more inexpensive prints in a small format that were produced for a wider audience being especially scarce. In the early 1830s this suddenly changed, perhaps as part of a revival of interest in the period 1800–5. The seeds of such a revival may be found in the de luxe albums of *kyōka* poems of the 1820s, of which famous places in Edo commonly constitute the main theme. At the same time, these albums bear witness to increasing interest in other places in Japan, and a further indication of a fairly wide-ranging change in taste may perhaps be seen in the fact that the publishers Suharaya Mohei and Ihachi appear to have stepped up pressure on writers and illustrators to complete *Famous Places in Edo* (12 vols.), a large-scale undertaking initiated at the end of the eighteenth century and finally brought to a conclusion in 1834.

The major innovation of the 1830s in prints of famous places in Edo was to issue them in the standard *ōban* format. This is no doubt primarily attributable to the success of Hokusai's *Thirty-six Views of Mount Fuji*, the series, published by Nishimuraya Yohachi from 1830 onwards, that marks the recognition of the landscape print as an independent genre. The influence of the *Thirty-six Views* on Hiroshige's earliest major series, *Famous Views in the Eastern Capital*, published *c.* 1831–2 by Kawaguchiya Shōzō, is unmistakable (cat. 6, 7). Hiroshige's series does not seem to have been reprinted often enough for it to be counted an overwhelming success. Perhaps the prints were rather too expensive for that: surviving impressions are often meticulously printed in fine pigments on high-quality paper.

Hiroshige became *the* artist who recorded the famous places in Edo only with the group of prints published by Sanoya Kihei (Kikakudō), probably commencing in 1832 (cat. 8–10). The difference in success between *Famous Views* and this second group may be explained in part by the location of their publishers' shops: Kawaguchiya's was in the centre of the city, at Ryōgoku Hirōkōji, close to Ryōgoku Bridge, while Sanoya's shop was at Shiba Shinmeimae, which all travellers to or from Edo along the Tōkaidō Road had to pass. No doubt tourists on this route ensured a good turnover of prints of this kind, which were eminently suitable as souvenirs. Certainly, the series published by Sanoya was issued in very large editions and was often reprinted even fifteen or twenty years later. Sales of some prints must have exceeded fifteen or twenty thousand.

The different clientele targeted by these publishers is reflected in the various formats in which they issued prints of famous places in Edo. Kawaguchiya—and Fujiokaya Hikotarō, another publisher whose shop was in the centre of the city—also used the tall, narrow *tanzakuban* format, while Kihei strove for diversity in smaller formats, such as the *aiban*, *chūban* and *koban*, aimed at the tourist with a smaller purse. It is difficult to determine whether or not a series of thirty prints by Hiroshige of famous places in Edo, published in the *koban* format by Enshūya Hikobei at Nihonbashi, the starting-point of the Tōkaidō Road, was intended primarily for the tourist market. The same applies to a few dozen other designs by Hiroshige that were issued in small formats by various minor, virtually unknown publishers. Yet it may well have been the diversity of markets catered for by publishers in different parts of the city that enabled Hiroshige to continue producing successful views of Edo for the rest of his career. Undoubtedly, the enormous popularity of this theme—which accounts for roughly a quarter of the artist's entire oeuvre of prints—and of such other topographical subjects favoured by Hiroshige as the stations of the Tōkaidō Road and views of Lake Biwa in Ōmi Province was aided by the fact that, in the course of the nineteenth century, increasing numbers of people in Japan were able to travel.

In view of the rather limited range of subjects, Hiroshige's success in keeping alive interest in images of Edo was no mean achievement. Although the number of famous locations expanded somewhat over the years, some ten or twelve remained 'musts'. For instance, of a total of almost eight hundred prints in the standard *ōban* format, Hiroshige devoted more than fifty to the Ryōgoku Bridge, over forty to Ueno, Takanawa and the Kinryūzan Temple at Asakusa, and more than thirty to the Yoshiwara, Susaki and Gotenyama.[1] These subjects were often combined with almost equally obligatory features, such as snow (Sumida River and Asakusa), moonlight (Takanawa), evening light (naturally enough, in the Yoshiwara, Edo's pleasure district), fireworks (above Ryōgoku Bridge) and cherry blossom (beside the Sumida, in Gotenyama or in Ueno). That Hiroshige was concerned to maintain his reputation as the leading artist for views of Edo's famous places can be deduced from his last great series of prints, *One Hundred Famous Views in Edo*, which is an impressive demonstration of vigorous powers of invention by a sixty-year-old artist (cat. 93–106).

BIRDS AND FLOWERS

Some of the above remarks also apply to Hiroshige's prints of birds and flowers, which probably began to appear in 1832: the number of different birds is limited and here, too, there are regular combinations, such as kingfishers and irises, tits and camellias, nightingales and cherry blossom, hawks and pine trees, the Indian peacock and the equally exotic peony, originally imported from China. Hiroshige tried to achieve a virtual monopoly of this field, as he had of views of Edo. It was a theme, however, that possessed a longer tradition: already found in Chinese and traditional Japanese painting, it was first made the subject of prints—either in albums or as single sheets—by Koryūsai (*c.* 1770), Utamaro (1790), Kitao Masayoshi (1789) and Kitao Shigemasa (1805). Subsequently, it formed an important part of the emergent interest in naturalism evidenced by such innovators as the Chinese-influenced Nagasaki school of painting and the Dutch-influenced tradition of the Akita Ranga, supported by the *daimyō* of Akita.

Yet fascination with naturalism is not sufficient to explain the large demand for prints of birds and flowers. An important part was also played by the considerable interest that poets, both of the traditional *haiku* and, especially from the 1780s on, of the more popular *kyōka*, displayed in birds, fish, insects and flowers. In addition, aviaries both reflected and contributed to the popularity of birds, not only those constructed by many a *daimyō* or

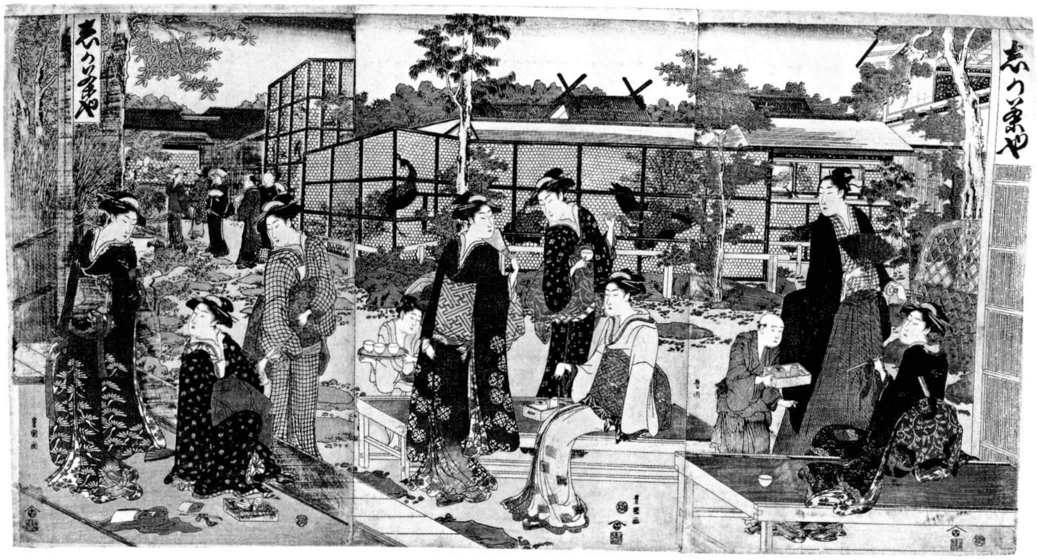

Fig. 1 Utagawa Toyokuni, *The Garden of the Kachō Tea-house in Edo*, *c.* 1792. Museo d'Arte Orientale, Genoa

samurai, but also those kept by some of the larger tea-houses, especially in Edo. (Aviaries of the latter kind, in which exotic birds naturally stole the show, can be seen in prints from the 1780s and 1790s by Kiyonaga, Shunchō and Toyokuni [fig. 1].[2]) Hiroshige was thus able to study at first hand even the many foreign birds depicted in his prints. The naturalness of his birds as they fly through the air or perch on a branch is astonishing and the artist's extraordinarily sharp powers of observation are revealed in his ability to 'freeze' wings in flight.

In their books on Hiroshige, neither Uchida Minoru (1932) nor Suzuki Jūzō (1970) attempted to estimate the number of the artist's designs on the theme of birds and flowers. Yoshida Susugu did so in his article of 1967, but that has been superseded by a study written by Ōkubo Junichi, who gives the following figures: twenty-five designs in the *ōtanzaku* format (the widest of the tall, narrow sheets favoured for this genre), most of them published by Wakasaya Yoichi, and a total of sixty-three in the slightly narrower *chūtanzaku* format, forty-two of them published by Kawaguchiya Shōzō, eight by Fujiokaya Hikotarō and thirteen by minor or unknown publishers. Ōkubo mentions a further 105 designs, in the much narrower *aitanzaku* format, bringing the total number of tall, narrow-format designs alone to almost two hundred. The majority of these contain a poem. It is sometimes claimed that such prints were often pasted on screens or sliding doors as a form of interior decoration. This cannot be ruled out entirely, but I have never come across an instance of the practice and, if it was as common as has been suggested, one would expect to find more copies in mediocre or poor condition, soaked off the screens or doors after having been exposed to smoke and cooking vapours for decades.

Hiroshige no doubt achieved a fair degree of success in the early 1830s with his views of famous places in Edo and his images of birds and flowers, yet his decisive breakthrough came with *The Fifty-three Stations of the Tōkaidō Road* (cat. 17–28, 110–13). Tradition has it that the origins of this series of prints lay in the artist's being selected to escort the white horse that was presented each year to the emperor by the shogun. On this mission he travelled the Tōkaidō Road from Edo to Kyoto in the Eighth Month of 1832. Upon returning to Edo in the Ninth or Tenth Month, the traditional narrative continues, he approached the publishers Takenouchi Magohachi and Tsuruya Kiemon, offering them designs for prints that he had made on the basis of sketches done during the journey. This account, culminating in sudden recognition of a hitherto neglected talent, has greatly appealed to the romantic imagination and has remained largely unchallenged. Yet it is based solely on the biography of Hiroshige written in 1894 by Iijima Kyōshin, whose only evidence was an unconfirmed statement by Hiroshige III (1843–94), a pupil of Hiroshige's who adopted the name of his teacher some seven years after the latter's death. If the course of events described by Iijima is apocryphal, this would have important consequences for the dating of the Tōkaidō series.

It cannot be emphasised too strongly that ascribing precise dates to individual prints is virtually impossible before 1852, when date seals replaced the *kiwame* seal as part of the Japanese censorship regulations. In the case of *The Fifty-three Stations of the Tōkaidō Road* we do at least have a *terminus ante quem*: in 1834 the series was published in two albums with a foreword, dated in the First Month of that year, by Yomo Ryūsui and a list of contents. If the traditional story of its genesis is correct, the entire series of fifty-five prints must have been issued over a period of little more than a year. Although the publication of the series was a collaborative enterprise between the hitherto totally unknown Takenouchi Magohachi and the more established Tsuruya Kiemon—they issued eleven designs jointly, while the rest were produced by Takenouchi alone—this is still a quite exceptionally fast rate of production. It appears unlikely that the work of a designer who can hardly be said to have 'arrived' would be put on the market at such speed and it is also improbable that a beginner like Takenouchi would have had the resources or credit to invest so heavily in woodblocks and paper. It therefore seems natural to assume that the publication of *The Fifty-three Stages of the Tōkaidō Road*, an undertaking on a virtually unprecedented scale, was spread out over a longer period, commencing, say, in 1831, if not in 1830.

This more plausible chronological framework allows Hiroshige's participation in the mission to the emperor—if that, too, is not mythical—to fall during the period before he relinquished his official position as fireman in 1832 in favour of Andō Nakajirō (who then became head of the Andō family). A further advantage is that one can imagine a keener rivalry, or at least reciprocal influence, between Hiroshige's Tōkaidō series and Hokusai's *Thirty-six Views of Mount Fuji* of *c.* 1830–5. That said, it is hard to point to parallels between the two series, beyond, perhaps, similar ideas in, for example, Hokusai's

Mishima Pass and view of Ejiri, on the one hand, and Hiroshige's stations of Hamamatsu and Yokkaichi on the other. The revised dates for the Tōkaidō series do, however, make the advertisement that appeared with the publication of the series as a whole in 1834 less surprising than it would otherwise seem. This advertisement announces publication of similar, yet smaller series, of places along the routes to Ōyama, Enoshima, Akibayama and Ise. Only two of these prints—both of the route to Enoshima—have survived,[3] though a few others have possibly been preserved in the form of drawings. The advertisement also announces two further series, *Eight Views in Ōmi Province* and one devoted to the stations of the Kisokaidō Road, both of which have survived, as well as some books on the theme of 'One Hundred Poems of a Hundred Poets', which have not been preserved, at least not under the titles given in the advertisement. The publisher Takenouchi would hardly have advertised such an impressive list of forthcoming work by Hiroshige if he had not seen drawings for at least some of the projected series, yet the customary dating of the *Fifty-three Stations* makes it unlikely that the artist could have found time to design other prints. Everything points, in fact, to a working relationship between Takenouchi and Hiroshige that could scarcely have become so well established in the short time allegedly taken to produce the Tōkaidō series.

The advertisement describes the Kisokaidō prints as 'a series of naturalistic views, with landscapes and people'. The express mention of people would seem to suggest that they had been the key to the success of the Tōkaidō series: the human presence in the prints enabled viewers everywhere to speculate about people's activities in the places depicted. Such speculation, and discussion, must have played an important part in the reception of practically all types of print. It is not difficult to imagine how prints of kabuki actors, for example, could serve as a pretext for friends to gather together of an evening and compare notes on various actors' performances. Hiroshige's landscapes will have encouraged similar discussions. Who is the man in the palanquin in *Travellers Passing a Shrine in the Mist*, for instance, and what are the figures on the left doing (cat. 19)? Or again, *A Roadside Restaurant* may have elicited debate on where the best *tororoshiru* could be eaten (cat. 23). And just what is happening in Seki (cat. 27)? The subtitles of the prints went some way to providing an explanation, but much was left to the viewer's imagination. The latter was no doubt also fed by an extremely popular novel by Jippensha Ikku (1765–1831), published serially between 1802 and 1809, which describes the doings of two adventurers from Edo during their journey along the Tōkaidō Road. The novel spawned a sequel and all kinds of imitations, ensuring that it retained its popularity with a large public until the late nineteenth century.

Publication of the Kisokaidō series, which was begun by Keisai Eisen and was issued jointly by Takenouchi and Iseya Rihei, is usually held to have started in 1835. As with the Tōkaidō prints, Hiroshige's contribution to the series maintains a balance between images that emphasise the landscape and those that favour the human figure (cat. 35–40). Eisen's designs, on the other hand, are far more strongly orientated towards the latter and feature all kinds of figures engaged in a variety of activities, including a group of blind people attacking one another with their sticks. Indeed, the advertisement's 'naturalistic views, with landscapes and people' might almost be taken as a description of Eisen's designs. If that were so, not only would Eisen have begun the series earlier than generally supposed—probably *c.* 1831–2—but also Hiroshige's involvement in the project could have dated from 1834, the year of the advertisement. The traditional date of 1835 for commencement of publication of the series is based on a reference to that year on an umbrella in Eisen's design for the station of Nihonbashi. Yet with more reason this can be interpreted as marking the beginning not of the series, but of the collaboration between Takenouchi and Iseya, since both their trademarks appear on this print.

THE 'EIGHT VIEWS IN ŌMI PROVINCE' AND WESTERN INFLUENCE

In contrast to the Tōkaidō and Kisokaidō series, the prints in *Eight Views in Ōmi Province* (cat. 68–75), advertised as 'in ink with light colour washes', do not encourage speculation on the part of the viewer: they are pure landscapes with an almost classical atmosphere, completely in accordance with the traditional poems printed on them. The *Eight Views* thus represent a new departure for Hiroshige, who perhaps wished to demonstrate the breadth of his talent. This series is one of his most coherent and impressive, and the fact that the artist later devoted more than fifteen series to the same theme, most of them in smaller formats, may indicate that he himself regarded it as particularly suited to his talents.

The series consists of eight views of Lake Biwa in Ōmi Province. Series of eight depictions of a certain place originated in Chinese poetry and painting in connection with the Hsiao and Hsiang rivers near Lake Tung-T'ing in Hunan Province, but the genre was absorbed by Japanese painting at an early date. Japanese places were gradually substituted for the Chinese ones, as in one of the earliest known examples in woodblock printing, which dates from the late seventeenth century. The genre became more common in prints during the early eighteenth century, which often bore the same poems as Hiroshige's prints. By the end of the eighteenth century such series of eight images were often displayed in the street in viewers that were fitted with a special lens, producing the illusion of depth. By the early years of the next century, therefore, the genre was familiar to a large section of the public, as evidenced by a few rather experimental prints in a small format by Hokusai. Such images had become a focus of Japanese interest in Western-style perspective and remained so until the 1820s, several series of views in Ōmi, such as those by Shinsai, Shuntei and Kunitora, displaying strong Western influence.

Against this historical background, Hiroshige's *Eight Views* emerge as specifically 'Japanese' landscapes in their adoption of more traditional perspective and in their use of colour woodblock printing techniques. Comparison of Hiroshige's series with Shinsai's *Eight Views in Ōmi Province* of *c.* 1820, for example, reveals striking compositional similarities between both artist's views of Ishiyama and Seta. Although Hiroshige retains the bend in the shore of the lake (cat. 69, 70), his horizon is a straight line. Shinsai's horizon is curved, a specifically Western element derived, of course, from the knowledge that the earth is spherical (fig. 2). Another point of difference is that, while in Shinsai's images the cliffs around the lake are coloured in a variety of bright tints, Hiroshige tries to

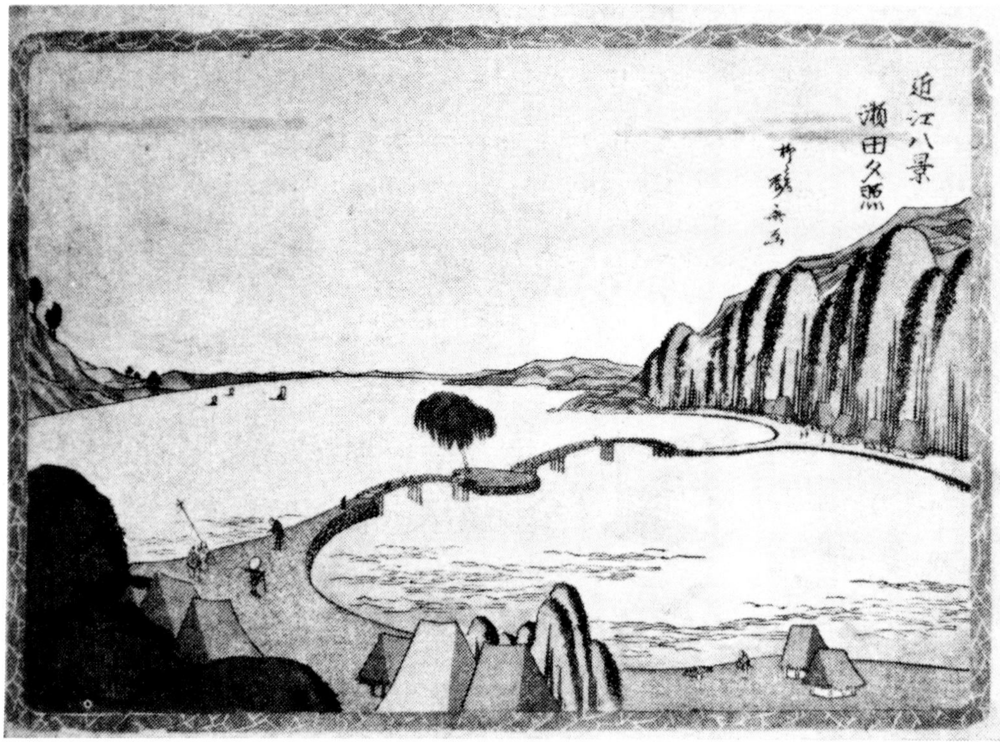

Fig. 2 Ryūryūkyo Shinsai, *Evening Glow at Seta Bridge*, c. 1820

create the impression of successive outcrops of mountain. By allowing distant mountains to emerge above the fog or mist, he approaches traditional Chinese perspective, in which the various sections from top to bottom correspond to increasing degrees of proximity to the viewer. Moreover, Shinsai's relatively aggressive colour contrasts give way, in Hiroshige's prints, to sequences of transitional shades. A significant part in all this is played by light or uncoloured areas, which Hiroshige employs not only descriptively, but also as a means of conveying depth. Similar comparisons can be made between Hiroshige and his predecessors in the field of views of Edo. Again, antecedents existed in the form of prints designed to be seen through special viewers and here, too, Hiroshige manages to modify the tradition in a subtle way, not by giving the impression that he had no understanding of Western perspective, but by applying it more sparingly and in a generally less striking way.

There would seem to be two main exceptions to Hiroshige's reticence towards Western influence, the so-called *Reisho Tōkaidō* of *c.* 1848–9 (cat. 29–33, 127–30) and *One Hundred Famous Views in Edo* of 1856–8 (cat. 93–106). In the former series we often seem to be looking down from a high vantage point, into a street, into shops or a harbour. Yet it is debatable whether this represents Western influence at all and was not derived, instead, from the kind of perspective frequently encountered in the popular travel guides of the period, the *meishoki* (fig. 3). This bird's-eye perspective alternates in this series with broad panoramas that, with their low viewpoints (cat. 30, 129) and clear vanishing points,

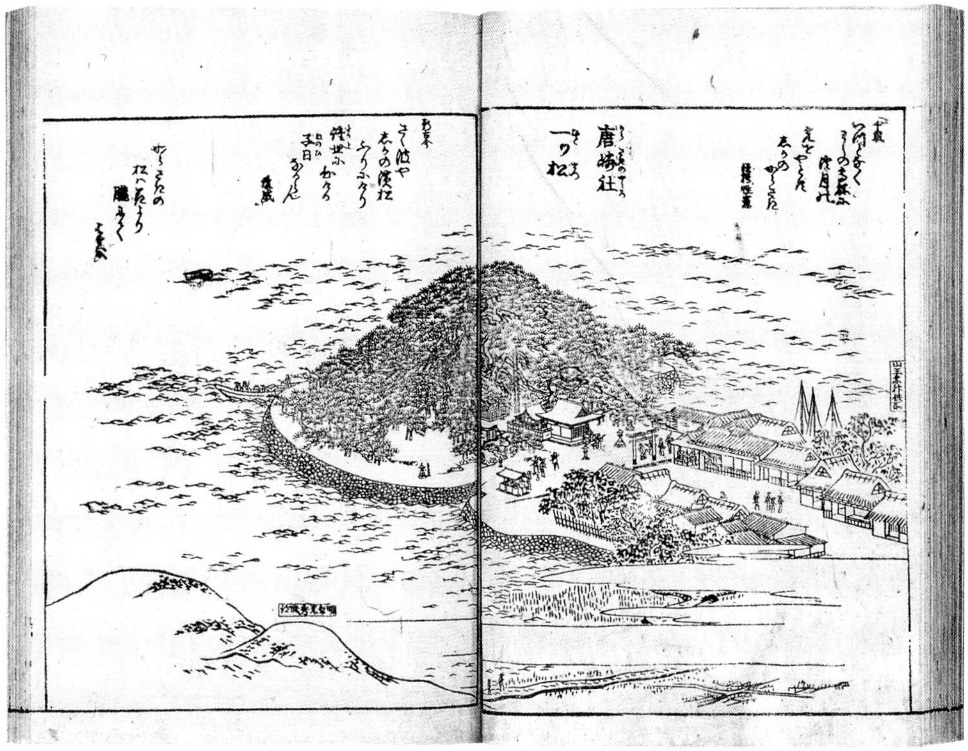

Fig. 3 *Bird's-eye View of the Pine at Karasaki*, from the album *Tōkaidō meisho zue*, illustrated by Kitao Masayoshi and Takehara Shunsensai, Edo, 1797. National Museum of Ethnology, Leiden

do unquestionably betray Western influence. On occasion, Hiroshige even ventures typically Western cloud formations (cat. 33).

In *One Hundred Famous Views in Edo* Hiroshige frequently places strikingly large-scale objects, people and animals, or parts of them, in the foreground. This device, doubtless derived from Western art, was obviously intended to add depth to the composition. The results in Hiroshige's prints, however, are seldom satisfactory, appearing exaggerated or even comical, as in the print of Yotsuya, where the viewer is confronted directly with the rear end of a horse—and more besides. Occasionally, this approach does work most effectively. In the print of Massaki, for example (cat. 102), we almost feel that we are guests in the tea-house, while in that of the Kameido plum orchard (cat. 93) we enjoy a better view of the tree than the other visitors, who are kept at a distance behind a fence.

Even in these two series, Hiroshige rarely gives overt expression to familiarity with Western artistic principles, certainly less so than such contemporaries of his as Kuniyoshi, Kunisada and even Hokusai. With the exception of some isolated examples—the clear shadows cast by the moon above Saruwakamachi, say, or the reflections in the water at Kyōbashi (cat. 98, 104)—Hiroshige's treatment of light, too, owes little to the bold Western effects admired in Japan. His concern was more with the subtle play of light (cat. 39, 56, 99), notably moonlight (cat. 35, 67, 69).

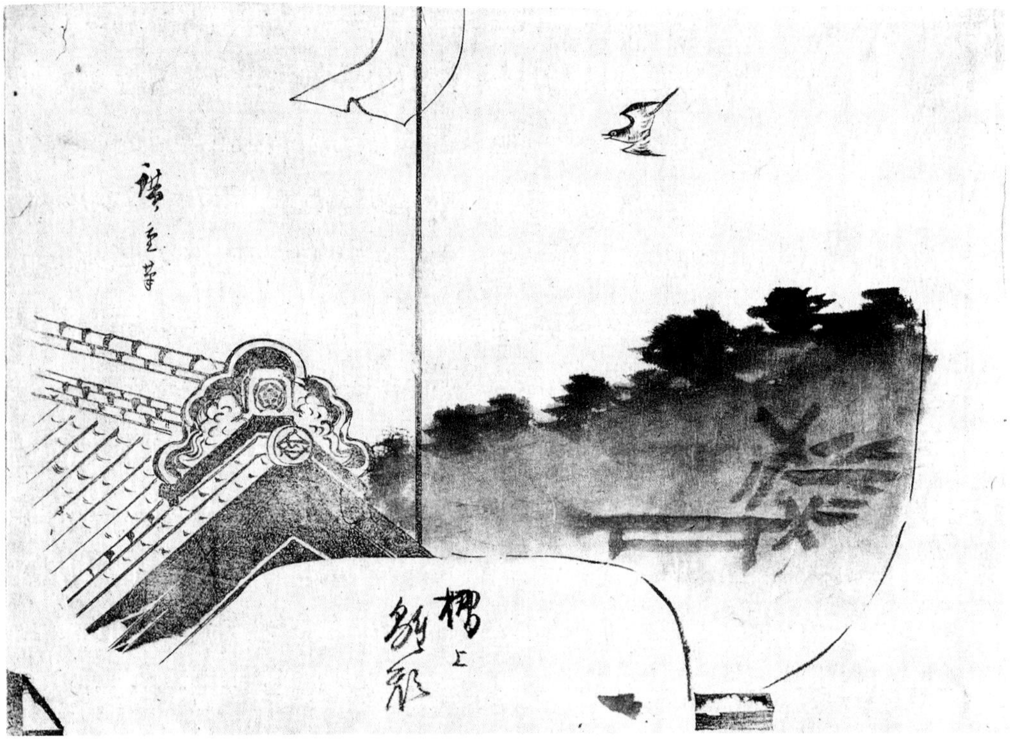

Fig. 4 *A Cuckoo and the Roof of the Komakatadō*, proof impression of a fan print, signed 'Hiroshige hitsu', *c.* 1857, with additions by the artist on the right-hand side. National Museum of Ethnology, Leiden

ARTISTIC INTENTIONS AND WOODBLOCK PRINTING TECHNIQUES

There has been much speculation about the intentions underlying Hiroshige's art, about the essence of that art and, therefore, about the personality of its creator. He has been termed a romantic, a humorist and even an Impressionist *avant la lettre*. Apart from his work, Hiroshige himself has left us with very little from which to gain an idea of his aims. In the preface to *A Hundred Views of Mount Fuji* he implies that he works in a different way from Hokusai when he writes that the illustrations are based on first-hand observation ('original sketches'), even though it was not possible to incorporate every detail. He has striven for realistic portrayals, since not everyone has the opportunity to visit the places depicted. He returns to the omission of details in the album *Landscape Views on the Tōkaidō* (*Tōkaidō fūkei zue*) of 1851, where he writes that 'everything lacking in taste and grace must be omitted'. In 1849, in the drawing manual *Ehon tebikigusa*, which unfortunately was never completed, Hiroshige had the following to say: 'Paintings are based on the form of things. So if you copy the form and add style and meaning, the result is a painting', and also: 'To depict a beautiful view the artist must know how to combine with one another each of the elements that constitute that view'.

Perhaps these few written statements are more valuable than they appear at first sight. Hiroshige's mention of 'original sketches' is certainly not in line with classical Chinese ideals, according to which an image reproduces the 'idea' of a landscape, not a specific

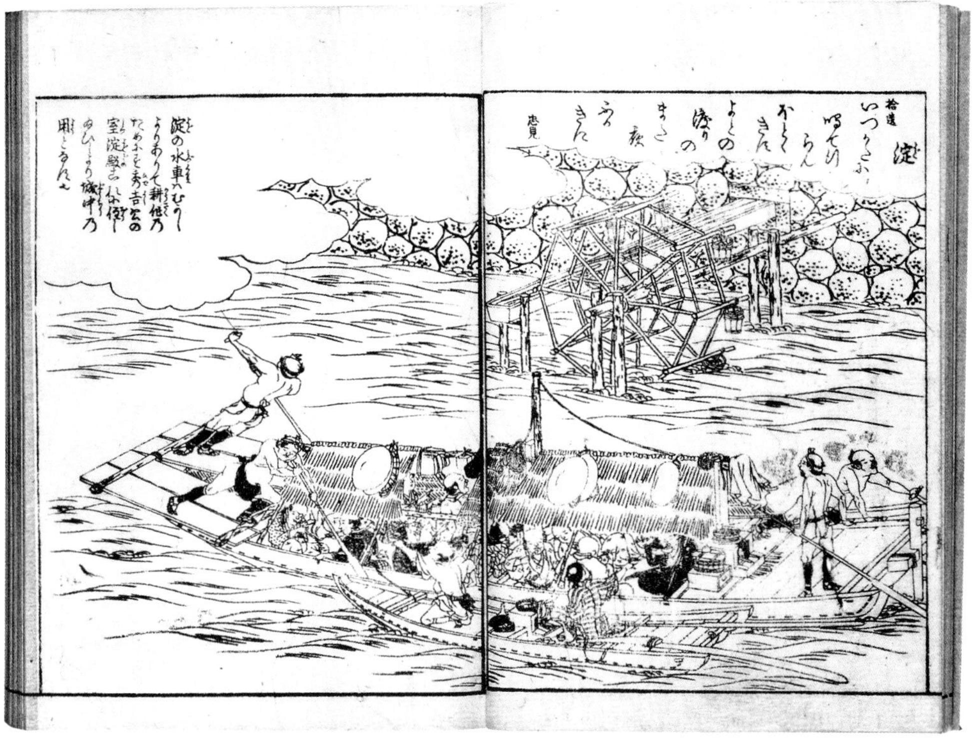

Fig. 5 *Ferry on the Yodo River*, sheets 12b/13a of volume 5 of *Miyako rinsen meishō zue*, various illustrators, Kyoto, 1799. National Museum of Ethnology, Leiden

location. Similarly, the exhortation to 'copy the form', then 'add style and meaning' reverses Chinese notions, which held that 'form' can result only from an 'idea' that has led to an understanding of 'meaning'. Hiroshige seems almost to be at pains to disassociate himself from the ancient tradition of Chinese painting and it is even conceivable that, in the preface to *A Hundred Views of Mount Fuji*, he is implicitly accusing Hokusai of subservience to that tradition.

Hiroshige's statements are reflected in his prints in a more concrete way, too. Many of his landscapes do indeed tell of a reality that has been manipulated, for example by the selection of a particular vantage point or by the omission of parts that make the view lack 'style' or 'meaning'. 'Style and meaning' were then 'added to the form' by skilful exploitation of the full potential of the woodcut medium. Although some of the sketches included here do not permit this procedure to be traced in detail—the final prints were never made—they do offer a clear illustration of Hiroshige's ideas. In particular, the very sketchy views of Lake Biwa (cat. 131–4) betray a firm grasp of all the constituent elements of the landscape, enabling the essence of the scene to be recorded in a few flowing brushstrokes.

It is not known whether rough sketches of this kind were worked up into more precise drawings—cat. 136, for example—by a professional copyist, employed by the publisher, or by a pupil of the artist, under the latter's direct supervision. Neither can we be certain that it was at Hiroshige's own request that a sizeable part of the boat in the foreground of cat. 136 was corrected on a piece of paper and then pasted on the drawing in place of the rejected area. We do know that the publisher had to submit such drawings to the censor, who added his seal of approval. The block-cutter then pasted the drawing face down on a woodblock and, woodcut being a form of relief printing, proceeded to cut away everything except the lines of the drawing and any areas that were to appear black in the final print, destroying the original drawing in the process (see cat. 138, 139). A number of proofs were taken from this line, or key, block, all of them including the marks—a corner and a straight line along which to align the paper—that the printer would later require to print the various colour blocks properly 'in register' (fig. 4). Since these markers from the line-block were printed on every proof and since the colour blocks were cut from those proofs, the markers always ended up in exactly the same place. The artist noted the desired colours on the proofs, taking a different proof sheet for each colour. Thus a print with eight colours called for the cutting of one line-block and eight colour blocks, with a series of nine proofs. This obviously meant that different colour areas—usually two—might overlap.

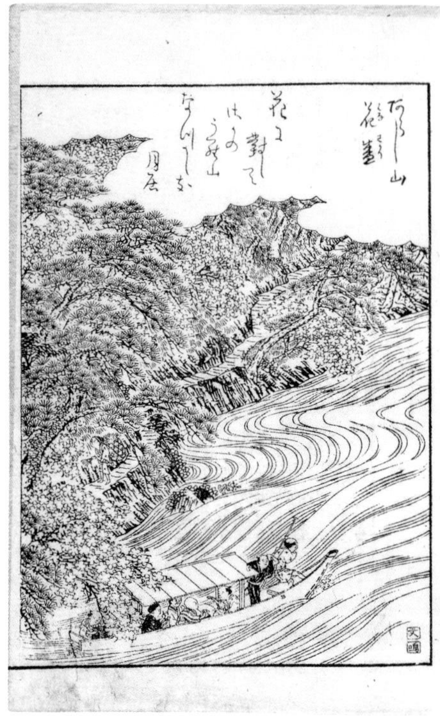

Fig. 6 *Pleasure Boat near Arashiyama*, sheet 15a of volume 5 of *Miyako meisho zue*, illustrated by Takehara Shunchōsai, Osaka, 1787. National Museum of Ethnology, Leiden

During the actual production process, each block—line-block and colour blocks—had to be inked anew for each sheet. It was therefore particularly important for the printer to apply the pigments, generally vegetable-based, with the greatest care, nowhere more so than in gradation printing (*bokashi*). Often employed in areas of sky or water, but not exclusively there, the latter required particular patience and skill. For example, if the sky was to become a progressively lighter blue towards a horizon line that was pierced by the sails of boats, the boats were drawn in ink on the blue colour block so that the printer could see how far down to apply the ink. All the same, the printer occasionally took the liberty of applying ink more or less extensively than necessary. Publishers took liberties too. Hiroshige's instructions for grey *bokashi* on the proof of a print from the *Eight Views in Ōmi Province* show that he wished the grey to be applied from the foot of the mountains upwards (cat. 137), yet impressions exist in which the grey has been applied from the top. Comparable differences can be observed in the two states of Kanbara (cat. 21, 112) and the numerous variants of Shōno (cat. 25, 110).

Hiroshige himself may not have wished to be regarded primarily as an artist of mist, rain, moonlight and snow, but investing these climatic and atmospheric conditions with 'style and meaning' in terms of the woodcut medium does appear to have been a source of endless fascination to him. Certainly, it is hard to think of any other artist who explored the potential of *bokashi*—probably first employed in 1774, by Toriyama Sekien in the *Sekien gafu*—as fully as he did. It is almost as though he was attempting to compete with painting, in which gradations of tone are, of course, infinitely easier to achieve. By frequently incorporating the grain of the woodblock in the final print did Hiroshige perhaps wish actually to draw attention to his ability to transcend woodcut in images that approached painting (cat. 29, 56, 96, 103)? Be that as it may, woodblock printing had the enormous advantage of virtually unlimited reproduction, enabling thousands of people to enjoy his art.

Comparison of the work of Hokusai and Hiroshige, already undertaken by countless scholars, may possibly be reduced to the difference between form and mood. Hokusai's

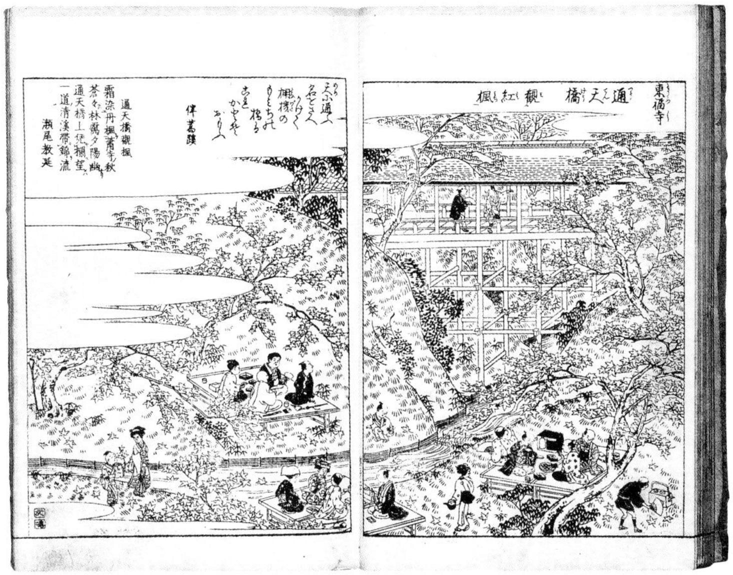

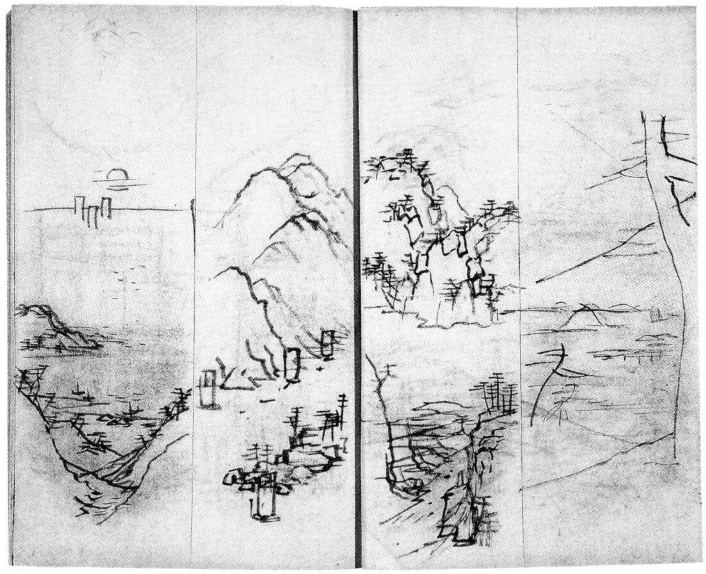

Fig. 7 *View of Tōfukuji with the bridge known as Tsūtenkyō*, sheets 21b/22a of volume 3 of *Miyako rinsen meishō zue*, various illustrators, Kyoto, 1799. National Museum of Ethnology, Leiden

Fig. 8 Two pages from an album of landscape sketches by Hiroshige. The British Museum, London

chief concern is form. Surprising yet firmly structured compositions of well-defined forms—that is where his innovative strength lies. Hiroshige, on the other hand, eschews depicting everything down to the last detail. Reality, for him, is to be sought in a highly refined range of colours, orchestrated to articulate mood (cat. 38).

EXTENT OF OEUVRE AND WORKING METHOD

It is often said that Hiroshige was extraordinarily productive—figures of up to 12,000 designs have been quoted—and that he was the victim of unscrupulous publishers who continually expected him to come up with new designs and who carried on printing the existing ones until the blocks were completely worn out. Both claims are exaggerated. The number of prints that Hiroshige designed can be estimated at between 4,000 and 4,500, plus illustrations for slightly more than 120 books. The majority of these prints—almost 1,000—are of places in Edo. Other large groups are the stations of the Tōkaidō Road (almost 800) and views in the various provinces (again almost 800). Subjects less generally associated with Hiroshige, such as beautiful women, actors and historical figures, account for some 600 prints, birds and flowers for slightly more than 200 and fan prints, assuming many to have been lost, for about 350.

It seems rather unlikely that Hiroshige was under continual pressure to supply new designs. Both the artist and his publishers were subject to economic laws that neither party could afford to ignore. In calculating their risks, publishers examined retail possibilities closely and, especially in an age that was sometimes very turbulent, will naturally have been forced to recognise that a print is not an essential element in day-to-day survival. Of course, they tried to find as broad a market as possible and that no doubt explains the large number of series of small-format prints that Hiroshige designed. This market was, therefore, also important to the artist, who was paid individually for each design. The publisher had first to recover the considerable cost of investing in the copyist, blocks, block-cutters, pigments, paper and printers, so it should come as no surprise that a number of Hiroshige's successful designs were reprinted time and again. If we assume a standard edition of between ten and fifteen thousand sheets (at a time when the population of Edo alone was already 1.5 million), a total of twenty to thirty thousand impressions for a best-selling print would seem to be nothing out of the ordinary.[4]

Hiroshige himself, as we have seen, claims to have based at least some of his designs on direct observation, and sketchbooks and diaries have indeed survived from journeys that he undertook. Yet he certainly did not travel the length and breadth of Japan. As both Uchida and Suzuki have shown, several of the artist's views of Kyoto and Osaka, and many of those from the series *Famous Views in the Sixty-odd Provinces*, are based on images in contemporary travel guides, the *meishoki* (figs. 5–7). A comparison between the models and Hiroshige's treatment of them provides an insight into his approach, which is more wide-ranging than one might have supposed. While in some images he obeys his own rule that elements lacking in 'style and meaning' should be omitted, in others he follows his model almost down to the last detail. Of greater importance to an understanding of Hiroshige's working methods are his sketches (fig. 8). Unfortunately, much research remains to be done in this area. Apart from a few early sketches that are unmistakably by Hiroshige, there are innumerable albums in various collections that would repay careful study. Suzuki has demonstrated that one group of albums containing travel sketches is a recent forgery. The sensationalism that accompanied another recent discovery, that the models for Hiroshige's great Tōkaidō series can be found in a sketchbook claimed to be by Shiba Kōkan,[5] has obscured rather than illuminated the issues: the sketchbook, even if not a forgery, cannot possibly have anything to do with Kōkan.

CRITICAL HISTORY

Western interest in Hiroshige dates from the end of the last century. Many painters would have concurred with Pissarro, who in 1893 wrote to his son after visiting an exhibition of 300 prints by Utamaro and Hiroshige: 'Hiroshige is a marvellous Impressionist.' The numerous Western paintings in which Japanese prints appear on walls almost always include a few typical Hiroshige designs. In 1887 Van Gogh painted copies in oils of two images from *One Hundred Famous Views in Edo* (cat. 93, 94) and there can be little doubt that the work of Hiroshige was a source of inspiration for Whistler's *Nocturne in Blue and Gold: Old Battersea Bridge* (*c.* 1872–5).

It was the American connoisseur Ernest Fenollosa (1853–1908) who, in 1896, first tried to fix Hiroshige's position in the history of Japanese printmaking, characterising him as a landscape artist *par excellence*.[6] From the outset, Western students of Hiroshige were in advance of their Japanese counterparts, especially as a result of the work of John Stewart

Happer and Edward F. Strange. In the catalogue of his own collection, auctioned in London in 1909, the former made the first serious attempt to establish a chronology for Hiroshige's work, thus laying the foundation for much later research into the various states and editions of the prints. This was the subject of an extensive study by Will E. Edmunds in 1922, and in 1925 Strange, too, built on Happer's work in what remains the only large-scale Western monograph on the artist.

Early Japanese research on the artist, beginning with the pioneering work of Iijima Kyōshin (Hanjirō), who in 1894 published a number of biographical articles on Hiroshige and other artists of the Utagawa school, concentrated on piecing together biographical information. Critical reflection on Hiroshige's actual work dates from considerably later. The 'Memorial Exhibition' marking the sixtieth anniversary of the artist's death in 1917 was organised by Watanabe Shōzaburō, but the great pioneer in Japan of more comprehensive research was Uchida Minoru, whose monograph appeared in its definitive form in 1932. What is still regarded as the standard work on Hiroshige, Suzuki Jūzō's study, was published in 1970.

Important recent research has been devoted to specific areas of Hiroshige's oeuvre. Many problems remain to be solved, however, and it may be necessary for us to free ourselves from reliance on source material that is often untrustworthy and on the views of our predecessors. One of the great virtues of Hiroshige's art is the immediacy of its emotional appeal. It is to be hoped that, as in the past, this will inspire scholars and enthusiasts alike to fresh discoveries.

NOTES

1 Ishii Kendō, 'Shōdai Hiroshige no fūkeiga', *Bijutsu no Nihon*, 104 (1916), arrives at slightly different figures on the basis of a larger total number of prints, but the general outlines remain the same: Ryōgoku 65, Sumidagawa 60, Takanawa 53, Sensōji Asakusa 46, Shin Yoshiwara 45, Ueno 38, Susaki 38, Gotenyama 35, etc.

2 See also the triptych by Toyokuni illustrated in L. Smith, *Ukiyoe: Images of Unknown Japan*, London, 1988, no. 154 (two sheets only).

3 See Forrer, 1994, G458.

4 These figures are based partly on contemporary sources relating to popular novels and partly on an interesting experiment conducted earlier in this century, in which a printer cut a Hiroshige design and printed from the blocks for as long as the prints were what the art dealer terms 'good impressions'. Eight thousand such impressions were taken before the blocks showed noticeable signs of wear.

5 See, for example, Tainaka Joun, *Hiroshige 'Tōkaidō gojūsan tsugi' no himitsu*, Tokyo, 1995, issued, appropriately enough, in the 'NON Book' series.

6 In the catalogue accompanying the exhibition 'Japanese Paintings and Colour Prints', held in January 1896 at the American Fine Arts Society Galleries, New York.

Some Observations on Hiroshige

SUZUKI JŪZŌ

The work of Utagawa Hiroshige, more than that of any other Japanese woodblock print artist, appeals profoundly and directly to the modern viewer, regardless of his or her knowledge of *ukiyoe*.[1] After an uncertain start, Hiroshige soon realised that his artistic inclinations were best suited to the genre of print then known as 'pictures of famous places' (*meishoe*) but more recently given the descriptive name 'landscape prints' (*fūkeiga*). This genre, founded by Utagawa Toyoharu (1735–1814)[2] and enriched by the highly original style and vision of an artist of a different school from Hiroshige, Katsushika Hokusai (1760–1849), took as its theme the historic sites of Edo (present-day Tokyo) and other cities or scenic views along famous highways.

The series of prints that made Hiroshige's name, *The Fifty-three Stations of the Tōkaidō Road* (*Tōkaidō gojūsan tsugi*), published by Hōeidō in the early 1830s, was permeated with an entirely new expressive poetic sensibility and enjoyed great critical acclaim (cat. 17–28, 110–13). Its success was followed up by further series on a broader range of subjects, such as *Famous Views of Kyoto* (*Kyōto meisho*; cat. 50–3, 125) and *Famous Views of Our Country* (*Honchō meisho*; cat. 54–6) as well as several sets of views of Edo. Hiroshige established the landscape print as a genre that could be universally appreciated, imbuing all these works with a uniquely Japanese lyricism that, in my view, demonstrates that he was gifted with refined taste and wit (*haikai*). His great series *The Sixty-nine Stations of the Kisokaidō Road*

Fig. 1 Double-page spread from *A Purple Volume of Kyōka Poems*, c. 1818. Private Collection

Fig. 2 *Fireworks at Ryōgoku*, from *Famous Views of Edo Reflected in Water*, 1840s. Private Collection

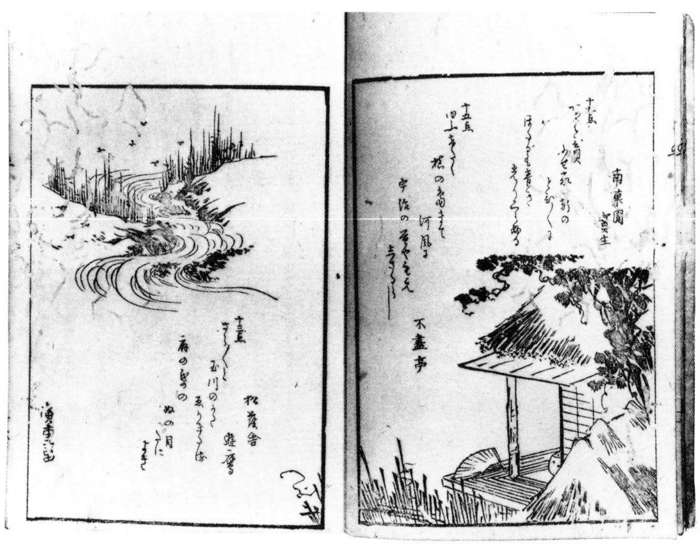

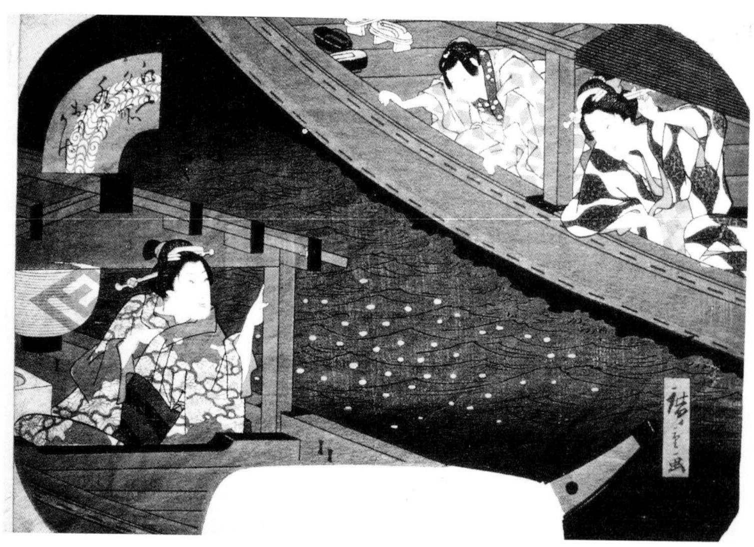

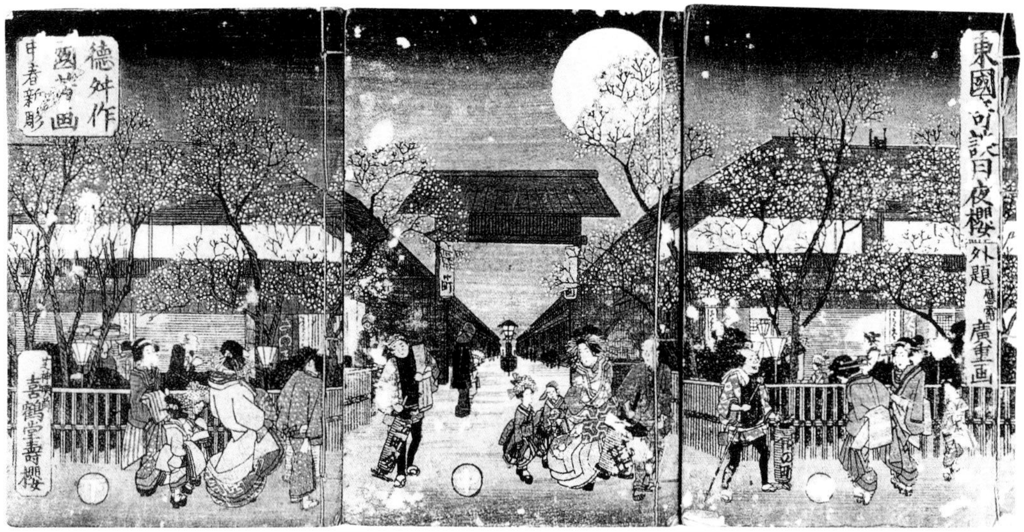

Fig. 3 Covers of *Strange Tales of Night-time Cherry Trees under the Eastern Moon*, 1836. Private Collection

(*Kisokaidō rokujūkyū tsugi*; cat. 35–40, 115–17) is full of the spirit of travel, while another masterpiece, *Eight Views in the Environs of Edo* (*Edo kinkō hakkei*; cat. 63–7), reveals the refinement and precision of his mature style. The draughtsmanship and use of colour printing techniques in the series entitled *One Hundred Famous Views in Edo* (*Meisho Edo hyakkei*; cat. 93–106) and other major works of his later years opened up new and challenging expressive vistas, setting the seal on his creative achievement and fully justifying the description 'master of the Japanese landscape print'. Hiroshige's understanding of narrative and the immediacy of his depiction of natural beauty in all its manifestations became almost second nature to him and have been often and widely praised. As a result, most of us take for granted his mastery of the traditional aesthetics of 'Snow, Moon and Flowers' (*setsugekka*) and his artistry in conveying the ever-shifting moods of the Japanese seasons or depicting such natural phenomena as wind, rain, clouds and mist. This aspect of his output has contributed to the popular image of Hiroshige as an artist whose designs are filled with poetic sentiment and the romance of travel.

There is little to disagree with in this conventional view, but an examination of the whole of Hiroshige's career reveals that it offers a less than full account of his achievement: Hiroshige is more than just a 'poetic painter'. He was, among other things, an artist of the common people, depicting the everyday life of Edo with great humanity, and also a tireless perfectionist, constantly refining his artistic sensibility and expressive techniques. An examination of a few examples of his work in book illustration and genres other than landscape will broaden our view of his art and throw light on other aspects of his personality.

Fig. 1 shows his earliest work, an illustration from a book entitled *A Purple Volume of Kyōka Poems* (*Kyōka murasaki no maki*) with an introduction dated 1818. Drawn in an immature, imperfectly assimilated version of the Kanō style of academic ink painting, it shows, on the left, a clump of reeds growing in a river and above it a group of fireflies placed so as to give a sense of depth. Even here there are some indications of Hiroshige's

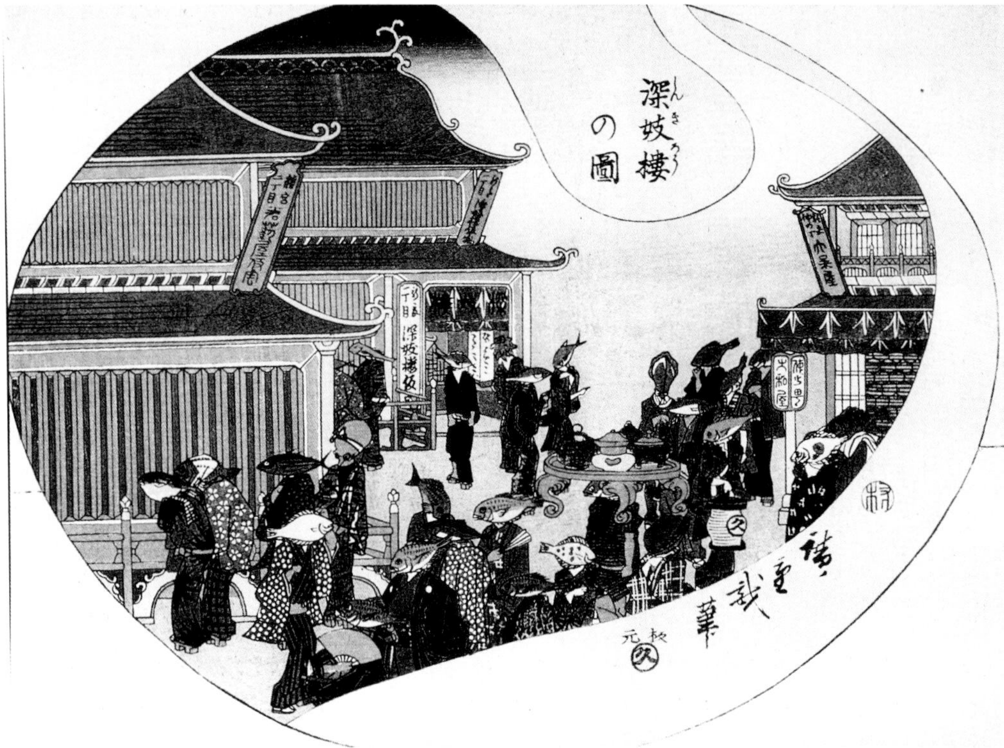

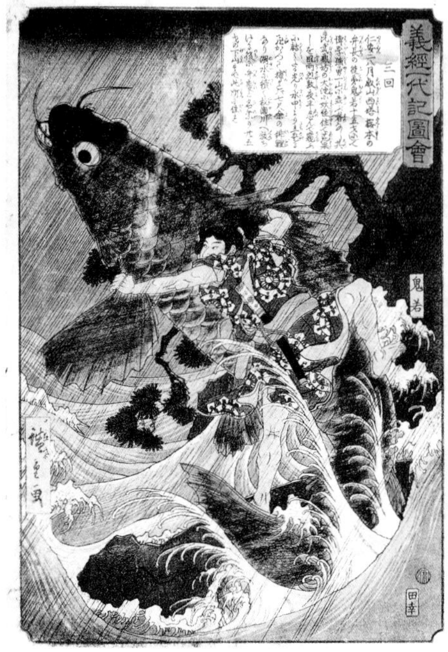

Fig. 4 *The House of the Mirage at Fukagawa*, 1846. Private Collection

Fig. 5 *Oniwakamaru*, from *The Illustrated Life of Yoshitsune*, c. 1843–7. Museo d'Arte Orientale, Genoa

future potential, yet this and the artist's other early works have yet to be systematically analysed. Fig. 3 reproduces the covers of a three-volume novel of the *gōkan* type entitled *Strange Tales of Night-time Cherry Trees under the Eastern Moon* (*Tōgoku kidan tsuki no yozakura*)[3] with illustrations by Utagawa Kuniyoshi (1797–1861). Hiroshige's covers form an atmospheric depiction of the top rank of prostitutes (*oiran*) parading in the main street of the Yoshiwara, Edo's pleasure quarter. It was published in 1836 at the height of his career, when he had already begun to specialise in landscape prints, and is noteworthy for its skilful combination of figures in typical *ukiyoe* style with a background of rows of houses drawn in strict Western-style perspective. The foreign mode of composition is also deployed to divide the picture plane into three bands divided by imaginary horizontal lines. A large lantern is placed at the focal point in the centre of the line between the lower and middle bands, while the line between the middle and upper bands coincides with the ridge of the roof on the main gate. By carefully observing this orthodox compositional device, called 'dividing into three' (*mitsuwari*),[4] Hiroshige shows his continuing commitment to perfecting his pictorial technique. Because of strong similarities in both subject-matter and mood, this book cover offers valuable comparative evidence for the dating of a print entitled *Evening Cherry at Nakanochō in the Yoshiwara* (*Yoshiwara Nakanochō yozakura*) from the series *Famous Views in the Eastern Capital* (*Tōto meisho*) published by Sanoya Kihei (Kikakudō) (cat. 8), but there is still room for further research into the details of Hiroshige's assimilation of Western pictorial methods.

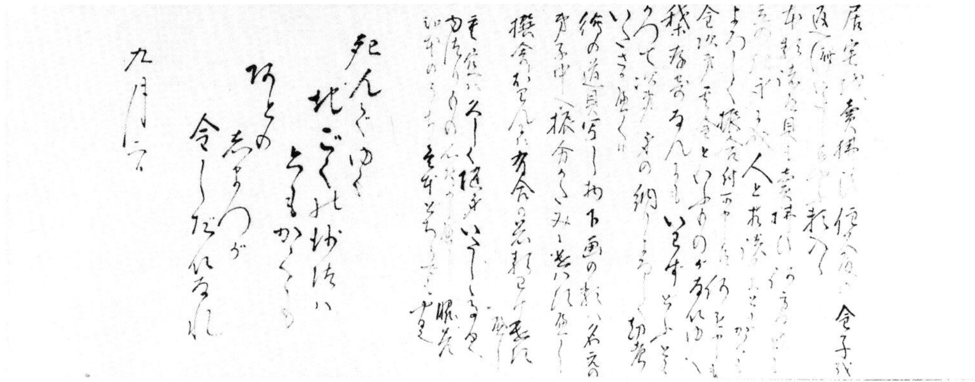

Fig. 6 Hiroshige's last will and testament, 1858

Another aspect of the assimilation of European ideas, the use of light, is illustrated by the fan print *Fireworks at Ryōgoku* (*Ryōgoku hanabi*) from a series called *Views of Edo Reflected in Water* (*Edo meisho mizu no omokage*) (fig. 2). Hiroshige was so highly skilled at conveying a sense of volume by means other than chiaroscuro that he seldom had recourse to this Western technique. Occasionally, however, he obtained a wonderful relief effect, with the illusion of light shining from one side, by having his printer partly wipe off the pigment after it had been applied to the block, a technique called *bokashi*. (A fine example of this is the view of Maruko from the Hōeidō Tōkaidō series, in which the pale red background colour conjures up an atmosphere of sunlight in springtime [cat. 23].) In this fan print, Hiroshige even tries to capture the effect of light as it is momentarily reflected in water. The blue shades off into darkness at both sides of the strip of river between the two boats and a great circle of light, radiating from the fireworks in the sky, is reflected in the remaining bright patch of water. Moreover, even the individual fragments of exploding gunpowder are shown as dots of red glittering on the waves. Hiroshige's fascination with light as a means of adding a relief effect to already striking compositions is worthy of further research.

The fan print *The House of the Mirage at Fukagawa* (*Shinkirō no zu*) is an example of the unusual pictorial fantasies so admired by the people of Edo (fig. 4). The main part of the design shows a crowd of people with fish for heads walking around in front of a Chinese pavilion that looks like the Dragon King's palace at the bottom of the sea. The title, which hints that the pavilion is, in fact, a brothel, shows that the image is a humorous allusion to the temporary relocation of the Yoshiwara, Edo's pleasure district, in the Fukagawa neighbourhood following a disastrous fire in 1846, a date corroborated by the censor's seal. Under strict regulations in force during the 1840s it was forbidden to publish pictures of the Yoshiwara, so Hiroshige put fish and Chinese buildings in place of real people's heads and real brothels.[5] When written with different characters the word '*Shinkirō*', used by Hiroshige in the title of the print, signifies a legendary Chinese undersea building that is supposed to have been exhaled by a giant clam. Hiroshige drew the whole design in the shape of a shell, applied a traditional subject of painting to the

Yoshiwara and, more skilfully still, drove home the message of the composition by means of an optical illusion: the two areas around the main design can be viewed as the flesh and outer membrane of a clam. Even without specialist knowledge, the sense of fun conveyed by the print is readily apparent, its clever urbanity revealing another facet of Hiroshige's genius.

Hiroshige produced masterpieces even in genres in which he did not specialise, as indicated by a warrior print (*mushae*) from the series *The Illustrated Life of Yoshitsune* (*Yoshitsune ichidaiki zue*) showing Oniwakamaru wrestling with a giant carp (fig. 5). The censor's seal suggests that it dates from about the same time as fig. 4 and, although the rather hard-edged drawing shows the signs of work done under pressure, this is more than a simple picture of a fight: both the composition as a whole and the torrential rain are pure Hiroshige. The robes worn by Oniwakamaru, later to become the warrior-monk Benkei, are decorated with Benkei's mark, the eight-pointed sacred Buddhist wheel (*rinbō*), proving that the artist shared with other designers of warrior prints a deep knowledge of ancient lore.

Fig. 6 is Hiroshige's last will and testament, the autograph of which has fortunately been preserved and conveys something of his character. Emended only the day before his death, it is written in a serene, untroubled hand and shows Hiroshige making provision for his friends and relations, in particular his pupil Shigenobu, who was to become Hiroshige II.

In conclusion, I should like to stress that it is essential to base one's assessment of Hiroshige's achievement on prints in good condition and from the earliest possible editions, preferably the first. This point, so often ignored, is an integral part of my aim here, which has been to demonstrate that we should try to understand Hiroshige as a whole, not simply as the poetic artist he is commonly taken to be, and to draw inspiration from the forceful as well as the lyrical aspects of his personality.

NOTES

1 Utagawa was the artist's school name, but he has sometimes been wrongly called Andō, using his family name. Hiroshige himself never used the names Andō and Hiroshige together.

2 Toyoharu was the founder of the Utagawa school and his pupils included Toyokuni and Toyohiro; Hiroshige was Toyohiro's pupil. Toyoharu is famous for his *ukie*, interior and landscape prints using strict Western-style perspective.

3 The term '*gōkan*' refers to a late Edo-period form of the popular illustrated novels called *kusazōshi*. This developed from the simple *akahon*, *kurohon* and *aohon* into the somewhat more sophisticated *kibyōshi*, which represented an improvement in both content and design. *Gōkan* are distinguished by their carefully produced woodblock-printed covers.

4 The term '*mitsuwari*' is defined and illustrated in volume III of the *Hokusai manga* (1815), a series of printed books based on sketches by Katsushika Hokusai.

5 From 1841 to 1843 the samurai bureaucrat Mizuno Tadakuni enforced a series of austerity measures known as the Tenpō reforms (*Tenpō kaikaku*).

Hiroshige in History

HENRY D. SMITH II

'We are already all Hiroshige', proclaimed the poet Yone Noguchi in 1917 at the ceremony commemorating the sixtieth anniversary of Hiroshige's death, a decisive moment in the early twentieth-century apotheosis of 'the only one native and national artist of Japan'.[1] Noguchi related the epiphany that he had experienced some years earlier, probably in the spring of 1905, shortly after his return from an extended period in America, where he had earned a reputation as an English-language poet.[2] Anxious 'to get a true sense of perspective toward Nature', Noguchi took a boat trip on the Sumida River to view the cherry blossoms at Mukōjima and discovered that the scene before him appeared exactly as in Hiroshige's many landscape prints of the spot: Nature was imitating art! It is a perfect example of the literal sense of 'picturesque'.

And so, in similar fashion, history has come to imitate art. Most of us today, Japanese and non-Japanese alike, are 'all Hiroshige' when we strive to visualise the landscape of the final decades of the Tokugawa period (1600–1868). For the city of Edo (present-day Tokyo) and the Tōkaidō Road in particular, we inevitably conjure up his prints in our mind's eye, drawing on the memory of countless book illustrations, tourist souvenirs and media recreations of the woodblock originals. If anything, the image has become even stronger in the course of the twentieth century, with continuing proliferation and improvement in the technologies of colour reproduction. For better or for worse, 'traditional Japan' has been envisioned for all posterity by Hiroshige.

In the process, the Japan of Hiroshige's own times has in critical ways been *removed* from history. Or, more precisely, his times have been subsumed into a timeless space of 'Japanese tradition', according to a logic that really began only in the twentieth century. During the first few decades after Hiroshige's death in 1858, his landscape images were consumed habitually in Japan and exotically in the West. In the great wave of Japonisme that swept Europe and then America in the later nineteenth century, it was Hokusai rather than Hiroshige who garnered the most attention, and both were admired not for the descriptive content of their images, but rather for their graphic skills, their composition, line and colour.

It was only after the turn of the century that Hiroshige came into his own, among a generation of romantic and spiritual seekers to whom his work seemed particularly attuned. Of considerable importance was the effusive essay by Mary McNeil Fenollosa, *Hiroshige: The Artist of Mist, Snow and Rain*, published in San Francisco in 1901. She and her husband, Ernest Fenollosa, seem to have developed an enthusiasm for *ukiyoe* as a genuine art of the Japanese people, overcoming Ernest's own earlier denigration of the genre as unrefined. Liberated from the sinified art of the aristocracy, *ukiyoe*, Mary Fenollosa declared, was 'the spontaneous art of a joyous nation' and Hiroshige one of its great practitioners.[3] She proceeded to single out Hiroshige's skill in expressing the atmospheric effects of mist, snow and rain as his greatest accomplishment—an opinion that rightly continues to hold sway among connoisseurs today.

The two features of Hiroshige's art emphasised by Mary Fenollosa—his specially 'Japanese' qualities and his skill as an artist of 'Nature' (always with a capital 'N')—became entrenched over the next two to three decades as the inevitable framework for thinking about the artist. In the same memorial ceremony of 1917 at which Yone Noguchi spoke, for example, the budding Hiroshige scholar Uchida Minoru, whose biography *Hiroshige* of 1932 remains the definitive work on the artist, proclaimed that, whereas most of the art of Japan's past was derived from China and hence, by implication, artificial, only Hiroshige was 'absolutely loyal to Nature'. Hiroshige, declared Uchida, was able to transmit 'Nature itself' in his art, so that through his prints the viewer could come into direct contact with Nature as a transcendent religious experience.[4]

Implicit in this highly romantic appreciation of Hiroshige was the notion that he was able to rise above the decadence and frivolity of his own times. Since Nature itself was Hiroshige's true teacher, as Uchida proclaimed, it followed that the artist was not really a part of his own era, but rather subject to the more universal and timeless laws of adherence to Nature itself. It was precisely this affinity for Nature that accounted for Hiroshige's popularity in the West, Uchida observed. Kojima Usui, the banker and pioneer alpinist who wrote the first extended Japanese scholarly study of Hiroshige in 1914, similarly argued that Hiroshige's landscapes offered the sole 'glimmer of revival' in an age of decadence and that his depictions of Nature made him the closest of all traditional artists to twentieth-century man.[5]

This removal of Hiroshige from his historical milieu was achieved, in a sense, by suppressing time and enhancing space, particularly the geographical and climatic space of the Japanese nation. Removal from the historical context was paralleled by an emphasis on the integration of Japanese society and culture into the 'natural' landscape of rivers, coasts, forests and mountains. These natural features of the land, and the urge to celebrate them in art and poetry, were considered to be timeless characteristics of Japan and its people. Such an emphasis was a source of particular consolation to young urban intellectuals in the rapidly industrialising Japan of the early twentieth century, as well as to many Westerners, who observed the process from without, lamenting the destruction of Japanese 'tradition'.

THE BEST OF TIMES, THE WORST OF TIMES

How, then, can we return Hiroshige to his own times, and what new perspectives on his art would this yield? It is no simple matter, since the times in which he actually lived, from his birth in 1797 until his death in 1858 at the age of sixty-two, were both contradictory and constantly changing. As with the England of 1775 with which Dickens began *A Tale of Two Cities*, 'it was the best of times, it was the worst of times'—depending on which observer, in which year, one chooses to heed.

The 'best of times' perspective is supported by various objective features of the age and by a persistently optimistic tone in many popular writings of the time. It is a view that focuses on the first three decades of the nineteenth century, the central years of the fifty-year reign of the eleventh Tokugawa shogun, Ienari, from 1787 to 1837. Ienari's rule began with the turmoil of the Kansei reforms of the early 1790s and ended, as we shall see, in the famine years of the mid-1830s, but in between, Japan was singularly prosperous and peaceful—at least on the surface. Later historians have singled out the two eras of Bunka (1804–18) and Bunsei (1818–30), often combining the second syllables into the singular 'Kasei'.

The optimistic view of Kasei-era Japan was reflected at the time in a rhetoric that was most conspicuous in the shogun's capital city of Edo, stressing the 'prosperity' (*hanjō*) of the city, which was often referred to in these years as 'Great Edo' (Ō-Edo). This general view has been broadly corroborated by certain historians in recent years, both in Japan and in the West. The so-called 'modernisation' school of American historians, for example, has emphasised certain late Tokugawa trends as instrumental to the success of the rapid industrialisation after 1868, under the new Meiji regime. These include the growth of per capita income, rapid advances in popular education and literacy, increasing knowledge of the outside world and a thriving urban popular culture. Many Japanese as well, particularly in the last two to three decades, have been disposed to take a sanguine view of late Tokugawa 'civilisation' (the preferred term) as a time of peace and growing prosperity.

In general, however, the weight of both élite sentiment in Hiroshige's own time and of modern historiography falls decidedly on the side of 'the worst of times'. The prosperity of Kasei Japan, it is argued, was superficial, masking deep structural contradictions in the socio-political system and in the economy, as well as radical inequities in the distribution of wealth. Most of the critics in Hiroshige's own day were of a traditionalist bent, typically, samurai intellectuals bemoaning the fate of their own élite class under the steady encroachment of a money economy that impoverished the warrior rulers while enriching the merchants, who were officially at the bottom of the status hierarchy. The same critics were also distressed by the spread of popular culture, which was seen as materialistic, coarse and shallow. In the twentieth century, a similar critique was taken up by social and economic historians in the very different language of Marxist argument, but the emphasis on structural contradictions and the decadence of popular culture remained.

What do these two very different perspectives suggest about the art of Hiroshige? If we accept the peace-and-prosperity line, then the untroubled landscapes of the artist appear as a direct reflection of reality. Even the most ardent advocate of the 'best of times', however, is obliged to admit that Hiroshige's image of the country is highly idealised, revealing little of the frequently harsh realities of life in late Tokugawa Japan. By the argument that Mary Elizabeth Berry has advanced in connection with the great screen paintings of the capital Kyoto that appeared in the sixteenth century, landscape becomes an art of 'consolation' that 'excises the pain' of contemporary reality.[6] Indeed, precisely the three techniques of consolation specified by Berry are to be found at the core of Hiroshige's appeal: an emphasis on place, presented with integrity; a focus on the cyclical time of the seasons and the ritual calendar; and a preoccupation with people and their everyday customs.

Yet the fact remains that Hiroshige's Edo was far less troubled than war-ridden Kyoto of the sixteenth century, and elements that served as consolation three hundred years earlier had become conventional formulas by Hiroshige's time. And whereas the Kyoto screens were commissioned by the most powerful aristocratic patrons at huge expense, Hiroshige's colour landscape prints could be purchased for not much more than the price of a bowl of noodles. The power of printed reproduction and the sale through a large network of commercial publishers (see fig. 1) had worked to create a far broader base for the consumption of visual images, which now constituted a common culture for the city of Edo and increasingly for much of the rest of Japan, as prints and books were constantly carried back to the provinces as souvenirs of Edo.

In the end, we cannot grasp the dynamics of Hiroshige's art as it evolved from the 1820s to the 1850s without considering both the best and the worst of his times. It is, in fact, precisely the conjunction of dynamic growth and mounting crisis that helps to relocate his art in history. Contrary to the image propagated by later enthusiasts, Hiroshige was not a genius who transcended his times, but a skilful artist who took advantage of the opportunities offered to him.

BETWEEN SAMURAI AND ARTISAN

The deepest and most ominous crisis of Tokugawa Japan in the era of Hiroshige, both in the view of critics at the time and of historians later, was that within the ruling samurai estate. Accounting for as much as seven per cent of the total population, this hereditary military estate had been almost completely removed from direct control of land and was now concentrated in the cities of the shogun and the provincial *daimyō*, or feudal lords, as administrative and police functionaries. Those at the top of the social pyramid that constituted the estate were very wealthy, sometimes continuing to hold landed fiefs and controlling dozens of sub-retainers and servants. The majority of the estate, however—those typically described as 'lower' samurai—lived on meagre hereditary stipends that, even when supplemented with salaries for specific jobs, were often inadequate to raise a family.

It was into these lower reaches of the samurai estate that Hiroshige was born in 1797. His father had been born into the Tanaka family of retainers of the Tsugaru domain in northern Japan, but had married the daughter of Andō Jūemon, a direct retainer of the Tokugawa shogun in Edo, and became his heir, assuming the Andō family name. Jūemon's status within the shogunal retainer band, which with families and servants accounted for about a quarter of Edo's million-plus population, was that of 'houseman' (*gokenin*), below the élite 'bannermen' (*hatamoto*) class. His particular job was that of fireman of the *dōshin* rank, comparable in status to a non-commissioned officer in a

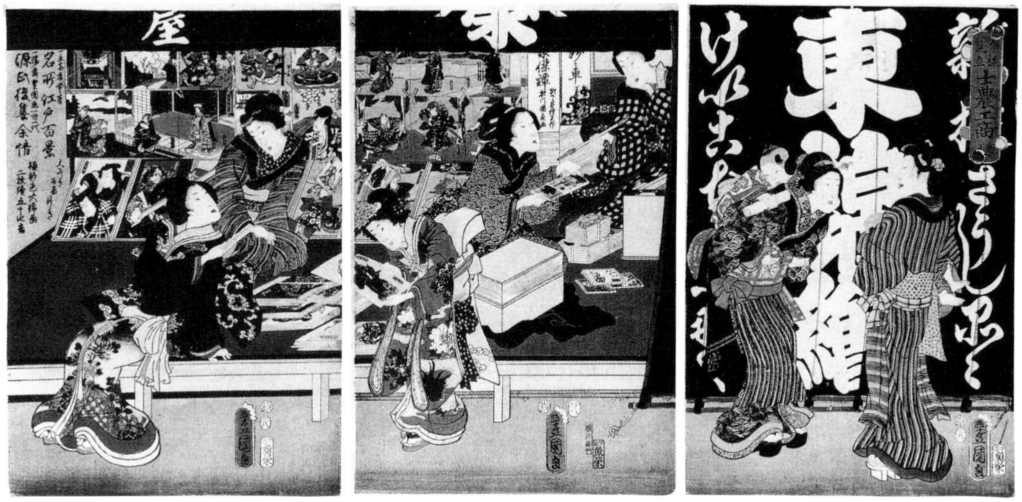

Fig. 1 The print shop of Uoya Eikichi, publisher of Hiroshige's *One Hundred Famous Views in Edo*, two prints from which are hanging at upper left in the left-hand panel. *Ōban* triptych by Utagawa Kunisada, dated 1857/VIII. Baur Collection, Geneva

modern military organisation. Hiroshige himself succeeded to this post at the age of fifteen, when he was orphaned by the successive deaths of his mother and father in 1812.

The only surviving scrap of evidence about Hiroshige's life as a fireman for the shogun is a commendation that he received for his performance at a fire on a winter's night in late 1818 at the age of twenty-one.[7] At the time, he was already producing book illustrations as an *ukiyoe* artist, essentially an odd job to make ends meet. In this, he was like the majority of the *gokenin* retainers of the shogun, who engaged in a whole range of artisanal pursuits to supplement their stipends. Some took advantage of the space offered by their official residences to raise goldfish and singing insects or to start nurseries for the booming trade in flowering plants. Others manufactured umbrellas, fans, lanterns and lacquerware—all endeavours that involved skill in painting, which was part of samurai training.[8] Still others, like the roguish Katsu Kokichi, a shogunal retainer of precisely Hiroshige's class and generation who recorded his exploits in an autobiography at the age of forty-two, lived by their wits, engaging in sharp practices and confidence tricks.[9]

Hiroshige thus lived precisely on the border of the samurai élite and the commoner working class of Edo. In his own job as fireman, he was in direct command of a unit of *gaen*, the rowdy men with full-body tattoos who fought fires in nothing but loincloths. Hiroshige was born in the Yayosu barracks of the shogunal firefighting organisation, located in the very heart of the area just east of Edo castle where the most powerful *daimyō* and the greatest shogunal officials had their offices—today the Marunouchi business district. He remained in the barracks until 1842, when, at the age of forty-six, he moved into the centre of the 'downtown' (*shitamachi*) section of commoner Edo about half a mile to the east, remaining there for the rest of his life.[10] To the last, Hiroshige retained a strong consciousness of his status, as indicated by his request, three days before he died, that 'the funeral be in samurai style'.[11]

Mary Fenollosa was thus misled in her conception of Hiroshige as representative of a native Japanese popular culture set apart from the 'haughty' samurai aristocracy and its

Chinese values. On the contrary, the artist was steeped in the Chinese learning that was basic to samurai education as well as in the refined pursuits of painting and poetry in both the Chinese and Japanese manner. At the same time, his ways of thinking and habits of life were probably not that different from the countless skilled artisans who made up the majority of commoner Edo. It was within this hybrid zone of artisan and samurai that Hiroshige was able to create an art that was at once elevated and deeply rooted in popular culture, both poetic and adept at craft technique.

THE 'CULTURE OF MOVEMENT'

For a persuasive account of the optimistic view of change in late Tokugawa Japan, we may turn to the writings of Nishiyama Matsunosuke and their emphasis on the emergence of a 'culture of movement' (*kōdō bunka*).[12] The term '*kōdō*' suggests not just physical movement, but also 'conduct' or 'performance', referring to a wide range of cultural activities that were booming in nineteenth-century Edo and spreading throughout provincial cities and rural Japan as well. Some were private indoor pursuits, such as the practice of tea ceremony or nō chanting, but in Nishiyama's conception the 'culture of movement' consisted primarily of outdoor leisure activities, conducted for pleasure and with at least a veneer of religious dedication. Most such activities involved paying money to a variety of purveyors, not the least of them the priests of shrines and temples. In short, it was a thriving culture of commercialised leisure, driven by general economic prosperity.

For a detailed pictorial record of such activities, no better source is available than the landscape prints of Hiroshige, which provide a virtual catalogue of the late Tokugawa 'culture of movement' described by Nishiyama. To the classical 'floating world' (i.e. fleeting) pastimes of the theatre and entertainment at the Yoshiwara brothel are now added a whole array of outdoor activities: flower-viewing and other seasonal pastimes, pilgrimages to temples and shrines, periodic festivals, trips to hot springs and sightseeing. The 'famous places' (*meisho*) were always depicted in Hiroshige's views in conjunction with a particular activity or range of activities. In Edo, Gotenyama and Asukayama would always be shown with picnickers viewing the spring cherries in bloom, while Ryōgoku featured summer sideshows and fireworks, the temple of Kaianji was seen amid maple trees in autumn and the famous Nihon Bridge appeared more often than not under an auspicious covering of New Year's snow.

In all such cases, the emphasis on leisure activities contrasts strikingly with the landscapes of Hokusai, which reflect the workaday world of human labour. People stop and play in the prints of Hokusai, of course, but more as a momentary respite from work; the figures in Hiroshige, on the other hand, seem more bent on relaxation. Whereas the most conspicuous travellers in Hiroshige's prints have their loads (or even themselves) carried by others, those on Hokusai's roads tend to bear their own burdens. We can easily detect the contrast of social origins here between Hokusai, the artisan, and Hiroshige, the man hovering between the world of the artisan and that of the samurai.

Another consequence of Hiroshige's emphasis on the leisure-orientated 'culture of movement' was a heavy stress on the surrounding landscape, which was itself often the focus of the activities, especially in the case of seasonal viewing pleasures. In some instances, of course, the landscape becomes an end in itself, in prints of lonely isolated figures huddled in the rain or snow or beneath a moonlit sky. While the aesthetic achievement of such works is not to be denied, they are in fact exceptional within the totality of Hiroshige's landscape oeuvre, some eighty-five per cent of which depicts busy activity in bright daylight under clear skies. Much of this activity depended on the surrounding landscape for its essential meaning, so that nature and culture were closely interdependent. In the end, Hiroshige was perhaps less an artist of Nature than of the culture of nature.

Although the majority of Hiroshige's landscape prints depicted activities in Edo, he also reached out along the highways of Japan, first in his famous series of the stations of the Tōkaidō Road, then in the stations of the Kisokaidō Road (in the series begun by Keisai Eisen) and, still later, in *Famous Views in the Sixty-odd Provinces*. A perpetual debate among those who have written about Hiroshige revolves around the extent to which he based his views of the highways and provinces on first-hand observation and direct sketching. Later anecdotes about the painter have tended to support the notion that he sketched from nature. There is, for example, the story, told to Matsuki Kihachirō by an old man whose father had allegedly been a close friend of the artist, that Hiroshige in his later years suddenly took off on a trip all the way to the island of Awaji just to sketch the Naruto whirlpools for his famous triptych view of the spot (cat. 119).[13] Common sense tells us that this is pure legend, but it is a legend that confirms the immediacy of Hiroshige's depictions of place.

Hiroshige did indeed travel from time to time, as did increasing numbers of his countrymen in the late Tokugawa period, and it was such travel that generated the demand for his prints. It is equally clear, however, that the majority of his prints of places outside Edo did not derive from direct observation. Most scholars agree that Hiroshige really did make the trip along the Tōkaidō Road to Kyoto in about 1832, as a member of an annual autumn mission from the shogun in Edo, the seat of actual governance, to the emperor, who resided in Kyoto and retained a strong ceremonial and symbolic role as the legitimator of the Tokugawa regime. This trip presumably served as inspiration for the famous series *The Fifty-three Stations of the Tōkaidō Road*, published by Hōeidō, probably in 1833, but Suzuki Jūzō has observed that Hiroshige probably did not rely on actual sketches, at least not for most of the stations more distant from Edo: those up to about Fujisawa (the sixth station from Edo) have a detailed quality of direct observation, but later views are more abstract and, after Okitsu (seventeenth station), he even relied for some views on a published gazeteer.[14] The sources for Hiroshige's Kisokaidō views are unknown, but certainly did not include direct experience, while the majority of his depictions in *Famous Views in the Sixty-odd Provinces* were modelled after illustrations in printed gazeteers.[15]

But none of this is of paramount importance: Hiroshige was selling images of places, not documentary photographs. His depictions of many places outside Edo are far more important in revealing how his work promoted the visualisation of a new national space in the later Tokugawa period. The groundwork was laid first in printed guidebooks and gazeteers, particularly the genre known as *meisho zue* ('views of famous places'), which began in 1780 with *Miyako meisho zue*, illustrating the imperial capital of Kyoto, and continued until 1862 in twenty-five more such works. Of these, ten were organised by specific provinces (mostly in western Japan), two by highways (the same two depicted by Hiroshige) and nine by pilgrimage circuits, while four were devoted to the great cities—three more to Kyoto and one to Edo.[16] This last, *Edo meisho zue*, appeared from 1835 to 1837, at the height of Hiroshige's activity, and was to provide the compositions for some of his own later depictions of Edo.[17]

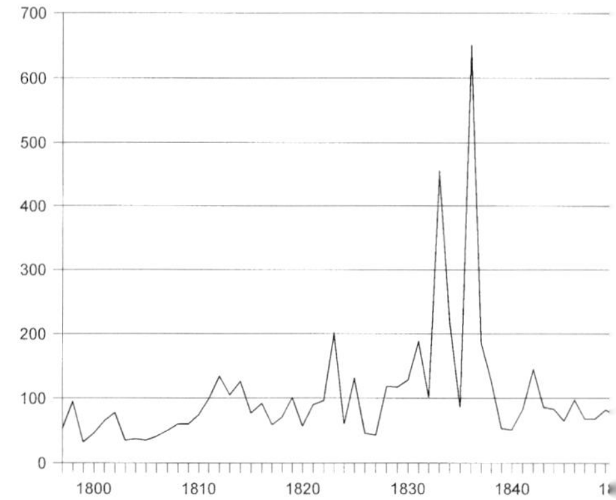

Fig. 2 'Magnitude' of national conflict in Japan during Hiroshige's life, 1800–58. Data courtesy of Professor James W. White, University of North Carolina. 'Magnitude' is an index that scales each recorded conflict according to severity

THE TENPŌ CRISIS

The era of peace and prosperity in which Hiroshige matured as an artist came to an end in the mid-1830s with the 'Tenpō crisis' (named after the Tenpō year-period, 1830–44), which is the focus of attention for those historians who take a 'worst of times' approach to late Tokugawa Japan. The Tenpō crisis was actually a succession of two related crises, first a prolonged period of famine, economic distress and political conflict throughout the country from 1832 to 1838 (see fig. 2), followed by a period of controversial political reforms by the Tokugawa government from 1841 to 1843, with the impact of each continuing well beyond the peak years.

On the face of it, the famine years of the 1830s do not seem to have set back Hiroshige as an artist: on the contrary, it was precisely in this period that he was at his creative peak, producing his most widely recognised masterpieces. The change in the weather that would lead to famine began in 1831, approximately the year of his first landscape success, the 'Ichiyūsai'-signed *Famous Views in the Eastern Capital* series (cat. 6, 7), while the Hōeidō *Fifty-three Stations of the Tōkaidō Road* (cat. 17–28, 110–13) is generally acknowledged to have been published in the course of 1833, the first truly disastrous year of crop failures and resultant famine. If we follow the customary dating schemes, these series were followed in the mid-1830s by such acclaimed works as *Famous Views of Kyoto* (cat. 50–3, 125) and *Eight Views in Ōmi Province* (cat. 68–75). Somewhat later, roughly coinciding with the peak of the famine from late 1836 on into 1838, came his lyrical *Eight Views in the Environs of Edo* (cat. 63–7) and his contributions to *The Sixty-nine Stations of the Kisokaidō Road* (cat. 35–40, 115–17). The cynical might suppose that Hiroshige's talent as 'the artist of mist, snow and rain' was nurtured by the excess of precipitation that lay behind most of the crop failures in this period.

A very different relationship between the famine and Hiroshige's art was proposed, however, by Roger Keyes in an essay of 1982.[18] He argued that Hiroshige took over the Kisokaidō series from Eisen shortly after it began in 1835, producing in short order some of his most memorable masterpieces (such as cat. 35, 38, 117). But then, Keyes speculated, from about the winter of 1835–6, the impact of the famine obliged Hiroshige to 'remain inactive as a print designer for two years, or even longer'. Moreover, when he then resumed activity in about 1838 or 1839, a dramatic change had occurred: his landscapes had lost their 'warmth and poetry' and were now 'flat and dull'. Only with *One Hundred Famous Views in Edo* in 1858 did he 'regain the power of his first vision'.

Putting to one side the problematic matter of dating Hiroshige's work on the Kisokaidō series (which most experts put considerably later than required by Keyes's theory), it is worth heeding the notion that the Tenpō famine produced a severe crisis in Japanese publishing. The evidence is mixed, but suggests in the end that the overall impact was modest, although somewhat greater in Osaka than in Edo.[19] The annual number of fiction titles published in Edo, for example, was fairly steady until 1837–8, when there was a decline of about one-third—noticeable but not dramatic.[20] Keyes claimed that *surimono* production fell off sharply in Edo after spring 1836, and it is indeed conceivable that the kind of extravagant entertainment for which *surimono* often served as announcements did in fact decline. Such entertainment certainly did not come to a halt, however, as demonstrated by the lavish painting party (*shogakai*) held by the writer Takizawa Bakin in the autumn of 1836, a 'nine-hour extravaganza' attended by over one thousand people.[21]

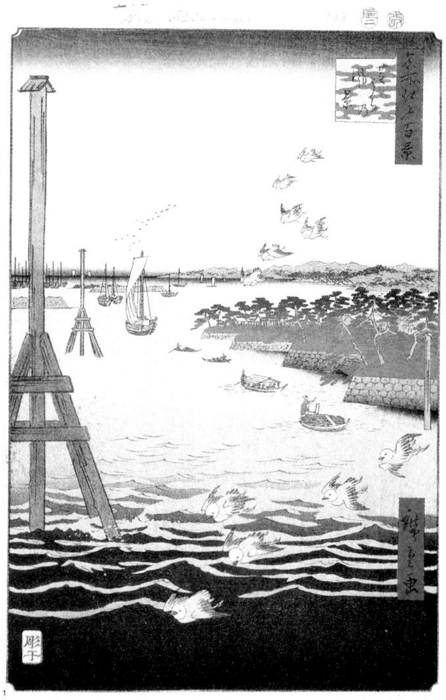

Fig. 3 *View of Shiba Coast*, from *One Hundred Famous Views in Edo*, dated 1856/X. The small islands in the distance on the left are the 'Odaiba' fortifications erected after Commodore Perry's arrival in Japan in 1853. The Brooklyn Museum, Brooklyn, NY

Andrew Markus comments on contemporary chroniclers' lack of disapproval of the 'contrast of penury and super-abundance' exemplified by such banquets in time of famine.[22] We must remember that the Tenpō famine was indeed a disaster of formidable proportions, with deaths numbering in the tens of thousands in parts of Japan. Yet, like most famines, it was a disaster with strongly differential effects by class and region, affecting the poor rather than the rich, the countryside far more than the cities, and certain parts of Japan—especially the Tōhoku region to the north—much more acutely than others. The capital of Edo weathered the crisis fairly well, in spite of acute increases in the price of rice, from two to four times the normal level in the five-year period from spring 1833.[23] The entertainment industry, in particular, suffered, with business falling off sharply in the pleasure quarters. Government authorities in Edo took aggressive and generally successful measures to alleviate the worst effects of the famine, providing free relief rice, selling cheap rice and sheltering the poorest. Hundreds died of famine in the city, but most appear to have been rural refugees who were already sick and starving. Edo was spared the rioting and protest that occurred in so much of rural Japan and in other cities (see fig. 2).

It is difficult to confirm, therefore, that the Tenpō famine had the impact on print production that Keyes claimed and even harder to demonstrate that Hiroshige, in Edo, was himself affected by the famine. It remains plausible, of course, that the crisis took a toll on his spirit, but a more persuasive reason for personal distress, as both Keyes and other scholars have suggested, was his wife's death in 1839/x. Most tend to agree that, sometime in the late 1830s, after Hiroshige had produced his greatest masterpieces, his art lost much of its poetry and inventiveness of design, but it remains a matter of speculation whether this was the result of social change, personal tragedy or simply of overwork.

There is general agreement, however, on the impact on art of the second phase of the Tenpō crisis: the reforms that the government instituted in the autumn of 1841, largely in response to the economic distress and political ferment occasioned by the famine years, had a major effect on the content of colour prints.[24] The brunt of the impact was born by prints of actors and courtesans, which were prohibited outright, and by de luxe prints (mostly of actors) that used large numbers of colour blocks. Hiroshige's landscapes, which already fell within the newly prescribed limits of seven to eight colours per print, could scarcely have been affected, although the restriction of the price for a single-sheet print to 16 copper *mon* may have required some cutting of corners.[25]

A further provision of the print-related Tenpō edicts, which were issued on three occasions over a year from 1842/VI, may have had a greater impact on Hiroshige's prints. This was the explicit demand, contained in the first reform edict, for prints on themes of 'loyalty, filiality and honour' (*chūkō setsugi*) so as to 'promote virtue for women and children' (*jijo kanzen*) in line with the moralistic emphases of the reforms as a whole. Partly as a result of this encouragement, and possibly also because publishers detected a genuine public interest, prints on historical themes and heroic figures grew in number. It was probably for this reason that the relative importance of figures in Hiroshige's prints showed a clear increase after the reform edicts. His many new Tōkaidō Road series, for example, in a variety of formats, generally featured larger figures than in the original series and also a heavier dose of local customs. In the end, this may all just reflect a growing public taste for images that were descriptive and historical. Judging from the large quantity of Hiroshige's work from the 1840s into the 1850s, it is also conceivable that he was simply too much in demand to pay close attention to quality and innovation.

THE WORLD STOOD ON END

The economic crisis of the Tenpō years relaxed in time, as did the effects of the reforms, which were forgotten within three to four years. Tension continued to mount, however, over the growing Western military presence in East Asian waters, particularly after the defeat of China in the Opium War of 1840–2, an event that deeply troubled Japanese leaders and intellectuals. The arrival of Commodore Matthew Perry's ships just over a decade later, in July 1853, set off a chain of diplomatic and political crises that would culminate in the political revolution of 1867–8, which restored the emperor to direct rule and ended the Tokugawa shogunate. Hiroshige's last years were thus marked by political ferment and also by various natural disasters, such as the great earthquake that struck Edo in the autumn of 1855. Nevertheless, he was spared the worst of this turbulent era, dying in the cholera epidemic in the autumn of 1858, prior to the opening of Yokohama the following year.[26] The crises of this new era found only the dimmest of reflections in the prints of Hiroshige. In his last great series, *One Hundred Famous Views in Edo* (cat. 93–106), for example, the only signs of danger are distant views of the fortifications in the Bay of Edo, erected in case of foreign attack (see fig. 3), and a single tiny depiction of Japanese soldiers wearing Western trousers.[27]

More symbolically, however, we might imagine a special meaning in Hiroshige's sudden turn to a vertical format in his final years, first on a large scale in *Famous Views in*

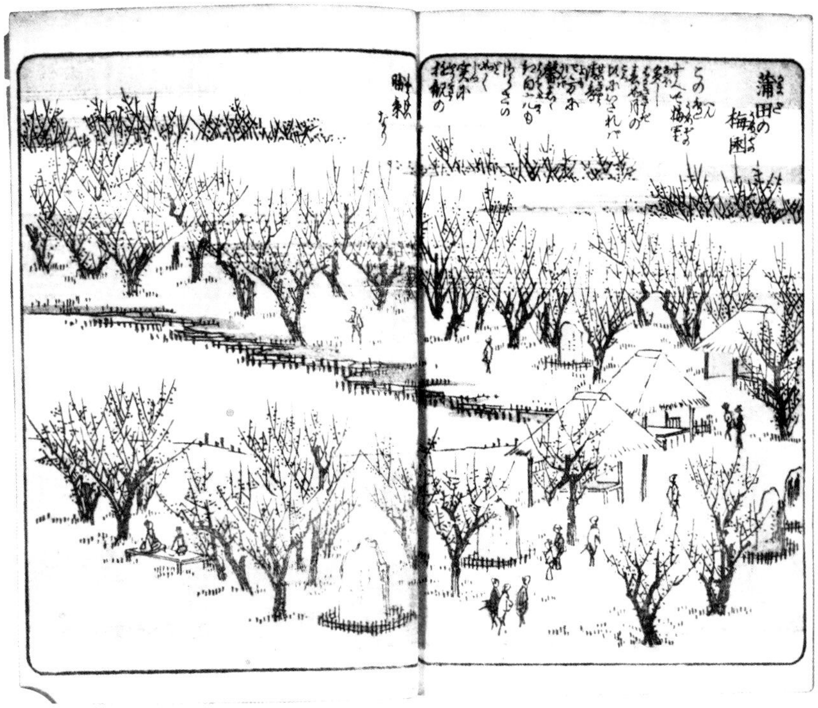

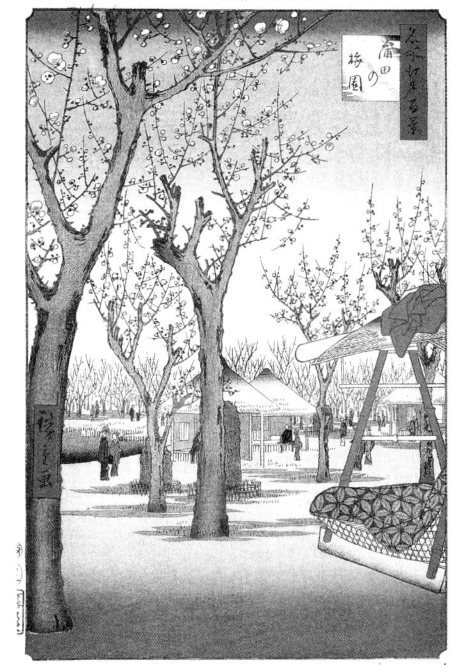

Fig. 4 *Plum Garden, Kamata*, from *Picture Souvenirs of Edo*, vol. 2 (1850). Columbia University, New York, C. V. Starr East Asian Library

Fig. 5 *Plum Garden, Kamata*, from *One Hundred Famous Views in Edo*, dated 1857/1. The Brooklyn Museum, Brooklyn, NY

the Sixty-odd Provinces, a series initiated just one month following Perry's arrival and completed three years later. It seems too simple to argue, as some have done, that Hiroshige was looking for a new selling point and, while I do not posit a causal connection between the political crisis and the pictorial format, there is little doubt that the stable, grounded quality of Hiroshige's classical, horizontal landscapes was now upset—literally stood on end.

This unsettling verticality was particularly evident in an unusual type of composition that is found in about one-third of the 118 prints in Hiroshige's *One Hundred Famous Views in Edo*, in which a dramatic and closely cropped foreground object was set against a distant view. I would argue that these are 'moving pictures', in which the artist effectively 'pans' across the picture surface in the manner of a movie camera.[28] Comparison of *Plum Garden, Kamata* (fig. 5), for example, with its model in Hiroshige's earlier *Picture Souvenirs of Edo* (fig. 4), reveals that the artist has deliberately obstructed our view of the three stone markers that had been clearly visible in the early print, impelling us mentally to shift viewpoint (either ours or the picture's) in order to discover the markers and their inscriptions. The strangely suspended palanquin in the foreground at right adds to the unstable tension of the scene, implying a hidden narrative. It is a strikingly cinematic composition, one wholly appropriate to unstable and quickly changing times.

Broadening this observation, we can see that, in fact, all Hiroshige's depictions of place were in a basic sense 'moving pictures'. This is partly a matter of compositional techniques, notably that of cropping objects along either the sides or, most unconventionally, the lower edge of the image (seen as early as the 1831-2 *Famous Views*;

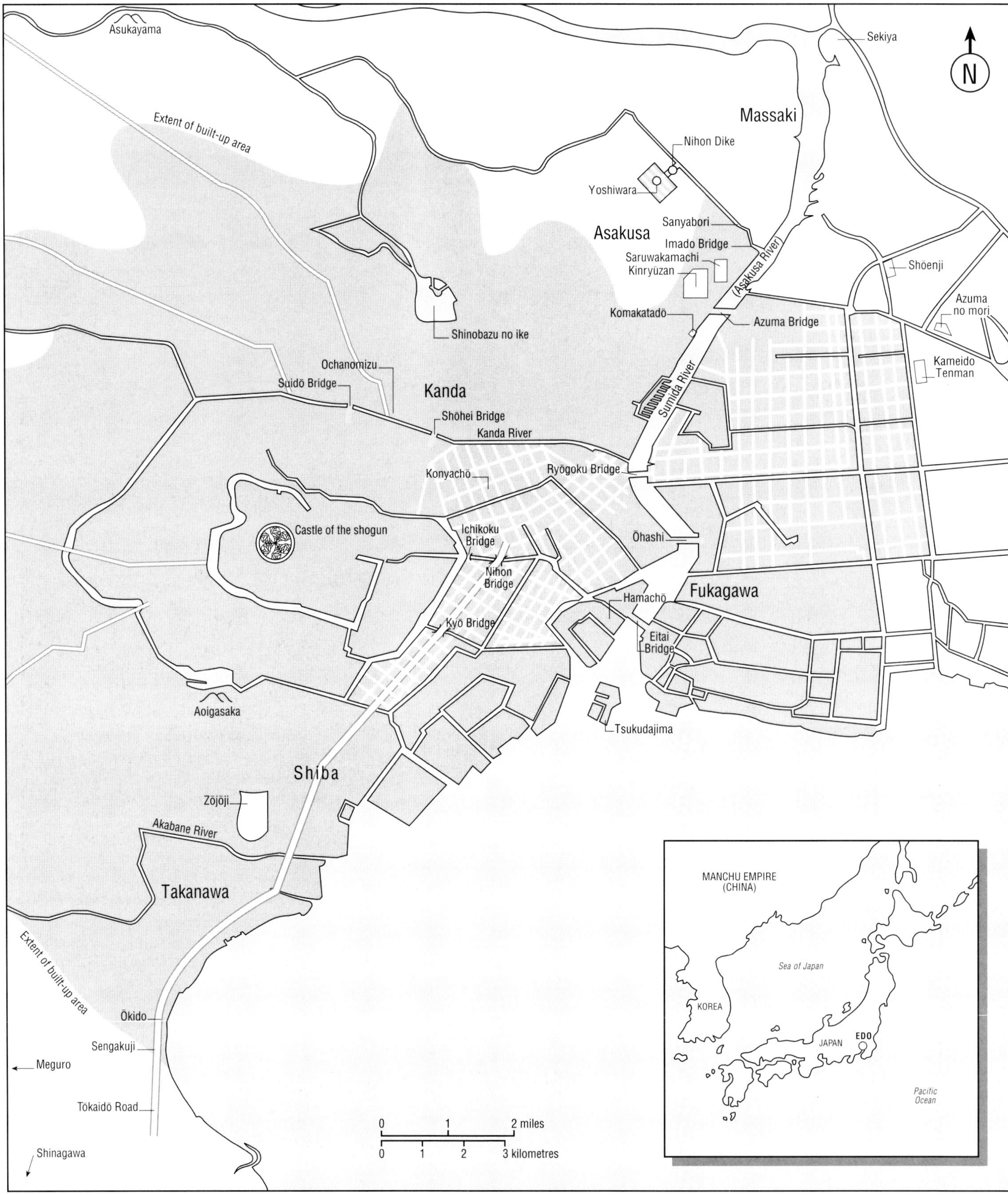

The City of Edo after a map of 1843

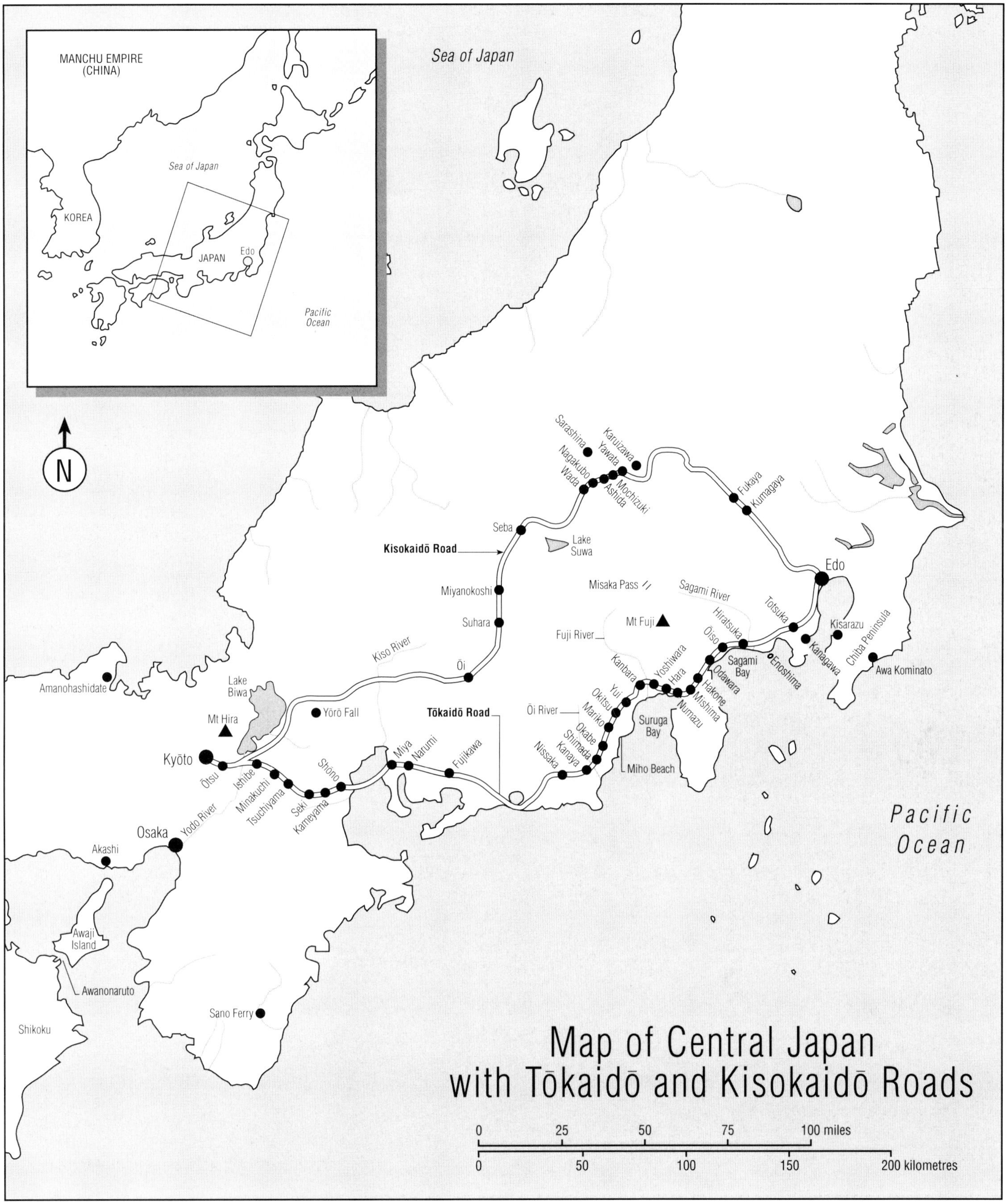

Map of Central Japan with the Tōkaidō and Kisokaidō Roads

CHRONOLOGY

	HIROSHIGE'S CAREER	CONTEMPORARY EVENTS
1797(?)	Born at Yaesugashi in Edo (present-day Tokyo) His early names are Tokutarō, Tokubei and Jūemon	
1802–9		Publication of Jippensha Ikku's novel describing a journey along the Tōkaidō Road
1806(?)	Possibly introduced to the Kanō style of painting by Okajima Rinsai Said to have painted delegates from the Ryūkyū Islands to the shogun in Edo	
1809	His parents die and he becomes head of the Andō family	
1810 (or 1811)	Said to have entered the studio of Utagawa Toyohiro (*b.* 1763?)	
1812	IX: Receives the name Utagawa Hiroshige Signs his early work 'Ichiyūsai Hiroshige'	
1818	Illustrations to a *kyōkabon* entitled *Kyōka Murasaki no maki* Starts designing prints of actors, influenced by Utagawa Kunisada (*b.* 1786)	
1819	*Surimono* print of a small drum and a hat used in nō dances	
1820s	Various series of prints of beautiful women	
1825		Death of Utagawa Toyokuni (*b.* 1769)
1828		V/23: Death of Utagawa Toyohiro Kuniyoshi (*b.* 1797) explores the new genre of historical prints
1830	Visits the writer Kyokutei Bakin, who introduces him to the publisher Bunkeidō	Publication begun of *Thirty-six Views of Mount Fuji* by Katsushika Hokusai (*b.* 1760)
1830(?)	VIII: Accompanies a ceremonial procession along the Tōkaidō Road	
1831	Changes signature to 'Ichiyūsai' (in different characters) Produces first landscape series, *Tōto meisho jukkei* and *Ōmi hakkei*	
1831–2	First large series of views of Edo, *Famous Views in the Eastern Capital*, is published by Kawaguchiya Shōzō	Hokusai publishes series of waterfalls and large flowers
1831–4	Publication of the series *The Fifty-three Stations of the Tōkaidō Road*	
1832	II/22: Visits Bakin to invite him to an exhibition of his art Changes name from Ichiyūsai to Ichiryūsai Publication begun of *Famous Views in the Eastern Capital* (issued by Sanoya Kihei) and of prints of birds and flowers	
1832–3	Publication of the series of large fish	
1832–7	Publication of the series *Famous Views of Our Country*	
1834	The complete Tōkaidō series published in a two-volume album with an advertisement for future projects Publication of the series *Famous Views of Kyoto* From this year on, he designs the illustrations to numerous *kyōka* albums	

1834–5	Publication of the series *Eight Views in Ōmi Province*	
1834–42	Publication of the series *The Sixty-nine Stations of the Kisokaidō Road*, begun by Keisai Eisen (*b.* 1791) earlier in the 1830s	
1835–6	Publication of the series *Eight Views in Kanazawa*	
1837–8	Publication of the series *Eight Views in the Environs of Edo*	
1839	X/23: His wife dies Interrupts publication of the Kisokaidō series	
1839–40	Publication of the *Kyōka Tōkaidō* series	
1841–2	Publication of the *Gyōsho Tōkaidō* series	
1842–3		The Tenpō reforms impose many restrictions on publishing, e.g. prints of actors and courtesans are banned
1844	Begins designing his many series on historical or mythological subjects; also collaborates on occasional projects with Kunisada and Kuniyoshi	Kunisada assumes the name of Toyokuni
1845		Censorship control starts to become tighter
1847	Marries Oyasu, a farmer's daughter Starts producing many prints of beautiful women in a landscape setting, mostly in the form of triptychs	
1848		Death of Keisai Eisen
1848–53	Publication of the drawing manual *Ehon tebikigusa*	
1849	Hiroshige moves to Kanōshindō, in the Nakabashi district of Edo, and borrows 100 *ryō* to build a new house	Death of Hokusai
1851–2	Publication of the *Reisho Tōkaidō* series	Peak in the production of outstanding prints, especially by Kunisada and Kuniyoshi
1852	Adds many prints of beautiful women and illustrated books to his constantly expanding output	
1853–6	Publication of the series *Famous Views in the Sixty-odd Provinces*	
1854		U.S. Commodore Matthew Perry arrives at Edo with a fleet, demanding the opening of Japanese harbours to foreign ships
1855	Publication of the vertical Tōkaidō series	
1856–8	Publication of the series *One Hundred Famous Views in Edo*	
1857	Publication of a group of three triptychs	
1857–8	Draws up his last will and testament	
1858	Publication of the series *A Wrestling Match between Mountains and Seas* IX/2: After a ten days' illness, draws up a second last will and testament IX/3: Draws up a third last will and testament IX/6: Dies	
1858–9	Publication of the series *Thirty-six Views of Mount Fuji*	
1861		Death of Utagawa Kuniyoshi
1865		Death of Utagawa Kunisada

CATALOGUE

BIRDS AND FLOWERS

CAT. 1–5

1 BLUE BIRD ON A HOLLYHOCK

from a group of more than forty prints of bird and flower subjects published by Kawaguchiya Shōzō, *c.* 1835

signed: *Hiroshige hitsu*, with seal: *Ichiryūsai*
censorship seal: *kiwame*
woodblock, *chūtanzakuban*, 384 x 128 mm
Private Collection, Denmark
(ex-Wakai Kenzaburō Collection)

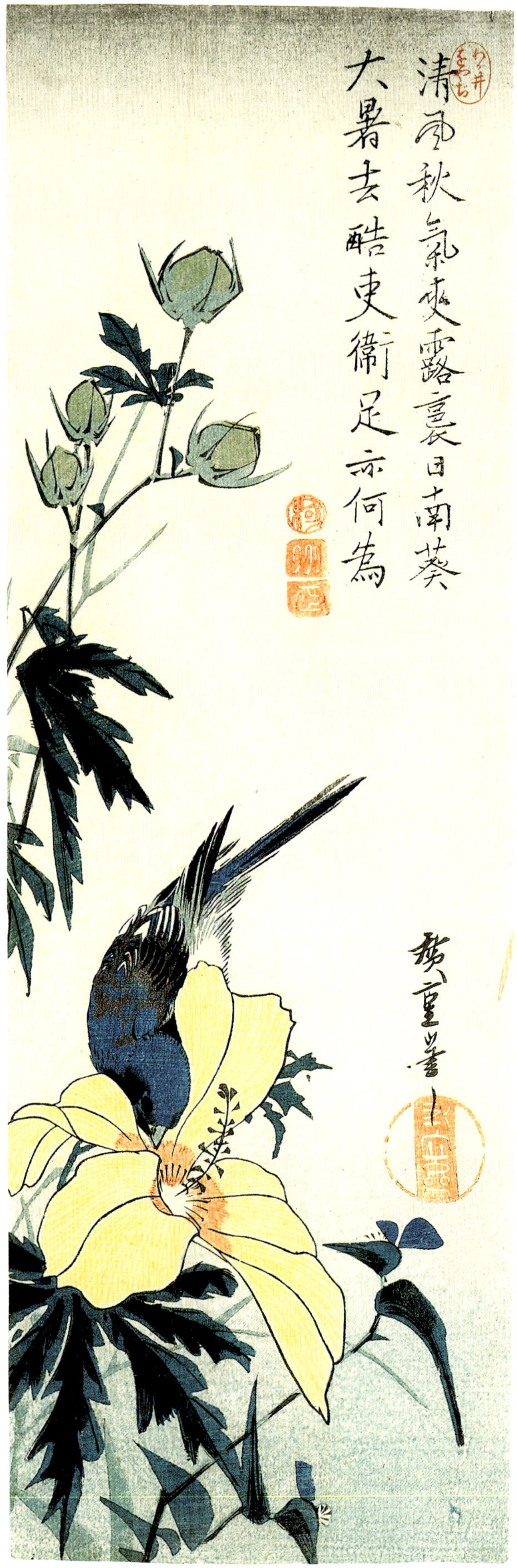

A blue bird is perched on a large hollyhock against a predominantly yellowish ground. The Japanese name of the bird is *ruricho*, literally 'lapis lazuli bird'. At upper right is a Chinese poem that can be translated as:

> The cool breeze refreshes the autumn air
> Laden with dew, the hollyhock turns towards the sun
> The summer heat has even driven away the tax
> collectors
> What, I wonder, am I doing here?

This bird is rare in Hiroshige's production of *kachōga*, prints of birds and flowers. He designed about two hundred such prints in a variety of formats at various times. Another example in the same format depicts a bird in an almost identical pose, on a hibiscus (Kobayashi, 1990, no. 292); a third example again shows the bird on a hibiscus, but seen from the rear (ibid., no. 119).

Hiroshige began designing *kachōga* in the early 1830s, probably around 1832, when Wakasaya Yoichi published about twenty prints in the tall, narrow *tanzaku* format, some of which were later reprinted by Sanoya Kihei. The artist regularly designed groups of prints in this format in the following years. This print is one of over forty in the *chūtanzaku* format issued by Kawaguchiya Shōzō, probably over a long period. For other examples, see cat. 2 and 5.

REFERENCES: Yoshida, 1967, A 810; Bogel and Goldman, 1988, no. 8; Kobayashi, 1990, no. 96; Ōkubo, 1992, no. 2; Copenhagen, 1993, no. 64 [this impression]

2 KINGFISHER AND IRIS

from a group of more than forty prints of bird and flower subjects published by Kawaguchiya Shōzō, *c.* 1835

signed: *Hiroshige hitsu*, with seal: *Hiroshige*
censorship seal: *kiwame*
woodblock, *chūtanzakuban*, 374 x 129 mm
Private Collection, Denmark
(ex-Wakai Kenzaburō Collection)

A kingfisher hovers above irises in bloom. At upper left is a *haiku* poem that reads:

Amadare ni
sode mo ayame ni
nioi ikeri

In raindrops, on sleeves as well as on the irises
the fragrance is true and real.

The poem, which may be by Hiroshige himself, is a welcome exception to that on innumerable prints of kingfishers and irises ('The kingfisher arranges his wings—The water is his mirror'), such as Kobayashi, 1990, nos. 170, 274, 289, 290 and 346.

REFERENCES: Yoshida, 1967, A 802; *Ukiyoe hakka*, 1984, no. 97; Bogel and Goldman, 1988, no. 59; Ōkubo, 1992, no. 10; Copenhagen, 1993, no. 69 [this impression]; Forrer, 1994, G543

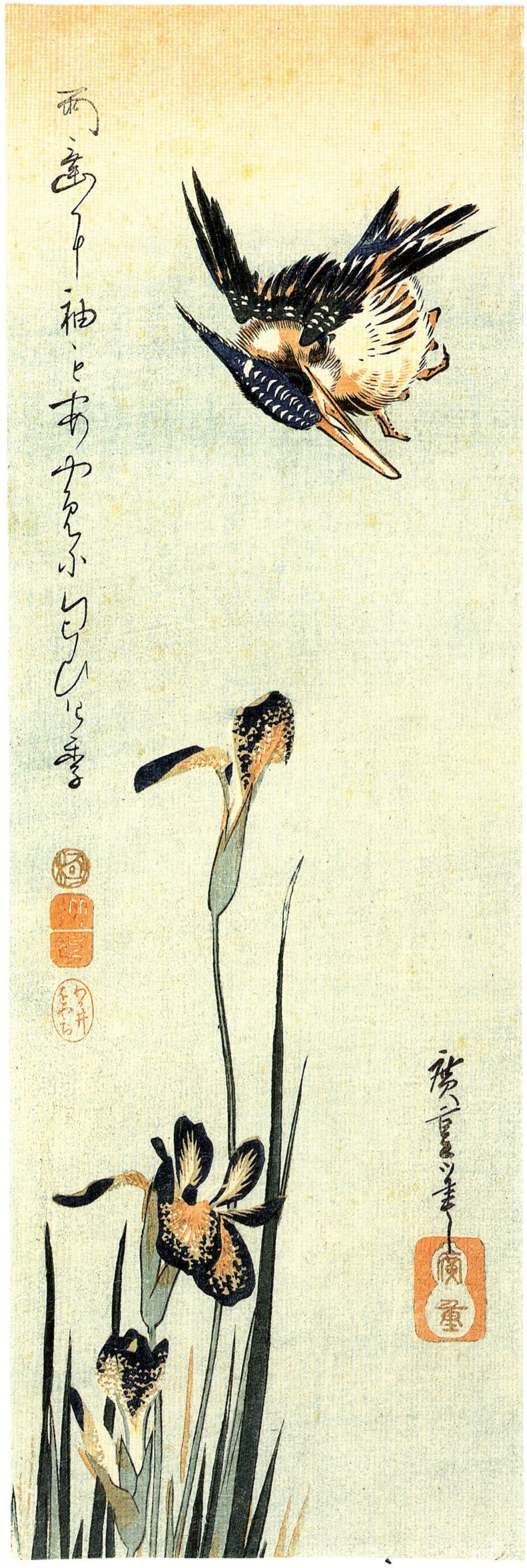

3 MOON AND FLOWERS

fan print
published by Sanoya Kihei, 1854

signed: *Ryūsai*, with seal: *Hiroshige*
censorship seal: *aratame*; date seal: Tiger 2 (1854/II)
woodblock, fan, 226 x 291 mm
Trustees of The Chester Beatty Library and Gallery of Oriental Art, Dublin (CBLJ 2730)

Throughout his career Hiroshige must have designed hundreds of prints that were later mounted on bamboo frames to be turned into fans. Their ephemeral nature—many fans did not survive the summer—means that these prints are extremely rare. Some were not cut to shape, however, but preserved as sheets, and it is possible that at least some of the prints in this format were not intended to be used as fans at all. This might explain the occurrence of fan prints in series with titles.

This print may belong to the kind that was intended to be made into fans, although the publisher Sanoya Kihei was not well known as a retailer of fans. The subject consists of the seven autumn flowers—pinks, *fujibakama*, *ominaeshi* and morning glory to the right, *kusu*, pampas grass and lespedeza to the left—seen against a blue sky with a large moon. Hiroshige had already treated this theme, which was not common in fan prints, in 1828, in a far more crowded composition with a larger selection of flowers (Matsuki, 1925, no. 11), and in 1853 (Kobayashi, 1990, no. 149).

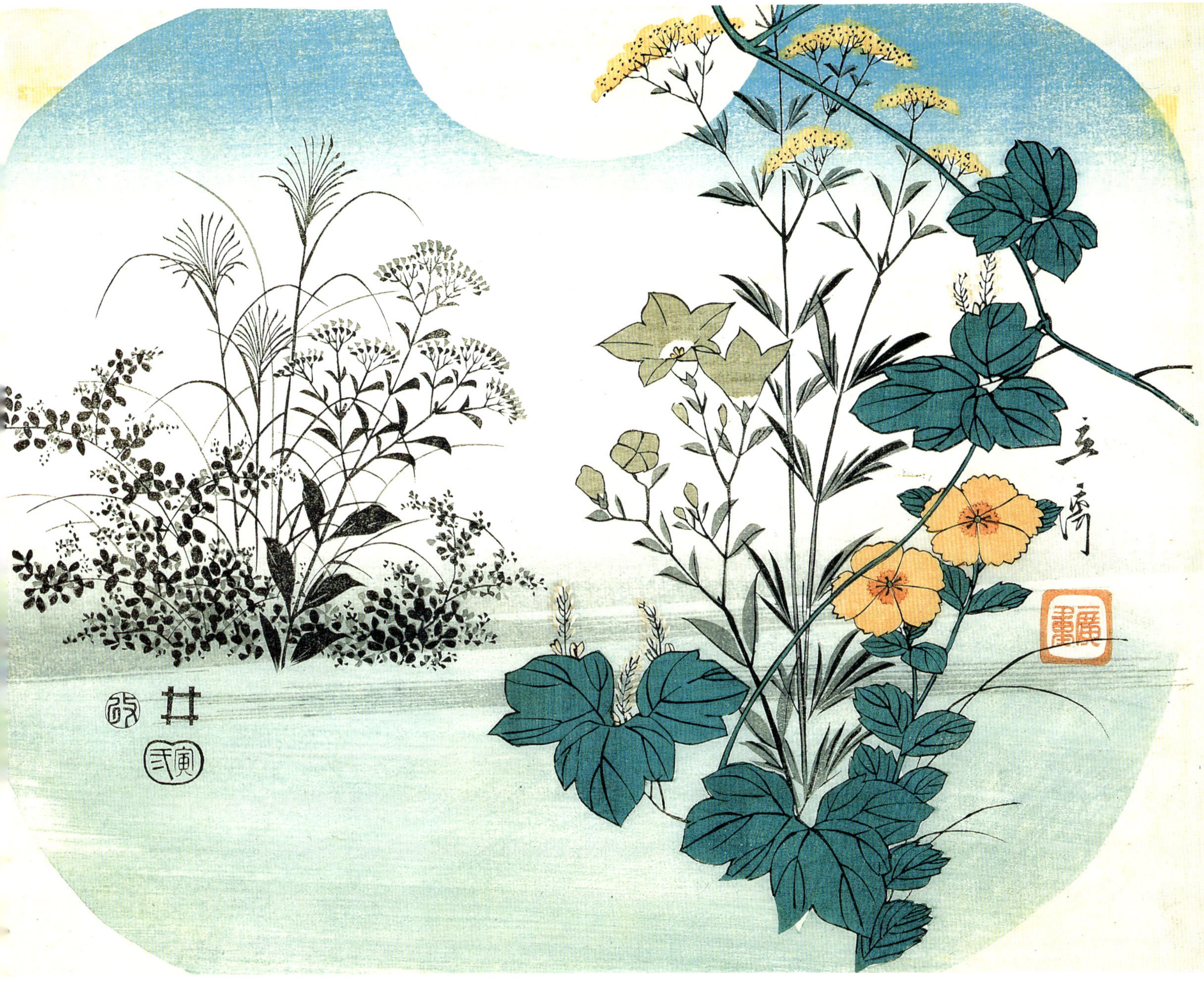

4 BIRD ON A CAMELLIA BRANCH

from a group of prints of bird and flower subjects probably published by Wakasaya Yoichi, *c.* 1832

signed: *Hiroshige hitsu*, with seal: *Ichiryūsai*
woodblock, *ōtanzakuban*, 380 x 176 mm (margins on all sides)
The Museum of Art, Rhode Island School of Design, Providence, Gift of Mrs John D. Rockefeller, Jr. (34.284.1)

In this carefully balanced composition, a bird, probably a tit, is hanging upside down from a camellia branch. There are two open flowers on the hanging branch, one seen frontally in the upper part of the print, one seen from the side at the tip of the branch. The *haiku* poem at lower right reads:

Tsubaki kare
ochiru shite kara
haki josō

The camellias are withering
and after they have fallen
the sweeping just goes on

Kojin [someone from the past].

The print includes a deliberate imitation of a brush-stroke at the top end of the camellia branch and the technique of overprinting is used with great refinement, especially on the leaves. In this second state of the print (b), the contours of the two open flowers that were visible in the first edition (a) have been removed from the line-block, further enhancing the subtle play of different tints of red. In addition, the publisher's trademark and the censorship seal on the left have been removed. There is a deceptively good facsimile of this image from recut blocks, on which the artist's seal has been replaced by something resembling a yin-yang seal; the seal below the poem is missing as well. Despite the absence of a publisher's trademark, Ōkubo attributes this print to the publisher Wakasaya Yoichi.

REFERENCES: Yoshida, 1967, Z 704; Keyes, 1984, no. 1300 [a]; *Ukiyoe hakka*, 1984, no. 72 [b]; Bogel and Goldman, 1988, no. 13 [b: this impression]; Kobayashi, 1990, no. 85 [b: this impression]; Ōkubo, 1992, no. 3

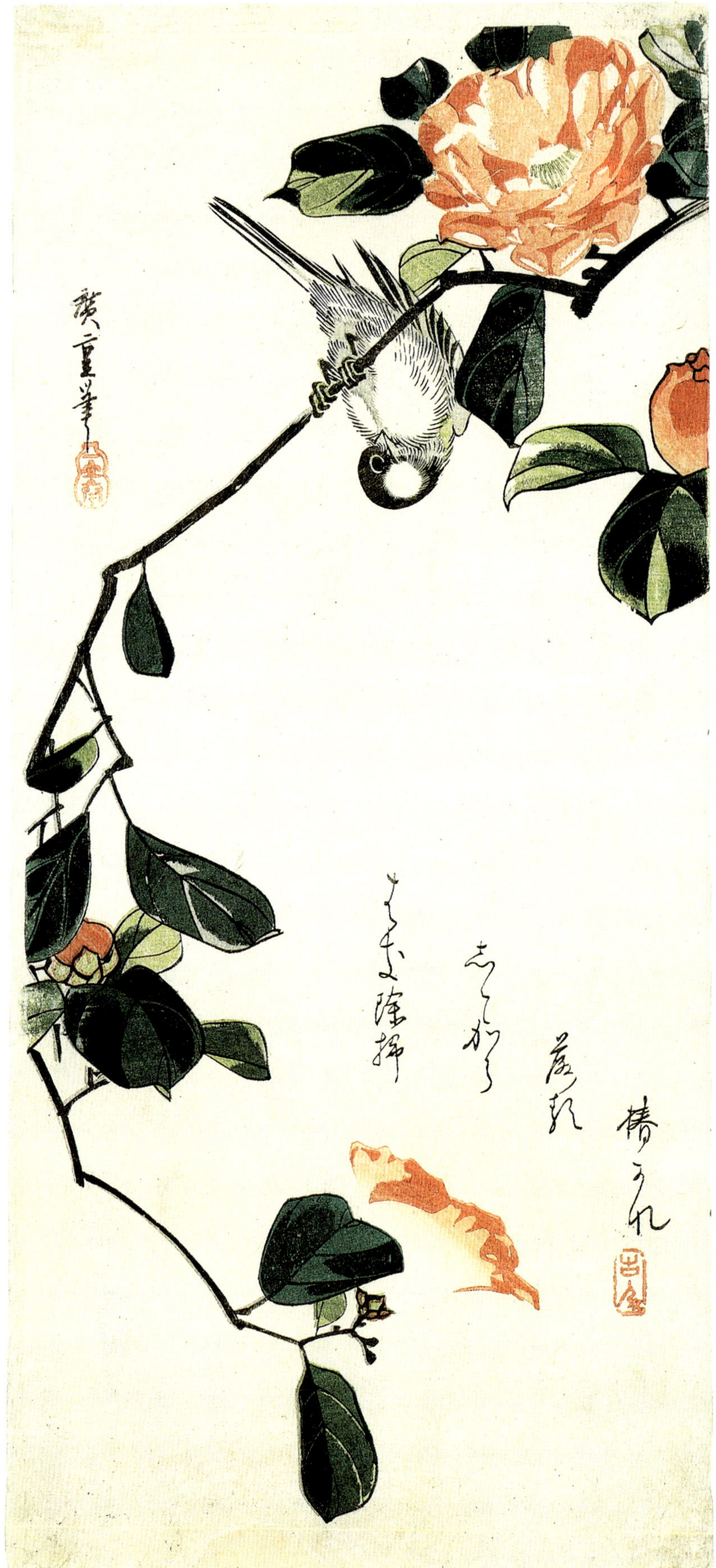

5 OWL ON A PINE BRANCH

from a group of more than forty prints of bird and flower subjects published by Kawaguchiya Shōzō (Shōeidō), *c.* 1832

signed: *Hiroshige hitsu*, with seal: *Yūsai*
woodblock, *chūtanzakuban*, 382 x 129 mm (margin at left)
Collection Pulverer, Cologne

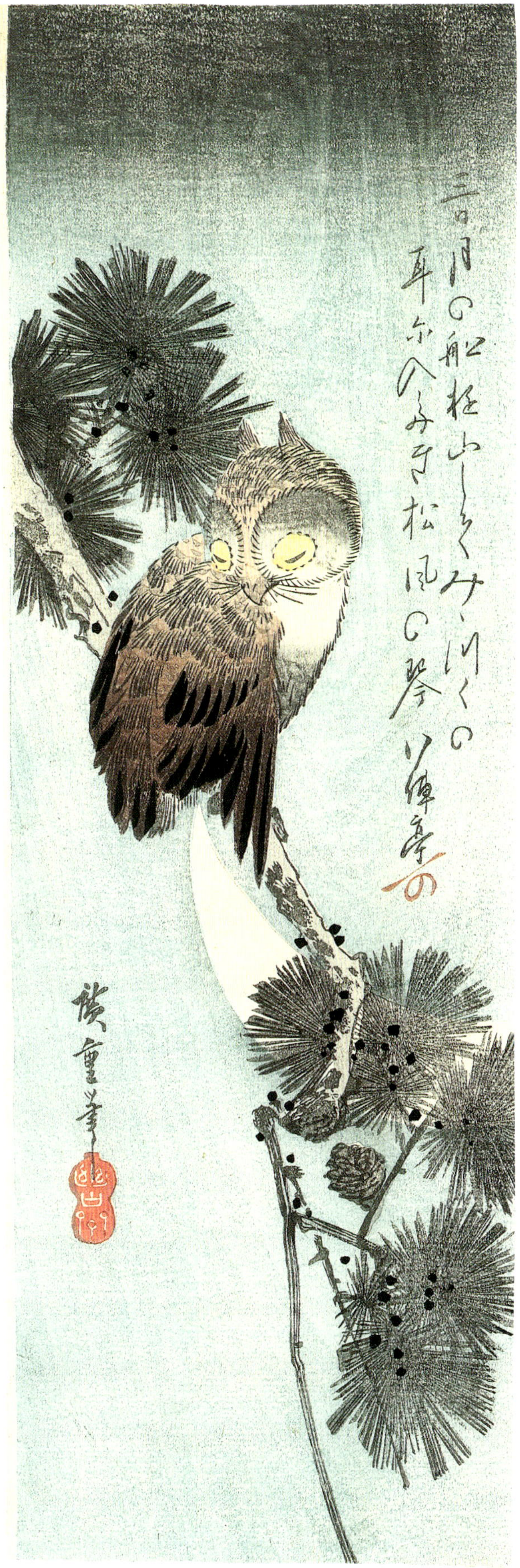

A small owl perches on the branch of a pine tree. Although the sky is blue, the grey strip along the top of the print and the crescent moon indicate the approach of evening. The composition of the branch, which runs diagonally across the sheet, and the almost recumbent moon echo the poem on the right, a *kyōka* by Hajintei Kataki:

Mikazuki no
funayusan shite
mimizuku no
mimi ni haitaki
matsukaze no koto

Making a boat ride on the crescent moon
the wind in the pines would love
to enter the long-eared owl's ears
—like the song of a harp

Hajintei [with his poet's emblem in red].

According to Suzuki (1970), Hajintei was a friend of Hiroshige. His poems are found on at least five other bird and flower prints, such as one of a cock on a snow-covered hill (Kobayashi, 1990, no. 99) or another with a sparrow among bamboo stems (ibid., no. 307). It is virtually certain that they were all published by Kawaguchiya Shōzō, which also indicates a link between the poet and the publisher. Although his trademark does not appear on this print, Kawaguchiya Shōzō was undoubtedly the publisher (see cat. 107).

Some impressions of this print (b) have a dark blue strip in *bokashi* along the upper edge. The dark grey strip in this impression (a) and in that in the Ledoux Collection is more in keeping with the time of day depicted. The naturalistic rendering of the bird is enhanced by the delicate draughtsmanship, with brown *bokashi* on the back and grey *bokashi* above the eyes.

REFERENCES: Yoshida, 1967, Z suppl. no. 9; Suzuki, 1970, no. 58 [b]; Suzuki, 1975, p. 91 [b]; *Ukiyoe taikei*, 11, no. 6 [b]; *Ukiyoe hakka*, 1984, no. 86 [b]; Bogel and Goldman, 1988, no. 2 [b]; Kobayashi, 1990, no. 103 [b]; Pulverer, 1990, no. I-79 [a: this impression]; Ōkubo, 1992, no. 26

VIEWS OF EDO I

CAT. 6–16

6 BOATS AT ANCHOR OFF AN ISLAND

The First Cuckoo at Tsukudajima Island (Tsukudajima hatsu kakkō)

from the series *Famous Views in the Eastern Capital* (*Tōto meisho*)
published by Kawaguchiya Shōzō, *c.* 1831–2

signed: *Ichiyūsai Hiroshige ga*
censorship seal: *kiwame*
woodblock, *ōban*, 255 x 364 mm
Collection Pulverer, Cologne (ex-John St. Happer and F. Tikotin Collections)

A few boats are lying at anchor off the island of Tsukudajima in the Bay of Edo. The vantage point is in the north, probably Eitai Bridge or the district of Hatchōbori. To the right the Shiba district can be seen in a curve in the bay, and the southernmost tip of Honjo Fukagawa is visible on the left. Several masts in the foreground emphasise the high viewpoint and serve to give the scene added depth.

Wisps of cloud are reddened by the setting sun, and the approach of evening is indicated by the dark blue strip along the top of the print, against which a slender crescent moon is sharply delineated. The 'first cuckoo' of the title, which can be seen under the tip of the moon, traditionally heralds the arrival of summer. Prints showing a cuckoo in combination with masts or the moon are a regular feature of Hiroshige's oeuvre (see cat. 14). The composition in this print is undoubtedly heavily influenced by Hokusai's view of Tsukudajima from the series *Thirty-six Views of Mount Fuji* of *c.* 1830–5. In fact *Famous Views in the Eastern Capital* seems to have been largely inspired by Hokusai's famous publication, which is one of the reasons for dating Hiroshige's series of ten prints to 1831–2. Some of these were reissued in an exclusively blue palette and this may also reflect the influence of Hokusai's Fuji series.

The name and address of the publisher and the censorship seal *kiwame* in the right-hand margin have been partly cropped. Early impressions such as this (a) have a decorative ochre border and the water is not printed in blue right up to the horizon. Subsequently, a terracotta meander pattern was printed in the margin and the entire surface of the water appeared dark (b), while still later states (c) lack the decorative margin and all the inscriptions in the right-hand margin and show the tail and wing of the bird totally merged.

REFERENCES: Narazaki, 1975, no. 2 [a]; Nagata, 1986, fig. 1 [c]; Pulverer, 1990, no. I-77 [a: this impression]; Sakai, 1996, nos. 447 [b], 448 [a]

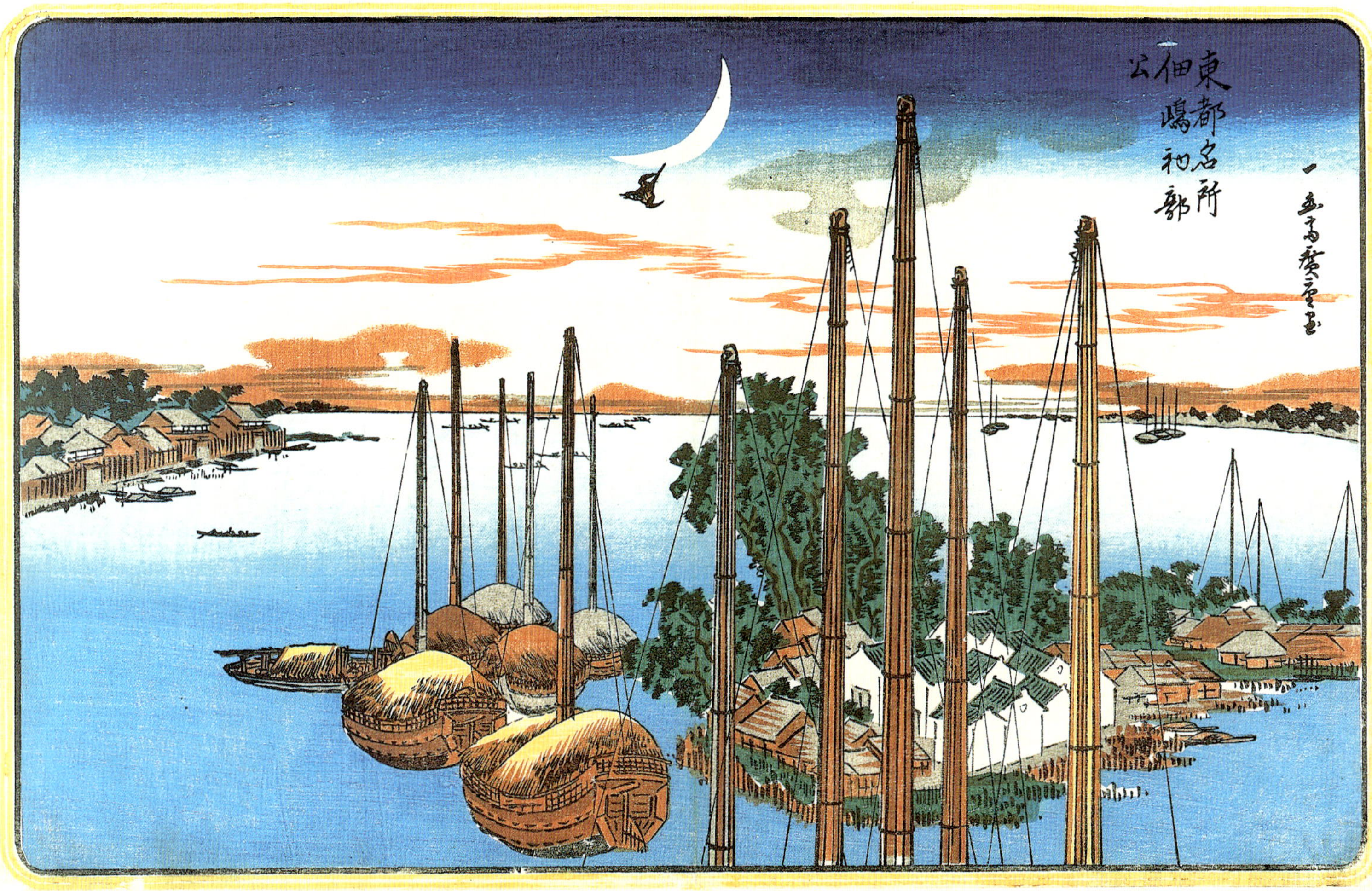
東都名所
佃嶋初郭公

7 GEESE DESCENDING OVER A BAY

Full Moon over Takanawa (*Takanawa no meigetsu*)

from the series *Famous Views in the Eastern Capital* (*Tōto meisho*)
published by Kawaguchiya Shōzō, *c.* 1831–2

signed: *Ichiyūsai Hiroshige ga*
censorship seal: *kiwame*
woodblock, *ōban*, 248 x 378 mm
The Mann Collection, Highland Park, Illinois

A flight of geese descends over the bend in the Bay of Edo near the southern district of Takanawa. To the left a few fishing boats are lying at anchor. A large full moon is silhouetted against the *bokashi* blue sky that runs across the upper edge of the print. Both the decorative border—probably an allusion to the frames of Western paintings—and the wisps of low-hanging clouds contribute to the Western feel of this composition. The position of the flight of geese, the stone gate and the signs, which are all conspicuous in the foreground, clearly suggest the influence of Western-style perspective, to which Hiroshige was to return at a later date.

Takanawa was a long, narrow strip of coastland between Ōkido, the gate that marked the border of the city of Edo, and Shinagawa. Every traveller along the Tōkaidō Road to Kyoto had to pass it. This accounts for the signs and the stone gate, built in 1710 to replace a wooden gateway, where travellers had to show their travel documents. Supplies for the journey could be purchased from the row of stalls along the coastal road and, of course, there were innumerable tea-houses and restaurants. In some impressions (a) the water is dark blue only up to the lowest of the flying geese, as here; in others (b) it is blue right up to the horizon.

REFERENCES: Narazaki, 1960, no. 33 [a]; Yoshida, 1973, no. 2 [b]; Suzuki, 1975, p. 10 [b]; *Ukiyoe hakka*, 1984, no. 28 [a]; Sakai, 1996, no. 446 [a: remargined]

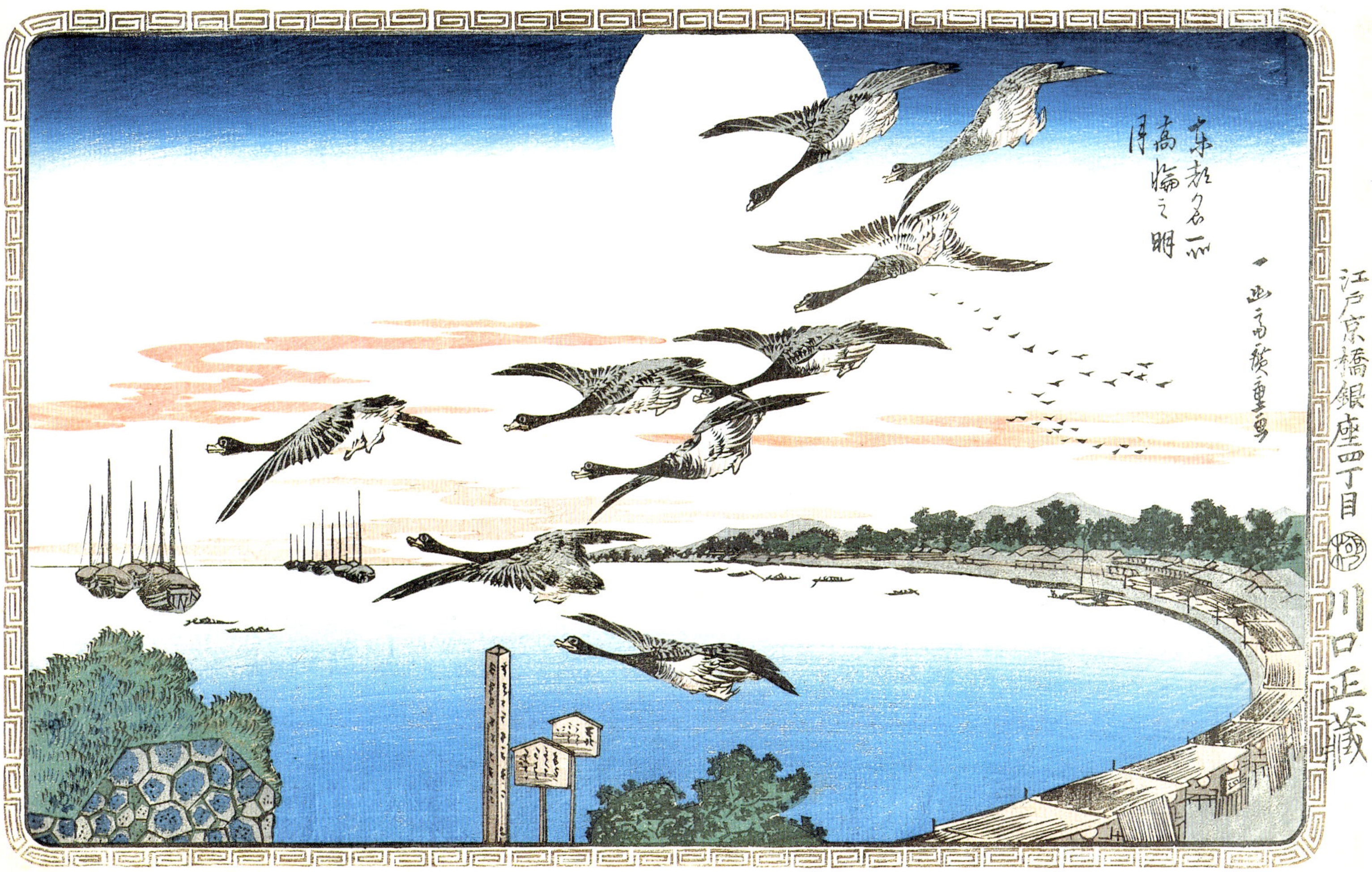
東都名所
高輪之明月
一幽斎廣重画
江戸京橋銀座四丁目
川口正蔵

8 PEOPLE WALKING UNDER CHERRY TREES AT NIGHT

Evening Cherry at Nakanochō in the Yoshiwara (*Yoshiwara Nakanochō yozakura*)

from the series *Famous Views in the Eastern Capital* (*Tōto meisho*)
published by Sanoya Kihei (Kikakudō), *c.* 1834–5

signed: *Hiroshige ga*, with seal: *Hiro*
censorship seal: *kiwame*
woodblock, *ōban*, 248 x 364 mm
Honolulu Academy of Arts, Honolulu,
Gift of James A. Michener, 1991 (23.572)

By the light of a full moon visitors and courtesans are walking under the flowering cherry trees at the gateway to the Yoshiwara, Edo's pleasure district. On the right a courtesan in full dress is followed by two trainee courtesans (*shinzō*). In the centre foreground is a courtesan with even younger assistants (*kamuro*). Further to the left are two geishas. A few visitors try to remain incognito by wrapping their heads in veils.

This is one of more than twenty prints, all with a series title and that of the individual print in a cartouche in the right-hand margin, that are often regarded as constituting a coherent series. Given the long period of publication—probably *c.* 1832 to 1838—and the fact that the same publisher continued to publish similar series (of twenty-one and sixteen designs) with the same title in cartouches of a slightly different shape, it is debatable whether this was planned as a series. It seems more likely that the publisher, Sanoya Kihei, whose store near Shiba Shinmei was passed by virtually every traveller along the Tōkaidō Road, had a constant demand for prints of the most famous places in Edo. No doubt such prints were the equivalent of present-day postcards.

The Yoshiwara, not far from the city centre, was founded in 1617 by an entrepreneur in an attempt to prevent the spread of prostitution throughout the city by confining it to a designated area. The district, which became a haven for the urban population to enjoy the flourishing nightlife, developed a culture of its own, including portraits of famous courtesans, the beauty queens of the time. It also offered a taste of the excessive, even to those who could not afford to visit the brothels, for the spectacle was always colourful and there were festivals in every season. One popular pastime was to admire the blossoms of the cherry trees in the main street, the Nakanochō. Hiroshige included a print of this same subject in an earlier series of views of the capital, published by Kawaguchiya Shōzō (cat. 6, 7). In that print he used an elevated vantage point to introduce a degree of depth into the design (*Ukiyoe hakka*, 1984, no. 29), but here he has chosen a low angle, so that the perspective is different and both the building on the right and the main street extend off the sheet (see also fig. 3, p. 29).

In later impressions (b), which lack the clouds in the sky at left, there are many differences in the colour of the clothes, and the ground and cherry leaves, which are grey here (a), are green in spite of the moonlight.

REFERENCES: Tanba, 1965, no. 25 [b]; Suzuki, 1970, no. 11 [a]; Suzuki, 1975, p. 6 [a: geisha in blue]; *Meihin soroimono ukiyoe*, 10, no. 166 [a]; Satō, 1994, no. 2 [a]; Sakai, 1996, no. 502 [a]

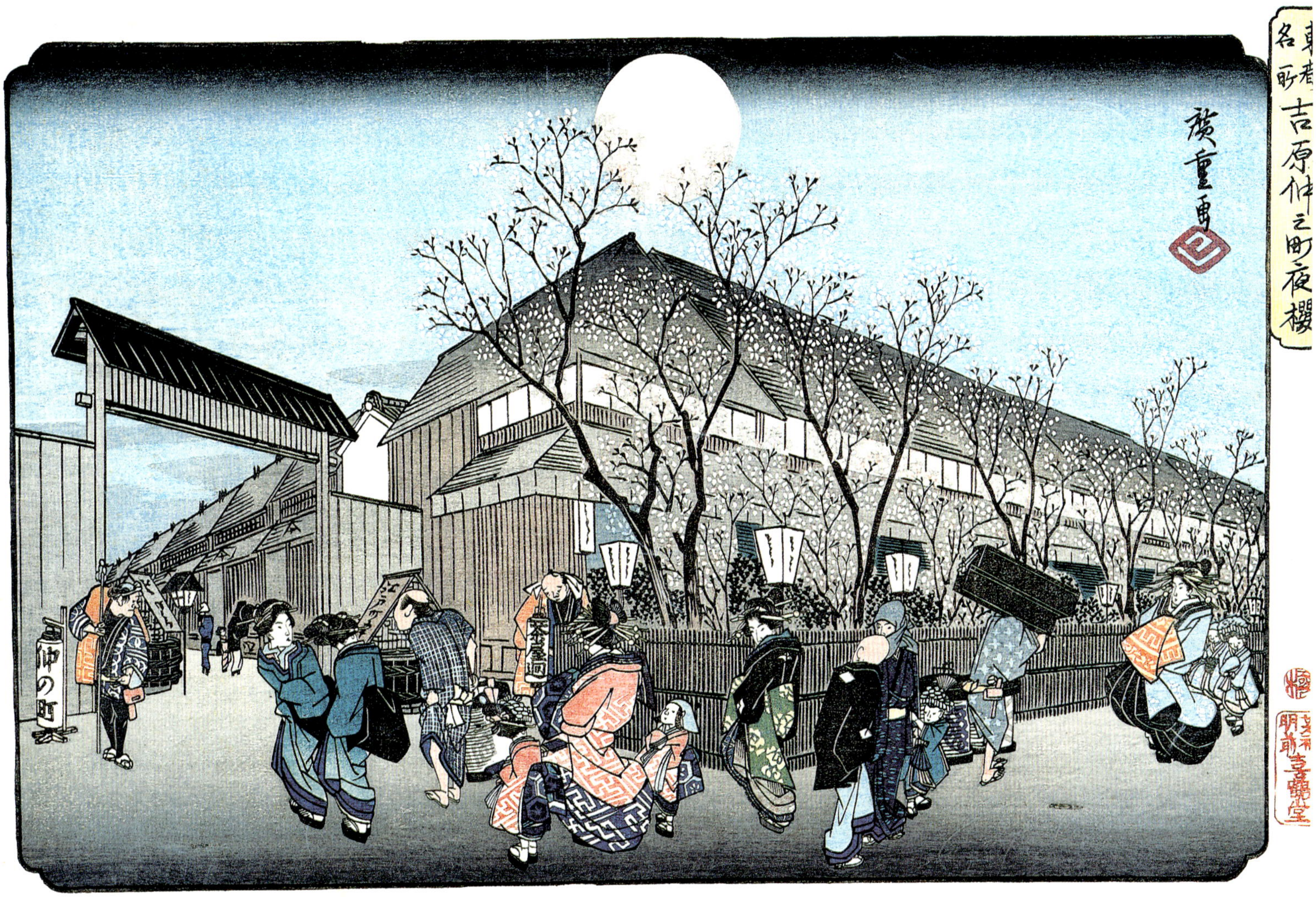
東都名所
吉原仲之町夜桜
廣重画
仲の町

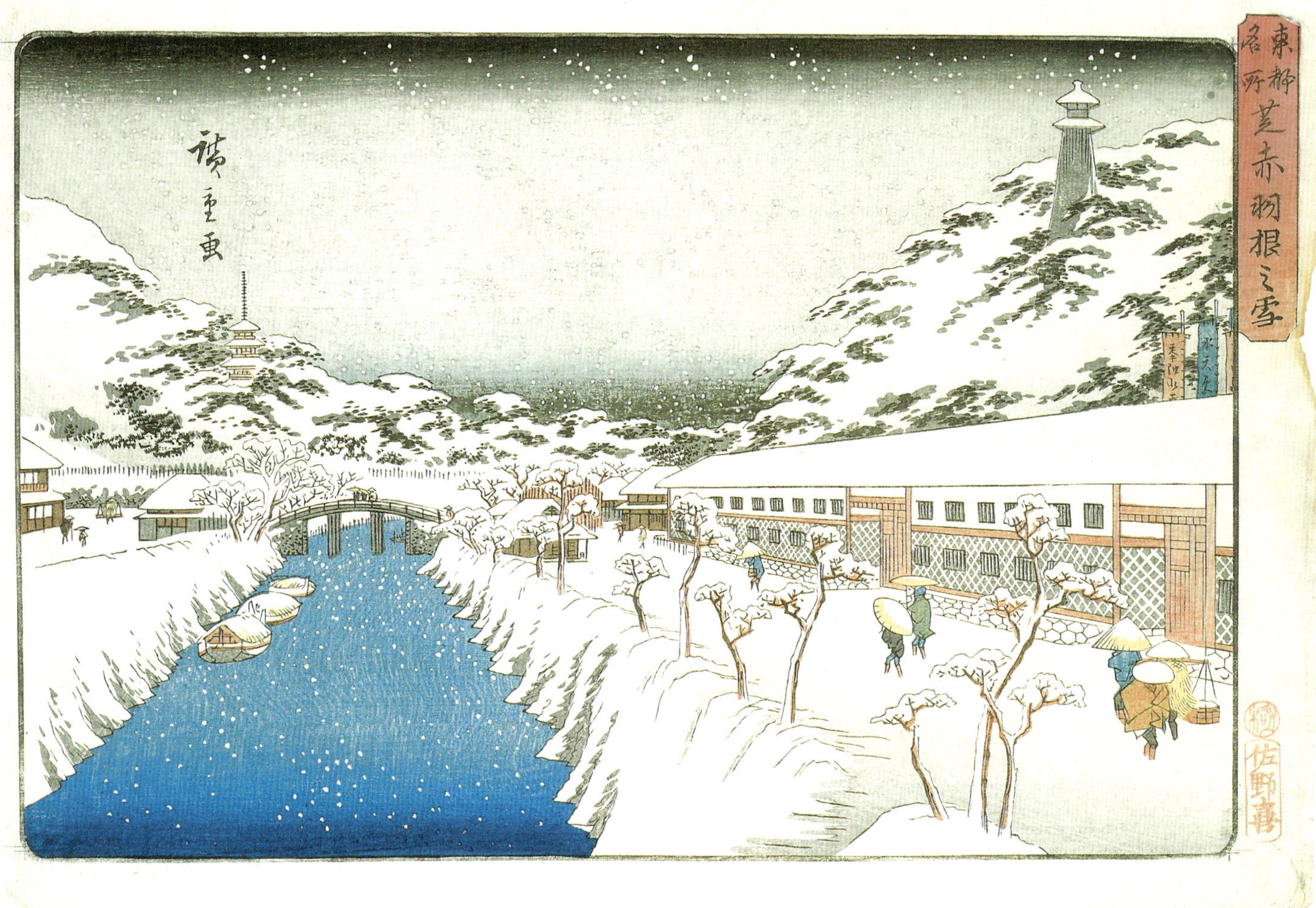

9 VIEW OF A CANAL IN THE SNOW

Snow at Akabane in the Shiba District (*Shiba Akabane no yuki*)

from the series *Famous Views in the Eastern Capital* (*Tōto meisho*)
published by Sanoya Kihei, *c.* 1834–5

signed: *Hiroshige ga*
censorship seal: *kiwame*
woodblock, *ōban*, 251 x 378 mm
The Art Institute of Chicago, Chicago,
The Clarence Buckingham Collection (1925.3464)

A view of the Akabane River under snow with Akabane Bridge in the distance. To the left, rising between the trees, is the pagoda of Zōjōji, the largest temple in the southern Shiba district of Edo. On the right is the side of chancellor Arima's mansion; the extremely tall fire-tower was said to be the most expensive in the whole of Edo.

This print, which is a fine example of Western-style perspective with a single vanishing-point, exists in two states. The earlier (a) has the name of the publisher and the *kiwame* censorship seal in red; the later state (b) has the seal of the censor Tanaka in black. There are few other differences between them, apart from the substitution of a violet tint for the original blue sky.

REFERENCES: Sakai, 1996, nos. 514 [a], 515 [b]

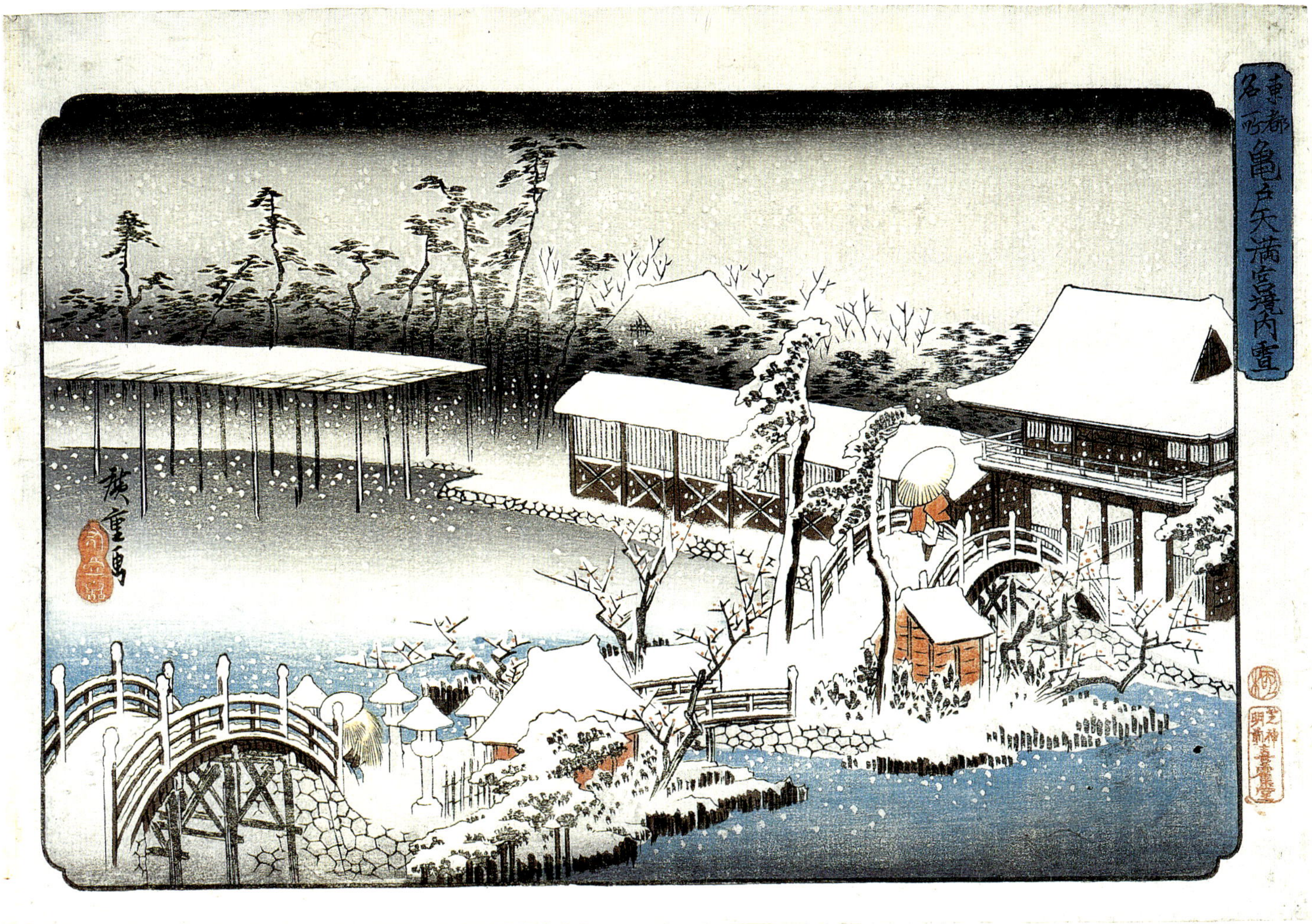

10 TEMPLE COMPLEX IN THE SNOW

The Compound of the Tenman Shrine at Kameido in the Snow (*Kameido Tenmangū keidai no yuki*)

from the series *Famous Views in the Eastern Capital* (*Tōto meisho*) published by Sanoya Kihei (Kikakudō), *c.* 1834–5

signed: *Hiroshige ga*, with seal: *Ichiryūsai*
censorship seal: *kiwame*
woodblock, *ōban*, 260 x 382 mm
The Mann Collection, Highland Park, Illinois

The Kameido Tenmangū, or Saifu Tenmangū, as the shrine now known as Kameido Tenjinsha used to be called, was one of the best known places in Edo. Famous for its pergola with wisteria and for the two drum bridges over the lake, the shrine was especially popular in the Fifth Month, when the wisteria flowered.

This print depicts the shrine in winter. A visitor is crossing the second bridge, another is returning from a visit to the shrine. The snow seems to fall ceaselessly from the dull sky.

There are various states of this print, and it is difficult to say which is the earliest. The clothing of the man on the bridge is sometimes red and white, with a purplish or blue cartouche for the title, as here (a); in other states (b) his clothing is brown and blue, with a greenish cartouche. Early impressions have the publisher's trademark and the censorship seal in red in the left-hand margin; later (c) these were printed in black with the abbreviated name of the publisher, Sanoki, and with a brown title cartouche.

REFERENCES: Suzuki, 1970, no. 12 [a]; Suzuki, 1975, p. 12 [a]; *Ukiyoe taikei*, 11, no. 40 [a]; Link, 1991, no. IV-6-A [b]; Satō, 1994, no. 1 [a]; Sakai, 1996, nos. 485 [a], 509 [c]

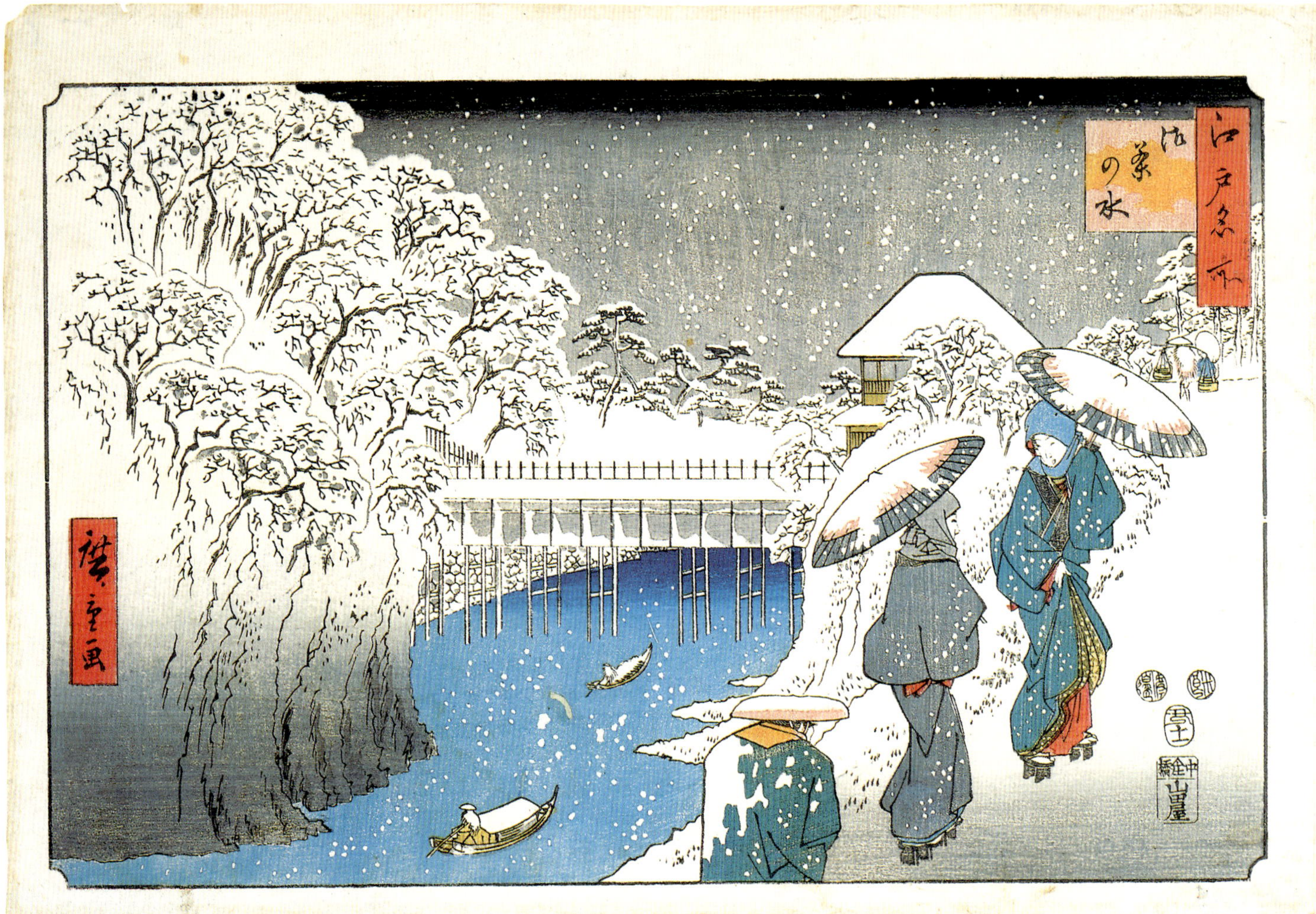

11 TWO LADIES CONVERSING IN THE SNOW

Ochanomizu

from the series *Famous Views in Edo* (*Edo meisho*)
published by Yamadaya Shōjirō, 1853

signed: *Hiroshige ga*
censors' seals: Mera and Watanabe; date seal: Ox 11 (1853/XI)
woodblock, *ōban*, 249 x 372 mm
Honolulu Academy of Arts, Honolulu,
Gift of James A. Michener, 1992 (22.088)

Ochanomizu is the name given to the bank of the Kanda River roughly between the Shōhei and the Suidō bridges. Two women stand there conversing, holding umbrellas to protect themselves from the snow. There are a few boats on the water, and in the distance is an aqueduct for the city water supply.

In early impressions such as this (a) the line-block is grey rather than black and a grey *bokashi* extends from the foreground. The sky is predominantly grey as well. The two women are dressed in blue and grey kimonos, and the water is a lightish blue. In later impressions (b), made with a black line-block, the women's kimonos are green and violet. Later still, the kimonos are green and blue, and the water is deep blue.

REFERENCES: Suzuki, 1975, p. 28 [b]; Sakai, 1996, nos. 870 [a], 871 [b]

12 MAN POLING A FERRY ON A RIVER IN THE RAIN

Asakusa River and Distant View of Kinryūzan Temple (Asakusagawa Kinryūzan no enbō)

from the series *Famous Views in Edo* (*Edo meisho*)
published by Wakasaya Yoichi, 1852

signed: *Hiroshige ga*
censors' seals: Mera and Watanabe; date seal: Rat 2 (1852/II)
woodblock, *chūtanzakuban*, 369 x 126 mm (margins at top and right)
Honolulu Academy of Arts, Honolulu,
Gift of James A. Michener, 1979 (17.512)

A ferry crosses the river in the rain. In the distance can be seen the pagoda and other buildings of the Kinryūzan Temple in Asakusa, the district after which this stretch of the Sumida River was named. The Komakatadō is visible in the left foreground (cf. cat. 103). Although Azuma Bridge was not far from here, just beyond the Komakatadō, the ferry continued to operate from the Onmayagashi, as this part of the river-bank was called. Eight designs for this series are extant (Sakai, 1996, nos. 1052–9).

REFERENCE: Sakai, 1996, no. 1052

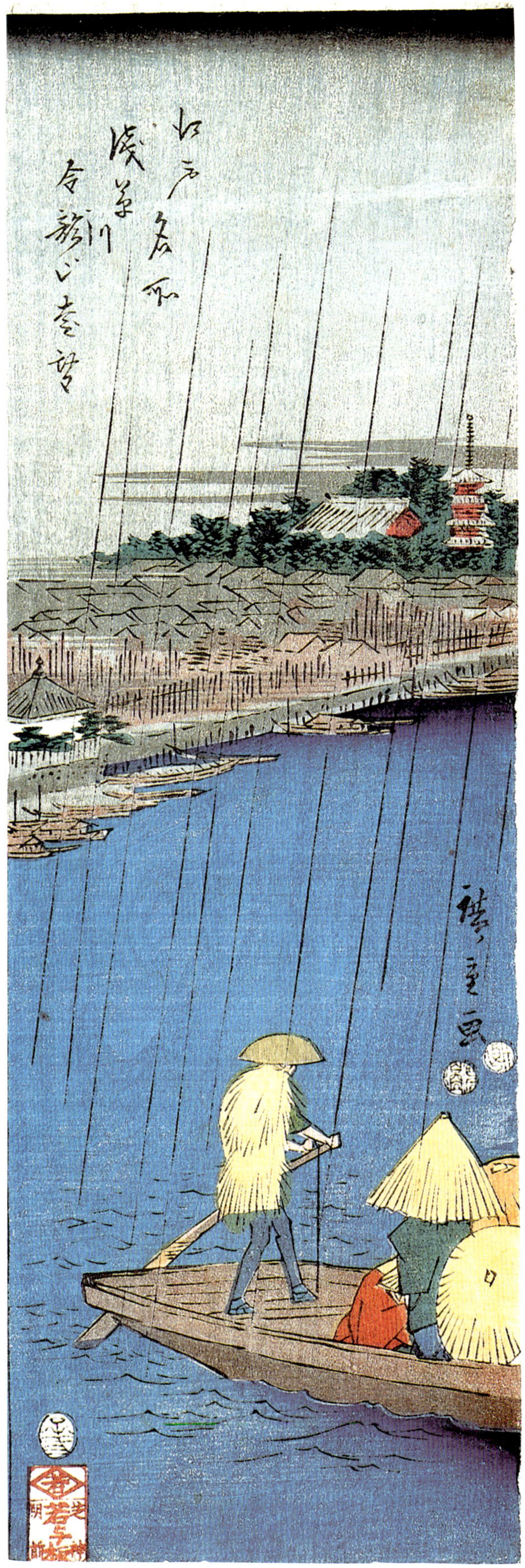

13 MAN POLING A RAFT

Winter (*Fuyu*)

from the series *Famous Views in Edo in the Four Seasons* (*Shiki Kōtō meisho*)
published by Kawaguchiya Shōzō, *c.* 1834–5

signed: *Hiroshige ga*
censorship seal: *kiwame*
woodblock, *chūtanzakuban*, 373 x 127 mm
(margins at top and right)
The Metropolitan Museum of Art, New York, H. O. Havemeyer Collection, Bequest of Mrs H. O. Havemeyer, 1929 (JP1889)

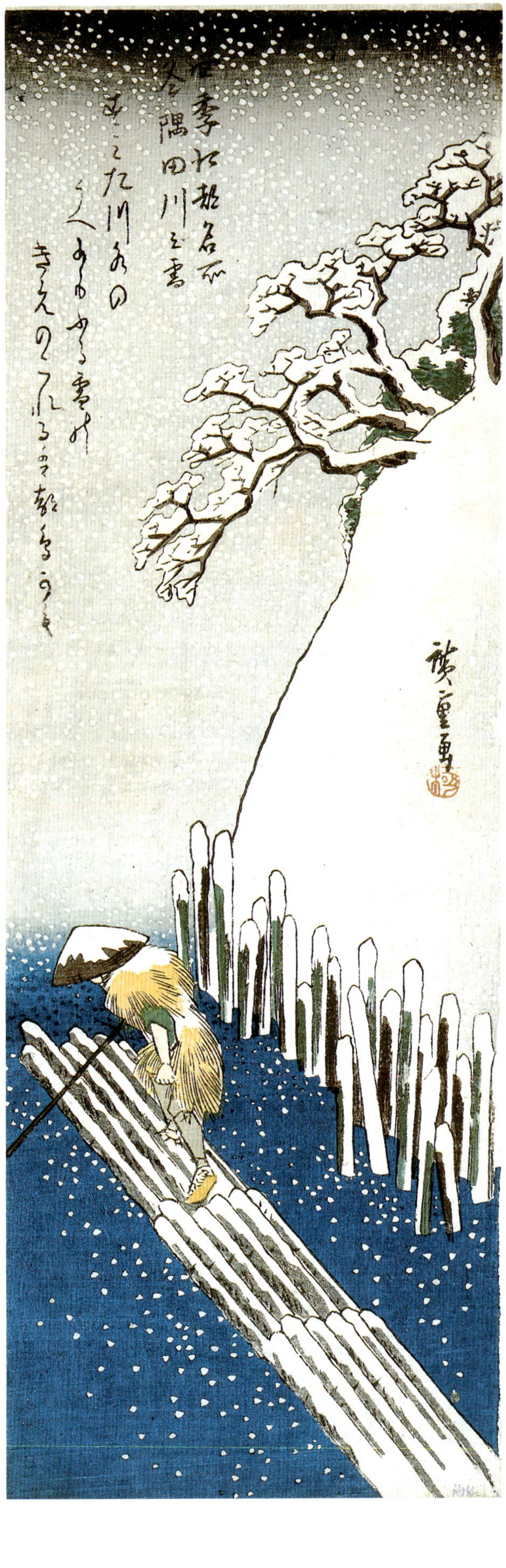

Perhaps in response to the popularity of his prints of bird and flower subjects in the *tanzaku* format, Hiroshige designed a number of landscape prints in the same narrow vertical format. In the *chūtanzaku* format it was customary to print two designs from a single block, with four designs fitting a single sheet of standard paper. As here, the format was often used for series of the four seasons. The present series consists of this design as an illustration of Winter, a view of cherry blossom near Gotenyama for Spring, the moon above Ryōgoku Bridge for Summer and maple trees near Kaianji Temple for Autumn (Suzuki, 1975, pp. 14–15; *Ukiyoe hakka*, 1984, nos. 38–40; *Meihin soroimono ukiyoe*, 10, nos. 26–28).

This print shows a lone man in a straw raincoat and hat poling a raft along the Sumida River. The falling snow provides a sharp contrast to the predominantly blue and grey tints of the print. At upper left is an anonymous *kyōka* poem:

Sumidagawa
mizu no ue nimo
furu yuki no
kienokoreru wa
miyakodori kamo

Even on the waters of Sumida River
the snow that falls fails to melt
—Or could they be seagulls?

There are impressions of this print with both the publisher's seal and the *kiwame* censorship seal (a), with the censorship seal but without the publisher's seal, as here (b), or without either (c).

REFERENCES: Suzuki, 1970, no. 17 [a]; Suzuki, 1975, p. 15 [a]; Izzard, 1983, no. 31 [c: trimmed at bottom]; Keyes, 1984, no. 740 [c]; Rappard-Boon, 1984, no. 35 [b]; *Ukiyoe hakka*, 1984, no. 41 [a]; *Meihin soroimono ukiyoe*, 10, no. 29 [a]; Sakai, 1996, no. 1027 [c]

14 A CUCKOO FLYING PAST MASTS

Eitai Bridge (*Eitaibashi*)

from the series *New Famous Views in the Eastern Capital* (*Shinpan Tōto meisho*)
published by Murataya Ichigorō (or Murataya Jirōbei), *c.* 1840

signed: *Hiroshige ga*
woodblock, *chūtanzakuban*, 364 x 123 mm
The Museum of Art, Rhode Island School of Design, Providence, Gift of Mrs John D. Rockefeller, Jr. (32.246)

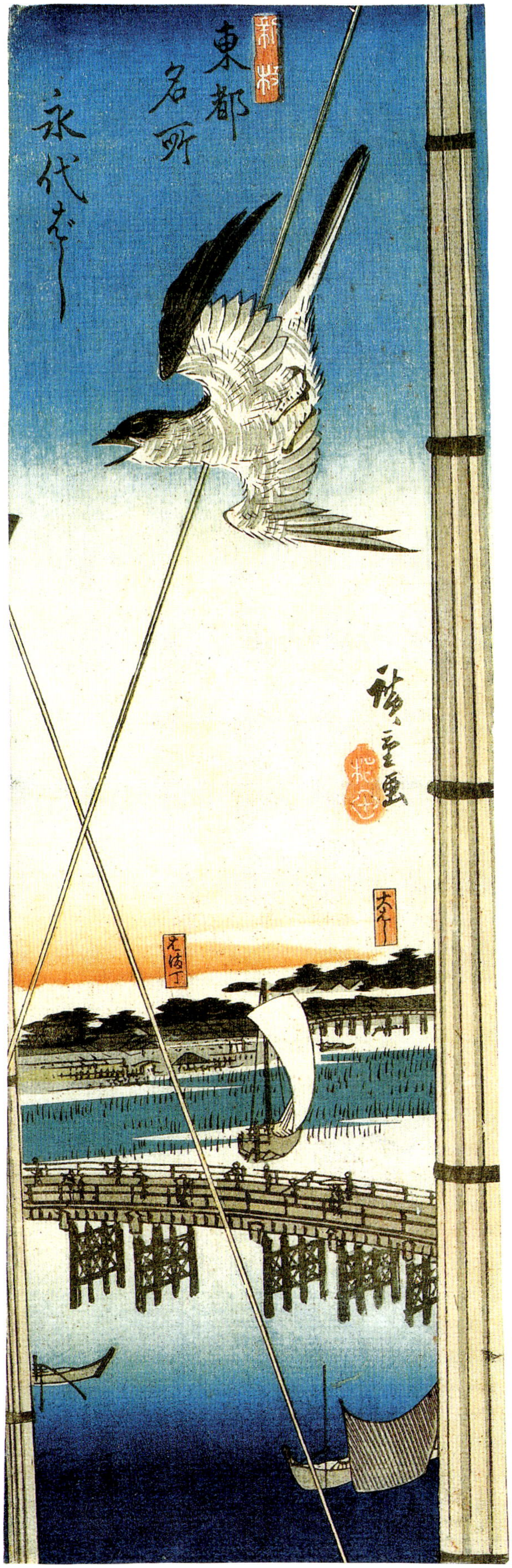

This startlingly close view of a cuckoo flying between the masts of boats near Eitai Bridge is probably intended to indicate the approach of summer. Eitai was the last bridge over the Sumida River, and the slightly wider Ōhashi (or Shin Ōhashi) can be seen in the distance. On the left is the Hamachō district. At the horizon the sky is red from the setting sun, implying that the boats are making for their mooring place.

The print is known in two impressions: the present one (a), in which the water around Eitai Bridge has been left white, and a variant (b) in which the water has been printed in a continuous blue.

Following Suzuki (1970), Link groups the print with the *Tōto meisho* series prefaced with the words *Fūryū shinchō* (*A Fashionable New Edition*). Given that this design is the only one in the group of six prints that does not bear these words, Link's assumption seems justified. Perhaps the series began with this print and the first words of the title were altered later.

REFERENCES: Kobayashi, 1990, no. 112 [a: this impression]; Link, 1991, no. IV-16-A [b]; Sakai, 1996, no. 1048 [a]

VIEWS OF THE TŌKAIDŌ AND KISOKAIDŌ ROADS

CAT. 17–49

17 RAIN ON A TOWN BY THE COAST

Ōiso—Tora's Rain (*Ōiso—Tora ga ame*)

from the series *The Fifty-three Stations of the Tōkaidō Road* (*Tōkaidō gojūsan tsugi no uchi*)
published by Takenouchi Magohachi (Hōeidō), *c.* 1831–4

signed: *Hiroshige ga*
censorship seal: *kiwame*
woodblock, *ōban*, 245 x 367 mm
Trustees of The Chester Beatty Library and Gallery of Oriental Art, Dublin (CBLJ 2672)

Beneath a black sky, a shower of rain surprises a small group of travellers as they enter the town of Ōiso in Sagami Province. To the right of the road is Mount Kōrai, which could also be seen from Hiratsuka, the previous station. To the left is a view of the sea. The dark rainstorm hangs menacingly above the horizon in the yellowish sky.

The town of Ōiso had been the residence of Tora Gozen, also known as Ōiso no Tora, a courtesan and the mistress of Soga no Jūrō, the oldest of the two Soga brothers who slew Kudō Suketsune in 1193 and thereby avenged the death of their father. Jūrō was killed almost immediately, while his brother Gorō was later beheaded with a blunt sword. This historical event was subsequently elaborated in innumerable plays for the nō and puppet theatre, later also for the kabuki theatre, where it became the traditional New Year's performance in the three theatres of Edo. Tora Gozen was later metamorphosed into a stone, one of the sights of Ōiso, and cried on the 28th day of the Fifth Month, the day of Jūrō's death. The printed title of the image, *Tora's Rain*, is a reference to this.

The colour of the sky and the general tone of the print are darker in later impressions (b), which seems less appropriate in view of the subject's allusion to the Fifth Month. There is no further difference in colour between these impressions.

REFERENCES: *Ukiyoe taikei*, 14, no. 9 [b]; Shiraishi, 1988, p. 29 [a]; Link, 1991, no. I-1-J [a]; *Meihin soroimono ukiyoe*, 11, no. 9 [a]

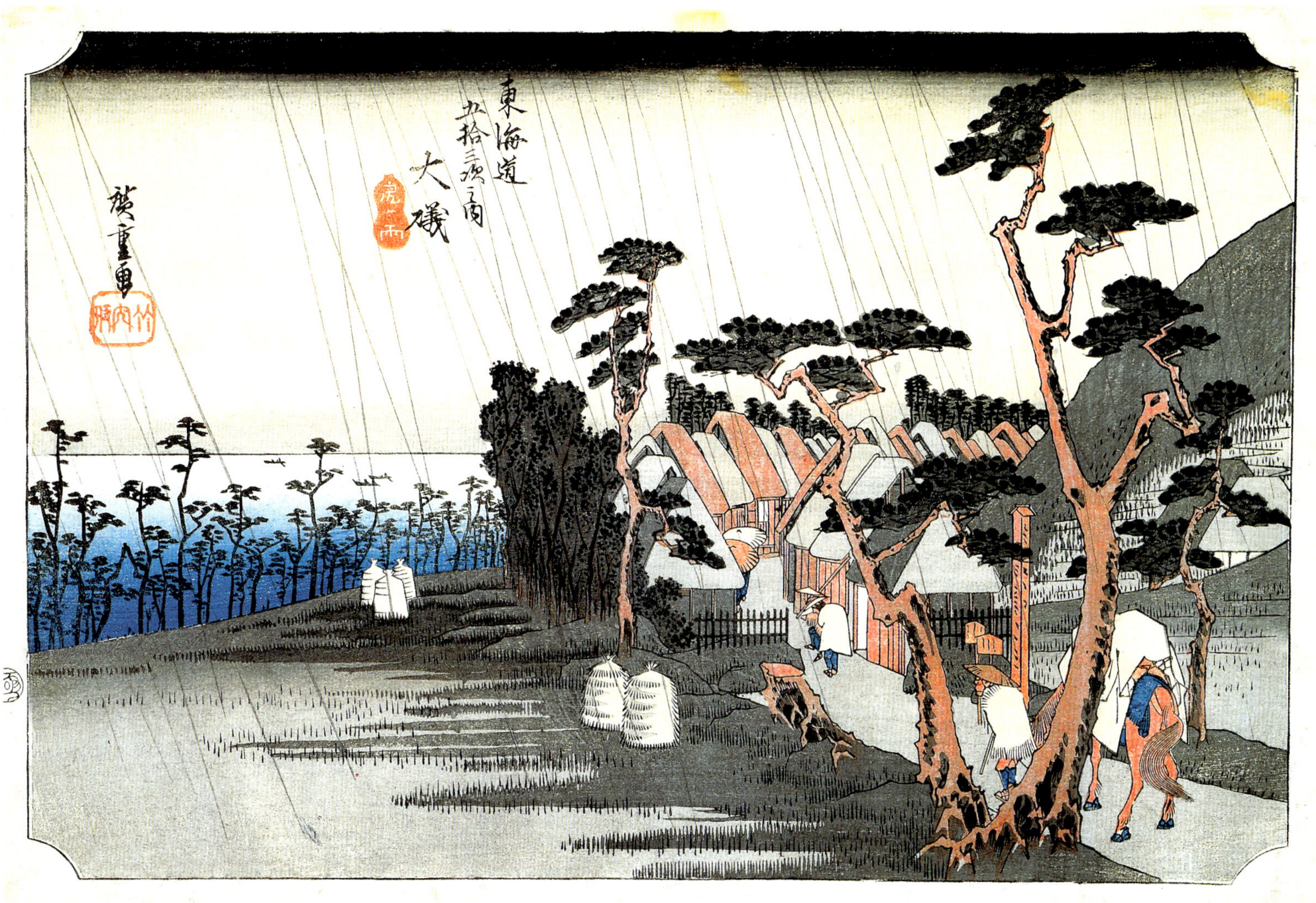
東海道
五拾三次之内
大礒
虎ヶ雨
廣重画

18 HIGH ROCKS BY A LAKE

Hakone—View of the Lake (Hakone—Kosui no zu)

from the series *The Fifty-three Stations of the Tōkaidō Road*
(*Tōkaidō gojūsan tsugi no uchi*)
published by Takenouchi Magohachi (Hōeidō), *c.* 1831–4

signed: *Hiroshige ga*
censorship seal: *kiwame*
woodblock, *ōban*, 248 x 372 mm
The Art Institute of Chicago, Chicago,
The Frederick W. Gookin Collection (39.1362)

The route between the stations of Odawara and Mishima takes the traveller through the mountainous region near Hakone, in Sagami Province, with peaks of more than 1,000 metres. The road continues up and down past the original site of Hakone, to Lake Ashi, and through Hakone Pass to the station of Hakone. In this print a *daimyō* procession is descending a steep mountain path, with Mount Futagoyama looming over them. To the left is Lake Ashi and beyond it Mount Fuji, silhouetted against the reddish sky. The buildings on the shore of the lake are probably part of the Hakone Gongen shrine complex.

This is an evocative composition, with rich variation in colour and an effective use of grey *bokashi* to suggest the mist in the valleys. It is certainly not an accurate topographical representation: Mount Fuji, for example, is not visible from this angle.

In this impression (a) the sky is simply printed as a thin reddish strip above the mountains—in others the red extends up to or even beyond the uppermost characters of the series title—and the grey *bokashi* has been kept fairly low down, so that the foreground appears remarkably clear and not, as in some impressions (b), strongly flecked with grey. In yet other impressions (c) the sky at the horizon, too, is almost purplish or ochre.

REFERENCES: Yoshida, 1973, no. 5 [b]; *Ukiyoe taikei*, 14, no. 11 [b]; *Ukiyoe hakka*, 1984, no. 2 [b]; Shiraishi, 1988, p. 35 [c]; Link, 1991, no. I-1-M [a]; *Meihin soroimono ukiyoe*, 11, no. 11 [a]

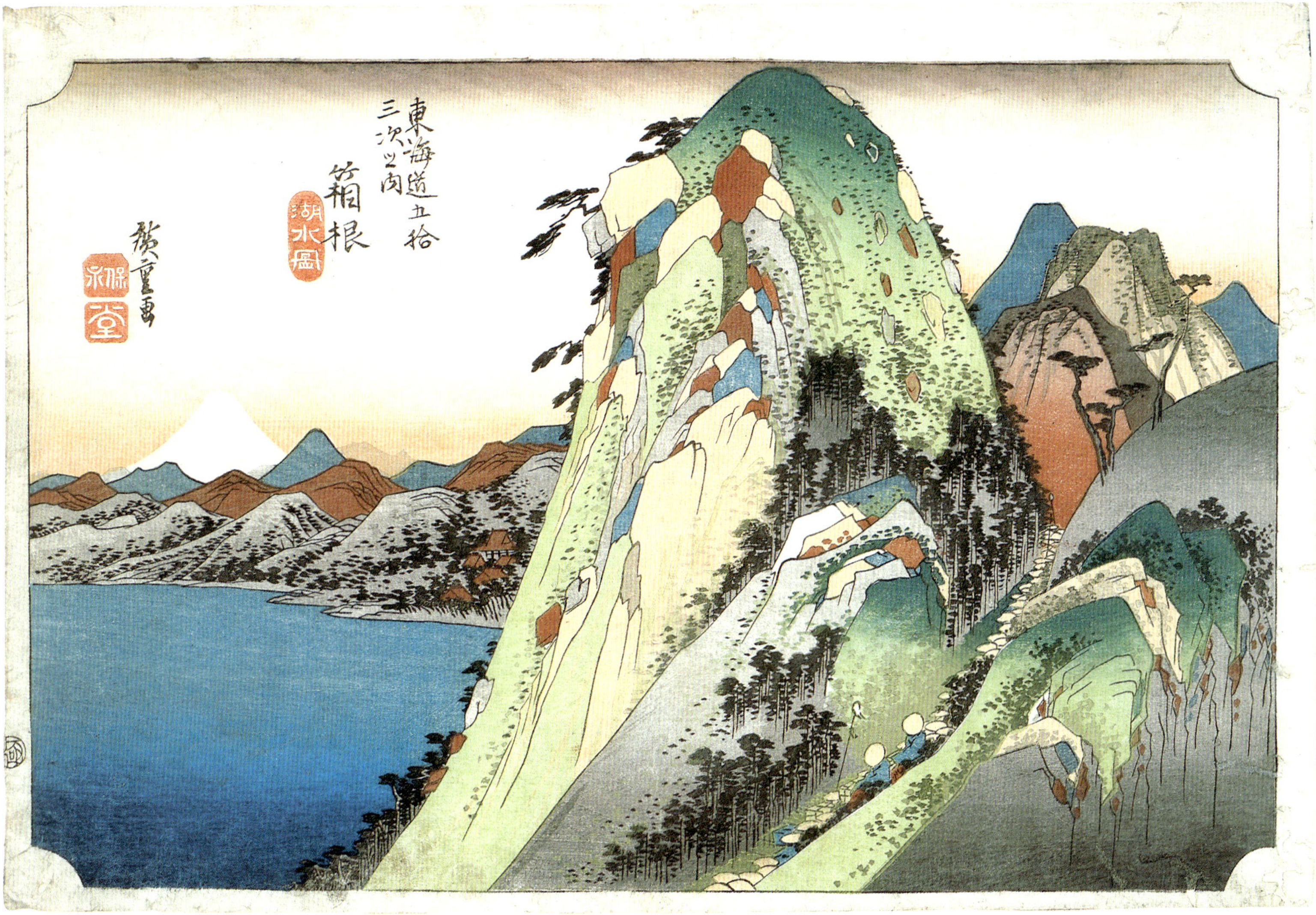
東海道五拾三次之内
箱根
湖水圖
廣重画

19 TRAVELLERS PASSING A SHRINE IN THE MIST

Mishima—Morning Mist (Mishima—Asagiri)

from the series *The Fifty-three Stations of the Tōkaidō Road* (*Tōkaidō gojūsan tsugi no uchi*)
published by Takenouchi Magohachi (Hōeidō), *c.* 1831–4

signed: *Hiroshige ga*
censorship seal: *kiwame*
woodblock, *ōban*, 252 x 378 mm
The Museum of Art, Rhode Island School of Design, Providence, Bequest of Isaac C. Bates (13.1057)

A small company of travellers is passing through the town of Mishima in Izu Province. The gateway and two stone lanterns of the Mishima shrine are clearly visible in the morning mist. To the left the roofs of the town and a few further figures are discernible in the middle distance. Since the shrine is to the right of the road, the travellers are heading for Edo, with Hakone (cat. 18) as the next station. This explains the simple construction of the litter, the most suitable type for the mountainous route ahead.

This print is the only misty landscape in the series and that aspect seems to have been emphasised in successive printings. In this early impression (a) the lower edge of The fence around the shrine, the lower edge of the houses on the left and the three figures on the left are visible. In some later impressions (b) the lower edge of the fence, the house furthest to the right and the figure furthest to the right are only indicated; in others (c) the lower edge of the fence and the two houses are no longer visible and two of the figures are only half-visible. In view of the detailed depiction of the travellers, including the pattern on their clothes, the transition to thick mist in these latter impressions seems too abrupt. In some impressions of the early state the strip of sky along the upper edge of the print is in black *bokashi* instead of blue. It is not certain whether or not this should be regarded as a characteristic of the first state. According to some Japanese scholars, a later impression included the inscription 'Senjokō' on the temple lantern, an advertisement for a popular brand of white face-powder (see cat. 27). However, this inscription was stamped on the print, not printed from the block, and does not, therefore, necessarily indicate a later state.

REFERENCES: Narazaki, 1960, no. 4 [a]; *Ukiyoe taikei*, 11, no. 13 [a: black at top], and 14, no. 12 [c]; *Ukiyoe hakka*, 1984, no. 3 [c]; Schindler, 1985, no. 168 [c]; Shiraishi, 1988, p. 37 [c]; Link, 1991, no. I-1-N [a: black at top]; *Meihin soroimono ukiyoe*, 11, no. 12 [b]; Copenhagen, 1993, no. 81 [b]

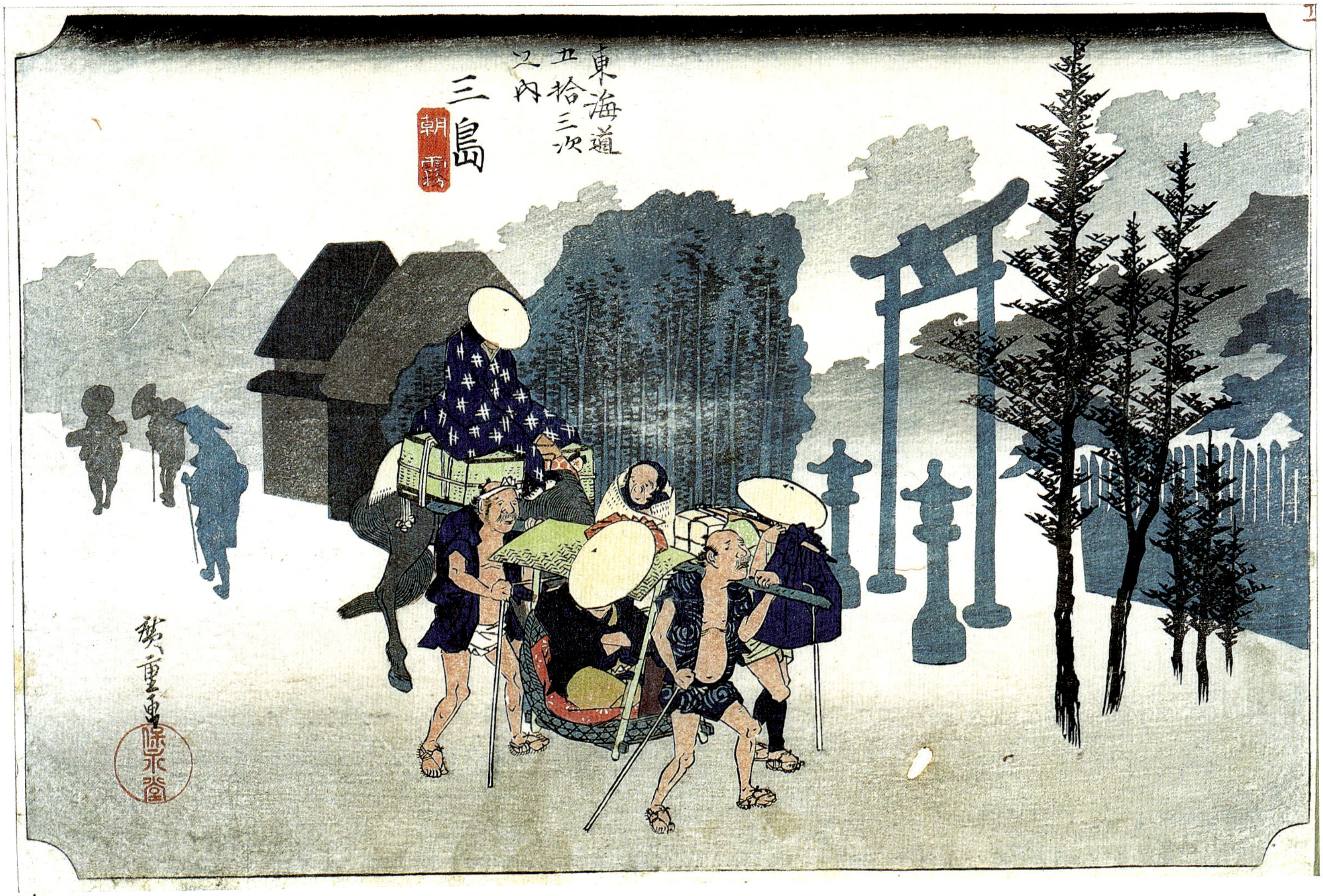
東海道
五拾三次
之内
三島
朝霧
廣重画
保永堂

20 TRAVELLERS PASSING MOUNT FUJI

Hara—Mount Fuji in the Morning (*Hara—Asa no Fuji*)

from the series *The Fifty-three Stations of the Tōkaidō Road* (*Tōkaidō gojūsan tsugi no uchi*)
published by Takenouchi Magohachi (Hōeidō), *c.* 1831–4

signed: *Hiroshige ga*
censorship seal: *kiwame*
woodblock, *ōban*, 255 x 383 mm
Honolulu Academy of Arts, Honolulu, Gift of James A. Michener, 1972 (17.252; ex-Matsuki Bunkio Collection)

Mount Fuji towers above a plain—and extends beyond the frame of the print—while two women in travelling dress speak to their porter. The early morning sun reddens the sky. Mount Fuji is partly hidden behind Mount Ashitakayama. The company has left the station of Hara in Suruga Province and would already seem to be close to Yoshiwara, the next station. The region contains many pools and eel is one of its specialities. Two cranes can be seen in the field to the right. The porter's jacket bears a pattern that later appears regularly on Hiroshige's prints as his seal, consisting of the two signs for 'Hiro'. In this Tōkaidō series it is otherwise found only in the prints for the stations of Shirasuka and Narumi.

Hara was the station with the best view of Mount Fuji. It is therefore hardly surprising that the mountain dominates the prints for this station in virtually all the major Tōkaidō series that Hiroshige designed. He repeats the device of extending it beyond the frame in the designs for the so-called *Gyōsho Tōkaidō* and *Kyōka Tōkaidō*, as well as in the vertical Tōkaidō series. In the other Tōkaidō series a comparable effect was achieved by making the frame cut off the mountain peak.

REFERENCES: *Ukiyoe taikei*, 14, no. 14; Shiraishi, 1988, p. 43; Link, 1991, no. I-1-P [this impression]; *Meihin soroimono ukiyoe*, 11, no. 14

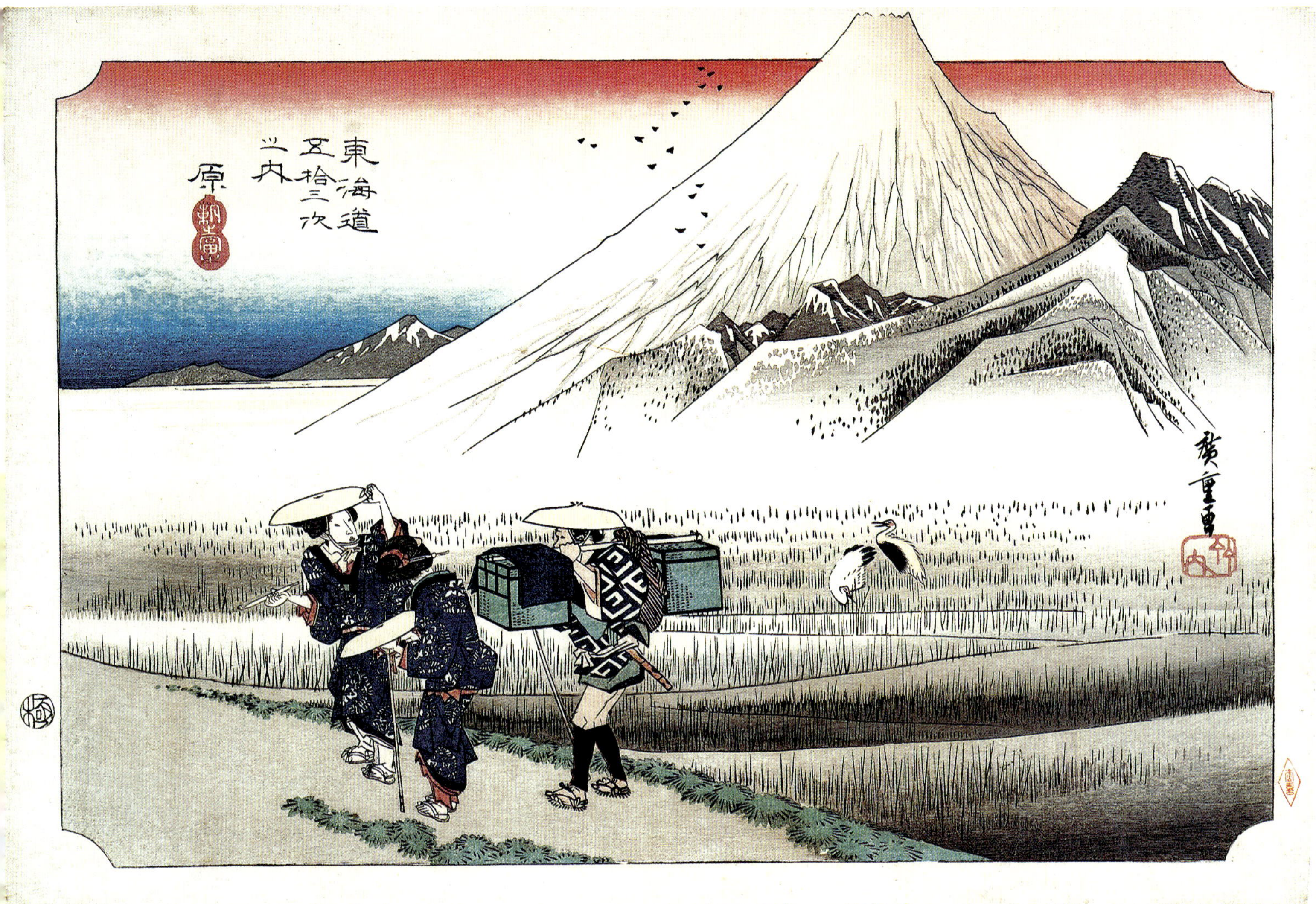

東海道
五拾三次
之内
原
朝之冨士
廣重画

21 A VILLAGE IN THE SNOW

Kanbara—Evening Snow (*Kanbara—Yoru no yuki*)

from the series *The Fifty-three Stations of the Tōkaidō Road* (*Tōkaidō gojūsan tsugi no uchi*)
published by Takenouchi Magohachi (Hōeidō), *c.* 1831–4

signed: *Hiroshige ga*
censorship seal: *kiwame*
woodblock, *ōban*, 259 x 386 mm
Honolulu Academy of Arts, Honolulu,
Gift of James A. Michener, 1971 (15.927)

Two figures in cloaks and hats are walking up a snow-covered hill. To the left is a man in blue with an umbrella and walking-stick. The mountains in the distance and the houses in the foreground stand out against a grey sky. It is evening: the strip of sky along the upper edge of the print is dark. Nevertheless, no light burns in the row of houses on the left: the figures in the print are apparently the only people in the town of Kanbara, in Suruga Province, who have not yet gone to bed.

In this impression the details of the houses and the roof supports can be seen clearly; in other impressions they are printed in a much darker tone. A far more significant difference, however, is that in most impressions the gradation-printed darkness usually starts behind the houses and the hills and ends roughly half-way up the sky (cat. 112). This, of course, provides no clue as to the date of an impression. Certainly, it cannot have been the intention to print the sky in a dark tone extending a long way down from the top of the print, for in that case the characters for the title of the series would have been white, as in the print for Miya (*Ukiyoe taikei*, 14, no. 42).

The first clear indication of a new state of this print is the appearance of a gap in the line above the right knee of the figure on the far right. Initially, the block-cutter made a mistake and did not cut away all the wood between the lines of this figure's legs. When this was made good later on, the gouge apparently slipped, producing the small break above the knee. The two states are generally referred to as 'dirty knee' and 'wounded knee'. 'Dirty knee' impressions, as here, usually have the sky dark at the upper edge of the print, while in 'wounded knee' impressions it becomes lighter from behind the houses upwards. The former impressions often display blue *bokashi* on the mountain in the background; this is generally grey in impressions where the sky is dark at the bottom. The grey *bokashi* became the norm, as is indicated by its appearance in an impression of the 'wounded knee' (i.e. later) state that has the sky dark at the top (Shiraishi, 1988, p. 47).

REFERENCES: Suzuki, 1970, no. 7; Yoshida, 1973, no. 3b; *Ukiyoe takei*, 11, no. 14 [this impression], and 14, no. 16-1 [with false left margin and therefore the *kiwame* seal in an unusual position]; Nagata, 1986, no. 9; Link, 1991, no. I-1-Q [this impression]; Copenhagen, 1993, no. 76

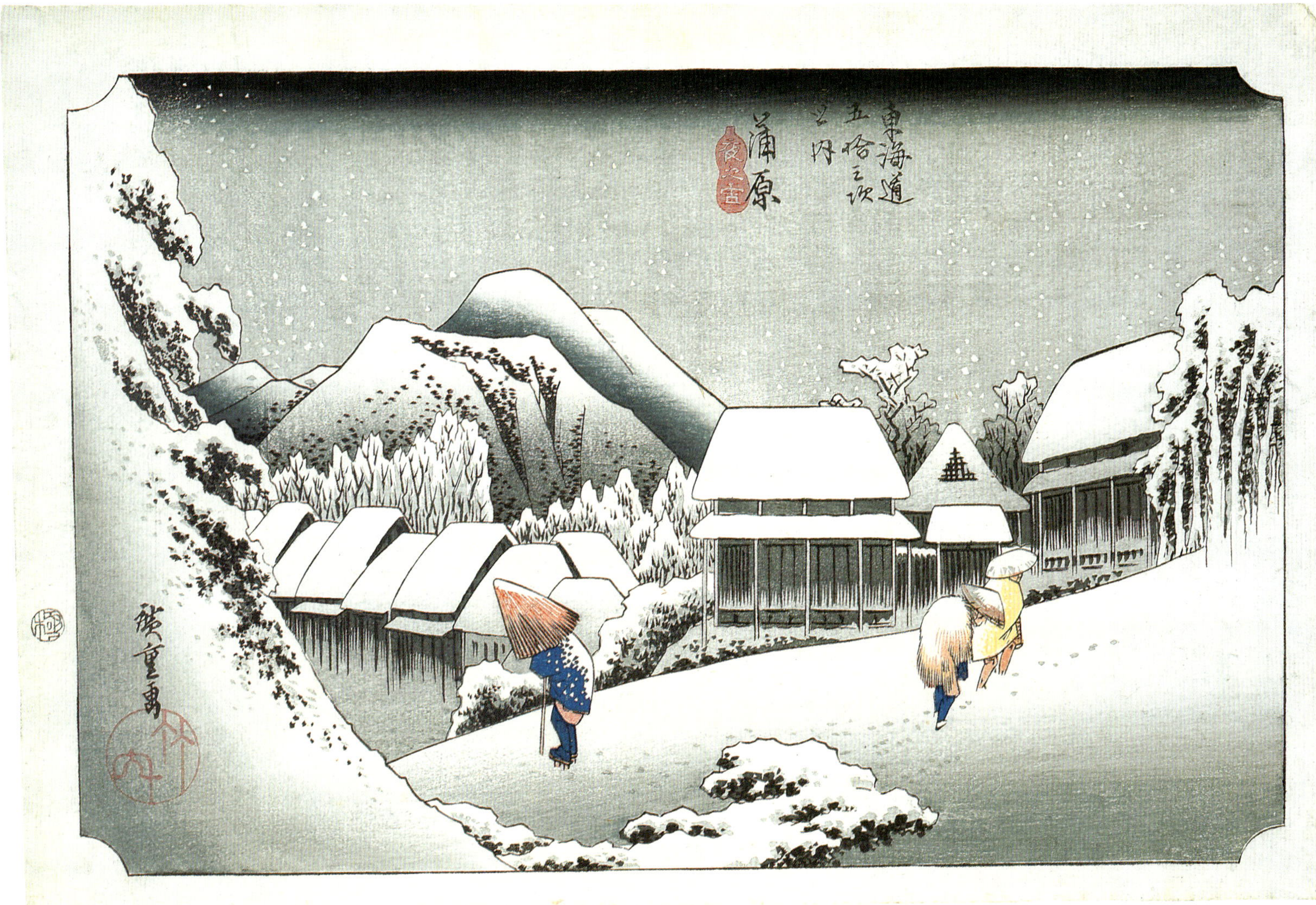
東海道
五拾三次
之内
蒲原
夜之雪
廣重画

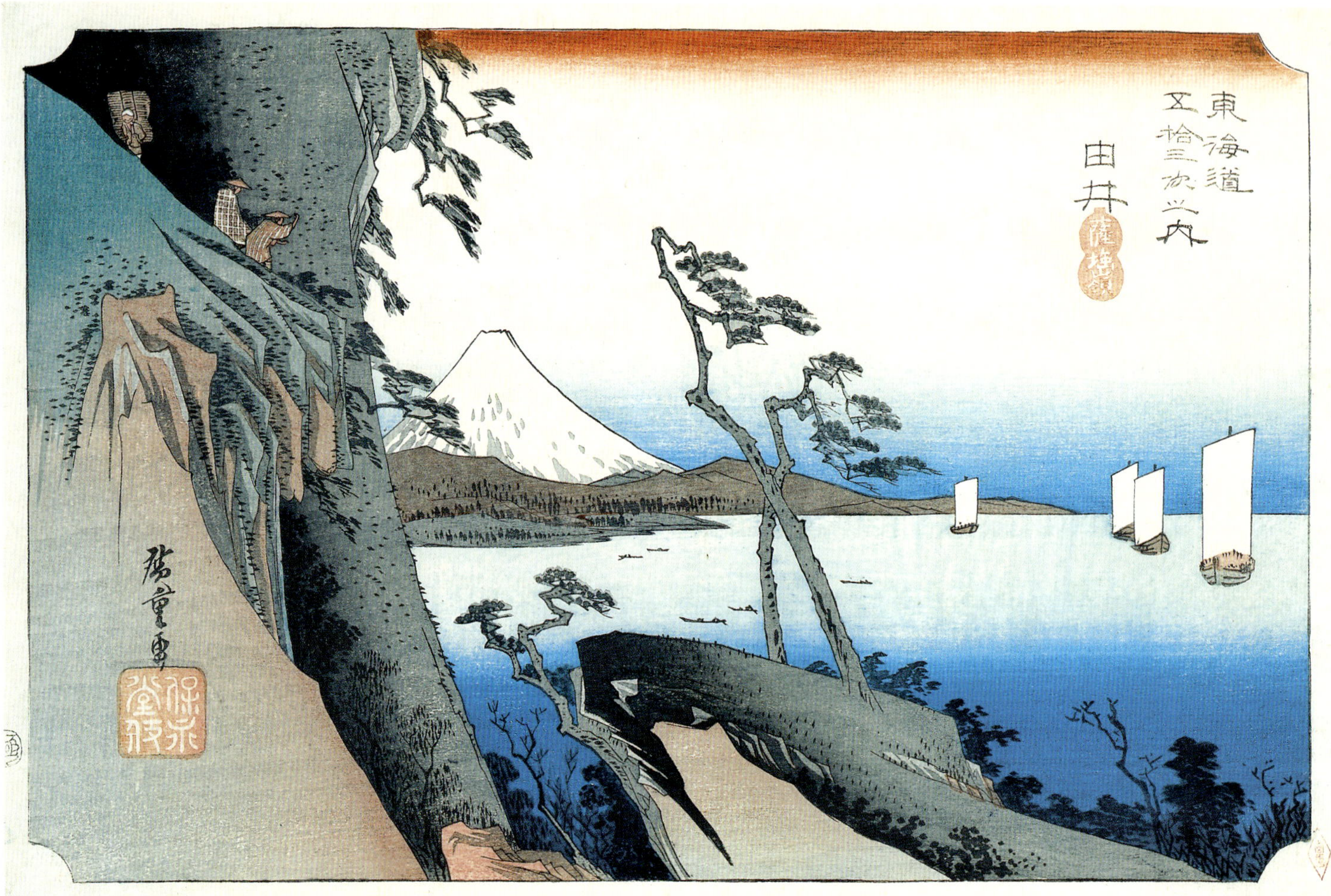

22 TRAVELLERS ON A HIGH CLIFF BY THE SEA

Yui—Satta Pass (*Yui—Satta mine*)

from the series *The Fifty-three Stations of the Tōkaidō Road* (*Tōkaidō gojūsan tsugi no uchi*)
published by Takenouchi Magohachi (Hōeidō), *c.* 1831–4

signed: *Hiroshige ga*
censorship seal: *kiwame*
woodblock, *ōban*, 242 x 368 mm
Honolulu Academy of Arts, Honolulu, Gift of James A. Michener, 1979 (17.423; ex-Matsuki Bunkio Collection)

A few travellers on a path above a steep cliff admire the panorama of Kiyomi Bay, as this section of Suruga Bay is called. We look past a rocky outcrop surmounted by two pine trees, twisted in the wind, to see Mount Fuji in the distance. Satta Pass was carved out of the rocks in 1655. It is the boundary between Yui in Suruga Province and Okitsu in the modern prefecture of Shizuoka. Yui is behind one at this point and Mount Fuji still further behind, in the direction of Edo. Nevertheless, this is regarded as one of the best places for a good view of the mountain. Hiroshige depicted more or less the same landscape in the vertical Tōkaidō series of 1855 (Shiraishi, 1988, p. 48), and the site also forms the subject of cat. 54.

In this and the other earliest impressions (a) the sea is printed in *bokashi* from the lower edge upwards, whereas in later impressions (b) the *bokashi* extends downwards from the horizon. Still later impressions (c) omit the reddish *bokashi* on the rocks in the left and centre foreground, while the lower mountains at the foot of Mount Fuji are dark grey instead of brown; the *bokashi* on the rocky outcrop in the foreground is replaced by overprinting in dark grey. Experiments were also made with the colour of the sky: early impressions have a yellow sky (*Meihin soroimono ukiyoe*); later it became orange (*Ukiyoe taikei*) or red (Forrer, 1994)

REFERENCES: *Ukiyoe taikei*, 14, no. 17 [b]; Shiraishi, 1988, p. 49 [c]; Link, 1991, no. I-1-S [a: this impression]; *Meihin soroimono ukiyoe*, 11, no. 17 [b]; Forrer, 1994, G445 [b]

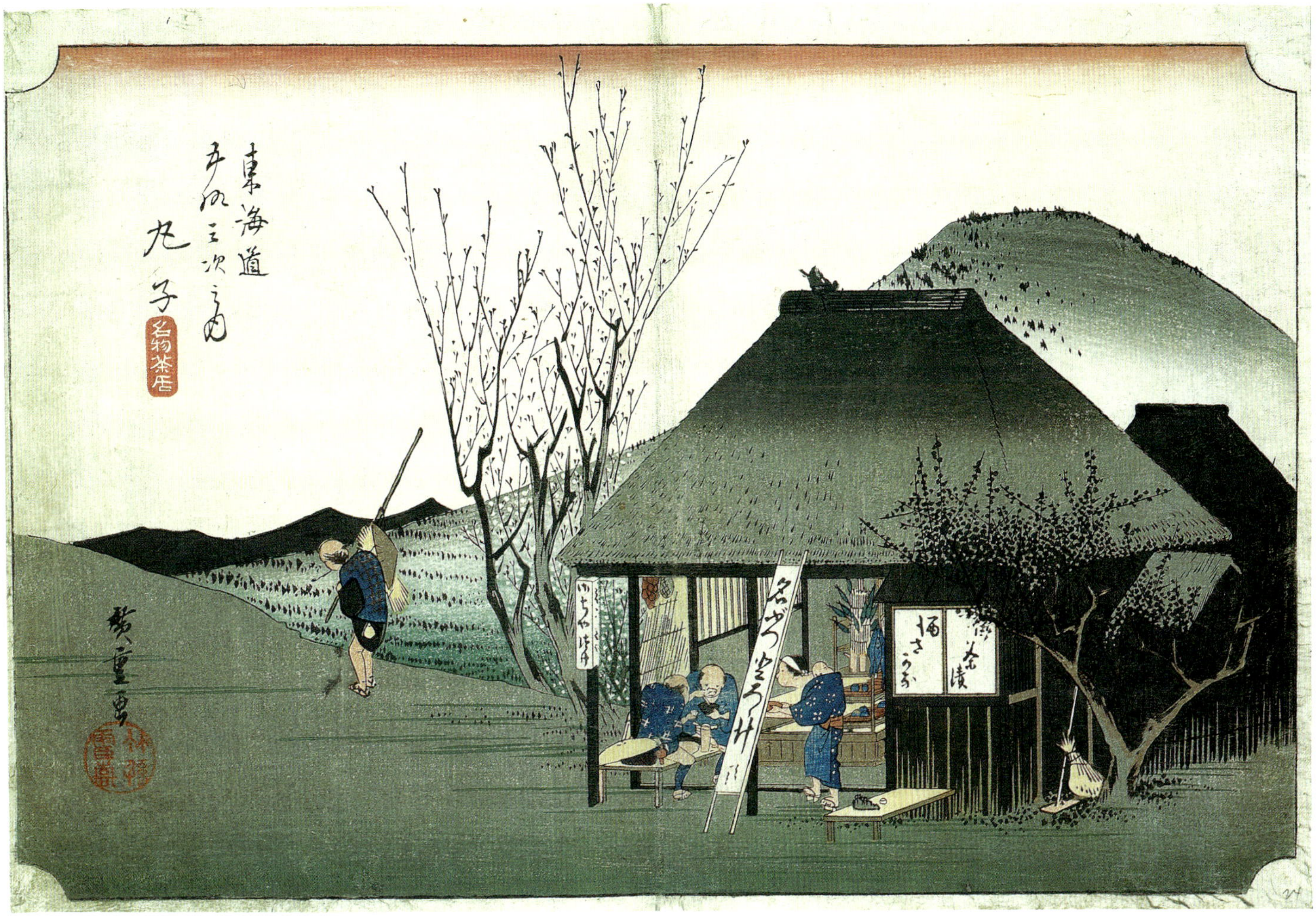

23 A ROADSIDE RESTAURANT

Mariko—Local Specialities Shop (*Maruko—Meibutsu chamise*)

from the series *The Fifty-three Stations of the Tōkaidō Road* (*Tōkaidō gojūsan tsugi no uchi*)
published jointly by Takenouchi Magohachi (Hōeidō) and Tsuruya Kiemon (Senkakudō), *c.* 1831–4

signed: *Hiroshige ga*
censorship seal: *kiwame*
woodblock, *ōban*, 243 x 360 mm
The Art Institute of Chicago, Chicago,
The Clarence Buckingham Collection (1925.3522)

Two travellers pause at a roadside stall near Mariko in Suruga Province where tea is served with a local speciality called *tororoshiru*, a paste made from grated yam. They are served by a woman who is carrying a child on her back. A third traveller passes by smoking a pipe, his hat and raincoat tied to a stick over his shoulder. This is one of the eleven prints that Takenouchi Magohachi originally published jointly with the more established Tsuruya Kiemon. The others were the stations: 1–Nihonbashi, 2–Shinagawa, 3–Kawasaki, 5–Hodogaya, 6–Totsuka, 7–Hiratsuka, 18–Okitsu, 23–Fujieda, 26–Nissaka and 28–Fukuroi. Five of these designs, including the present one, probably received an extra subsidy because they provided advertising for certain restaurants or inns. The speciality *tororoshiru* appears in the illustrations for Mariko in virtually all Hiroshige's major Tōkaidō series except the *Reisho Tōkaidō* and the *Tōkaidō fūkei zue* album, although the dish is mentioned in the text of the latter (Shiraishi, 1988, pp. 56–7).

This print is notable for its very soft tints and for the clarity of the scene in the tea-house that results from the balanced use of colour. This early impression (a) contains an error in the name of the station, which is written *Maruko* instead of *Mariko*. This mistake was later corrected (b).

REFERENCES: *Ukiyoe taikei*, 14, no. 21 [a]; *Ukiyoe hakka*, 1984, no. 5 [a]; Shiraishi, 1988, p. 57 [b]; *Meihin soroimono ukiyoe*, 11, no. 21 [b]

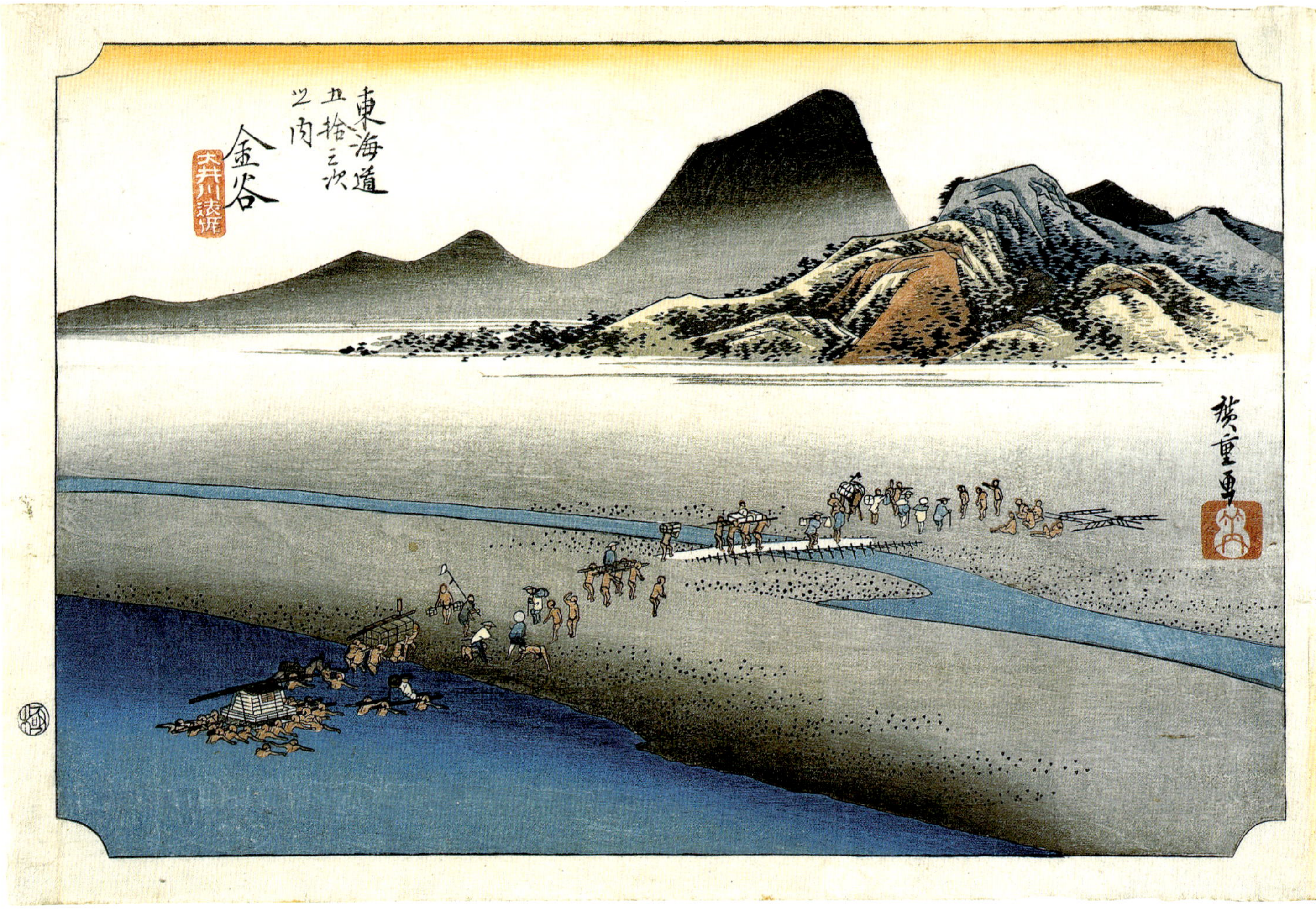

24 CROSSING A WIDE RIVER

Kanaya—The Distant Bank of Ōi River (Kanaya—Ōigawa engan)

from the series *The Fifty-three Stations of the Tōkaidō Road (Tōkaidō gojūsan tsugi no uchi)*
published by Takenouchi Magohachi (Hōeidō), *c.* 1831–4

signed: *Hiroshige ga*
censorship seal: *kiwame*
woodblock, *ōban*, 249 x 378 mm
Private Collection, Denmark

The Ōi River marks the boundary between the provinces of Suruga and Tōtōmi. There was no bridge in Hiroshige's day and, because of the dangerous current, people usually crossed the river on the shoulders of a wader or on a simple litter. This provided a livelihood for some 350 people on both sides of the river.

Hiroshige depicts the crossing of this imposing river for two stations: Shimada and Kanaya. The town of Kanaya in Tōtōmi Province is visible among the peaks of the Kanayasaka in the distance. The sun setting behind the hills reddens the sky slightly.

In early impressions of this print, as here (a), the river-bank is grey with dark grey *bokashi*, while the hills in the distance are yellow, brown and blue-grey. In later impressions (b) the river-bank is ochre with bluish grey *bokashi* and the hills green, brown and grey.

REFERENCES: *Ukiyoe taikei*, 14, no. 25 [b]; Nagata, 1986, no. 10 [a: this impression]; Shiraishi, 1988, p. 67 [b]; Link, 1991, no. I-1-W [a]; *Meihin soroimono ukiyoe*, 11, no. 25 [b]; Copenhagen, 1993, no. 79 [a: this impression]

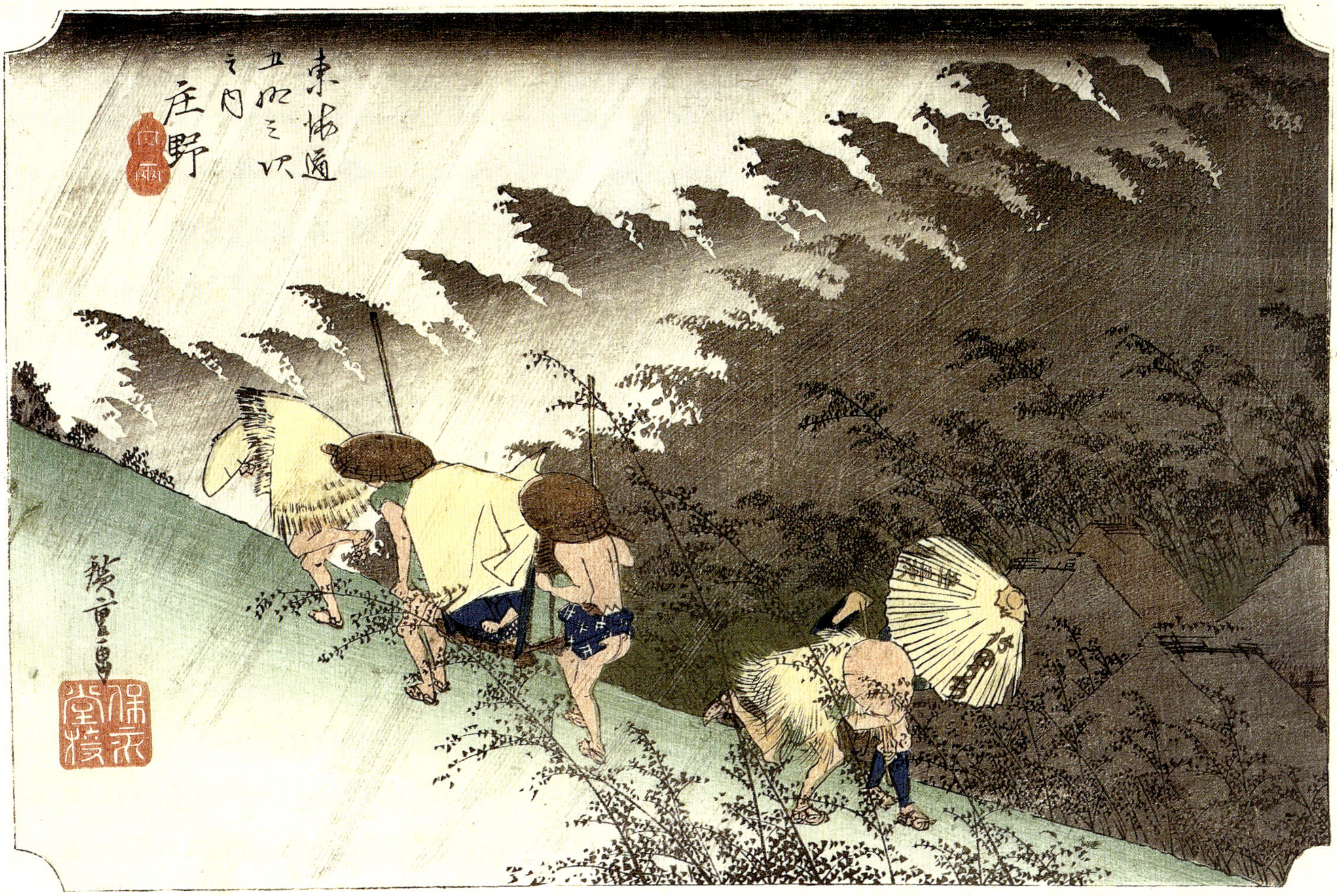

25 TRAVELLERS SURPRISED BY SUDDEN RAIN

Shōno—Sudden Rain (*Shōno—Hakuu*)

from the series *The Fifty-three Stations of the Tōkaidō Road* (*Tōkaidō gojūsan tsugi no uchi*)
published by Takenouchi Magohachi (Hōeidō), *c.* 1831–4

signed: *Hiroshige ga*
censorship seal: *kiwame*
woodblock, *ōban*, 239 x 370 mm
Berès Collection, Paris

Some travellers are surprised by a sudden shower of rain near the town of Shōno in Ise Province. To the right a man with an umbrella is followed by a man with a hat and cloak. The umbrella bears two inscriptions: *Takenouchi*, the name of the publisher of the series, and *Gojūsan tsugi*, part of the title of the series. Another man with a hat and cloak walks uphill, followed by two litter-bearers. The bamboo is bent low under the downpour.

This print underwent a number of changes in the course of time. In the earliest impressions (a), the rows of bamboo are printed uniformly in three different greys, with green *bokashi* between the roofs on the right and black *bokashi* extending upwards from the foreground on the right. The black *bokashi* in the foreground is missing from a slightly later impression (b), illustrated here. In a still later impression (c) the crests of the row of bamboo in the background are printed in *bokashi*, as if partly concealed by the rain. In all these impressions the falling rain is like a grey curtain; in the later ones it is given more emphasis by being printed in distinctly darker squalls (cat. 110).

REFERENCES: Narazaki, 1960, no. 35 [b]; Suzuki, 1970, no. 6 [a]; Yoshida, 1973, no. 4 [a]; Narazaki, 1975, no. 5 [b]; *Ukiyoe taikei*, 11, no. 16 [a], and 14, no. 46 [a: re-margined, hence the two censorship seals]; *Ukiyoe hakka*, 1984, no. 7 [a]; Shiraishi, 1988, p. 113 [a]; Link, 1991, no. I-1-Ab [c]; *Meihin soroimono ukiyoe*, 11, no. 46 [b]; Copenhagen, 1993, no. 77 [a]

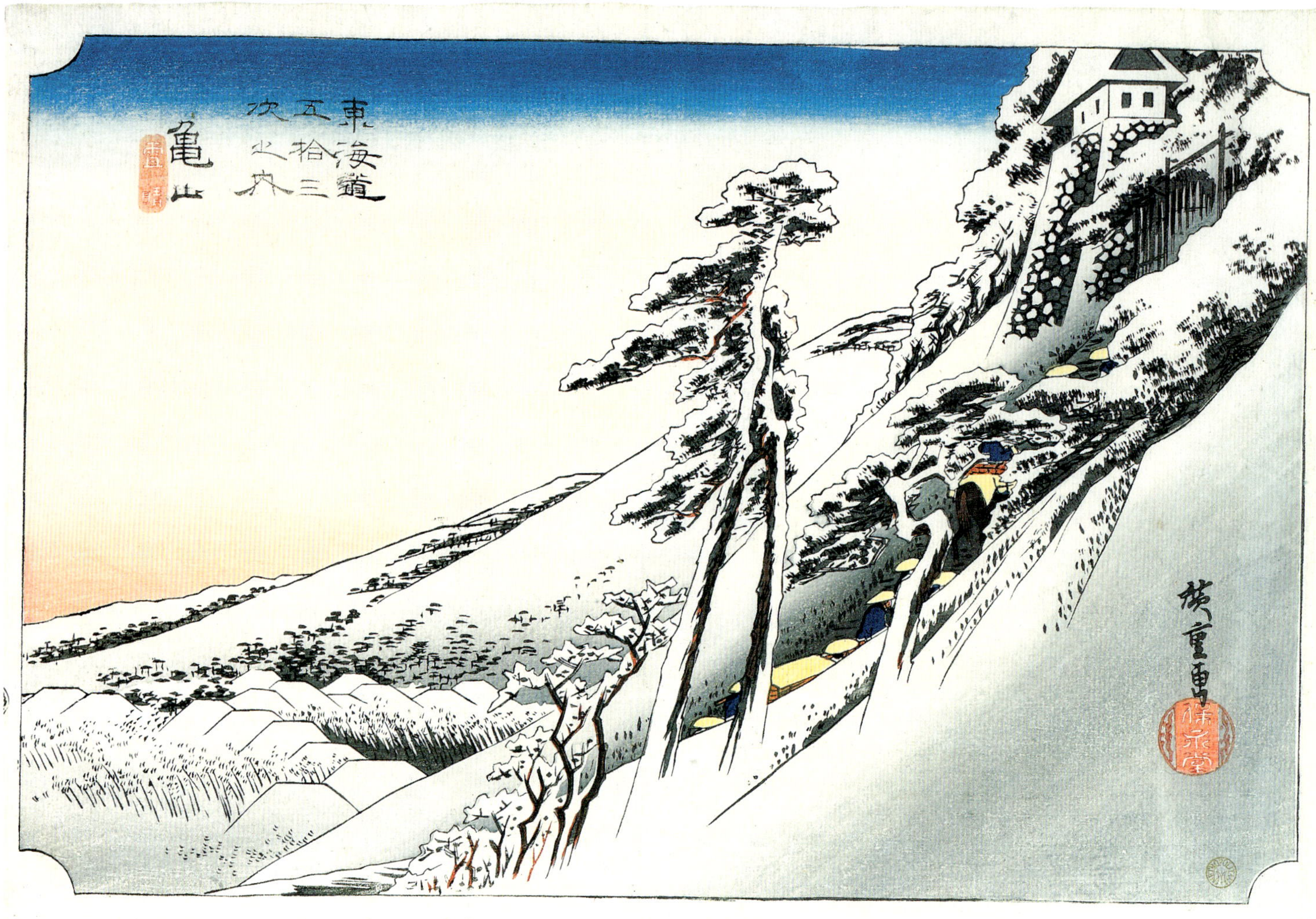

26 A CASTLE ON A SNOW-COVERED SLOPE

Kameyama—Weather Clearing after Snow (Kameyama—Yukibare)

from the series *The Fifty-three Stations of the Tōkaidō Road (Tōkaidō gojūsan tsugi no uchi)*
published by Takenouchi Magohachi (Hōeidō), *c.* 1831–4

signed: *Hiroshige ga*
censorship seal: *kiwame*
woodblock, *ōban*, 242 x 360 mm
The Metropolitan Museum of Art, New York, Rogers Fund, 1918 (JP517)

A steep path leads upwards past the castle of the Ishikawa *daimyō*, with the town of Kameyama in Ise Province in the valley to the left. The people ascending the path are probably taking part in a *daimyō* procession to the capital, Edo. The sky is red from the early morning sun. A strip of blue is printed in *bokashi* along the upper edge of the print.

Kameyama was a fortified city from the middle of the sixteenth century, when Seki Munekazu built a castle there. The castle was destroyed during the great Ansei earthquake of 1854/XI/4 and only the foundations have survived, yet Hiroshige depicted it as intact in the Kameyama illustration in his vertical Tōkaidō series of 1855 (Shiraishi, 1988, p. 116). He used practically the same image as the present one in the 1851 album *Tōkaidō fūkei zue* (ibid., p. 117).

This impression (a) is notable for a minor defect in the blue block, which resulted in a narrow white line appearing just below the frame above the tree-top. Occasionally, this has been coloured in by hand (Link, 1991). The sky is sometimes printed in red in later impressions taken from the block with the defect (b), possibly to emphasise the morning atmosphere.

REFERENCES: *Ukiyoe taikei*, 14, no. 47 [a]; Narazaki, 1975, no. 6 [a]; Shiraishi, 1988, p. 117 [a]; Link, 1991, no. I-1-Ac [a]; *Meihin soroimono ukiyoe*, 11, no. 47 [a]; Forrer, 1994, G451 [b]

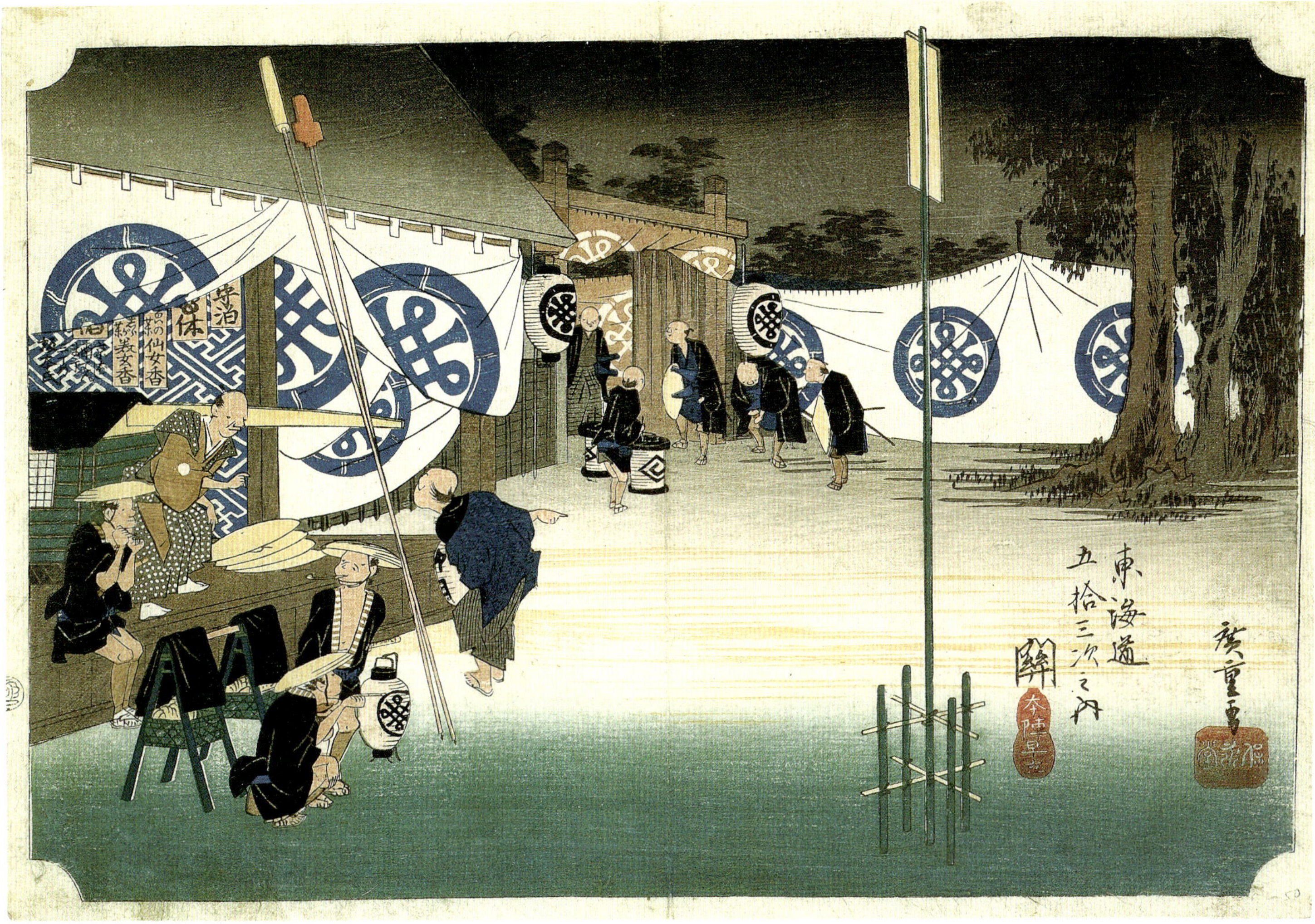

27 DEPARTURE FROM THE INN

Seki—Early Departure from the Daimyō's Inn (Seki—Honjin hayadachi)

from the series *The Fifty-three Stations of the Tōkaidō Road (Tōkaidō gojūsan tsugi no uchi)*
published by Takenouchi Magohachi (Hōeidō), *c.* 1831–4

signed: *Hiroshige ga*
censorship seal: *kiwame*
woodblock, *ōban*, 241 x 358 mm
The Art Institute of Chicago, Chicago,
The Clarence Buckingham Collection (1925.3555)

It is still dark as the *daimyō*'s procession leaves the inn in Seki, Ise Province. The innkeeper, dressed in *kamishimo*, is on the verandah giving instructions to a servant. A litter stands ready behind him. In the foreground a few litter-bearers still have time for a smoke. The banners hung around the inn probably bear the emblem of the *daimyō* who is spending the night there. According to the signs behind the innkeeper, the famous Senjokō and Bijokō brands of white face-powder was available here.

The lanterns are a light ochre in early impressions (a), as here; later (b) they are usually red.

REFERENCES: *Ukiyoe taikei*, 14, no. 48 [b]; Shiraishi, 1988, p. 119 [a]; *Meihin soroimono ukiyoe*, 11, no. 48 [a]

28 TRAVELLERS CROSSING A RIVER

Odawara—Sakawa River (*Odawara—Sakawagawa*)

from the series *The Fifty-three Stations of the Tōkaidō Road* (*Tōkaidō gojūsan tsugi no uchi*)
published by Takenouchi Magohachi (Hōeidō), *c.* 1831–4

signed: *Hiroshige ga*
censorship seal: *kiwame*
woodblock, *ōban*, 257 x 383 mm
The Art Institute of Chicago, Chicago, Gift of Mr and Mrs Harold Henderson (63.665)

Travellers crossed the Sakawa River on the backs of waders or, if they could afford it, in a litter. Travel guides of the time indicate that there was a bridge over the river from the winter to the Second Month, but from the Third Month on it had to be crossed by wading. Right of centre, on the plain on the opposite bank of the river, is Odawara, a prosperous town in Sagami Province; further to the right is the fifteenth-century castle of Odawara. The latter was conquered by Toyotomi Hideyoshi in 1590, putting an end to the Hōjō hegemony in the region. In Hiroshige's day it was the residence of the Ōkubo *daimyō*, who lived there from 1686 to 1868.

The scene in the print is probably set in the summer at the approach of evening. At least, this could be the implication of the dark strip along the upper edge of an otherwise yellow sky.

The blocks of this print may have been lost at some point, as there is a later version (b) for which all the blocks were entirely recut. The course of the river was altered and the number of travellers and porters increased—for example, there are two porters on the near river-bank in the original version, while in the later version there are three of them plus two travellers. In addition, the whole background was altered, with the mountain peaks replaced by rolling hills. Another change can be seen in the subtitle of the print: in all these later impressions it was printed in red positive instead of negative. Finally, as happened so often with late reprints, the *kiwame* censorship seal, which had always been printed in black in the margin, was brought into the picture and printed in the form of a red seal.

REFERENCES: Yoshida, 1973, no. 10A [a]; *Ukiyoe taikei*, 14, no. 10 [a]; Shiraishi, 1988, p. 33 [a]; Link, 1991, nos. I-1-K [a], I-1-L [b]; *Meihin soroimono ukiyoe*, 11, no. 10 [a]

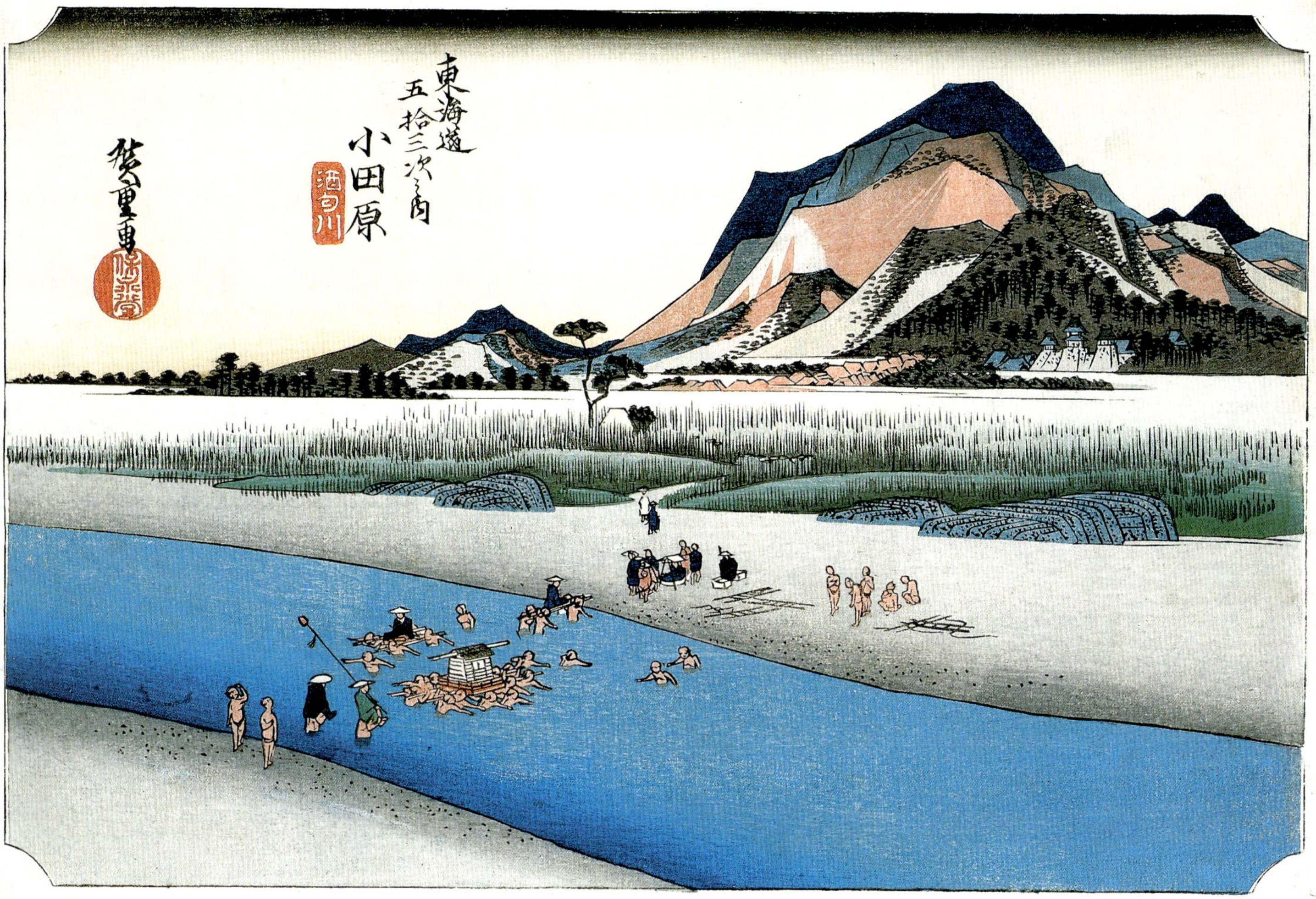
東海道
五拾三次之内
小田原
酒匂川
廣重画
保永堂

29 TRAVELLERS ON A MOUNTAIN PATH AT NIGHT

Hakone—No. 11—Holding Pine-torches in the Night (Hakone—Yonaka taimatsutori)

from the series *The Fifty-three Stations of the Tōkaidō Road (Tōkaidō gojūsan tsugi)*, the so-called *Reisho Tōkaidō*
published by Maruya Seijirō, c. 1851–2

signed: *Hiroshige ga*
censors' seals: Mera and Watanabe
woodblock, *ōban*, 231 x 363 mm
Honolulu Academy of Arts, Honolulu,
Gift of James A. Michener, 1992 (22.173)

Hakone is represented in the Hōeidō Tōkaidō series by an imposing mountain with a *daimyō* procession ascending a steep path (cat. 18), whereas here, in the so-called *Reisho Tōkaidō*, it has become a night scene with a close-up of a group of porters and servants with torches climbing a path littered with stones. The forms of the mountains lend a certain mystery to the scene, its atmospheric quality enhanced by the effective use of *bokashi*. The grain of the woodblock is incorporated in the image almost playfully, as if it were an element in the gradation printing—a technique known as *kimetsubushi*, in which the surface of the block is rubbed down or treated with stiff brushes so that the pattern of the grain is faintly impressed on the print.

The station of Hakone is represented almost identically in the so-called *Kyōka Tōkaidō*, although more of the mountains can be seen there (cat. 34). The same image recurs in a fan design by Hiroshige and there is a similar scene in his vertical Tōkaidō series of 1855, this time with a view of the mountains on the other side of the Haya River (or perhaps a much smaller river that runs largely parallel to it). This latter print, in particular, bears a resemblance to the illustration that Tani Bunchō (1763–1840) made of the Hakone Pass in his *Album of Famous Mountains* (*Meizan zufu*, 3 vols., 1804).

A mistake by the original block-cutter seems never to have been put right. Apparently, two of the grey stones on the path were accidentally cut from the block and they stand out as unprinted areas of paper. The series does not seem to have been reprinted very often. Later impressions (b) omitted the brown *bokashi* on the left-hand side of the far mountain and on a large part of the near one.

REFERENCES: Shiraishi, 1988, p. 35 [b]; Link, 1991, no. I-5-B [a]; Forrer, 1994, G456 [b]

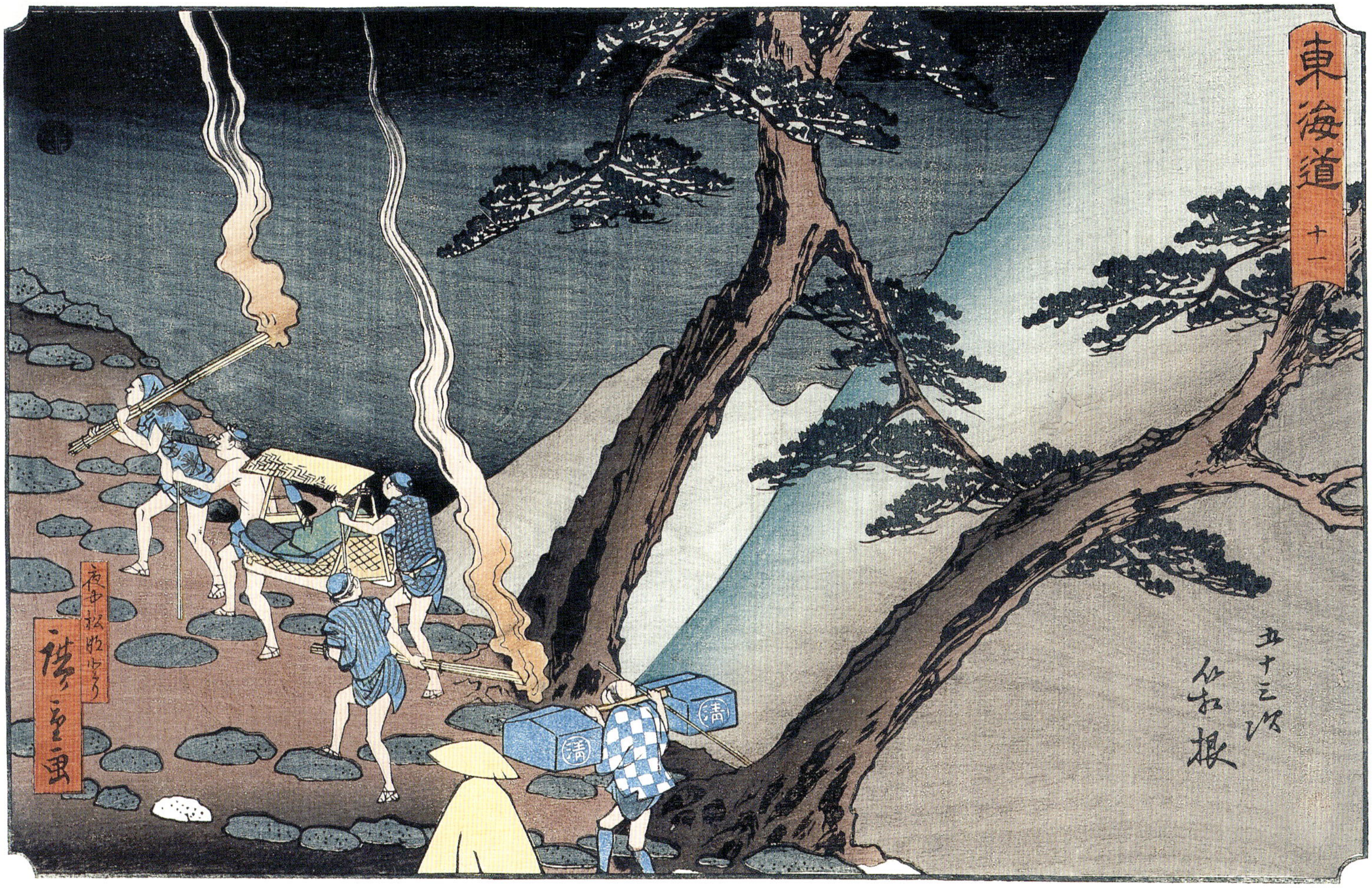
東海道
十一
五十三次
箱根
夜中松明とり
廣重画

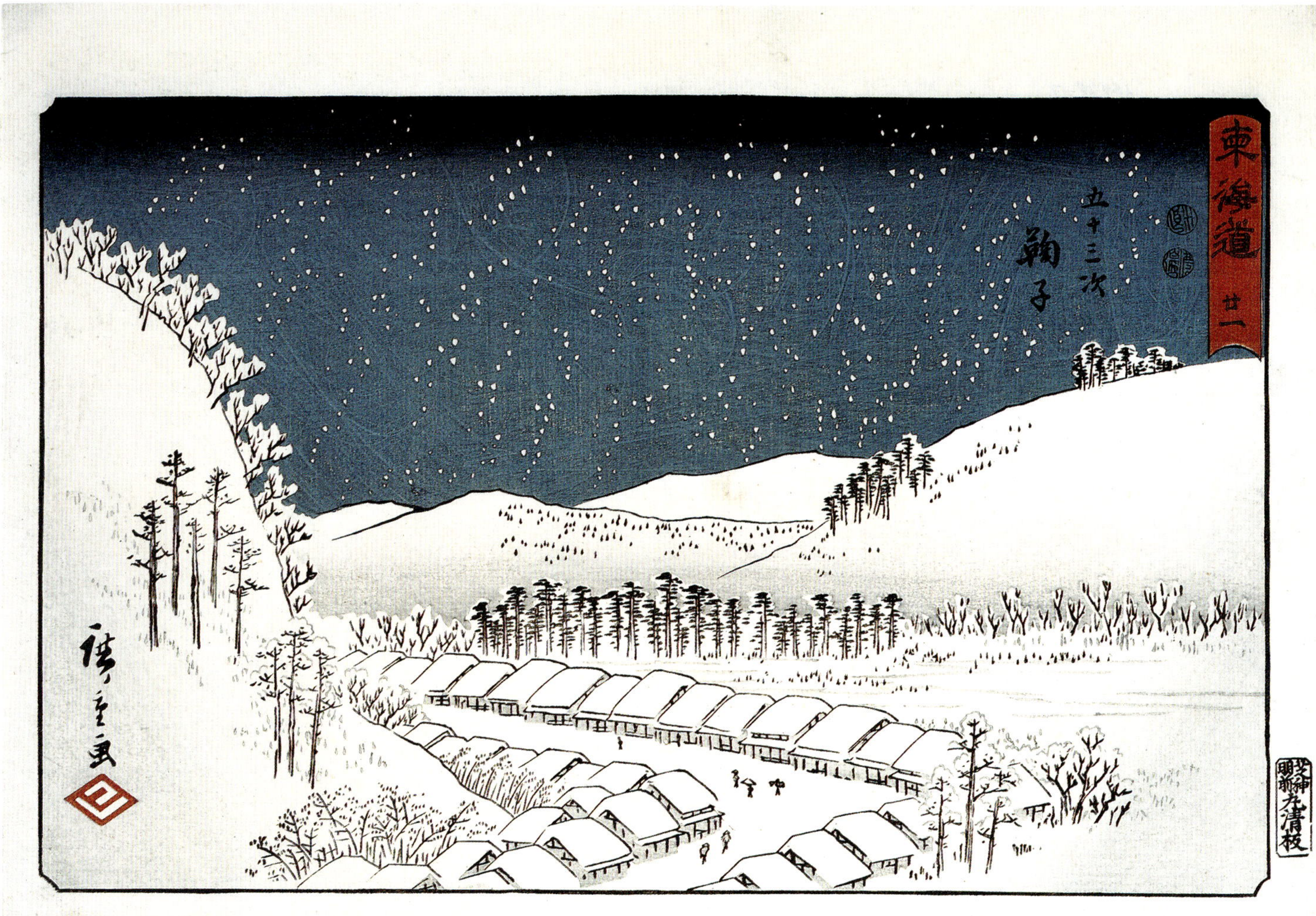

30 SNOW FALLING ON A TOWN

Mariko—No. 21

from the series *The Fifty-three Stations of the Tōkaidō Road* (*Tōkaidō gojūsan tsugi*), the so-called *Reisho Tōkaidō* published by Maruya Seijirō, *c.* 1851–2

signed: *Hiroshige ga*
censors' seals: Mera and Watanabe
woodblock, *ōban*, 252 x 373 mm
Honolulu Academy of Arts, Honolulu,
Gift of James A. Michener, 1992 (22.180)

Although this print illustrates the station of Mariko, it is very likely that it represents the mountain village of Utsunoya, half-way on the road to the next station, Okabe. This spot is also used for illustrations of Okabe in all Hiroshige's major Tōkaidō series (Shiraishi, 1988, pp. 60–1). According to the guidebooks, travellers at this point had to climb about a mile up and down the Utsunoya Pass. The guides recommended the local speciality, a kind of dumpling called *tōdango*, and, for those interested in tradition, there was the Narrow Ivy Path (*Tsuta no hosomichi*), described by the tenth-century poet Ariwara no Narihira in his *Tales of Ise* (*Ise monogatari*). The only comparable illustration of the Utsunoya Pass for the station of Mariko is in Hiroshige's album *Landscapes Along the Tōkaidō Road* (*Tōkaidō fūkei zue*, 2 vols., 1851; Shiraishi, 1988, p. 57).

REFERENCES: Shiraishi, 1988, p. 57; Link, 1991, no. I-5-E

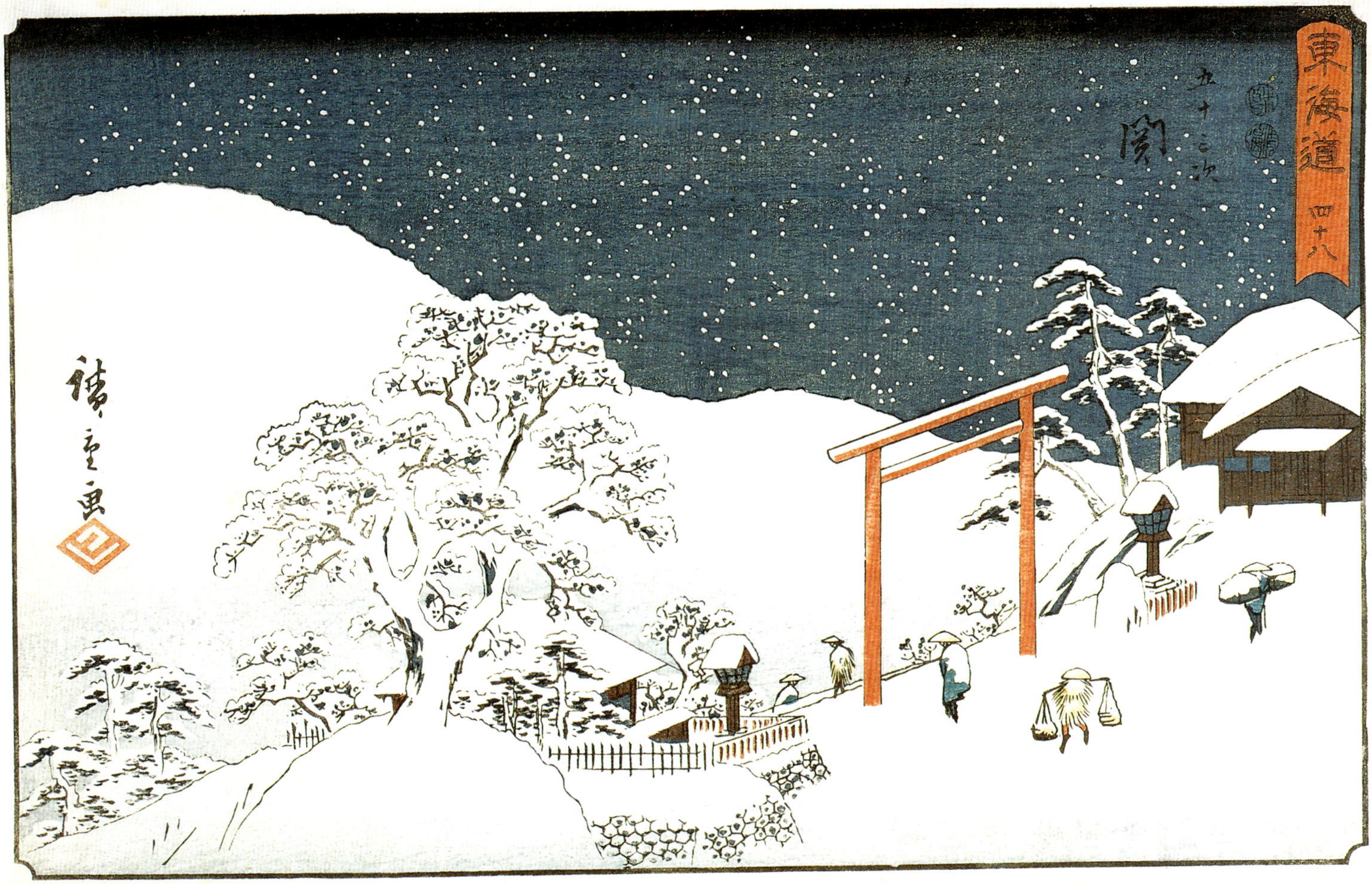

31 SNOW LANDSCAPE WITH GATE

Seki—No. 48

from the series *The Fifty-three Stations of the Tōkaidō Road* (*Tōkaidō gojūsan tsugi*), the so-called *Reisho Tōkaidō*
published by Maruya Seijirō, *c.* 1851–2

signed: *Hiroshige ga*
censors' seals: Mera and Watanabe
woodblock, *ōban*, 232 x 359 mm
Baur Collection, Geneva (G457)

In the late afternoon of a snowy day a few travellers pass the gate to the pilgrim's route to Ise. Some are tempted to descend the steps while snow falls from a dark blue sky above the hills.

Both in the Hōeidō Tōkaidō series (cat. 27) and in the *Kyōka Tōkaidō* (Shiraishi, 1988, p. 119) Hiroshige chose to represent the station of Seki by a *daimyō* procession leaving an inn, while in the *Gyōsho Tōkaidō* he opted to depict travellers at a commoners' inn (Shiraishi, 1988, p. 119). In his vertical Tōkaidō series of 1855, however, he presents a view that is virtually identical to the present one, but seen in the summer (Shiraishi, 1988, p. 118).

REFERENCES: Shiraishi, 1988, p. 119; Forrer, 1994, G457 [this impression]

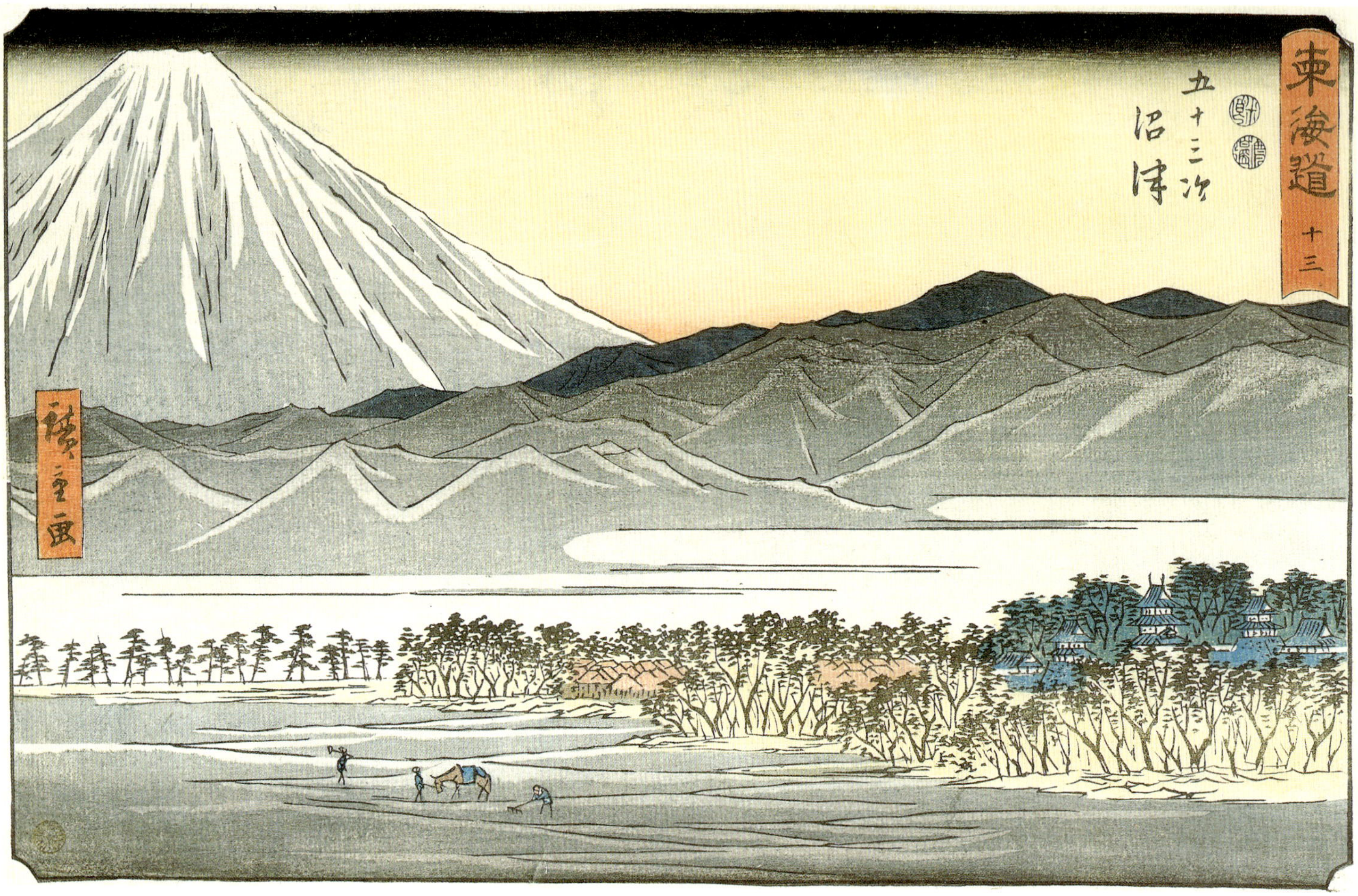

32 MOUNT FUJI SEEN ACROSS A PLAIN

Numazu—No. 13

from the series *The Fifty-three Stations of the Tōkaidō Road* (*Tōkaidō gojūsan tsugi*), the so-called *Reisho Tōkaidō*
published by Maruya Seijirō, *c.* 1851–2

signed: *Hiroshige ga*
censors' seals: Mera and Watanabe
woodblock, *ōban*, 219 x 346 mm
The Metropolitan Museum of Art, New York, The Francis Lathrop Collection, Purchase, Frederick C. Hewitt Fund, 1911 (JP763)

The most impressive view of Mount Fuji is to be had from the plain, in Suruga Province, that the Tōkaidō Road enters after passing through the mountains of Hakone. Here the mountains rise high against a yellow sky, with Mount Ashitaka on the right. Closer to the viewer on the right is the castle of Numazu, erected in 1579, later destroyed and rebuilt in 1777.

This print closely resembles that for the same station in the *Kyōka Tōkaidō* of *c.* 1840 (Shiraishi, 1988, p. 41). The latter, however, includes a tea-house in the foreground and the blue sky is broken by white patches of cloud, probably intended as a Western element. The present composition, dominated by bluish-purple tones, is more impressive in its serene simplicity.

REFERENCE: Shiraishi, 1988, p. 41

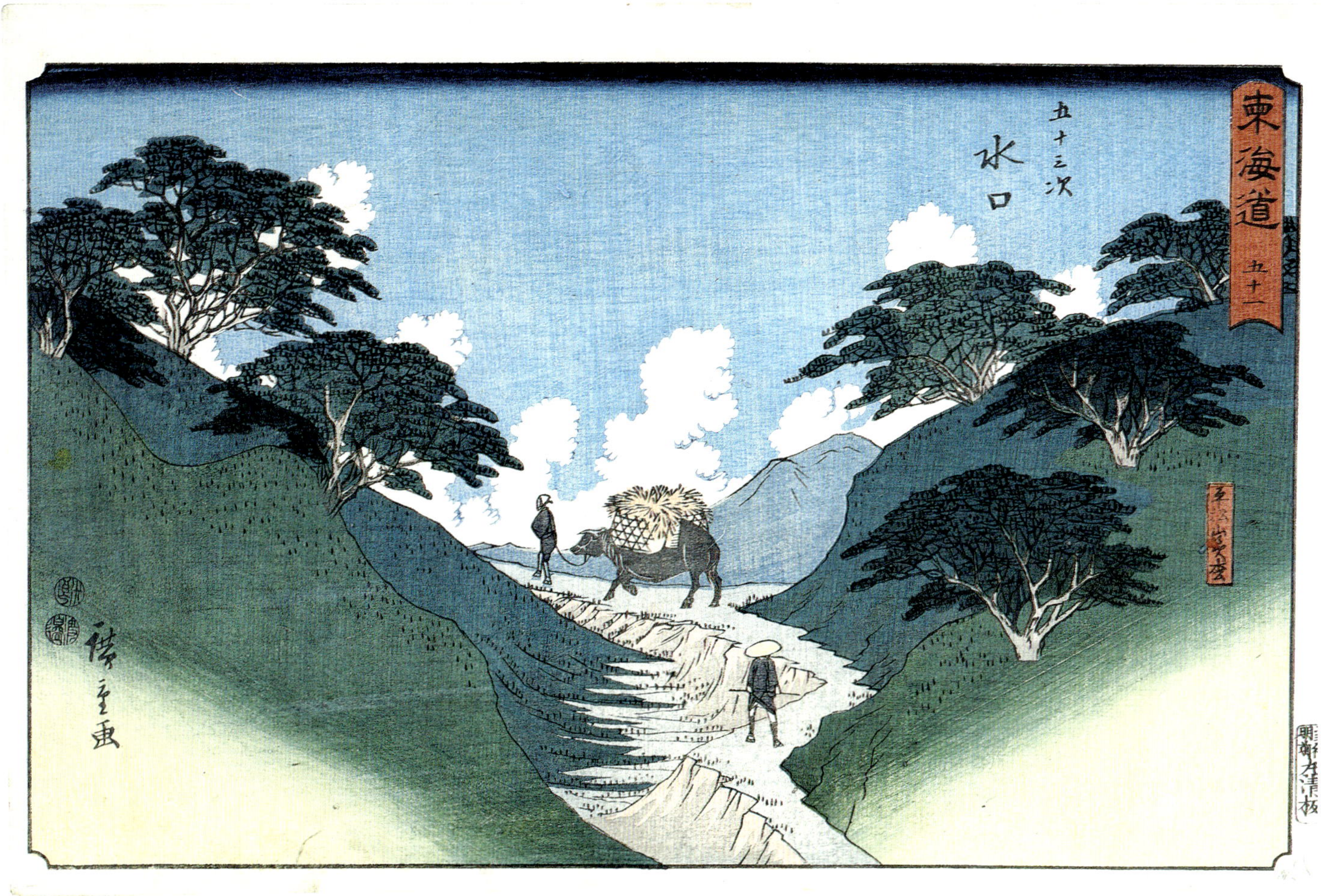

33 MAN LEADING AN OX BETWEEN MOUNTAIN SLOPES

Minakuchi—No. 51—The Beautiful Pines at Hiramatsuyama (Minakuchi—Hiramatsuyama no utsukushii matsu)

from the series *The Fifty-three Stations of the Tōkaidō Road (Tōkaidō gojūsan tsugi)*, the so-called *Reisho Tōkaidō*
published by Maruya Seijirō, *c.* 1851–2

signed: *Hiroshige ga*
censors' seals: Mera and Watanabe
woodblock, *ōban*, 236 x 356 mm
Honolulu Academy of Arts, Honolulu,
Gift of James A. Michener, 1992 (22.202)

Just before the station of Ishibe, to the left of the Tōkaidō Road between the villages of Harimura and Kōjibukuro, is a hill. Although only 228 metres high, it is known as Mount Hiramatsu. Reputedly, pine trees grew there of their own accord, whereas most of the pine trees beside the Tōkaidō Road had been planted. It is this landscape that inspired Hiroshige to make this print: a peasant leads an ox on a path that winds up the slopes of the hill, with pine trees on either side.

The print is notable for its depiction of cumulus clouds, which were introduced in Japanese prints or paintings only as a deliberate Western element. Such Western-style skies are particularly rare in Hiroshige's work and in this Tōkaidō series they are to be found only in the prints for the stations of Ejiri (Shiraishi, 1988, p. 53) and Nissaka (ibid., p. 69; Link, 1991, no. I-5-F).

REFERENCE: Shiraishi, 1988, p. 127

34 TRAVELLERS ON A MOUNTAIN PATH AT NIGHT

Hakone

from the series *The Fifty-three Stations of the Tōkaidō Road* (*Tōkaidō gojūsan tsugi*), the so-called *Kyōka Tōkaidō*
published by Sanoya Kihei (Kikakudō), *c.* 1839–40

signed: *Hiroshige ga*
censorship seal: *kiwame*
woodblock, *chūban*, 171 x 228 mm
Honolulu Academy of Arts, Honolulu,
Gift of James A. Michener, 1992 (22.399)

This scene of a group of travellers with torches climbing a mountain path is almost identical to that in the print for Hakone in the *Reisho Tōkaidō* of over ten years later (cat. 29). Each print in the present Tōkaidō series contains a *kyōka* poem—hence its popular name of *Kyōka Tōkaidō*. Like the other poems in the series, the *kyōka* on this print has its thirty-one syllables arranged in lines of 5-7-5-7-7. It reads:

> *Kotowaza ni*
> *kumo tomo ieru*
> *hito nare ya*
> *kakaru yamaji o*
> *yoru mo koshi yuku*
>
> As the saying goes, speaking of clouds
> it also happens to people—
> just when one approaches a mountain path,
> evening falls
>
> Fūkien Mitsuharu.

In contrast to this impression, that in the Mary A. Ainsworth Collection (Keyes, 1984) is printed in such light colours that the whole effect of the print is lost.

REFERENCES: Keyes, 1984, no. 941; Shiraishi, 1988, p. 35

Hakone.

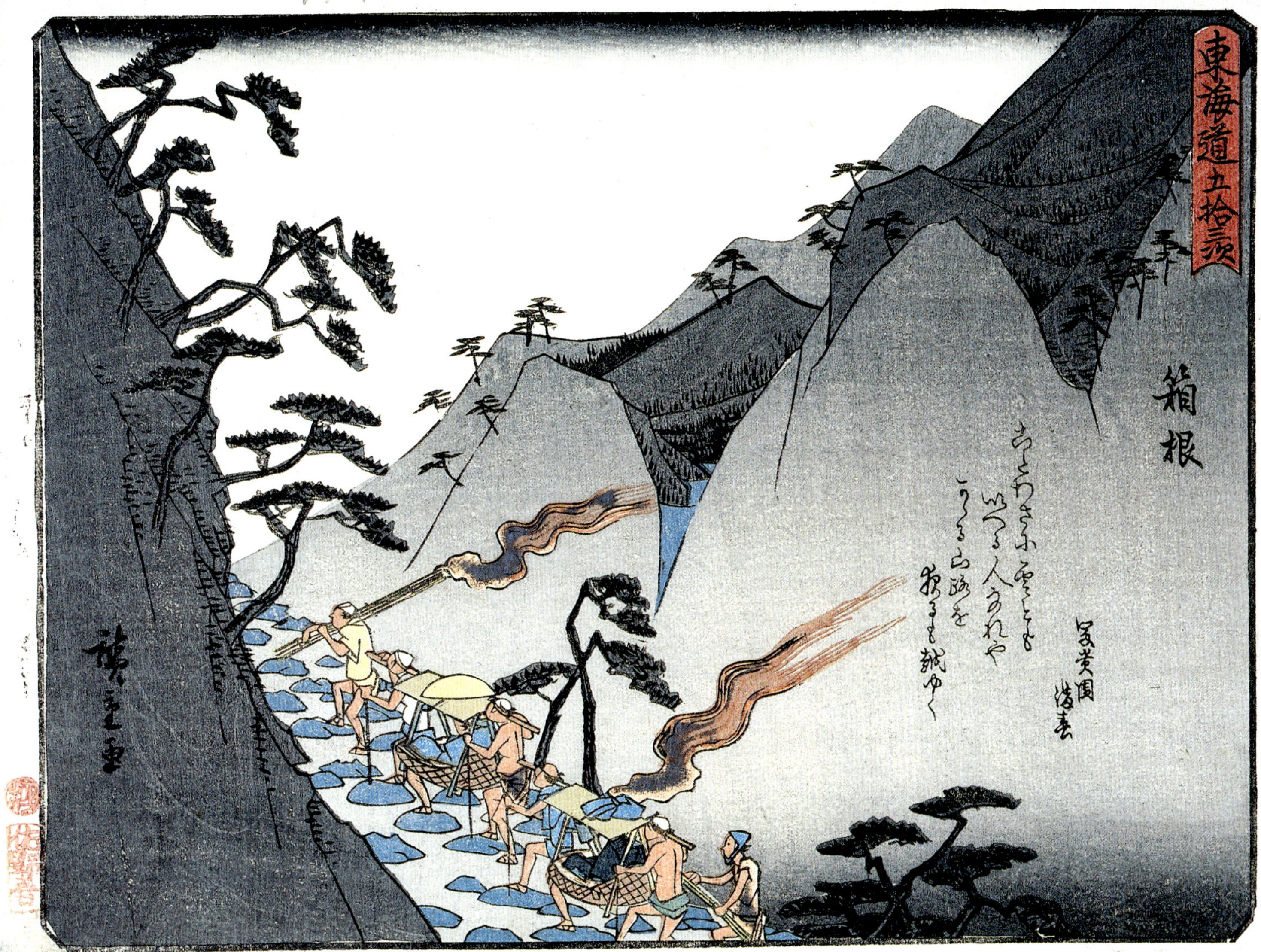

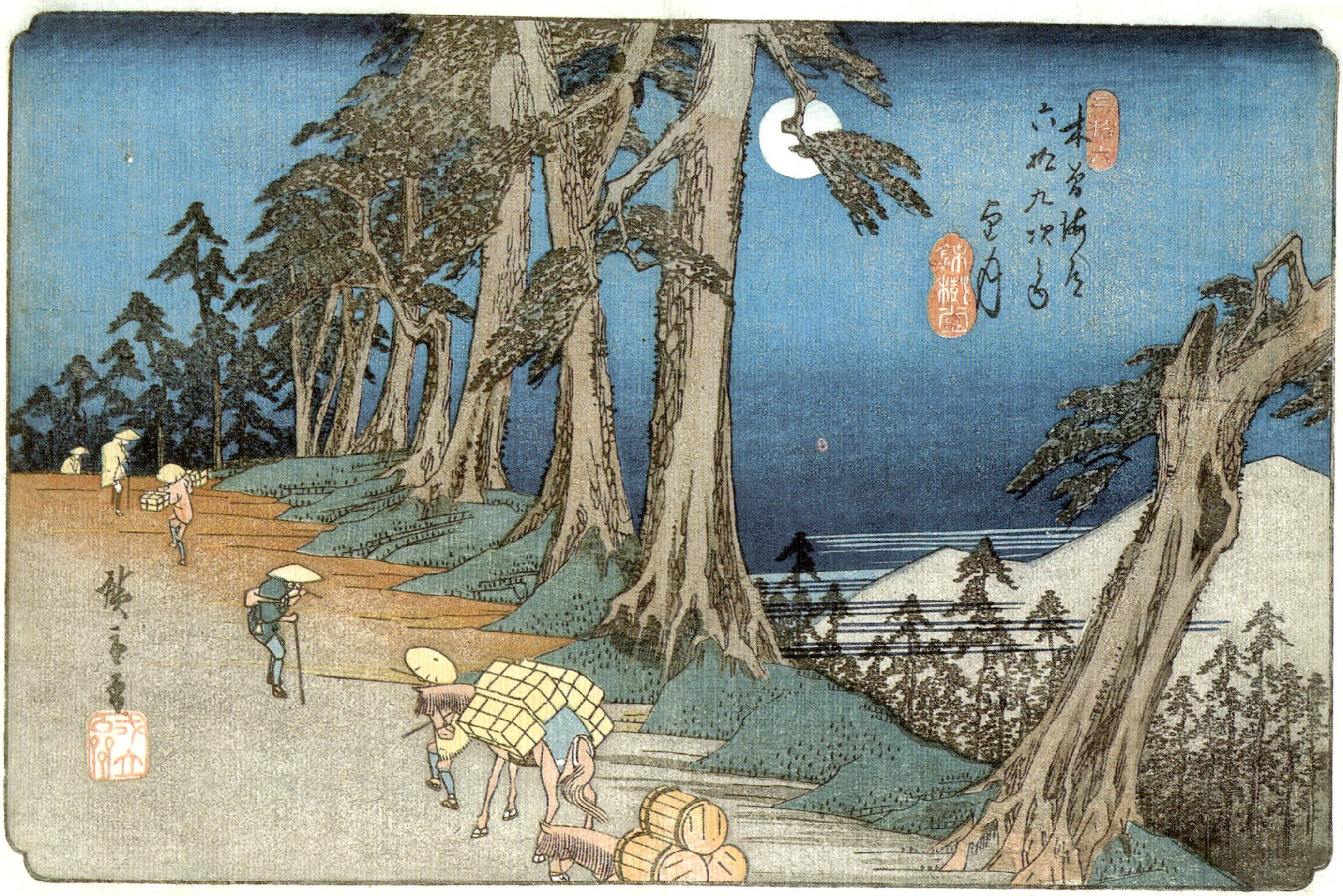

35 TRAVELLERS IN THE MOONLIGHT

Mochizuki—No. 26

from the series *The Sixty-nine Stations of the Kisokaidō Road* (*Kisokaidō rokujūkyū tsugi no uchi*)
published by Iseya Rihei (Kinjudō), *c.* 1834–42

signed: *Hiroshige ga*, with seal: *Ichiryūsai*
censorship seal: *kiwame*
woodblock, *ōban*, 232 x 373 mm
The Metropolitan Museum of Art, New York, The Henry L. Phillips Collection, Bequest of Henry L. Phillips, 1940 (JP2873)

Travellers walk along a mountain path with a row of pine trees on the right. The government planted pine trees along large sections of the national thoroughfares to protect travellers. On the right is a tree-lined valley with mountains behind. A full moon shines in the blue sky.

After passing the previous station of Yawata, the traveller crosses a bridge over the Momozawa irrigation canal and then follows a mountain path through the Uryū Pass before reaching the town of Mochizuki in Shinano Province. This is probably the path illustrated in this print. Perhaps it is no coincidence that the word *mochizuki* means 'full moon'.

It is sometimes stated that the moon is shaded on early impressions of this print. Since this depends entirely on how far down the *bokashi* extends from the upper edge of the print, it is not necessarily an indication of an early impression. A rather hazy moon has its own charm, but far more important for the coherence of the design is that the valley on the right be printed in black *bokashi* (a), in keeping with the depiction of nightfall. Impressions that have a shaded moon but lack the darkness in the valley (b) are therefore less convincing.

REFERENCES: Suzuki, 1970, no. 21 [c: moon not shaded]; *Ukiyoe taikei*, 15, no. 26 [a]; Nagata, 1986, no. 89 [c: moon not shaded]; Link, 1991, no. II-1-D [b]; *Meihin soroimono ukiyoe*, 11, no. 81 [b]

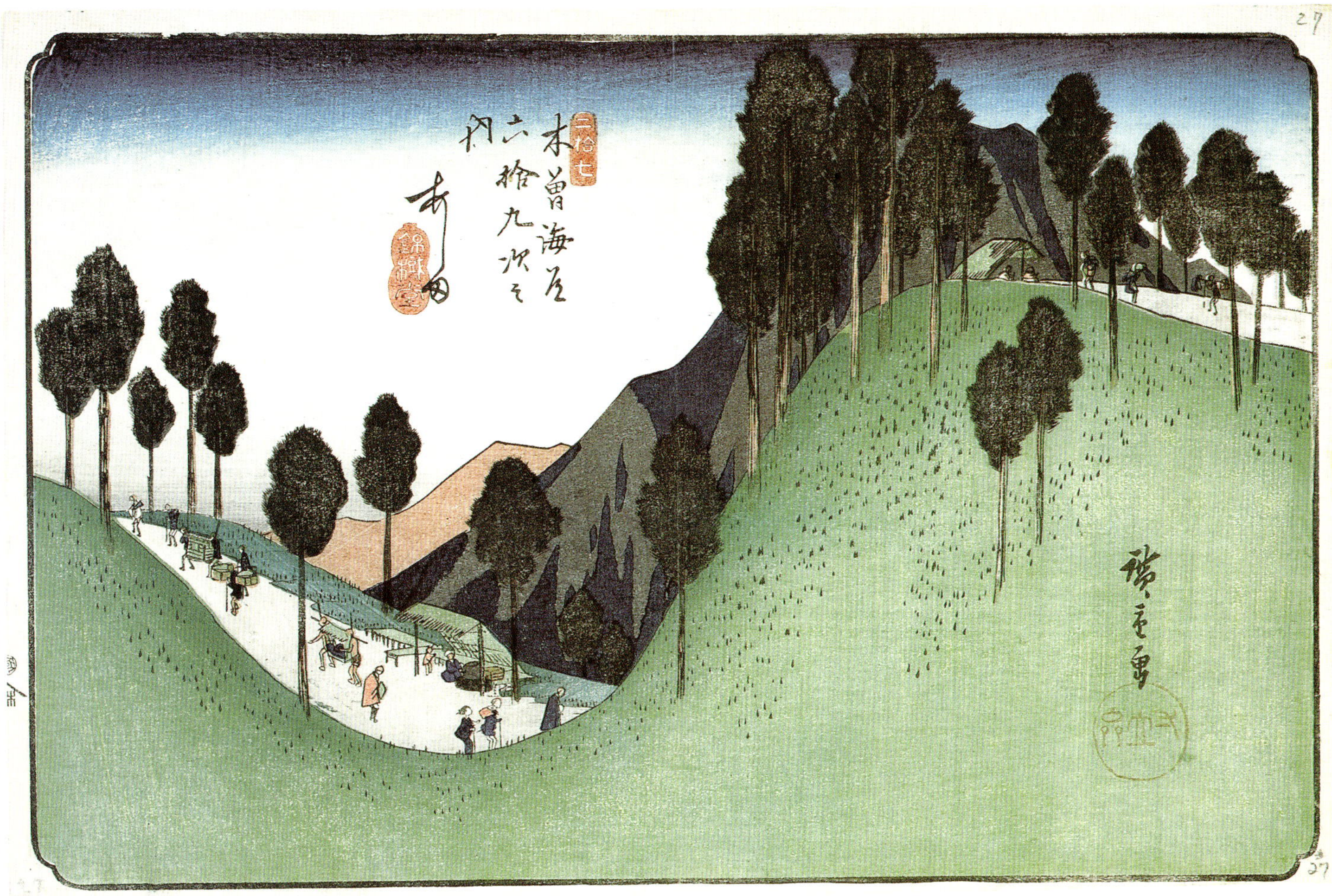

36 A GREEN VALLEY WITH TREES

Ashida—No. 27

from the series *The Sixty-nine Stations of the Kisokaidō Road* (*Kisokaidō rokujūkyū tsugi no uchi*)

published by Iseya Rihei (Kinjudō), *c.* 1834–42
signed: *Hiroshige ga*, with seal: *Ichiryūsai*
censorship seal: *kiwame*
woodblock, *ōban*, 236 x 368 mm
Honolulu Academy of Arts, Honolulu,
Gift of James A. Michener, 1970 (15.617)

After leaving Mochizuki, the traveller comes to the foothills of Mount Tateshina (2530 m) in Shinano Province, here visible in the distance. Beyond the station of Ashida lies the Kasatori Pass, opposite a valley with a very attractive row of pine trees, which is probably the location illustrated here.

This composition owes some of its almost abstract character to the sharp contrast between the large green area of the valley and the blue and grey mountain behind it. Such quasi-abstract landscapes are found elsewhere in Hiroshige's oeuvre, for example in the print for the station of Okabe in the Hōeidō Tōkaidō series and in the station of Ōkute (*Ukiyoe taikei*, 15, no. 48) and the village of Yase from *Famous Views of Kyoto* (cat. 50).

REFERENCES: *Ukiyoe taikei*, 15, no. 27; *Meihin soroimono ukiyoe*, 11, no. 81

37 MAN ON HORSEBACK CROSSING A BRIDGE

Nagakubo—No. 28

from the series *The Sixty-nine Stations of the Kisokaidō Road* (*Kisokaidō rokujūkyū tsugi no uchi*)
published by Iseya Rihei (Kinjudō), *c.* 1834–42

signed: *Hiroshige ga*, with seal: *Ichiryūsai*
censorship seal: *kiwame*
woodblock, *ōban*, 245 x 368 mm
Honolulu Academy of Arts, Honolulu,
Gift of James A. Michener, 1970 (15.618)

A man leads his horse along a path beside the Ida River, which is in fact closer to the next station, Wada, than to Nagakubo in Shinano Province. In the foreground two boys play with a dog. Evening approaches and the full moon is in the sky: the bridge, and particularly the trees and mountains in the distance, are visible only as shapes with no detail. Yet there is a certain lack of logic in the image, because the tree in the foreground seems to be more in darkness than the man leading the horse. Moreover, the mountains appear to be hovering because the *bokashi* has not been continued under the bridge. In what seems to be the earliest state of this print (cat. 115) the mountains in the distance are missing and the sky is considerably lighter; there is simply a blue *bokashi* circle around the moon. The red seals in impressions of this state have still printed very sharply. A second state would seem to be represented by an impression (a) that includes the mountains, added on a separate block, but omits the railing on the far side of the bridge. The red seals are still relatively sharp; the dominant tone is blue. The impression shown here (b), with the mountains and the bridge with the figures on it printed in a dark, almost black tone, is thus from a later state, although it is generally regarded as the first. Accordingly, the red seals have become much less sharp and are clogged with ink.

REFERENCES: Suzuki, 1970, no. 25 [b]; Yoshida, 1973, no. 4A [b]; *Ukiyoe taikei*, 15, no. 28 [b]; Izzard, 1983, no. 37 [a]; *Ukiyoe hakka*, 1984, no. 14 [b]; *Meihin soroimono ukiyoe*, 11, no. 86 [b]

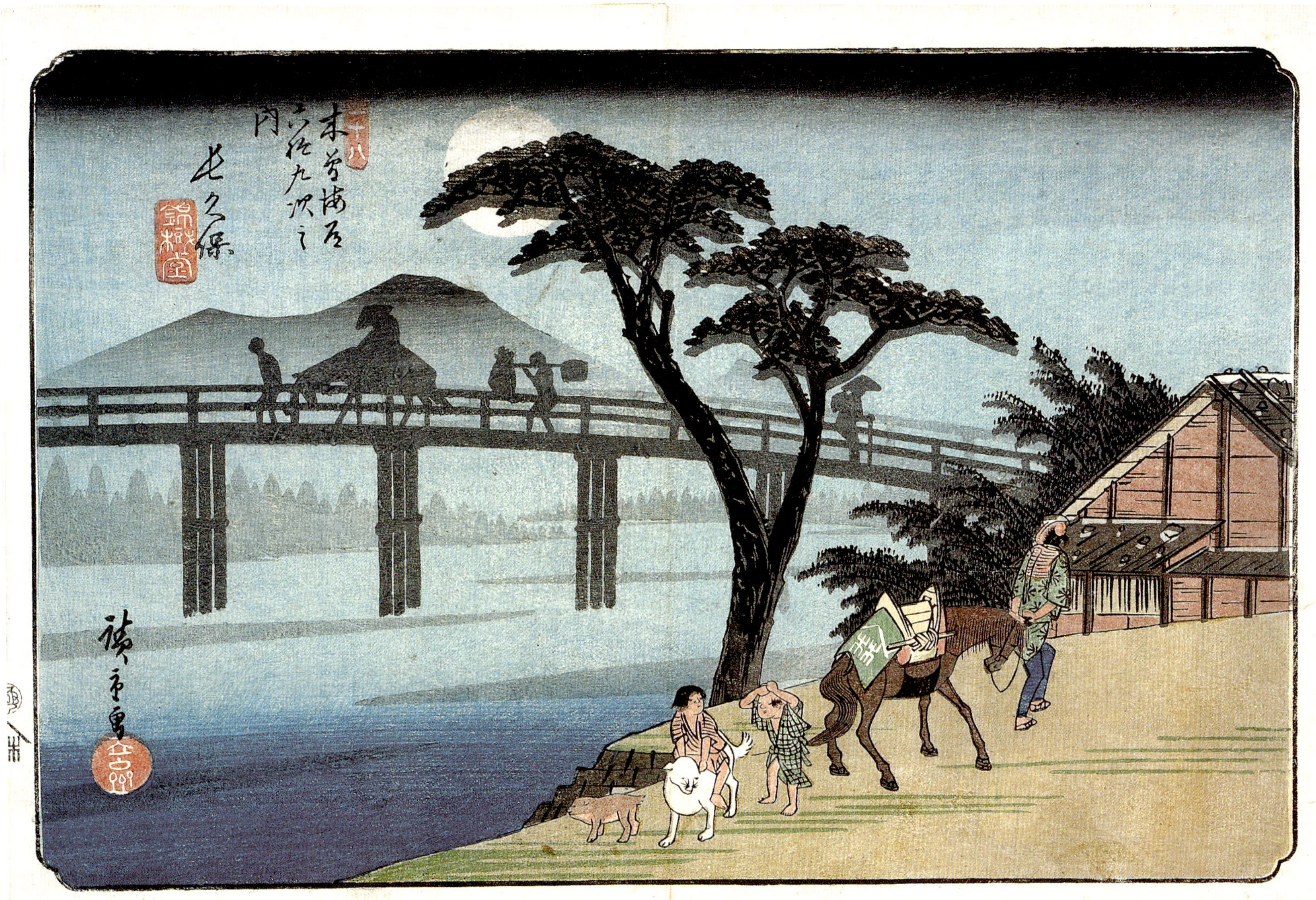
二十八
木曽海道六拾九次之内
長久保
錦樹堂
廣重画

38 MEN POLING BOATS PAST A BANK WITH WILLOWS

Seba—No. 32

from the series *The Sixty-nine Stations of the Kisokaidō Road* (*Kisokaidō rokujūkyū tsugi no uchi*)
published by Iseya Rihei (Kinjudō), *c.* 1834–42

signed: *Hiroshige ga*, with seal: *Ichiryūsai*
censorship seal: *kiwame*
woodblock, *ōban*, 253 x 362 mm
Honolulu Academy of Arts, Honolulu,
Gift of James A. Michener, 1970 (15.671)

Seba, literally 'washing the horse', was the place where the great general Minamoto no Yoshinaka (1145–84) was once supposed to have washed his horse, probably when he raised an army in Shinano Province to fight against the Taira.

In this print we see two men, one in a boat, the other on a raft, who appear to be trying to reach the town of Seba before dusk falls. The river is the Narai, which winds through the plains near Lake Suwa. The moon is already visible, and the setting sun colours the sky an orange-red. A subtly printed *bokashi* at the horizon heralds the approach of dusk; the strip of sky along the upper edge of the print is also in dark *bokashi*.

Like all Hiroshige's prints in which the time of day or the weather plays an important part, this one is known in many variants. There are light versions, as here (a), in which the approach of dusk is indicated merely by a grey *bokashi* strip along the upper edge of the print, while the sky below it is blue and, further down, red from the setting sun. The men are wearing brown jackets. The impression in the Matsuki Collection (b) is very light, but the uppermost part of the sky is printed grey, while the men wear blue jackets. In most impressions (c) the uppermost strip of sky is printed in black down to the tops of the willows and the men have blue jackets. Sometimes the sky at upper left is printed yellow, giving a somewhat menacing tone to the whole (*Ukiyoe hakka*, 1984). In a later state (d) the block with the trees on the horizon is omitted and the water is printed uniformly blue, without the stripes in the distance.

REFERENCES: Tanba, 1965, no. 68 [a]; Suzuki, 1970, no. 24 [a]; Narazaki, 1975, no. 7 [c]; *Ukiyoe taikei*, 11, no. 22 [c]; Suzuki, 1975, p. 124 [c]; *Ukiyoe taikei*, 15, no. 32 [c]; *Ukiyoe hakka*, 1984, no. 15 [c]; Link, 1991, no. II-1-F [a: this impression], and II-1-G [d]; *Meihin soroimono ukiyoe*, 11, no. 87 [b]; Copenhagen, 1993, no. 91 [c]; Forrer, 1994, G463 [a]

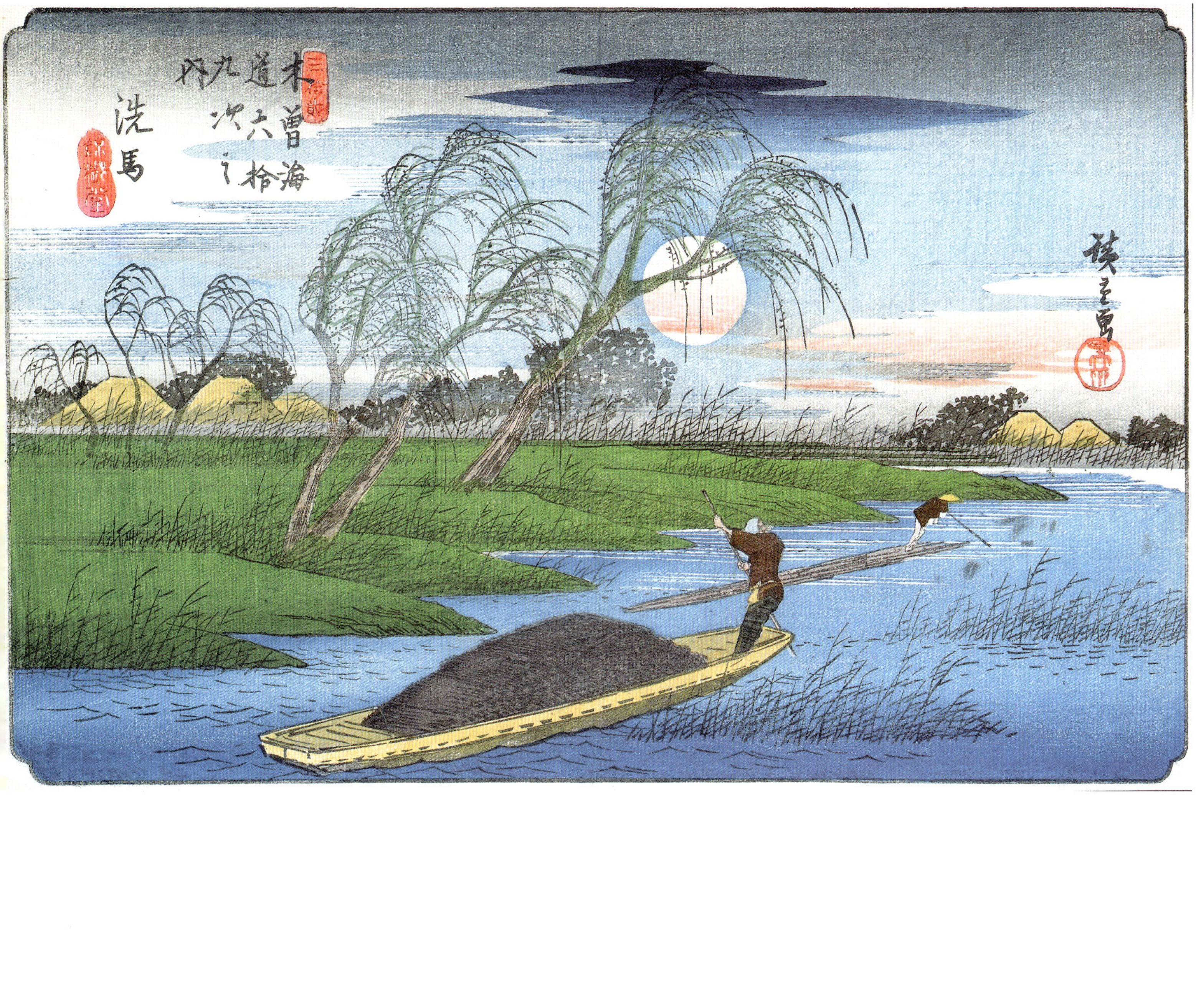
木曽海道六拾九次之内
洗馬
廣重画

39 TRAVELLERS LIGHTING THEIR PIPES BY A FIRE

Karuizawa—No. 19

from the series *The Sixty-nine Stations of the Kisokaidō Road* (*Kisokaidō rokujūkyū tsugi no uchi*)
published by Takenouchi Magohachi (Hōeidō) and Iseya Rihei (Kinjudō), *c.* 1834–42

signed: *Hiroshige ga*, with seal: *Tōkaidō*
censorship seal: *kiwame*
woodblock, *ōban*, 245 x 367 mm
Honolulu Academy of Arts, Honolulu,
Gift of James A. Michener, 1970 (15.607)

Evening approaches as a traveller on horseback arrives at the station of Karuizawa, visible in the middle distance on the right. He asks a passer-by for a light for his pipe, while his foot-servant lights his own pipe from a fire beneath a large cryptomeria tree. The smoke from the fire seems to illuminate part of the tree. Even more striking is the light from the lantern hanging from the baggage carried by the horse. The lantern bears the letters 'Iseri', an allusion to one of the publishers of this print, Iseya Rihei, whose trademark is just visible on the saddle-cloth. In the distance we see Mount Asama, on the border between the provinces Kōzuke and Shinano.

In early impressions of this print (a) there is a bluish haze over the fields, the houses and the mountain, with black *bokashi* on the mountain and on the roofs of the houses. The cloak wrapped around the man on horseback is green. The image becomes generally darker in later impressions (b) and the blue disappears. The cloak worn by the rider is green (*Ukiyoe hakka*, 1984) or blue (*Ukiyoe taikei*, 11 and 15; Forrer, 1994). Still later impressions (c), including the present one, are even darker, emphasising the light of the lantern hanging from the horse. The horse is no longer brown but grey, like the houses, and the man's cloak has become dark blue. These impressions also lack the red printed seal of the publisher Takenouchi Magohachi.

REFERENCES: Tanba, 1965, no. 69 [c]; Suzuki, 1970, no. 22 [a]; *Ukiyoe taikei*, 11, no. 21, and 15, no. 19 [both b]; *Ukiyoe hakka*, 1984, no. 13 [b]; Link, 1991, nos. II-1-B [a], II-1-C [c: this impression]; *Meihin soroimono ukiyoe*, 11, no. 75 [b]; Forrer, 1994, G461 [b]

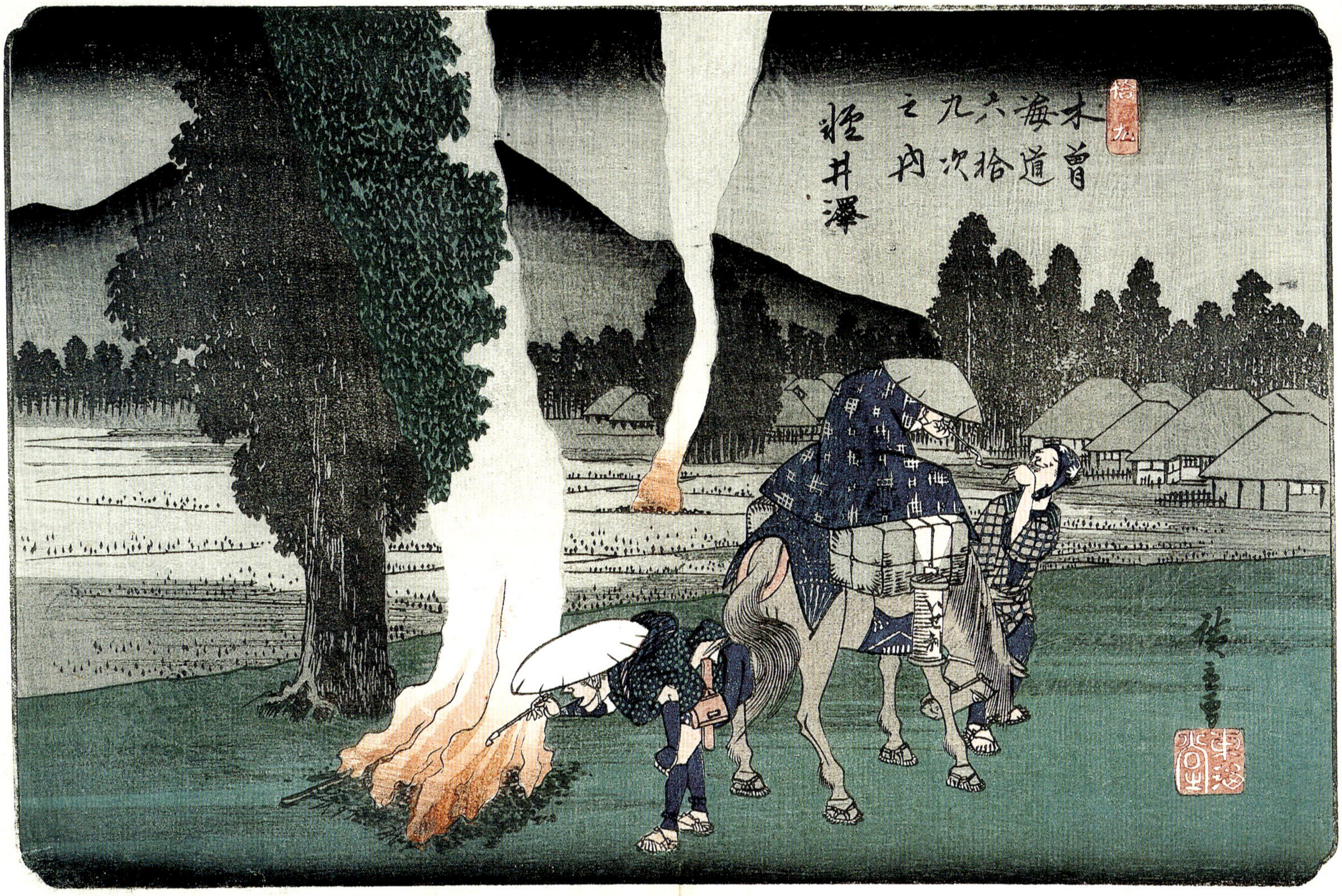
木曾海道六拾九次之内
軽井澤

40 PEOPLE SEEKING SHELTER FROM THE RAIN

Suhara—No. 40

from the series *The Sixty-nine Stations of the Kisokaidō Road*
(*Kisokaidō rokujūkyū tsugi no uchi*)
published by Takenouchi Magohachi, *c.* 1834–42

signed: *Hiroshige ga*
censorship seal: *kiwame*
woodblock, *ōban*, 246 x 367 mm
The Art Institute of Chicago, Chicago,
The Clarence Buckingham Collection (1925.3719)

Two samurai in the foreground run towards a small roadside shrine to shelter from a heavy shower of rain. Two pilgrims with large straw hats are already inside the shrine, while another traveller has taken out his writing set to write his name on the column supporting the roof. Yet another traveller is seated, waiting for the rain to stop. On the left a man on horseback and a man walking hold their cloaks over their heads to keep off the rain. Suhara is a small town at the foot of the Kiso Valley, just past Agematsu with the famous Ono waterfall.

This image of the Suhara station is one of Hiroshige's most popular rain prints and is known in a large number of variants. This would seem to be an early impression.

REFERENCES: *Ukiyoe taikei*, 15, no. 40; *Meihin soroimono ukiyoe*, 11, no. 99; Forrer, 1994, no. 99

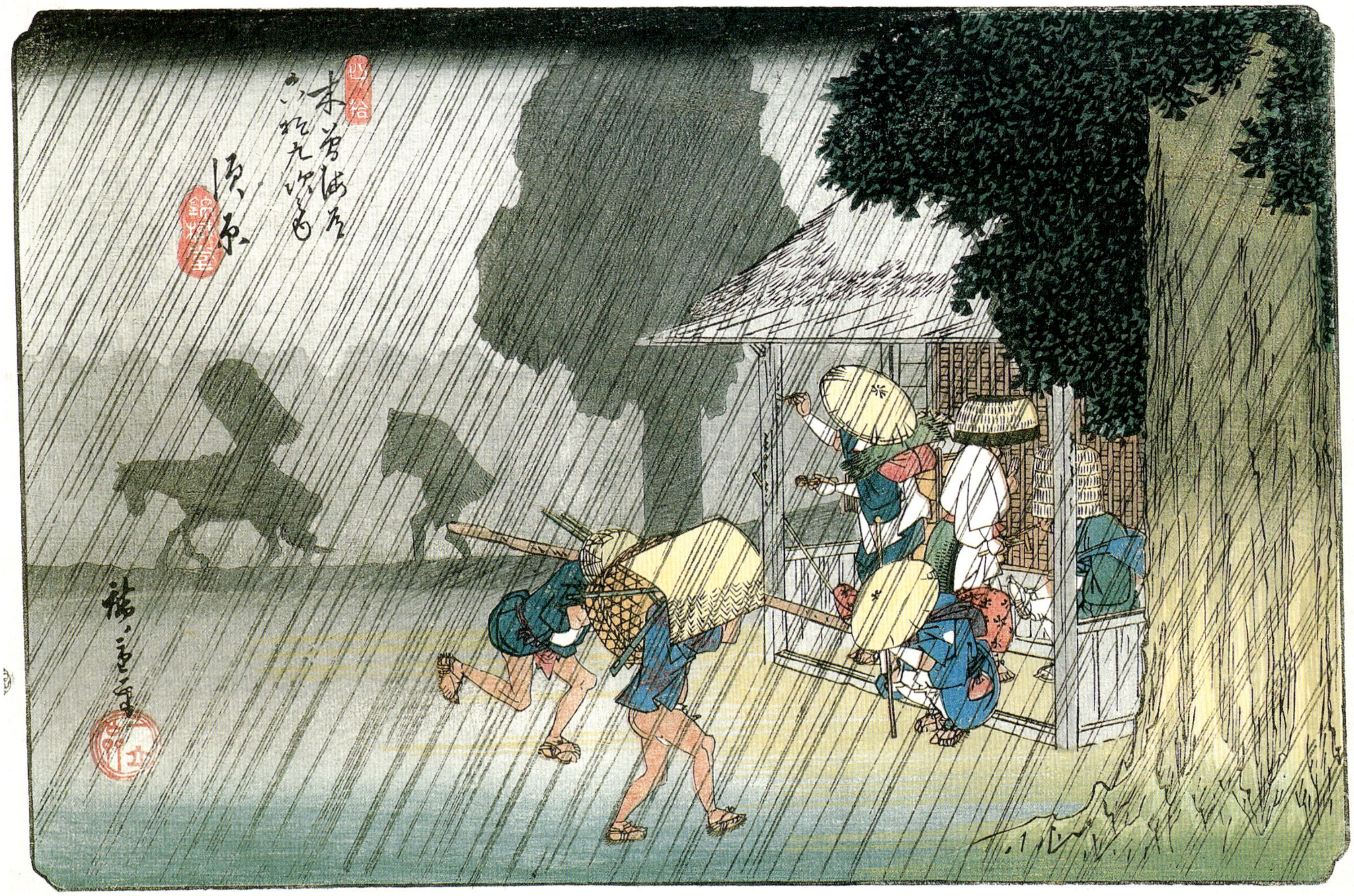

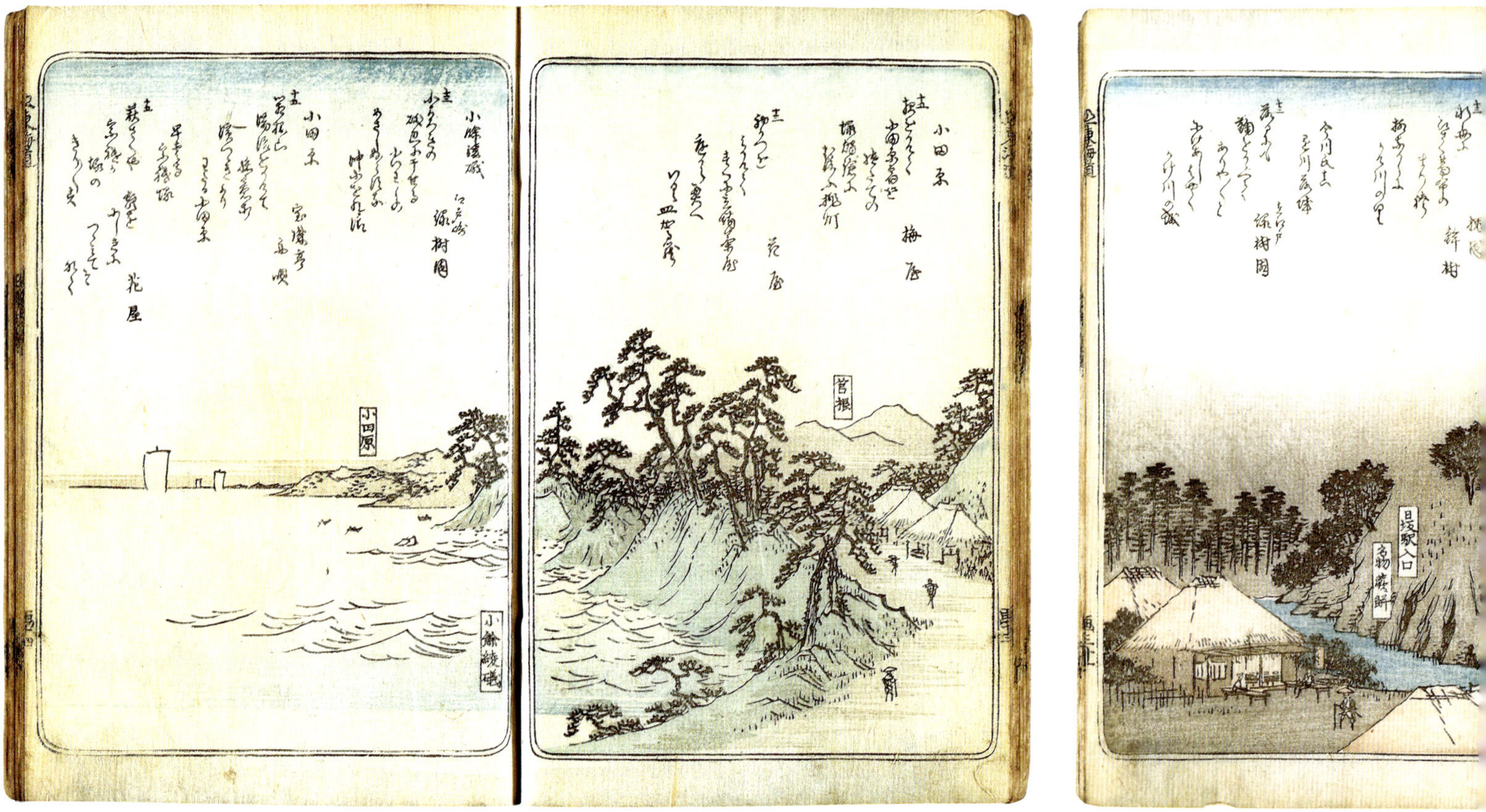

41 PEOPLE ON A WINDING ROAD

Odawara and Hakone

from the three-volume album *Famous Views on the Tōkaidō* (*Tōkaidō meisho zue*)
published by Shunyūtei Umehiko, *c.* 1849

signed: *Ichiryūsai Hiroshige*
from volume 1, sheets 13b/14a
woodblock, album plate, *hanshibon*, 225 x 157 mm
Collection Pulverer, Cologne

Some travellers follow a road that twists along the coast towards Odawara, seen in the distance. The Hakone range can be seen far away on the right. There are a few boats on the water. The upper part of the print contains five *kyōka* poems.

The poems in this *kyōka* album devoted to the stations of the Tōkaidō Road were selected by Hinokizono Umeaki (1793–1859), head of the Hinokizono poetry club, whose emblem can be seen in the white margin of each sheet. The publisher, Shunyūtei Umehiko (1822–96), was himself a famous poet. An undated foreword was written by Jippensha Ikku III (*d.* 1851).

The album consists of sequences of images containing poems alternating with sequences of poems only. The date Kaei 1 Eighth Month (1848/VIII) is indicated at the end of the last volume, followed by the comment that the illustrations were made in the Ninth Month of that year and that the blocks were cut in the Fifth Month of the following year, i.e. 1849/V.

REFERENCE: *Kokusho sōmokuroku*, 6-15-2

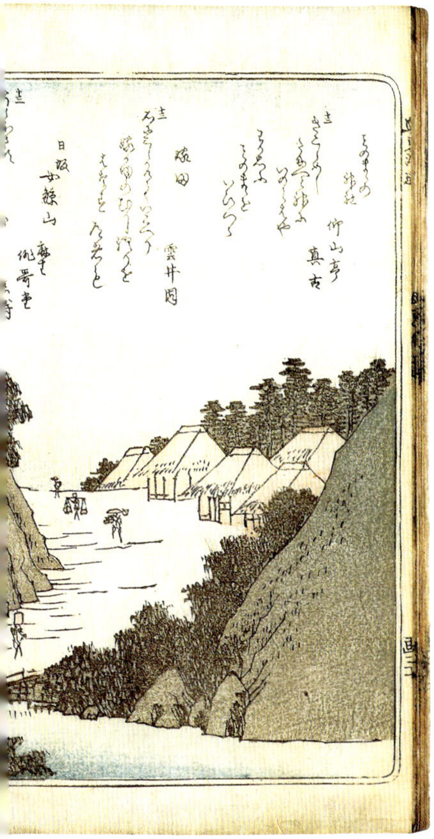

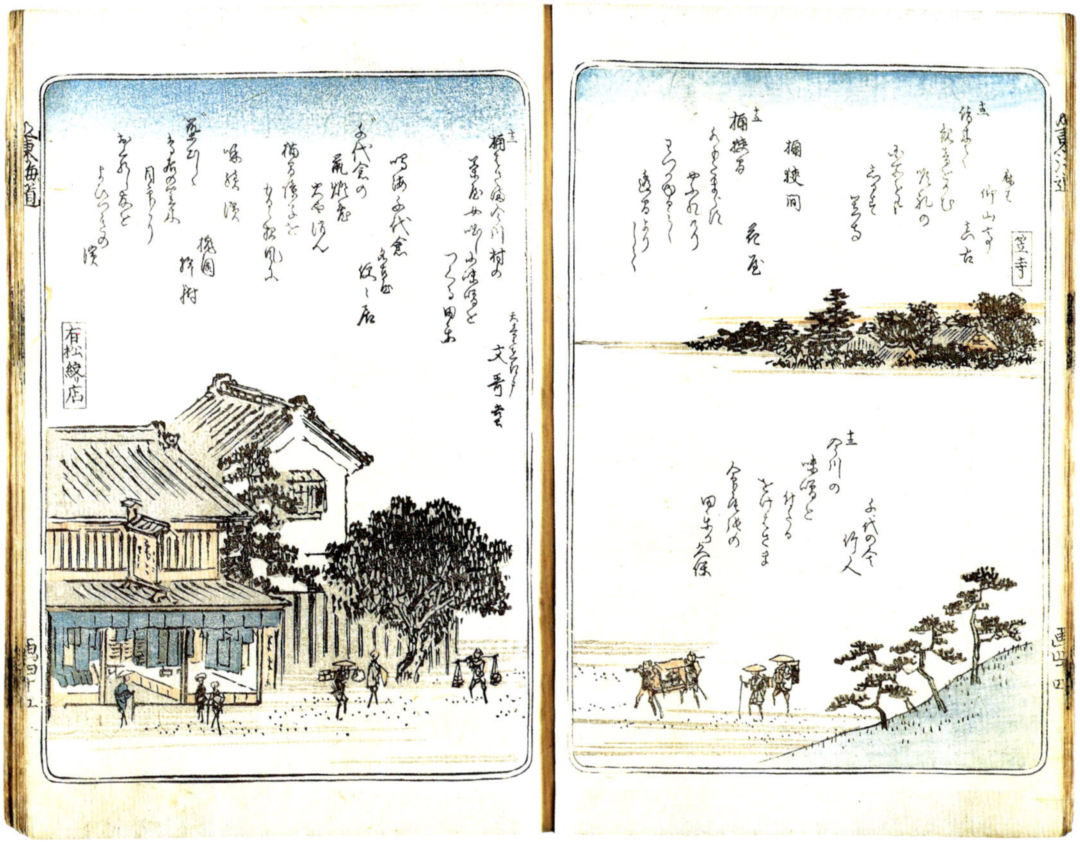

42 VIEW OF A VILLAGE BY A STREAM

Entering the Station of Nissaka; Famous Product Rice Cakes with Bracken (Nissaka eki iriguchi/meibutsu warabimochi)

from the three-volume album *Famous Views on the Tōkaidō (Tōkaidō meisho zue)*
published by Shunyūtei Umehiko, *c.* 1849

signed: *Ichiryūsai Hiroshige*
from volume 2, sheets 30b/31a
woodblock, album plate, *hanshibon*, 229 x 162 mm
Collection Pulverer, Cologne

A small bridge over the Kakarigawa leads the traveller into the town of Nissaka, whose houses can be seen beside the road on the right. In the foreground to the left is a small restaurant that sells the local speciality, rice cakes with bracken. The upper part of the print contains five *kyōka* poems.

The design shows similarities to that for Nissaka in the so-called *Kyōka Tōkaidō* (Shiraishi, 1988, p. 69).

REFERENCE: *Kokusho sōmokuroku*, 6-15-2

43 TRAVELLERS PASSING A SHOP

Kasadera Temple and a Shop for Arimatsu Shibori (Kasadera/Arimatsu shiboriten)

from the three-volume album *Famous Views on the Tōkaidō (Tōkaidō meisho zue)*
published by Shunyūtei Umehiko, *c.* 1849

signed: *Ichiryūsai Hiroshige*
from volume 3, sheets 44b/45a
woodblock, album plate, *hanshibon*, 229 x 162 mm
Collection Pulverer, Cologne

The Narumi district was famous for the manufacture of a particular variegated or dappled cloth, *shibori*. In this image travellers are passing a shop advertising *shibori* from Arimatsu, a village just before Narumi on the Tōkaidō Road. The Kasadera Temple can be seen among the trees in the distance. The sheet bears six *kyōka* poems.

REFERENCE: *Kokusho sōmokuroku*, 6-15-2

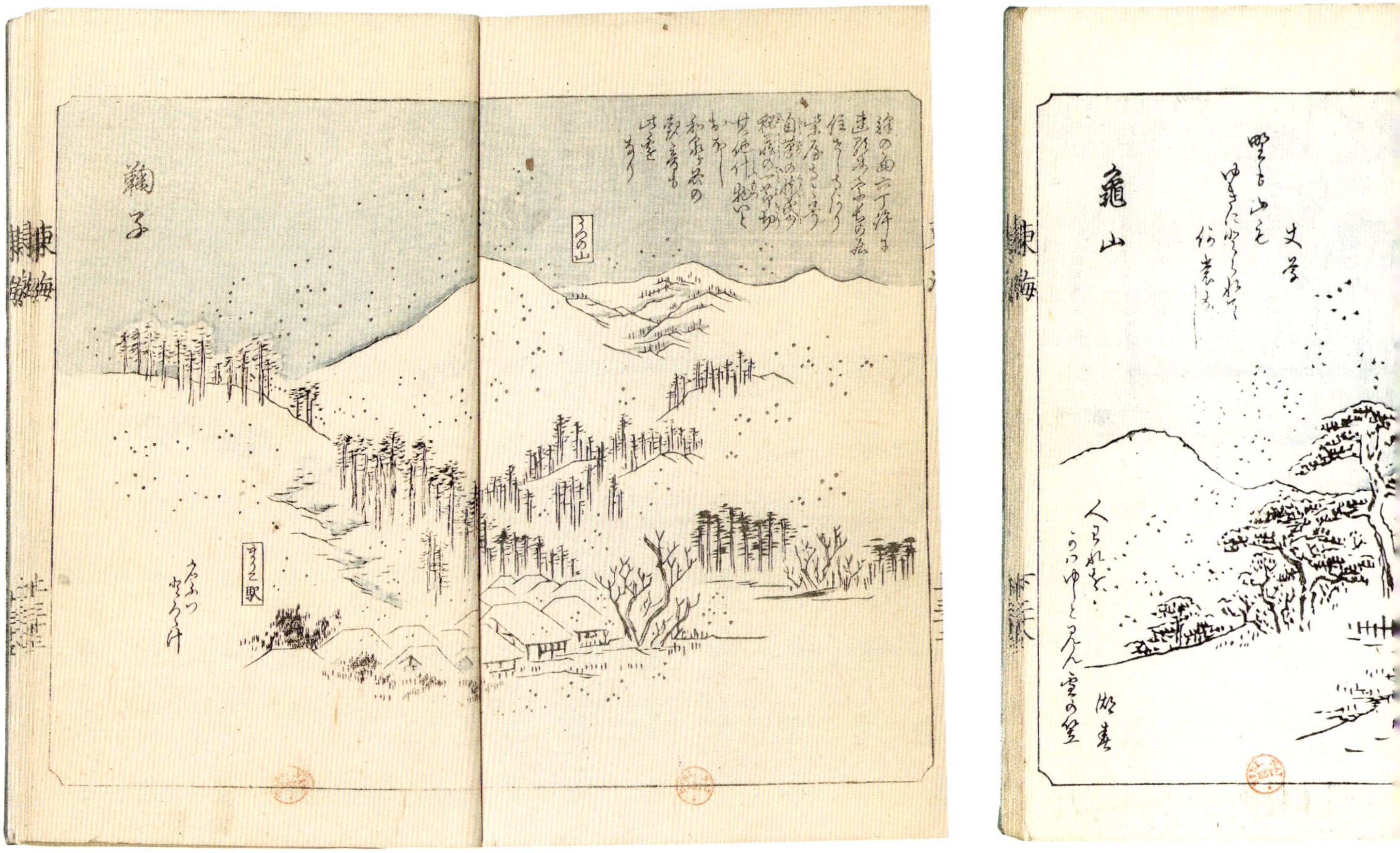

44 A VILLAGE IN THE SNOW

Mariko—Mount Utsunoyama and the Station of Mariko (Mariko—Utsunoyama/Mariko no eki)

from the four-volume album in two parts *Landscape Views on the Tōkaidō* (*Tōkaidō fūkei zue*)
published by Fujiokaya Keijirō (Shōrindō), 1851

signed: *Ichiryūsai Hiroshige hitsu*
from volume 1
woodblock, album plate, *hanshibon*, 175 x 120 mm
Bibliothèque Nationale de France, Département des Estampes, Paris (Dd390)

The snow-covered station of Mariko is surrounded by mountains, Mount Utsunoyama in the background. At upper right is information for travellers, directing them to the Murasakiya Temple, where the poet Morinaga lived, and to other sights. At lower left there is a reference to *tororoshiru,* the local speciality made of grated yams. The composition is very similar to the print of Mariko that Hiroshige included slightly later in the so-called *Reisho Tōkaidō* (cat. 31). In his preliminary remarks Hiroshige warned that the illustrations were rather sketchy and not intended as accurate representations of what could be seen on the journey.

This album was originally published by Fujiokaya Keijirō (Shōrindō). It was printed from a line-block in a soft bluish-grey tint. The parts were numbered *zen* and *gō*. Both the foreword, by Ryūkatei Tanekazu, and the colophon in the last volume are dated 1851/I. A reprint was published by Shōjuya Shōshichi (Kinshōdō), with the addition of rather harsh blue and green, and with the parts numbered *jō* and *ge*.

REFERENCES: Toda, 1931, no. 299; *Kokusho sōmokuroku*, 6-14-3; *Ukiyoe taikei*, 14, no. 181; Shiraishi, 1988, p. 57

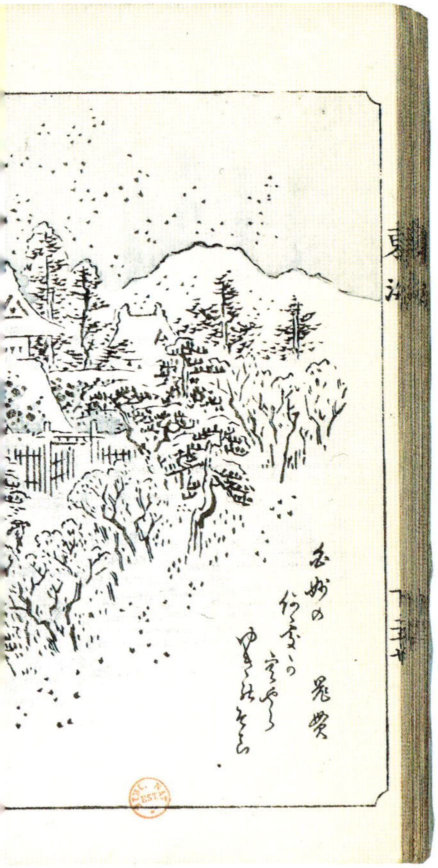

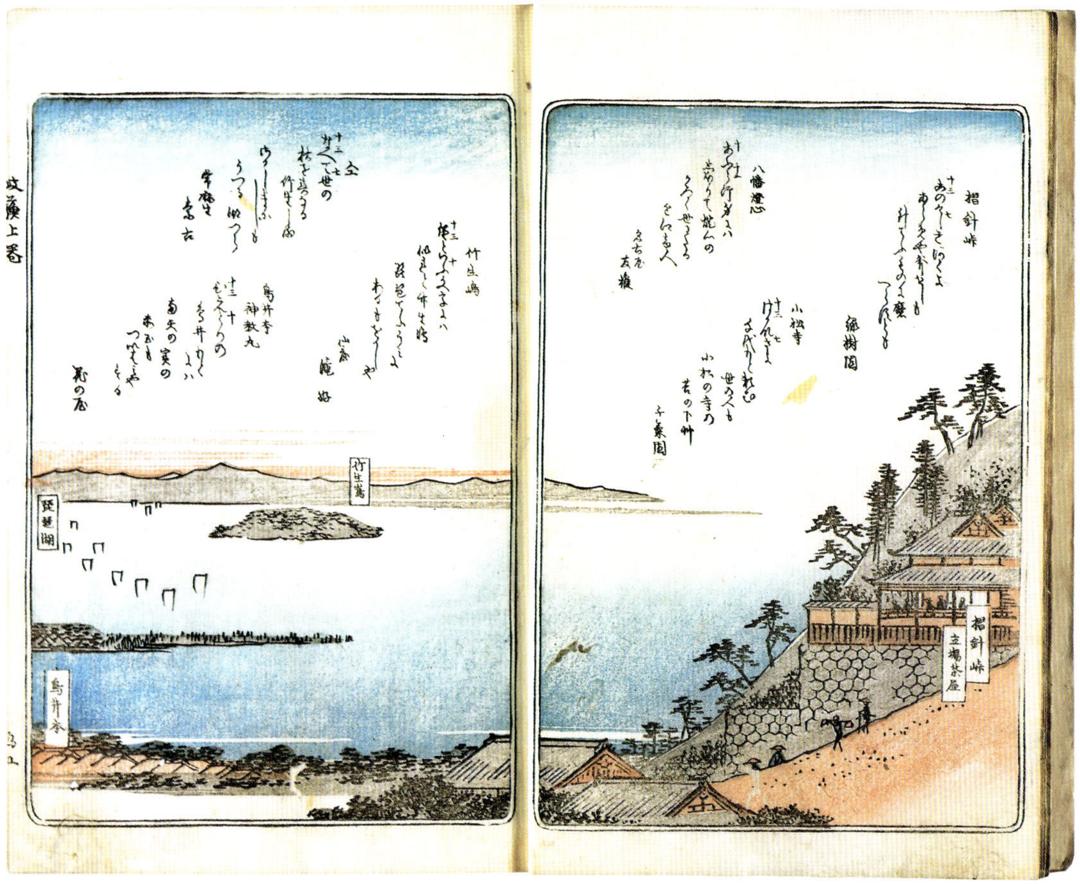

45 A CASTLE IN THE SNOW

Kameyama

from the four-volume album in two parts *Landscape Views on the Tōkaidō* (*Tōkaidō fūkei zue*)
published by Fujiokaya Keijirō (Shōrindō), 1851

signed: *Ichiryūsai Hiroshige hitsu*
from volume 2
woodblock, album plate, *hanshibon*, 175 x 120 mm
Bibliothèque Nationale de France, Département des Estampes, Paris (Dd390)

Two men climb a steep path through the snow to Kameyama Castle. The composition, which includes three *haiku* poems, recalls the print of Kameyama from Hiroshige's first great Tōkaidō series (cat. 26).

REFERENCES: Toda, 1931, no. 299; *Kokusho sōmokuroku*, 6-14-3; *Ukiyoe taikei*, 14, no. 183; Shiraishi, 1988, p. 117

46 VIEW OF A LAKE

Lake Biwa (*Biwako*)

from the three-volume album *Famous Views on the Kisokaidō* (*Kiso meisho zue*)
published by Shunyūtei Umehiko, *c.* 1851 (vols. 1 and 2)

signed: *Hiroshige hitsu*
from volume 1
woodblock, album plate, *hanshibon*, 230 x 160 mm
Collection Pulverer, Cologne

A view of Lake Biwa in Ōmi Province, with the small island of Chikubushima in the distance. In the right foreground are the Surihari Pass and a tea-house. The upper part of the image contains six *kyōka* poems. For the album, see cat. 47.

REFERENCES: *Kyōka shomoku shūsei*, p. 103 (2 vols.); *Kokusho sōmokuroku*, 2-422-1; Izzard, 1983, no. 104

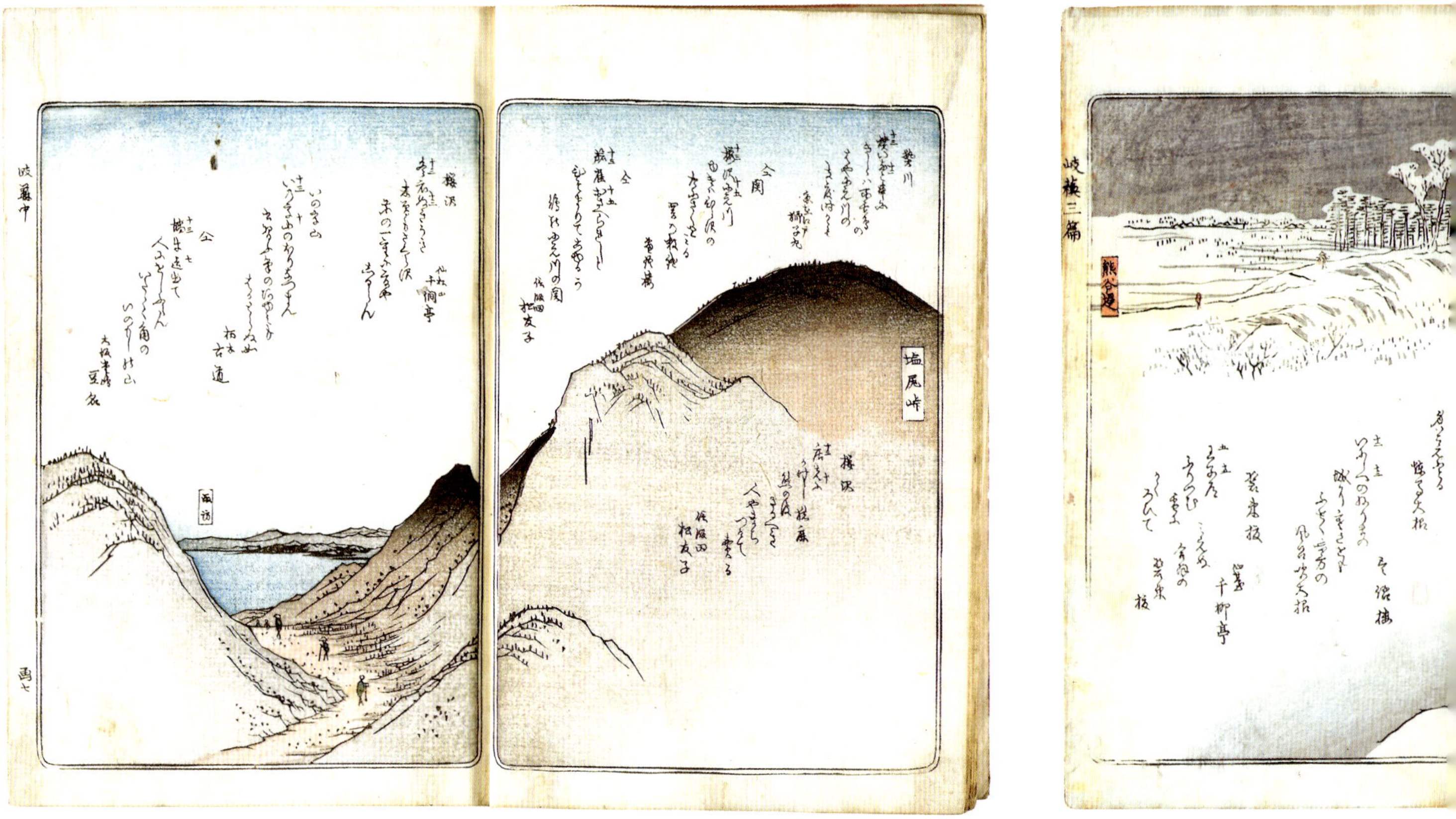

47 A ROAD THROUGH THE MOUNTAINS

Shiojiri Pass and Lake Suwa (*Shiojiritōge/Suwa*)

from the three-volume album *Famous Views on the Kisokaidō* (*Kiso meisho zue*)
published by Shunyūtei Umehiko, *c.* 1851 (vols. 1 and 2)

signed: *Hiroshige hitsu*
from volume 2
woodblock, album plate, *hanshibon*, 230 x 160 mm
Collection Pulverer, Cologne

One of the designs executed by Keisai Eisen, the print of this subject in the Kisokaidō series (*Ukiyoe taikei*, 15, no. 31), shows a man on horseback leaving the road and descending through the pass; it is winter and people are walking on the frozen Lake Suwa. In his illustration for the present album Hiroshige again used this tried and tested composition, with the road winding its way through the pass and the mountains to the right and left, opening out onto a prospect of the lake.

This album of the stations of the Kisokaidō Road follows the route from Kyoto (vol. 1) to Edo (vol. 3). The poems were selected by Umenoya Tsuruko and Hinokizono Umeaki (1793–1859), head of the Hinokizono poetry club. A comment at the end of volume 2, which applies to the first two volumes, states that the blocks were cut in the late summer of 1851.

REFERENCES: *Kyōka shomoku shūsei*, p. 103 (2 vols.); *Kokusho sōmokuroku*, 2-422-1; *Ukiyoe taikei*, 15, no. 87

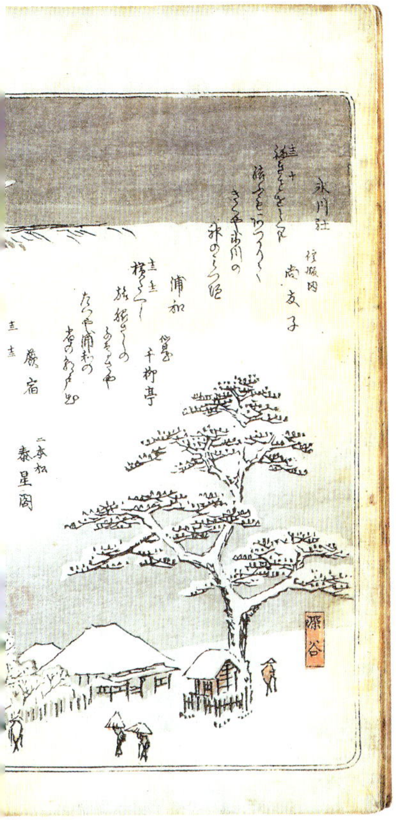

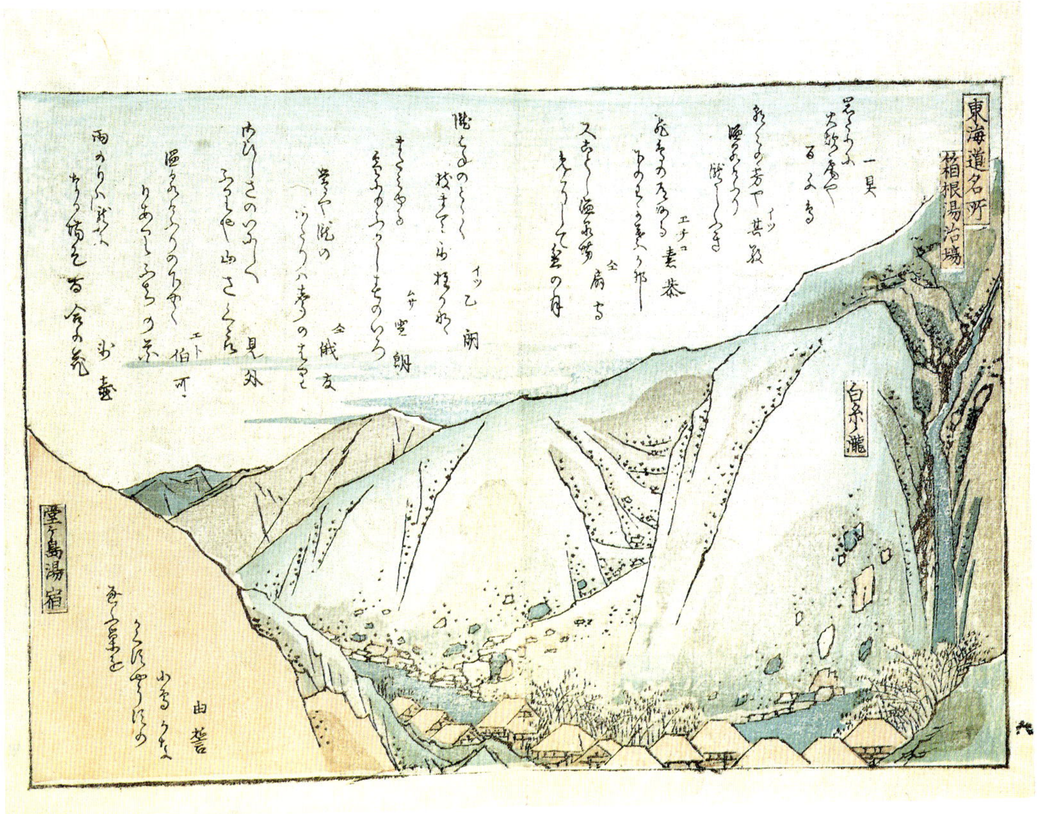

48 A VILLAGE IN SNOW WITH A DIKE

Fukaya and Kumagaya Dike (Fukaya/Kumagaya tsutsumi)

from the three-volume album *Famous Views on the Kisokaidō (Kiso meisho zue)*
published by Shunyūtei Umehiko, *c.* 1852 (vol. 3)

signed: *Hiroshige hitsu*
from volume 3
woodblock, album plate, *hanshibon*, 230 x 160 mm
Collection Pulverer, Cologne

The station Fukaya is in the foreground with a few people in the snow-covered street. In the distance, slightly to the left, is the Kumagaya Dike, leading to the next station, Kumagaya.

REFERENCES: *Kyōka shomoku shūsei*, p. 103 (2 vols.); *Kokusho sōmokuroku*, 2-422-1; *Ukiyoe taikei*, 15, no. 99

49 A MOUNTAIN VILLAGE

Famous Views along the Tōkaidō Road—Health Resort at Hakone (Tōkaidō meisho—Hakone tōjiba)

from the two-volume(?) *Album of Famous Views on the Tōkaidō (Tōkaidō meisho gajō)*
published by Tōkaidō, 1851

signed: *Ichiryūsai Hiroshige hitsu*
censors' seals: Fuku and Muramatsu
woodblock, album plate, *hanshibon*, 182 x 120 mm
The British Library, London, Oriental and India Office Collections (16114.a.7)

In a valley between mountains is a village with one of the famous hot springs for which the Hakone district is famous. The Shiraito waterfall can be seen on the right. Eleven *kyōka* poems are arranged above the mountains and at lower left.

The preface to this publication, assembled as a folding album, is dated 1850. Nothing is known of the publisher apart from the name of his firm, Tōkaidō.

REFERENCE: *Kokusho sōmokuroku*, 6-15-1

VIEWS IN THE PROVINCES I

CAT. 50–80

50 WOMEN WALKING ON A ROAD THROUGH THE FIELDS

The Village of Yase (*Yase no sato*)

from the series *Famous Views of Kyoto* (*Kyōto meisho no uchi*)
published by Kawaguchiya Shōzō (Eisendō), *c.* 1834

signed: *Hiroshige ga*
censorship seal: *kiwame*
woodblock, *ōban*, 243 x 366 mm
The Art Institute of Chicago, Chicago,
The Clarence Buckingham Collection (43.710)

A group of three women, followed by a fourth, walk through a deserted landscape. There is a single tree on a slope to the left. The three women are carrying a bundle of branches, a ladder and a wooden tray. Behind them, the fourth woman is leading a horse laden with branches. They are probably Ōharame, women from the village of Ōhara to the north-east of Kyoto, making their way to the city to sell their wares. The village of Yase lies between Ōhara and Kyoto, and the mountain towering above the horizon could be Mount Yokotake or Hieizan.

The print comes from *Famous Views of Kyoto*, a series of ten prints published by Kawaguchiya Shōzō, probably shortly after the completion of the Hōeidō Tōkaidō series. He had published Hiroshige's earliest large series, *Famous Views in the Eastern Capital* (cat. 6, 7), and had issued a series of ten prints, *Famous Views of Osaka,* at about the same time as the views of Kyoto. As an Edo publisher, his intentions in issuing views of other cities are difficult to fathom, especially as his shop was in the centre of Edo and his products therefore not aimed specifically at travellers. Perhaps he worked with a publisher in the Kansai region who sold the prints there.

The composition of the present print is given an almost abstract quality by the use of colour, with a red, white and yellow sky over surprisingly large areas of yellow, green and blue-grey. This rather unnaturalistic impression is reinforced by the repeated use of sharp contrast, occasionally toned down in *bokashi* before each new colour reaches its full intensity. This tendency towards abstraction, found in several Hiroshige compositions, has already been noted in connection with cat. 36. The effect in the present print is to increase the desolation of the landscape and, with only the tree on the left and the roofs of the distant houses on the right as guides, it is difficult to estimate the distance the women have travelled.

REFERENCES: Narazaki, 1964, p. 25; *Ukiyoe hakka*, 1984, no. 12; *Meihin soroimono ukiyoe*, 12, no. 9; Forrer, 1994, G507; Satō, 1994, no. 7

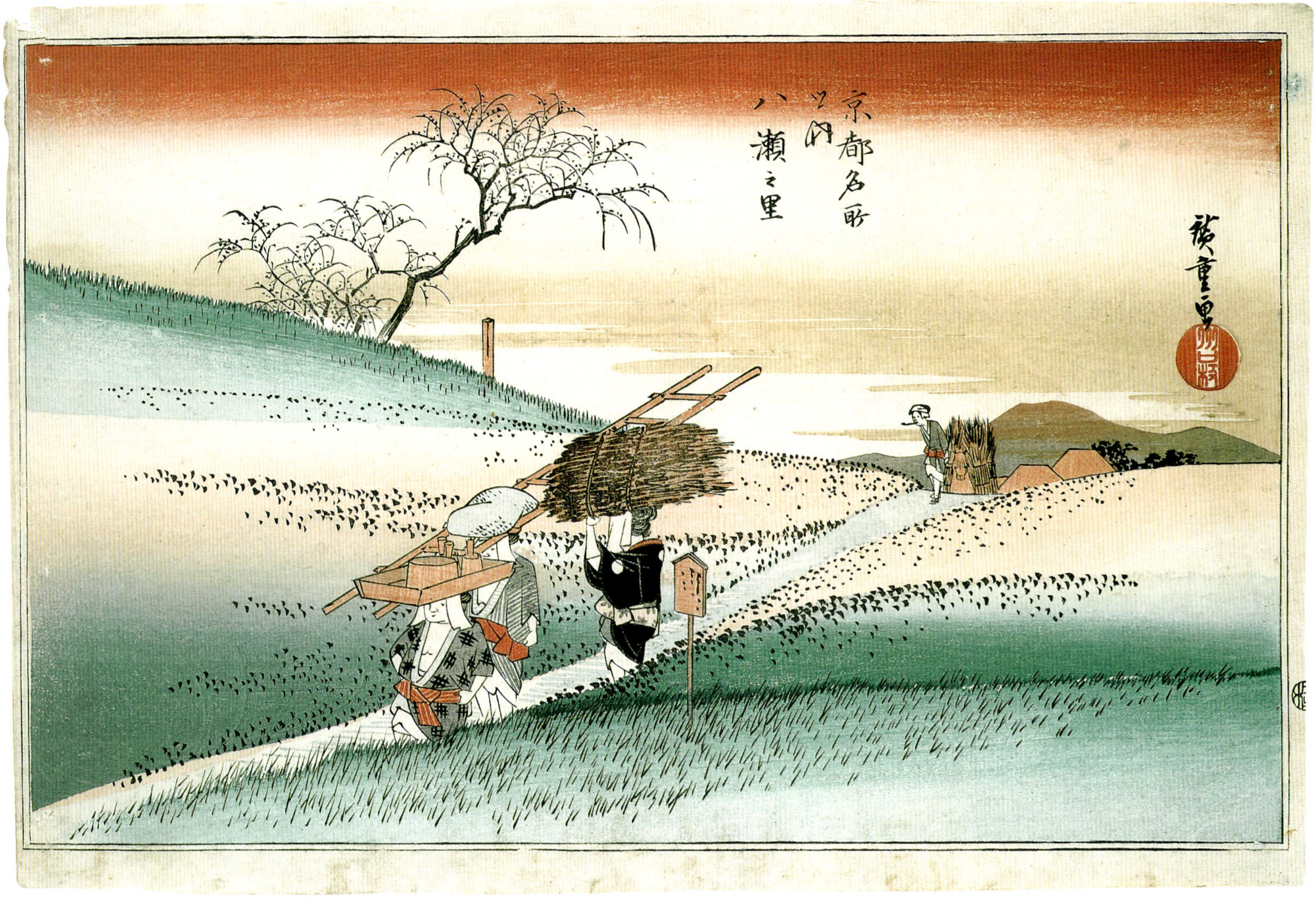
京都名所
之内
八瀬之里
廣重画

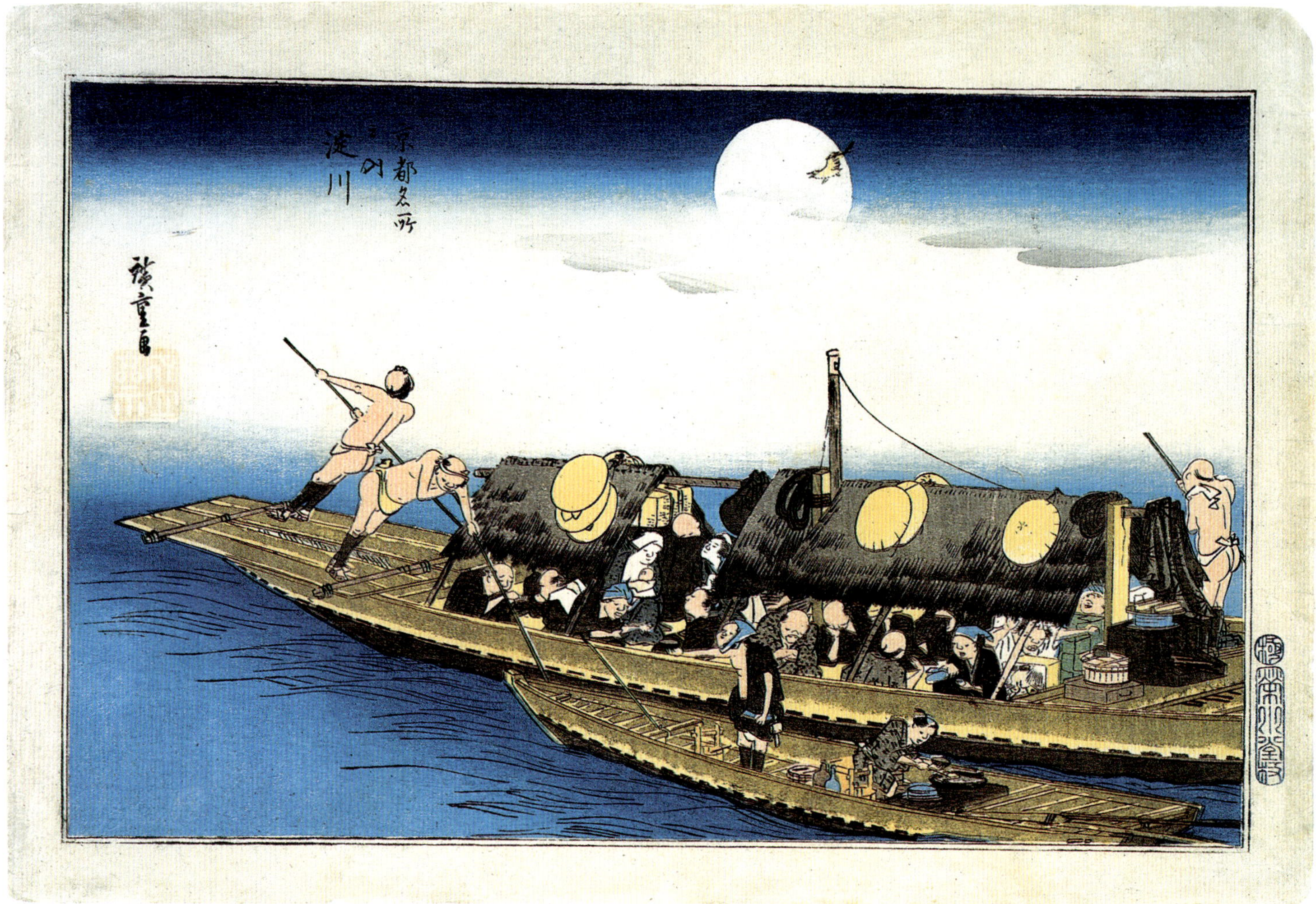

51 A FERRY ON THE RIVER

Yodo River (*Yodogawa*)

from the series *Famous Views of Kyoto* (*Kyōto meisho no uchi*)
published by Kawaguchiya Shōzō (Eisendō), *c.* 1834

signed: *Hiroshige ga*, with seal: *Ichiryūsai*
woodblock, *ōban*, 261 x 390 mm
Private Collection, Denmark

A provisions boat is tied alongside a ferry crossing the Yodo River, the major waterway between Kyoto and Osaka. The sutler offers a bowl of food, his assistant cooks and a man serves sake. The cuckoo flying past the moon seems to be noticed only by the two boatmen: some of the passengers concentrate on their food, others sit listlessly, while a woman suckles her baby. These boats left Osaka in the morning and reached Fushimi in the evening; there was also a night ferry.

Early impressions of the print (a) have the censorship seal and that of the publisher, Eisendō, in blue in the right-hand margin, as here. Later impressions (b) show the publisher's trademark in red within the design, in the place where Hiroshige's seal had been printed.

This composition was clearly inspired by the illustration of the Yodo River in a Kyoto city guide, the *Miyako rinsen meishō zue* of 1799 (fig. 5, p. 23), which had been illustrated by various designers. In particular, the two boatmen in the bows, and such details as the hats hanging over the roof, seem to have been taken directly from that work, which also includes a sutler's boat. In fact, this guide, like the similar *Miyako meisho zue* of 1786, provided Hiroshige with the inspiration for a number of designs in the Kyoto series.

REFERENCES: Narazaki, 1964, p. 20 [a]; Suzuki, 1970, no. 9 [a]; Narazaki, 1975, no. 11 [a]; *Ukiyoe taikei*, 11, no. 26 [a]; Izzard, 1983, no. 20 [a]; *Ukiyoe hakka*, 1984, no. 10 [a]; *Meihin soroimono ukiyoe*, 12, no. 4 [a]; Forrer, 1994, G503 [b]; Satō, 1994, no. 2 [a]

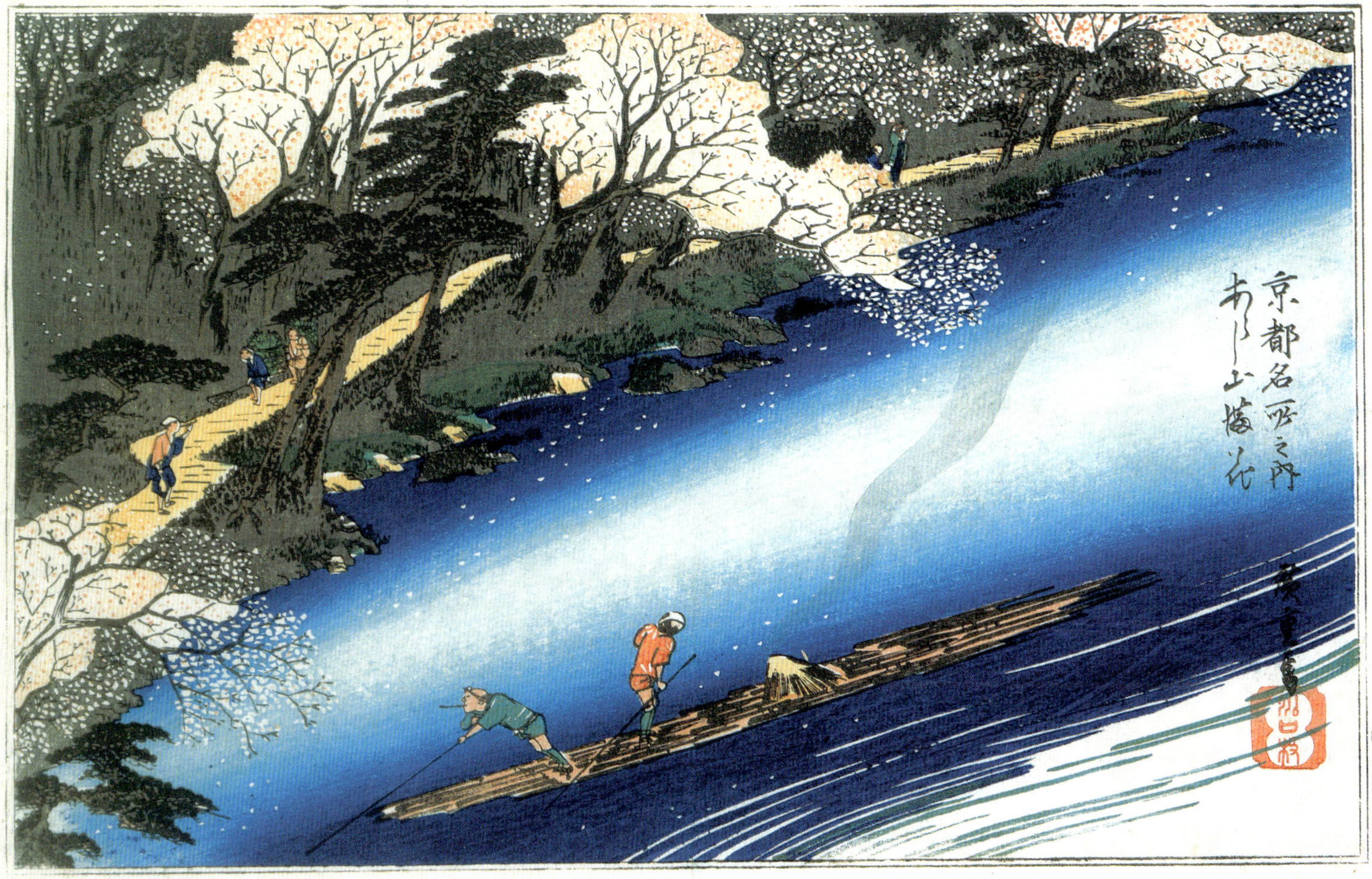

52 POLING A RAFT ON A RIVER

Cherry Trees in Full Bloom at Arashiyama (Arashiyama manka)

from the series *Famous Views of Kyoto* (*Kyōto meisho no uchi*)
published by Kawaguchiya Shōzō (Eisendō), *c.* 1834

signed: *Hiroshige ga*
censorship seal: *kiwame*
woodblock, *ōban*, 240 x 373 mm
The Mann Collection, Highland Park, Illinois

Arashiyama, west of Kyoto, was *the* place to admire cherry blossom or, in the autumn, the red maple trees. Some men on the path beside the Hosu River are taking time to look. Others, like the couple with baskets on their backs, are not interested. On the water two men are poling a big raft. Both are smoking pipes, and the man on the right cannot help looking at the impressive blossoms by the riverside. This print and a few others in the series somewhat resemble an illustration (fig. 6, p. 24) in *Miyako rinsen meishō zue* (see cat. 51). Although in that illustration it is a pleasure boat on the river, the distant river-bank looks very like the one in Hiroshige's print.

Some impressions of this print (a) have a wide uncoloured strip in the river, perhaps to suggest—none too convincingly, it has to be said—that the water is white from the fallen blossom. In others (c) the blue along the river-bank is absent. In the present impression (b) the river is almost entirely blue, with a lighter tint in the middle, as if light is reflected from the blossom. In some impressions the river-bank is fairly dark, resulting in a loss of detail in the trees and rocks.

REFERENCES: Vignier and Inada, 1914, no. 204 [c]; Narazaki, 1964, p. 4 [a]; Yoshida, 1973, no. 3 [a]; Suzuki, 1975, p. 120 [a]; *Ukiyoe takei*, 11, no. 25 [a]; Link, 1991, no. III-5-A [a]; *Meihin soroimono ukiyoe*, 12, no. 2 [a]; Forrer, 1994, G511, 512 [both b]; Satō, 1994, no. 6 [a]

53 PEOPLE UNDER MAPLE TREES BY A STREAM

Red Maple Trees at Tsūtenkyō (*Tsūtenkyō no momiji*)

from the series *Famous Views of Kyoto* (*Kyōto meisho no uchi*)
published by Kawaguchiya Shōzō (Eisendō), *c.* 1834

signed: *Hiroshige ga*
censorship seal: *kiwame*
woodblock, *ōban*, 246 x 362 mm
Trustees of The Chester Beatty Library and Gallery of Oriental Art, Dublin (CBLJ 2700)

Tsūtenkyō is a wooden bridge, some twenty-five metres long, that spans a mountain river in the precinct of the Tōfukuji Temple, originally built in 1597, in the eastern part of Kyoto. Beneath the bridge were benches for people to sit and enjoy the autumnal shades of the maple trees, as in this print. It is apparently late in the day, and the surrounding slopes are already in shadow. The red of the maple leaves was produced by deliberate oxidation in some impressions, as here.

Hiroshige again drew inspiration from an illustration in the *Miyako rinsen meishō zue* of 1799 (fig. 7, p. 25), not only for the construction of the bridge and the trees beside the water, but also for the man fanning a fire and the two girls on the right (although slightly differently positioned in the illustration).

REFERENCES: Narazaki, 1964, p. 24; *Kobijutsu*, 1983, no. 117; Link, 1991, no. III-5-C; *Meihin soroimono ukiyoe*, 12, no. 9; Forrer, 1994, G502; Satō, 1994, no. 8

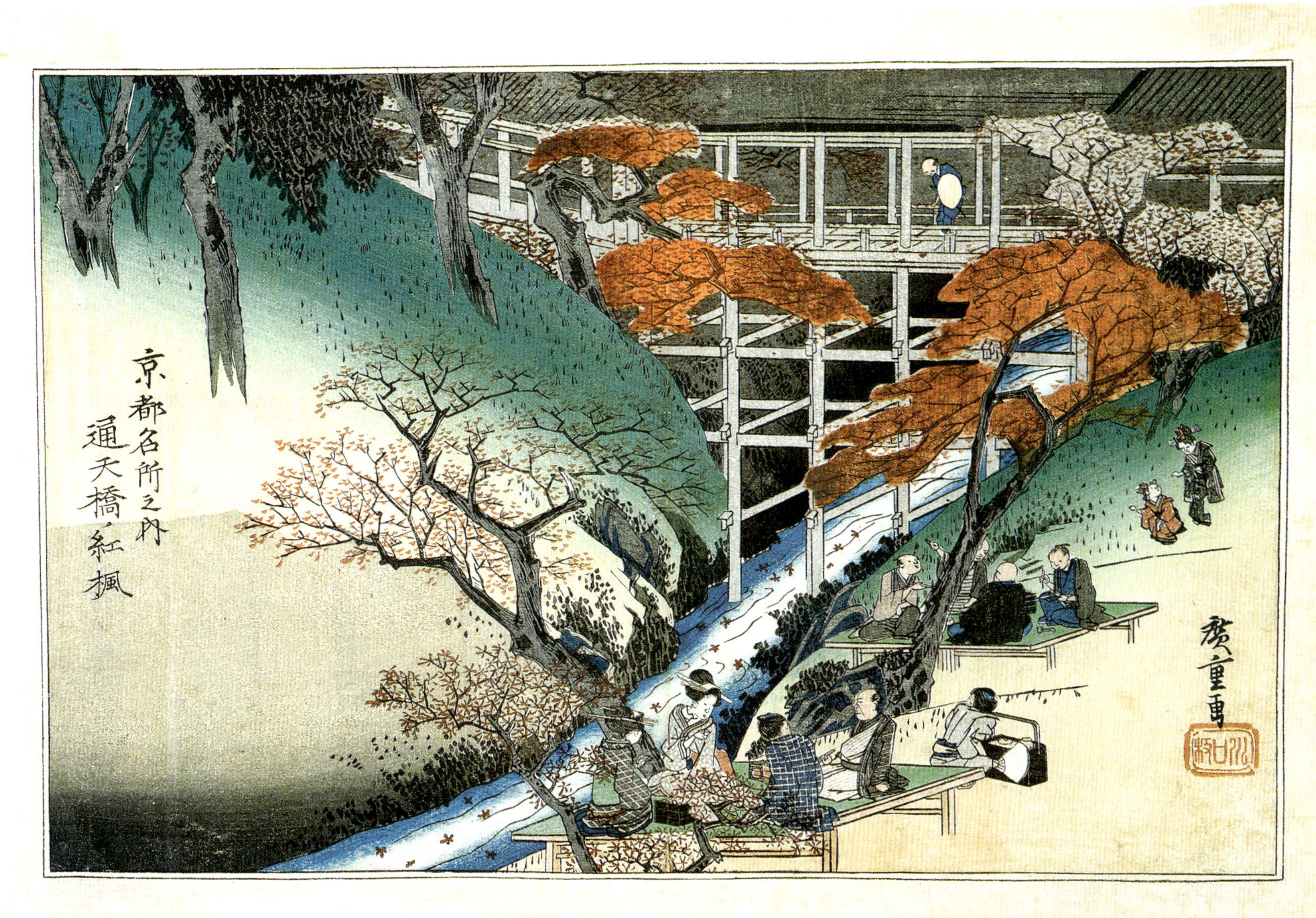
京都名所之内
通天橋ノ紅楓
廣重画

54 TRAVELLERS ON A MOUNTAIN PATH ALONG THE COAST

Mount Fuji from Satta (*Satta Fuji*)

from the series *Famous Views of Our Country* (*Honchō meisho*)
published by Fujiokaya Hikotarō, *c.* 1837

signed: *Hiroshige ga*, with seal: *Ichiryūsai*
censorship seal: *kiwame*
woodblock, *ōban*, 248 x 368 mm
Private Collection, Denmark

Until 1566, when a pass was made through the mountains, travellers along the Tōkaidō Road had to cross part of the shore of Shimizu Bay between the stations of Yui and Okitsu. Then, after a climb sheltered by trees, they enjoyed a wonderful view of Mount Fuji before proceeding down to the plain. In this print travellers are walking on the mountain path known as the Satta Pass, with a view of the sea on the right and Mount Fuji on the horizon. An idea of how difficult the descent beneath the cliff could be is provided by another print by Hiroshige (cat. 78).

Hiroshige probably began *Famous Views of Our Country* before the great Tōkaidō series. Fifteen prints from this *Famous Views* series are known; cat. 55 and two others, *Sōshū Enoshima Iwaiya* and *Sunshū Fujikawa watashibune*, probably date from around 1832. Publication may have been suspended owing to lack of success, but after the Tōkaidō series the public became interested in Hiroshige's prints and the publisher will have welcomed the opportunity to resume publication. The earlier prints bear the signature 'Ichiryūsai Hiroshige'; the later ones are simply signed 'Hiroshige', sometimes followed by the seal 'Ichiryūsai'. Another difference is that the early prints have the name of the publisher, Shōgendō, as a red seal, while the later ones bear his name in the abbreviated form of Fujihiko.

Although in a number of ways the composition of the present print resembles that for the station of Yui from the Hōeidō Tōkaidō series (cat. 22), the artist has chosen a very different vantage point. In the print from the Tōkaidō series there is more emphasis on the virtually impassable rocks on the left, with a few travellers admiring the view from an elevation. In this print, on the other hand, a path winds alongside a sheer cliff, with a calm sea below. The composition is of a type well represented in Hiroshige's oeuvre (see cat. 35).

REFERENCES: Narazaki, 1964, p. 37; Tanba, 1965, no. 60; Link, 1991, no. III-3-A; *Meihin soroimono ukiyoe*, 12, no. 24

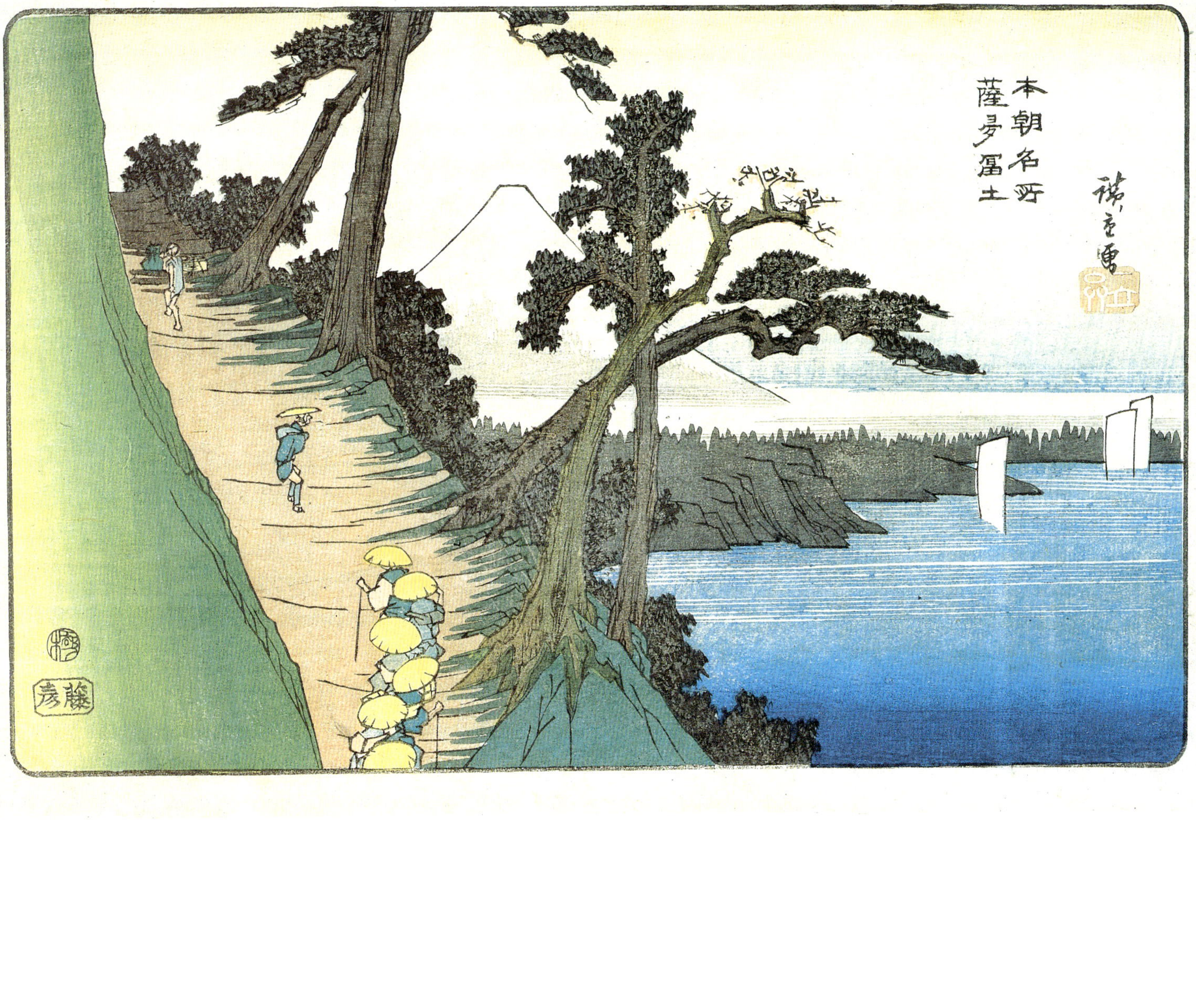
本朝名所
薩多冨士
廣重画

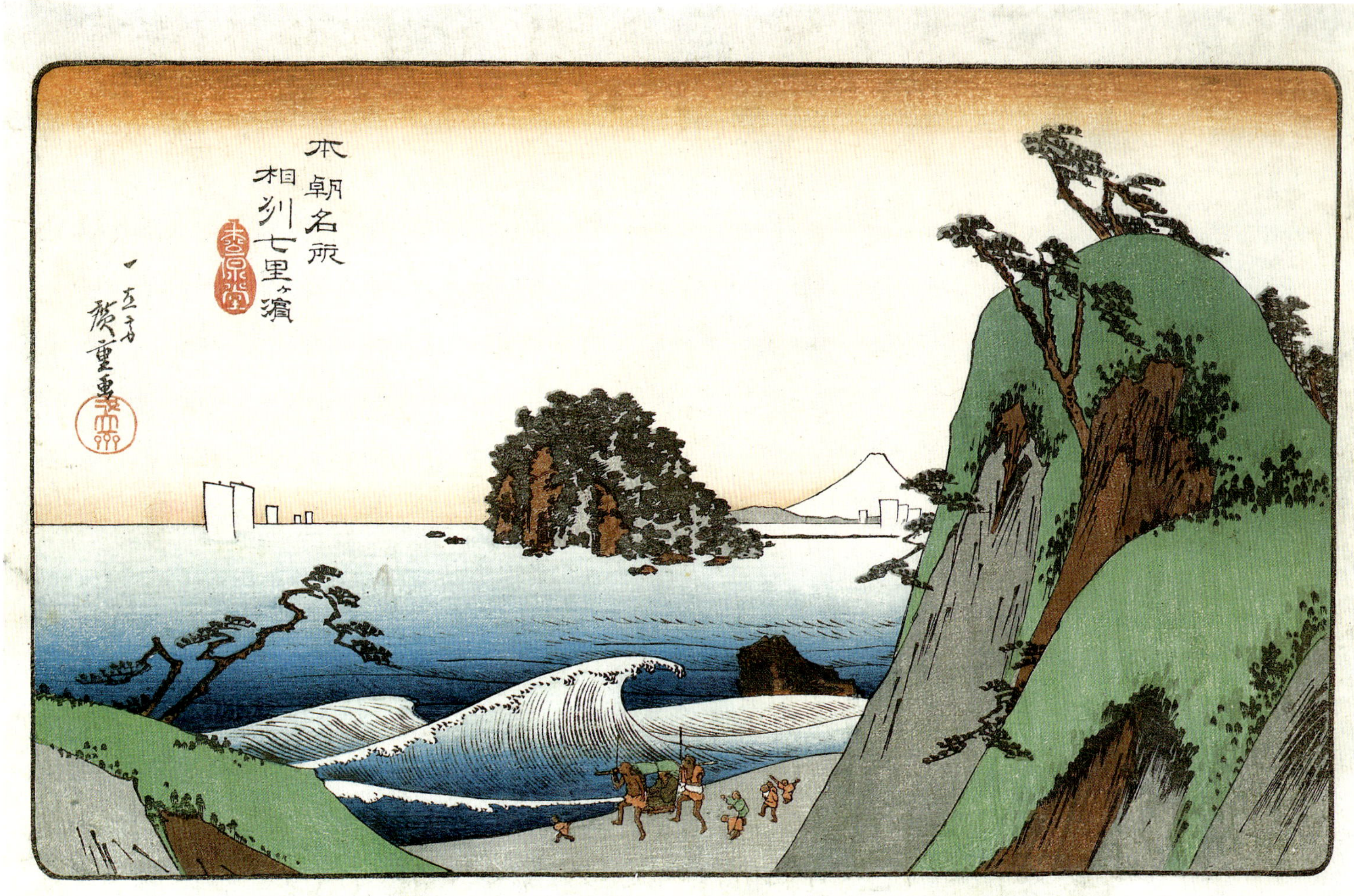

55 A GREAT WAVE BY THE COAST

Shichirigahama in Sagami Province (*Sōshū Shichirigahama*)

from the series *Famous Views of Our Country* (*Honchō meisho*)
published by Fujiokaya Hikotarō (Shōgendō), *c.* 1832

signed: *Hiroshige ga*, with seal: *Ichiryūsai*
censorship seal: *kiwame*
woodblock, *ōban*, 233 x 358 mm
The Metropolitan Museum of Art, New York, H.O. Havemeyer Collection, Bequest of Mrs H.O. Havemeyer, 1929 (JP1882)

The island of Enoshima, depicted in the foreground of this print, was roughly a day's journey from Edo. It was a popular pilgrimage site both because of the shrine dedicated to the goddess Benten on the rocky island and because of the refreshing breeze along the beach. The island could be reached from the mainland when the tide was out. It was a popular theme in landscape prints from the end of the eighteenth century and Hiroshige's version probably reflects paintings by Shiba Kōkan (1747–1818), which had already inspired Hokusai's famous *The Great Wave*. Hiroshige here chooses a more distant point of view, so that more of the rocks behind the beach are visible, but the shape of the wave is clearly inspired by Kōkan or Hokusai. An almost identical wave appears twice in a triptych of the island by Hiroshige that was published by Kawaguchiya Chōzō in 1833, at about the same time as this print (Tanba, 1965, no. 61).

REFERENCES: Tanba, 1965, no. 58; *Meihin soroimono ukiyoe*, 12, no. 20

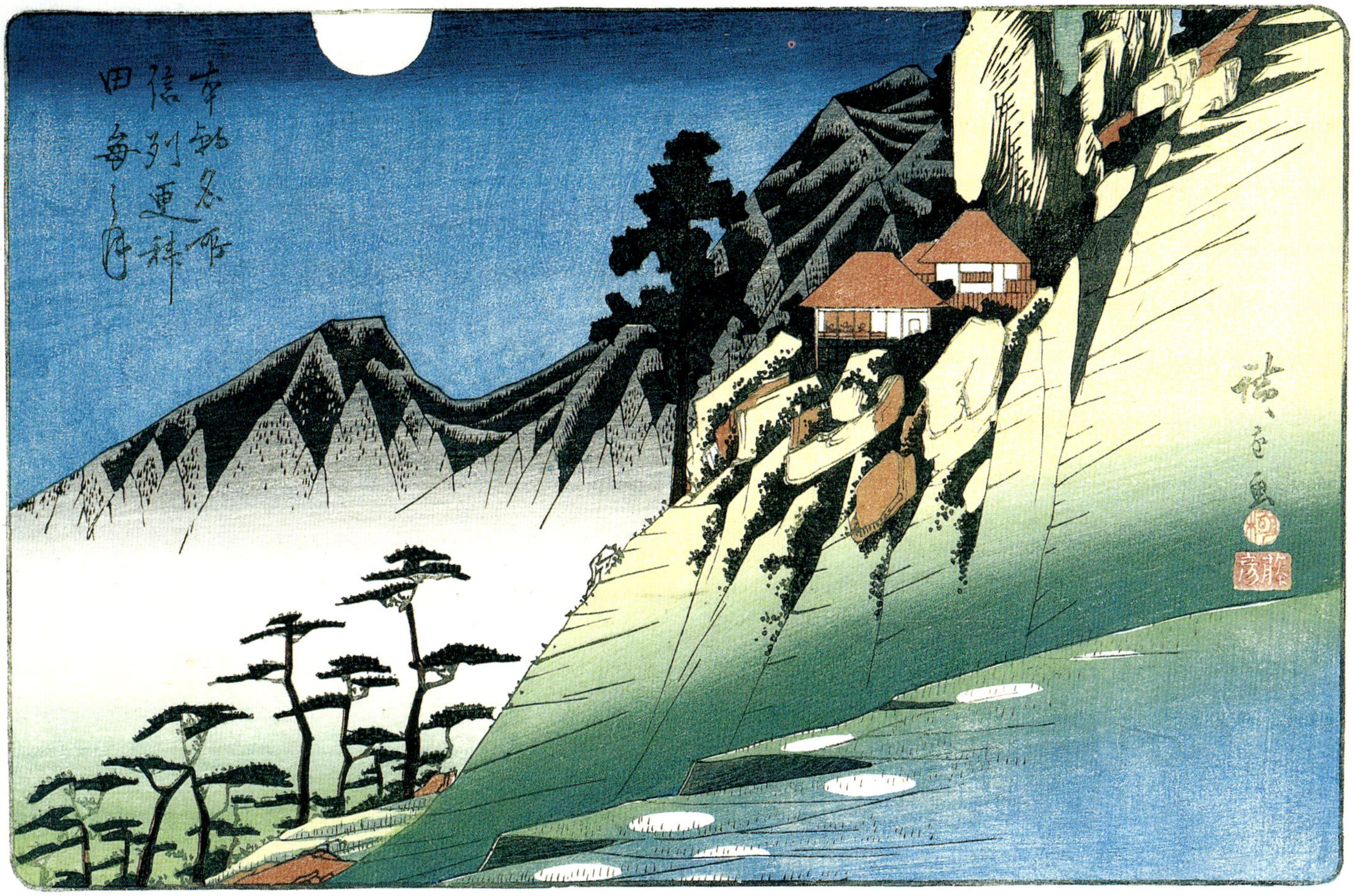

56 MOON OVER A MOUNTAIN LANDSCAPE

The Moon Reflected in the Rice-fields at Sarashina in Shinano Province (Shinshū Sarashina tagoto no tsuki)

from the series *Famous Views of Our Country* (*Honchō meisho*)
published by Fujiokaya Hikotarō, *c.* 1837

signed: *Hiroshige ga*
woodblock, *ōban*, 241 x 365 mm
Honolulu Academy of Arts, Honolulu,
Gift of James A. Michener, 1992 (22.382)

Multiple reflections of the moon in a waterfall or in rice-fields seem to have fascinated Hiroshige and he returned to the subject repeatedly in various series. These included *Famous Views in the Sixty-odd Provinces*, which contains another image of Sarashina, this time in a vertical composition. A striking feature of both that print and this one is that the moon is cut off by the upper edge of the print. The result is more remarkable in the horizontal composition than in the vertical one, where the moon is directly above the rice-fields. An attractive feature of this impression is the incorporation of the grain of the woodblock in the sky above Mount Kyōdai.

REFERENCE: *Meihin soroimono ukiyoe*, 12, no. 28

58 BOATS IN AN INLET

The Small Port and the Inlet in Awa Province (Awa kominato uchiura)

from the series *Famous Views in the Sixty-odd Provinces (Rokujūyoshū meisho zue)*
published by Koshimuraya Heisuke, 1853–6

signed: *Hiroshige hitsu*
block-cutter: Yokogawa Takejirō (Horitake)
censors' seals: Murata and Kinugasa; date seal: Ox 8 (1853/VIII)
woodblock, *ōban*, 368 x 250 mm
Collection Pulverer, Cologne (ex-Frank Lloyd Wright Collection)

People are descending a path between hills. A bay and some boats can be seen beyond. There is a small town in the middle distance on the left. In this early impression (a) the evening darkens the sky from the upper edge of the print—in a beautiful transition from brown to purple—while the setting sun reddens the yellow sky on the horizon. In later impressions this is simplified to a dark blue strip along the upper edge and an uncoloured sky with some orange on the horizon (b), or blue from the upper edge and red on the horizon (c).

In this print a special effect has been achieved by a slight sanding of the woodblock, permitting the grain to become an integral part of the final image. Hiroshige employed this technique in most of his later series, including *One Hundred Famous Views in Edo* (cat. 93–106). The effect is, of course, most striking in early impressions.

Awa is a small province at the southernmost tip of the Chiba peninsula. The port depicted here is probably near Tateyama. For convenience, this print was grouped with the Tōkaidō Road in the list detailing the contents of the series.

Compositions consisting of people on a path flanked by hills and a distant panorama occur regularly in Hiroshige's various Tōkaidō series and in that devoted to the Kisokaidō. This seems to have been one of his favourite ways of constructing landscape images and he returned to it several times in *Thirty-six Views of Mount Fuji* (cat. 76).

REFERENCES: Narazaki, 1964, p. 50 [b]; *Meihin soroimono ukiyoe*, 12, no. 51 [a]; Suzuki and Ōkubo, 1996, no. 18 [a: this impression]

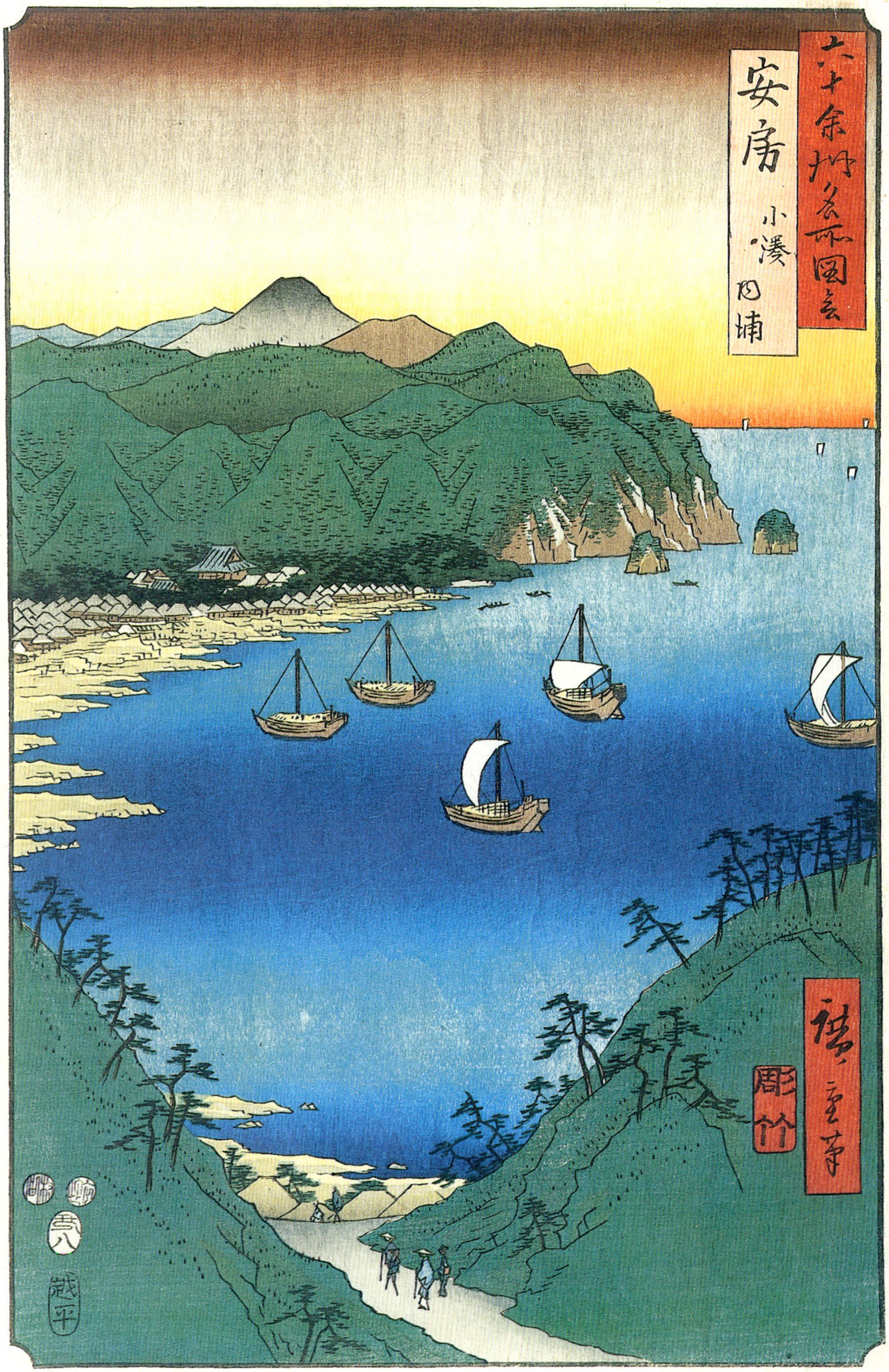
六十余州名所図会
安房
小湊 内浦
廣重筆
彫竹

59 A LARGE WATERFALL

The Yōrō Waterfall in Mino Province (Mino Yōrō no taki)

from the series *Famous Views in the Sixty-odd Provinces (Rokujūyoshū meisho zue)*
published by Koshimuraya Heisuke, 1853–6

signed: *Hiroshige hitsu*
block-cutter: Yokogawa Takejirō (Horitake)
censors' seals: Kinugasa and Murata; date seal: Ox 8 (1853/VIII)
woodblock, *ōban*, 368 x 246 mm
Collection Pulverer, Cologne (ex-Frank Lloyd Wright Collection)

The Yōrō waterfall in Gifu prefecture, Mino Province, cascades from a height of some thirty metres, and is four metres across. Hokusai included this waterfall in his series *Making the Rounds of the Waterfalls in All Provinces*, adding a few spectators. Hiroshige's composition is devoid of human beings, as the waterfall crashes down from the rocks and the upper edge of the print is bordered by low-lying clouds. Mino Province is grouped with the Tōsandō Road in the list of contents for this series.

In later impressions (b) the centre of the waterfall is white, with a faint light-blue tint at the sides, while the gradation printing on the lower part of the rocks turns a brownish yellow. Later still the waterfall is printed in light blue with deep blue *bokashi* along the sides, and the rocks are left unprinted from about two-thirds of the way down.

REFERENCES: Narazaki, 1964, p. 55 [b]; *Meihin soroimono ukiyoe*, 12, no. 59 [a]; Suzuki and Ōkubo, 1996, no. 23 [a: this impression]

60 A STRETCH OF LAND OVERGROWN WITH PINES

Amanohashidate in Tango Province (Tango Amanohashidate)

from the series *Famous Views in the Sixty-odd Provinces (Rokujūyoshū meisho zue)*
published by Koshimuraya Heisuke, 1853–6

signed: *Hiroshige hitsu*
block-cutter: *hori* Sōji (perhaps a member of the Muneoka family)
censorship seal: *aratame*; date seal: Ox 12 (1853/XII)
woodblock, *ōban*, 367 x 251 mm
Collection Pulverer, Cologne (ex-Frank Lloyd Wright Collection)

Amanohashidate is a sandbank overgrown with pine trees, extending about three kilometres into the Sea of Japan. It is in Tango Province, part of the Sanindō circuit, and, together with Miyajima and Matsushima, is considered one of the three most beautiful spots in Japan. Here the sandbank is seen from above, an example of Hiroshige's powerful visual imagination. In the foreground to the right is a Shinto shrine with a gate.

Essentially a simple scene, it acquires depth through skilful use of *bokashi*, in which the bands of mist familiar from other Japanese prints seem to hover over the water. This is probably intended to underline the literal translation of the place name, 'Bridge to Heaven'. When in later editions (b) the *bokashi* is simplified and the mist reduced to two strips, the whole composition becomes rather incongruous.

REFERENCES: Narazaki, 1964, p. 64 [a]; Link, 1991, no. III-14-C [a]; *Meihin soroimono ukiyoe*, 12, no. 75 [a]; Suzuki and Ōkubo, 1996, no. 38 [a: this impression]

61 WILD SEA BREAKING ON THE ROCKS

Rough Sea at the Whirlpools at Awa (Awa no naruto no fūha)

from the series *Famous Views in the Sixty-odd Provinces (Rokujūyoshū meisho zue)*
published by Koshimuraya Heisuke, 1853–6

signed: *Hiroshige hitsu*
censorship seal: *aratame*; date seal: Hare 9 (1855/IX)
woodblock, *ōban*, 366 x 253 mm
Collection Pulverer, Cologne (ex-Frank Lloyd Wright Collection)

Between Awa Province on the island of Shikoku and the smaller island of Awaji is a narrow strait, notorious for its whirlpools (see also cat. 119). In this print we see the whirlpools in the foreground, while the waves of the high sea foam as they break over rocks protruding from the water. Hiroshige probably intended the viewer momentarily to mistake the plovers flying above the water for specks of foam, an effect he repeated later in *Thirty-six Views of Mount Fuji* (cat. 78).

REFERENCES: Narazaki, 1964, p. 74; Suzuki, 1975, p. 117; Link, 1991, no. III-14-A; *Meihin soroimono ukiyoe*, 12, no. 88; Suzuki and Ōkubo, 1996, no. 55 [this impression]

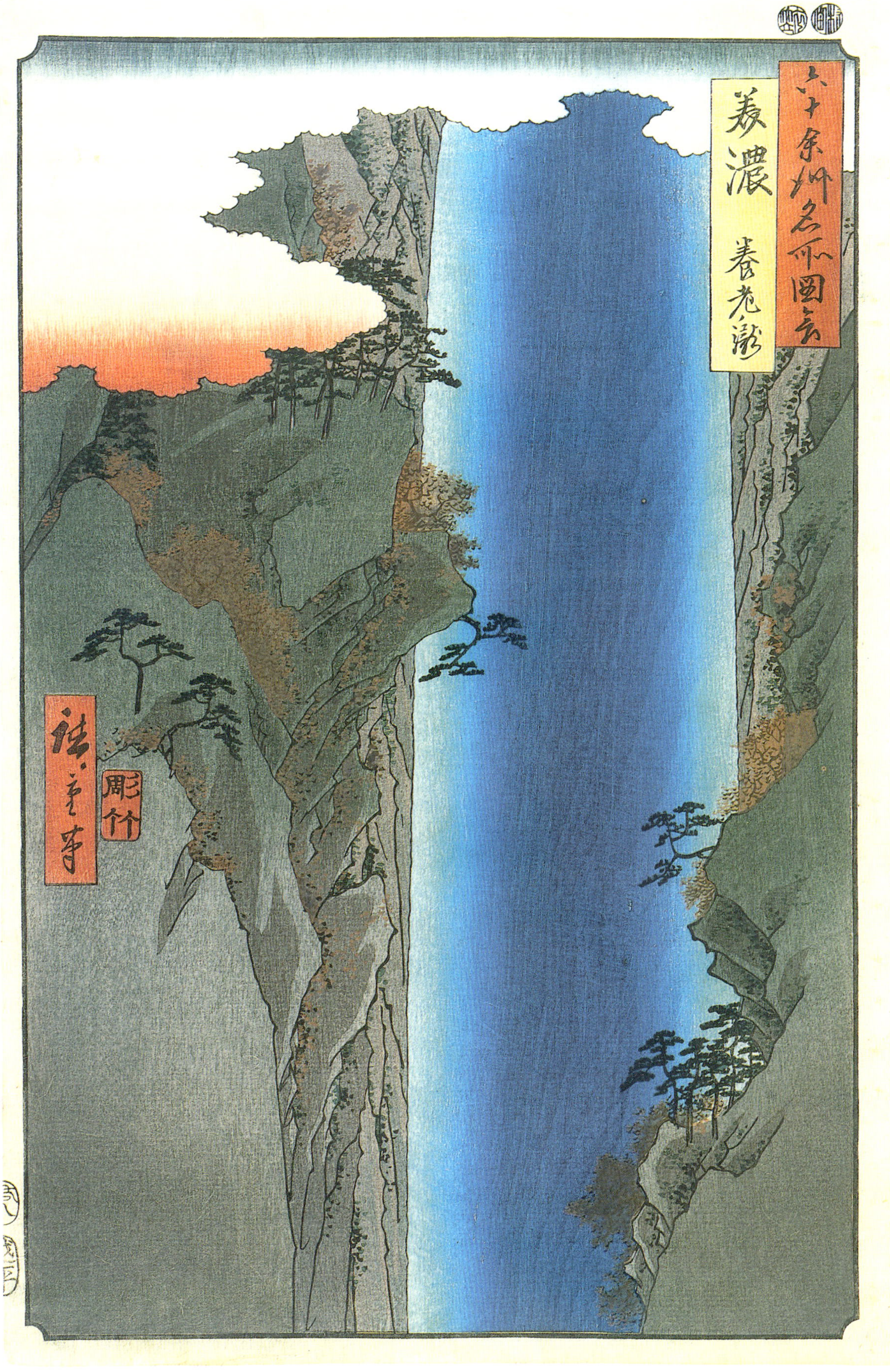
六十余州名所図会
美濃 養老瀧
廣重筆
彫竹

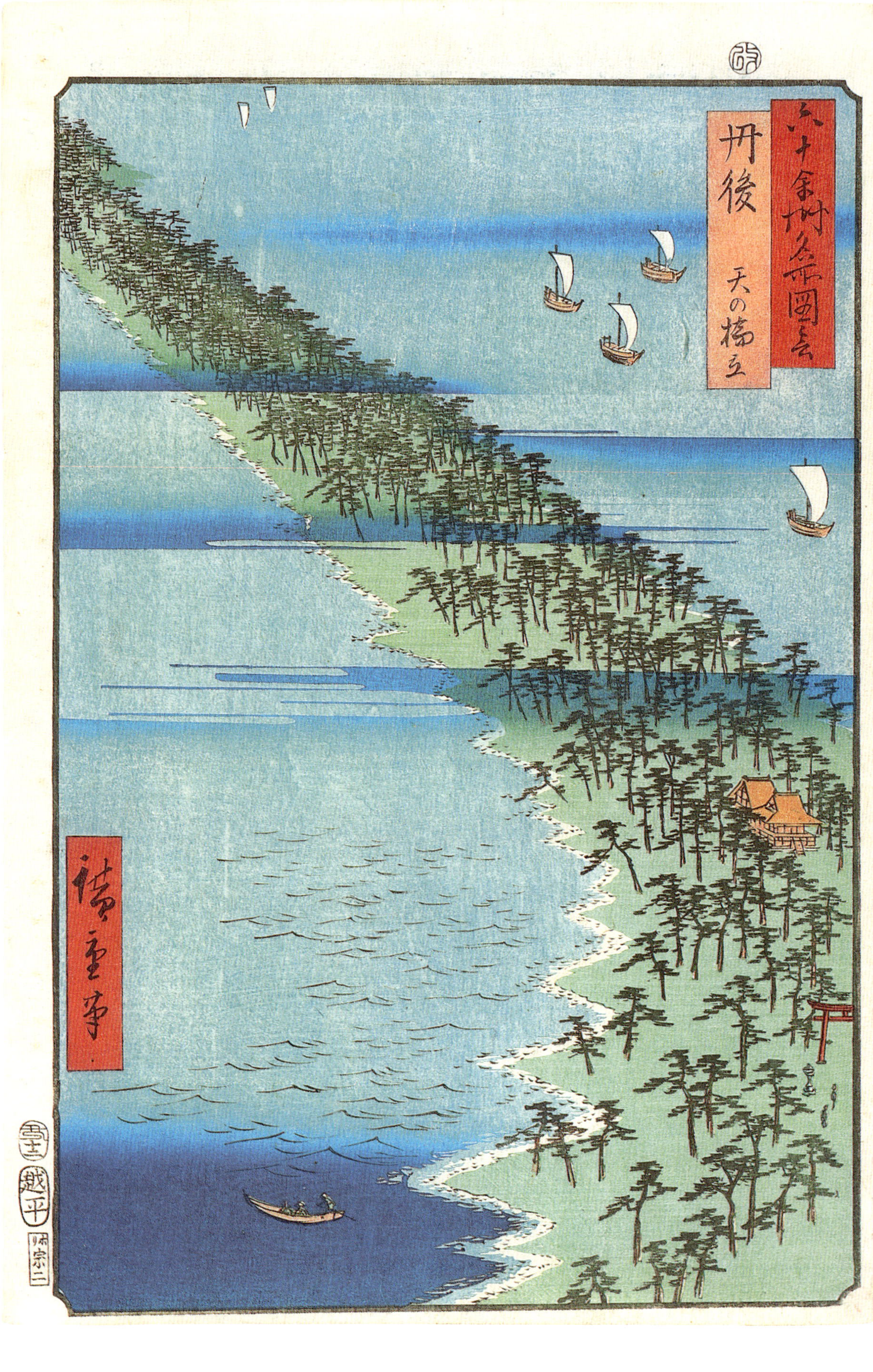
六十余州名所圖会
丹後
天の橋立
廣重筆

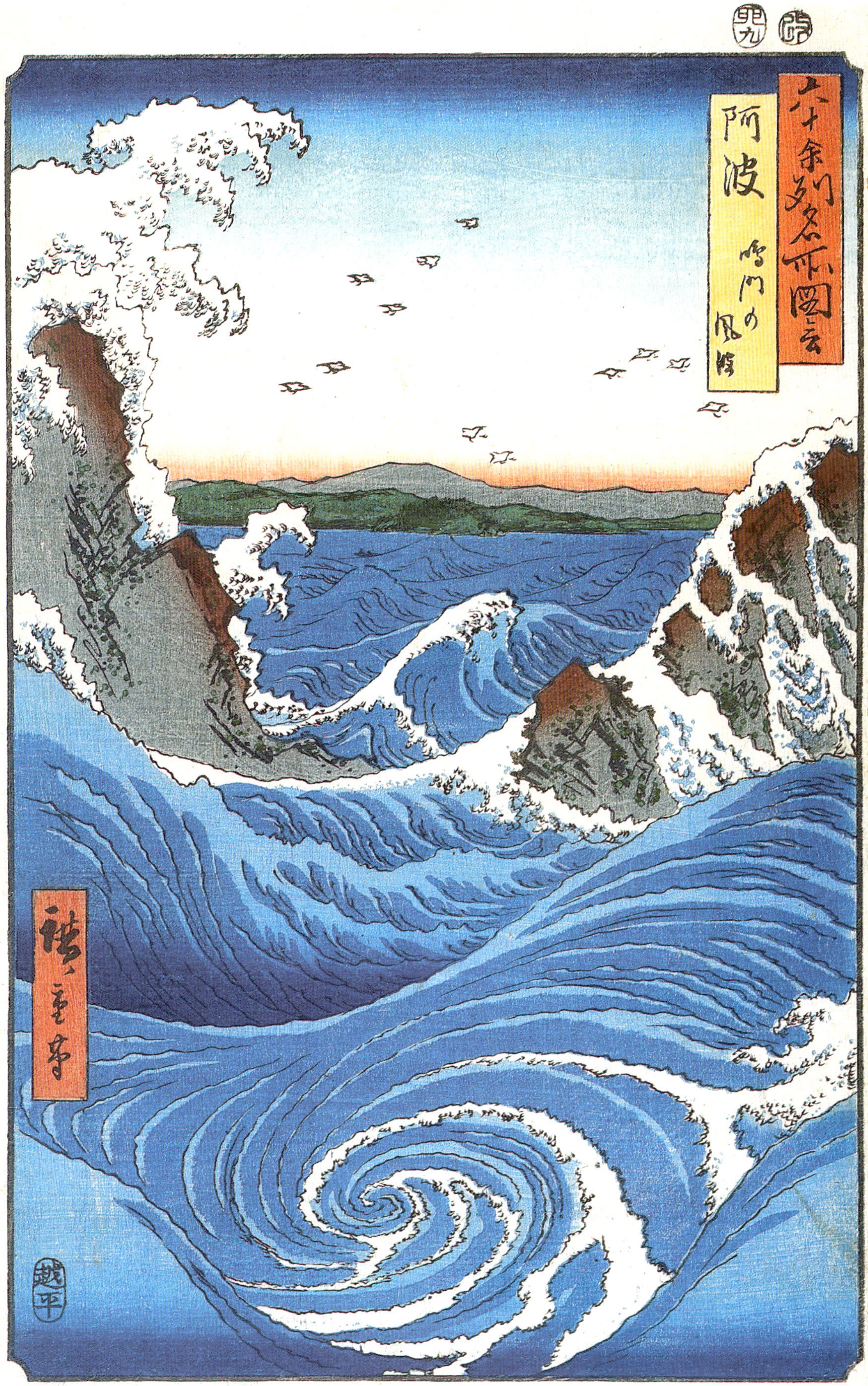
六十余州名所圖会
阿波
鳴門の風波
廣重筆
越平

62 A TEMPLE ON A HIGH ROCK

The Kannon Temple at Cape Abuto in Bingo Province (Bingo Abuto Kannondō)

from the series *Famous Views in the Sixty-odd Provinces (Rokujūyoshū meisho zue)*
published by Koshimuraya Heisuke, 1853–6

signed: *Hiroshige hitsu*
censorship seal: *aratame*; date seal: Ox 12 (1853/XII)
woodblock, *ōban*, 365 x 286 mm
Private Collection, Denmark

A view of the Buddhist Temple, dedicated to the god Kannon, perched on top of Cape Abuto in Bingo Province, which juts into the Inland Sea. Evening approaches, the moon is already silhouetted against the sky and lamps have been lit in the temple and the houses on the right. Bingo Province is grouped with the Sanindō circuit in the series's list of contents. As has been shown (Suzuki, 1970, figs. 33, 34), Hiroshige probably based this print on an illustration by Fuchigami Kyokkō (*d.* 1833) in the album *Remarkable Landscape Views* (*Sansui kikan*, 4 vols., 1800).

In early impressions, as here (a), the rock is built up of grey tints with some brown *bokashi* on the protruding section at the front and a bluish-green shade extending upwards from its foot. Later (b) this is simplified to two basic tints of brown and the clouds towards the top of the sky are omitted.

REFERENCES: Narazaki, 1964, p. 71 [a]; *Meihin soroimono ukiyoe*, 12, no. 82 [a]; Suzuki and Ōkubo, 1996, no. 49 [a]

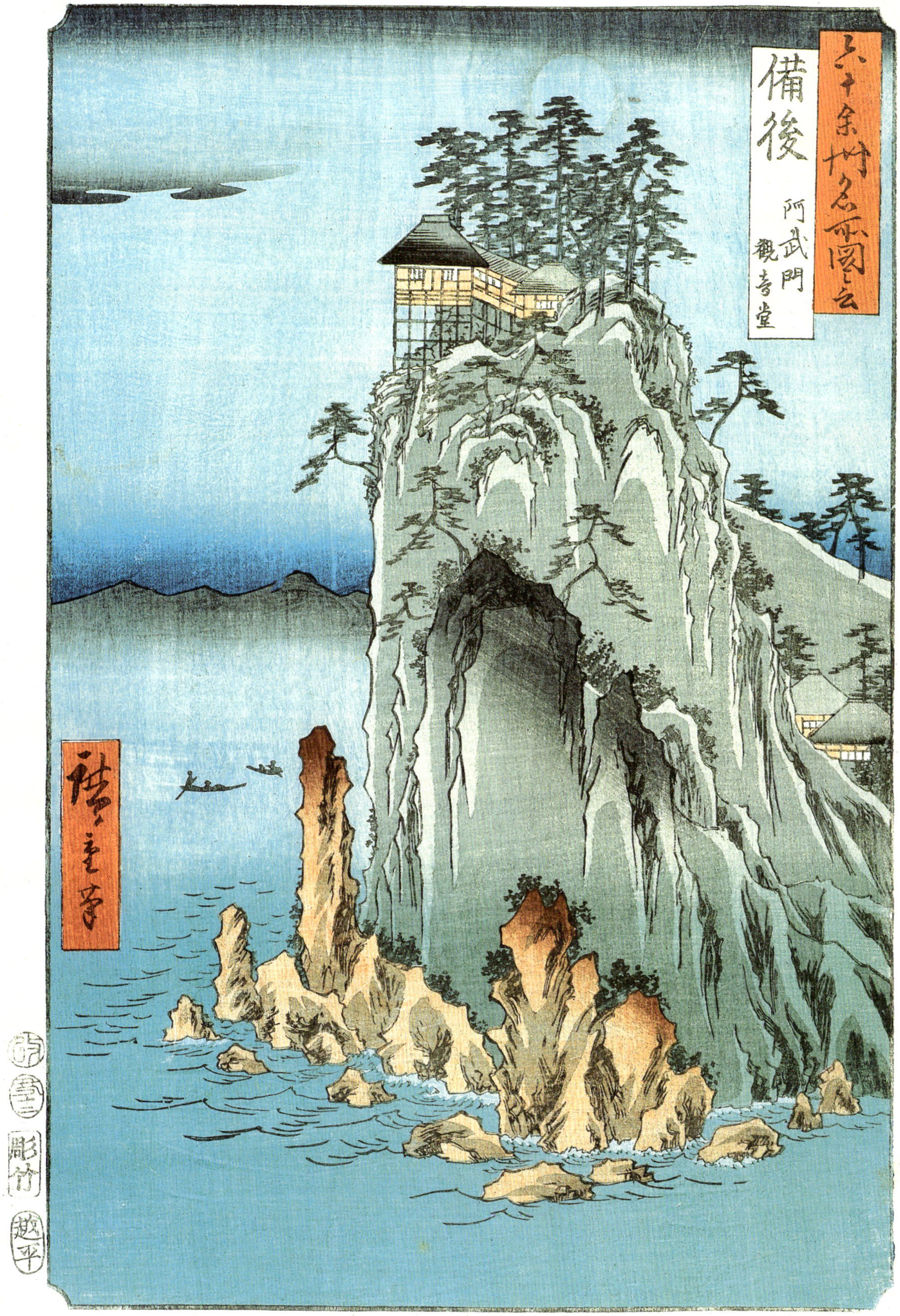
六十余州名所図会
備後
阿武門観音堂
廣重筆
彫竹

63 A SHRINE AMONG TREES ON A MOOR

Descending Geese at Haneda (*Haneda no rakugan*)

from the series *Eight Views in the Environs of Edo* (*Edo kinkō hakkei no uchi*)
published privately for the Taihaidō poetry club by Sanoya Kihei (Kikakudō), *c.* 1837–8

signed: *Hiroshige ga*
censorship seal: *kiwame*
woodblock, *ōban*, 255 x 372 mm
Baur Collection, Geneva (G492; ex-De Sartiges Collection; ex-Hayashi Tadamasa)

In a marshy landscape stand a cluster of trees and a few small buildings, including a shrine with a gate, dedicated to the goddess Benten. Boats can be seen to the left and right. Two flocks of geese descend from the sky. In the upper part of the print are four *kyōka* poems, one each by Momozono Michiki, Asayado Manao, Daiseirō Tsunagi and Taihaidō Nomimasu, head of the poetry club that commissioned the series to which this print belongs. The first of the poems is by Nomimasu and reads:

Haneda michi
saegiru kora ga
warusa yori
nawate wo yoko ni
ochisu karigane

The road to Haneda seems obstructed
as if naughty children
are holding a rope across—
the descending geese.

The first edition of this series was issued privately by the poetry club and Nomimasu's name is printed in the left-hand margin as the copyright owner. The publisher he used was Sanoya Kihei, whose seal is printed in red in the design, which contains four *kyōka* poems (a). On later editions there is only one poem on the print: first (b) the three poems on the left are omitted; later (c) a variant on the first poem by Nomimasu, composed by him, appears further to the left. The name of the original publisher is omitted in this latter edition and the blocks appear to have been acquired by Sanoya Kihei. By now the line on the horizon is damaged and the detail in the trees is missing, clearly reducing the impact of the print. Hiroshige represented Haneda in a virtually identical way in his album *Ehon Edo miyage*. Ironically, this later became the site of Tokyo International Airport.

REFERENCES: Narazaki, 1975, p. 14 [a]; Suzuki, 1975, p. 18 [a]; *Kobijutsu*, 1983, no. 179 [a]; *Ukiyoe hakka*, 1984, no. 36 [a]; Schindler, 1985, no. 173 [b]; Link, 1991, no. IV-10-C [c]; *Meihin soroimono ukiyoe*, 10, no. 10 [a]; Forrer, 1994, G492 [a: this impression]; Sakai, 1996, no. 582 [a]

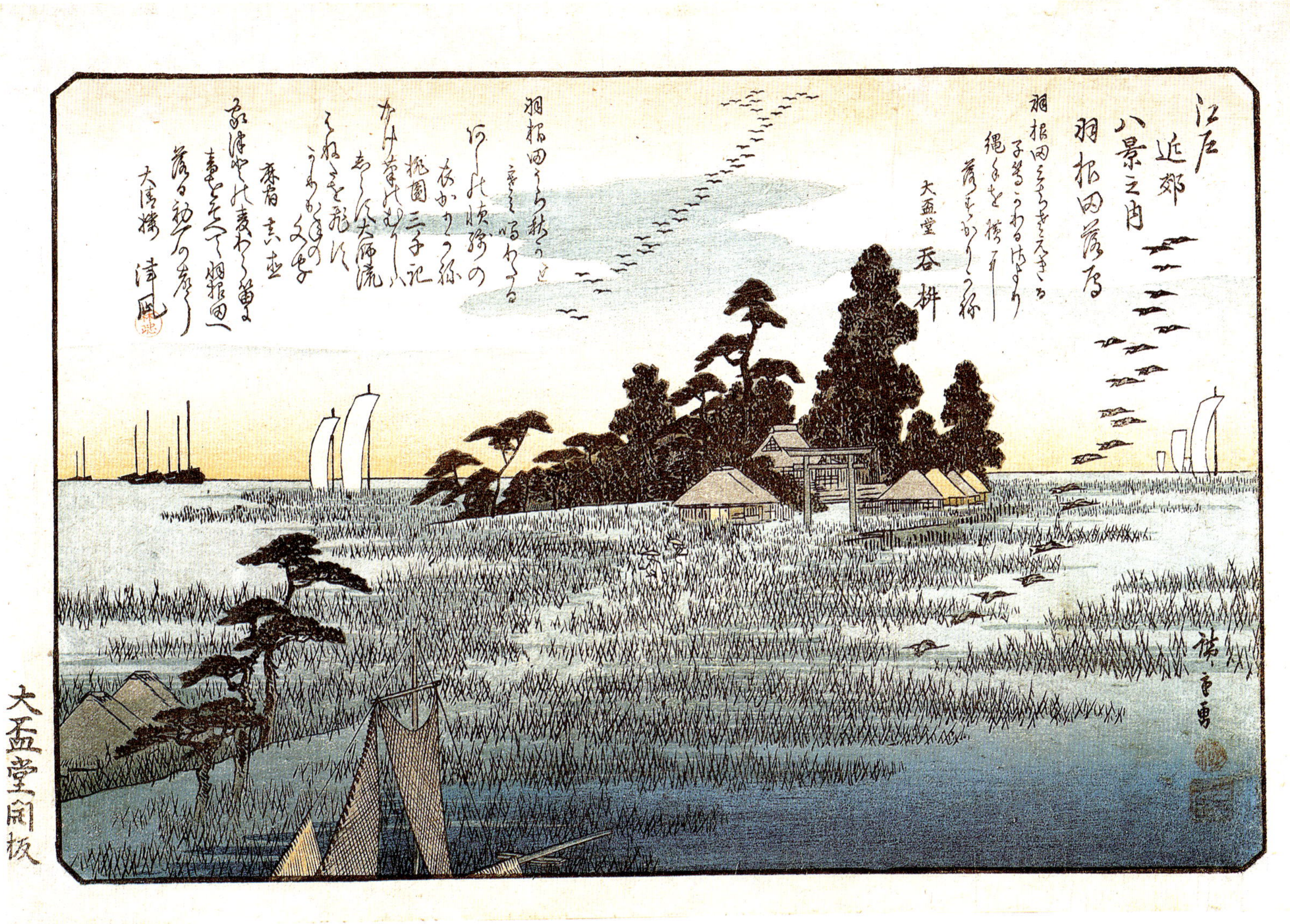
江戸近郊八景之内
羽根田落雁
大盃堂 呑桝
大盃堂開板

64 TEMPLE COMPOUND ON A HILL

Evening Bell at Ikegami (Ikegami no banshō)

from the series *Eight Views in the Environs of Edo (Edo kinkō hakkei no uchi)*
published privately for the Taihaidō poetry club by Sanoya Kihei (Kikakudō), *c.* 1837–8

signed: *Hiroshige ga*
censorship seal: *kiwame*
woodblock, *ōban*, 254 x 374 mm
Baur Collection, Geneva (G494; ex-De Sartiges Collection; ex-Hayashi Tadamasa)

A view of the Chōeizan Honmonji temple in the village of Ikegami in Senzoku, some twelve kilometres south of Edo. This temple of the Nichiren or Lotus sect was built in 1598. The large pond near the temple was a major attraction. A small bridge and a series of stone steps led to the Niōmon, a gateway, with a pagoda to the right.

In the upper half of the print are three poems by Shunkutei Tareyasu, Sakenoue Kisanji and Fūgetsuan respectively. The third reads:

Hibiki ni wa
hasu no kane koha
ugoku rashi
Ikegamidera no
iriai no kane

When it sounds,
the bell of the Lotus sect
seems to stir even the leaves on the trees—
announcing the sunset at Ikegami Temple

Fūgetsuan.

In this and other early impressions (a) the trees in the background have been overprinted to bring out the details. In later impressions (b) this block has not been used, the temple is printed in grey and the blue *bokashi* at the horizon on the left is omitted, as are the last two poems.

REFERENCES: Suzuki, 1975, p. 17 [a]; *Kobijutsu*, 1983, no. 185 [a]; *Ukiyoe hakka*, 1984, no. 32 [a]; Link, 1991, no. IV-10-B [b]; *Meihin soroimono ukiyoe*, 10, no. 11 [a]; Forrer, 1994, G494 [a: this impression]; Sakai, 1996, no. 577 [a]

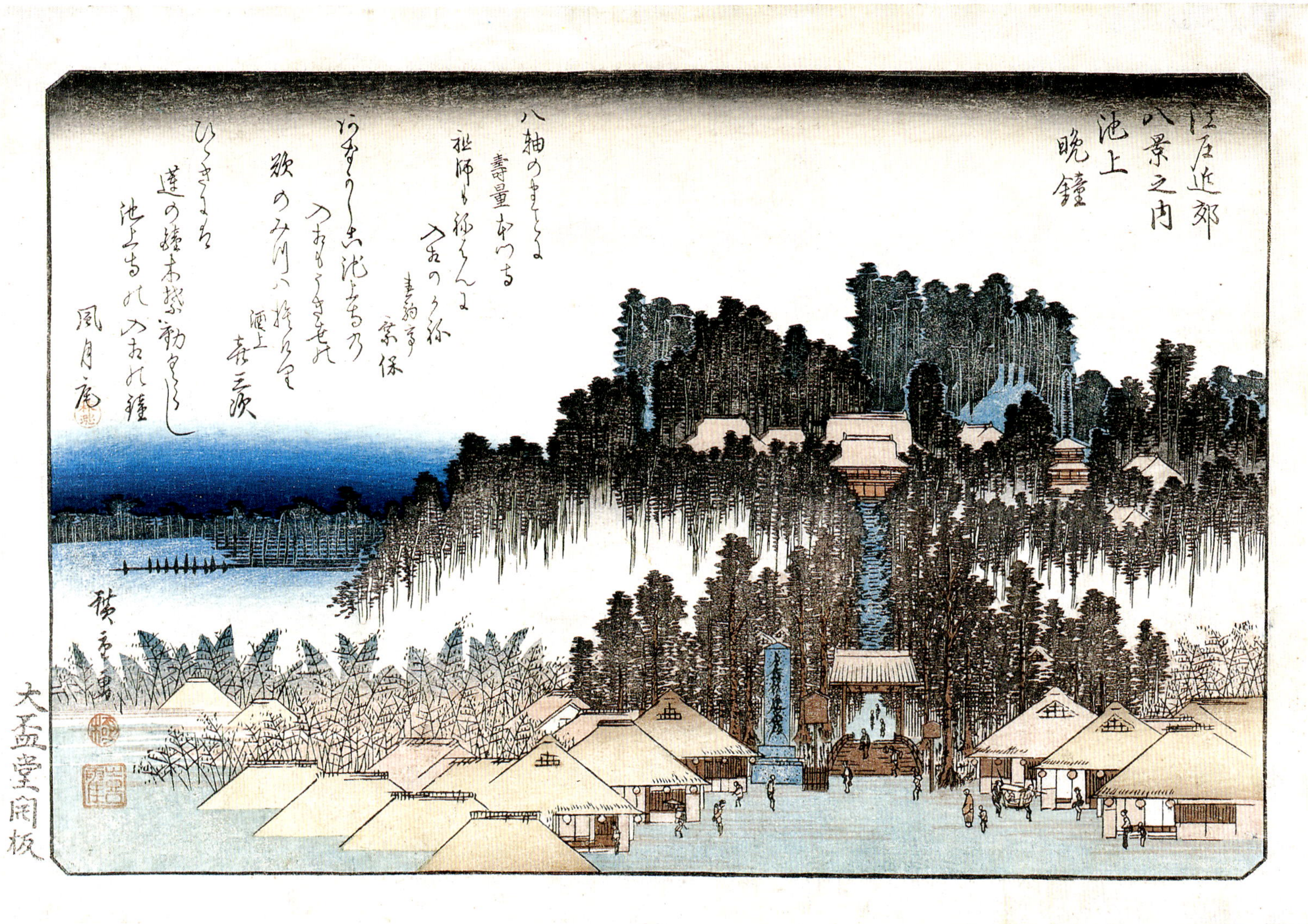
江戸近郊八景之内
池上晩鐘
大平堂開板

65 A DIKE ON A RAINY EVENING

Evening Rain at Azuma Shrine
(Azuma no mori yoru no ame)

from the series *Eight Views in the Environs of Edo*
(Edo kinkō hakkei no uchi)
published privately for the Taihaidō poetry club by Sanoya Kihei (Kikakudō), *c.* 1837–8

signed: *Hiroshige ga*
censorship seal: *kiwame*
woodblock, *ōban*, 243 x 373 mm
Baur Collection, Geneva (G498; ex-De Sartiges Collection; ex-Hayashi Tadamasa)

Two people, one with an umbrella, one with a cloak, walk along a dike beside the Kita Jumagawa during an evening shower. The Azuma Shrine can be seen in the middle distance to the left, among trees. The title refers to this shrine in the abbreviated form of Azuma no mori; it was actually called Azuma Gongensha. The shrine was in a remote part of Edo, on the still largely uncultivated eastern bank of the Sumida River, slightly north of the villages of Kameido and Yanagishima. It was particularly quiet here, with small villages, rice-fields and many temples and shrines. The much more famous Kameido Tenjin Temple was only a few hundred metres away.

In the sky are three poems, one each by Kanninsha Nijimori, Suichōdō and Shōbaitei Akiudo. The second reads:

Yanagishima
yanagi no mino o
karitemashi
Azuma no mori no
yowa no harusame

I borrowed a raincoat of willows
from 'willow island' Yanagishima
since the spring rain fell at midnight
at Azuma Shrine.

Suichōdō.

The last two poems were omitted in a later impression (b) and, later still (c), the design was reprinted with only the poem by Suichōdō. Hiroshige repeated this composition, which is very similar to the one in volume seven of *Edo meisho zue*, a quasi-encyclopaedic guide to the famous sites of Edo, in his album of famous places in Edo *Ehon Edo miyage* and, later still, in the series *One Hundred Famous Views in Edo*.

REFERENCES: Suzuki, 1975, p. 16 [a]; *Kobijutsu*, 1983, no. 184 [a]; *Ukiyoe hakka*, 1984, no. 30 [a]; Schindler, 1985, no. 172 [b]; Link, 1991, no. IV-10-D [c]; *Meihin soroimono ukiyoe*, 10, no. 7 [a]; Forrer, 1994, G498 [a: this impression]; Sakai, 1996, no. 575 [a]

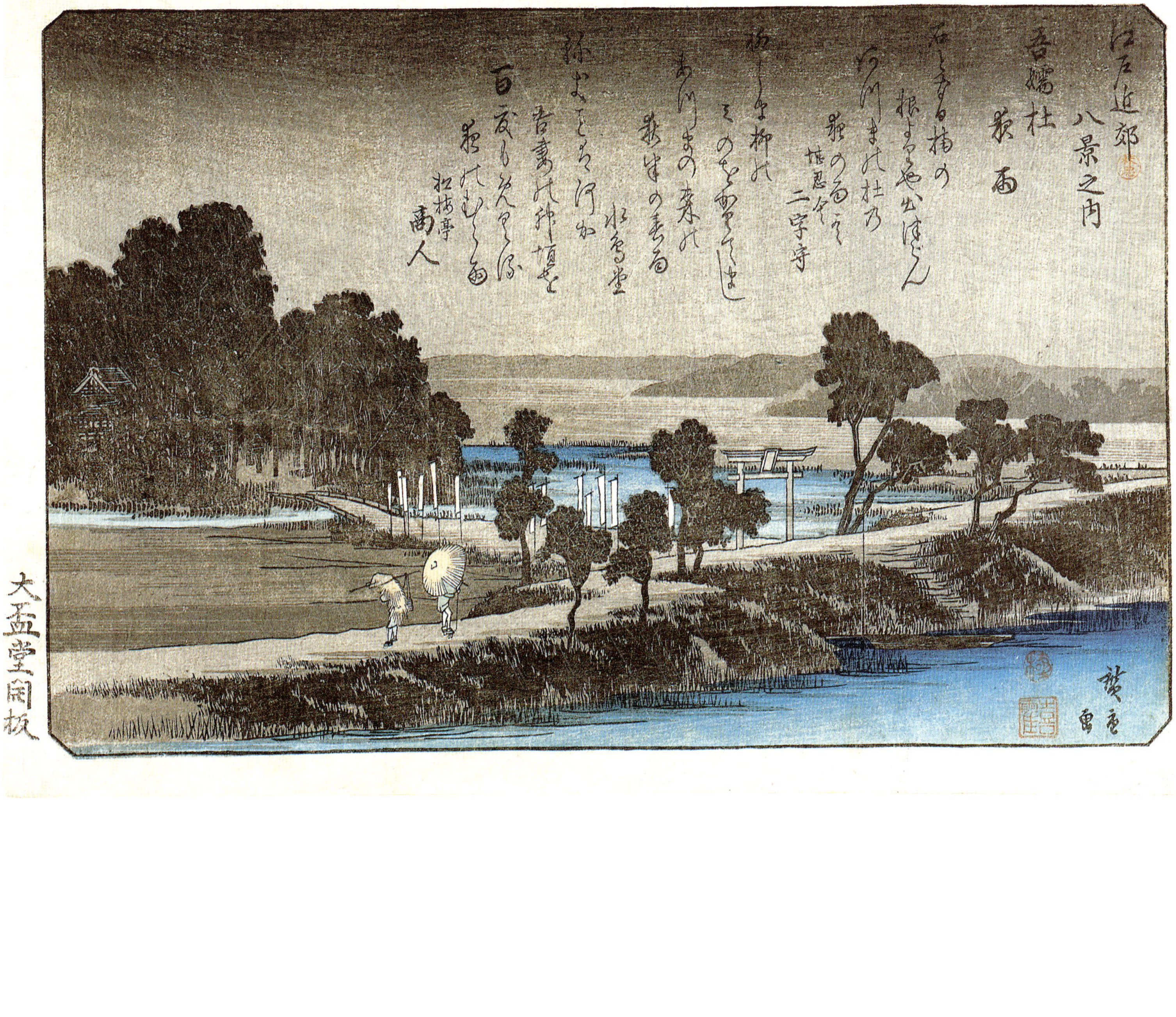
江戸近郊 八景之内
吾嬬杜 夜雨
廣重画
大盃堂開板

66 PEOPLE WALKING THROUGH SNOWY HILLS

Lingering Snow at Asukayama (Asukayama no bosetsu)

from the series *Eight Views in the Environs of Edo (Edo kinkō hakkei no uchi)*
published privately for the Taihaidō poetry club by Sanoya Kihei (Kikakudō), *c.* 1837–8

signed: *Hiroshige ga*
censorship seal: *kiwame*
woodblock, *ōban*, 247 x 367 mm
Baur Collection, Geneva (G493; ex-De Sartiges Collection; ex-Hayashi Tadamasa)

A man leads his horse past the wooded slopes of Asukayama in the north of Edo, passing a priest, possibly from the nearby Ōji Kumano Gongen Shrine. This spot is particularly popular in the spring when the hundreds of cherry trees planted there from 1720 are in blossom. In this print, however, the hills are covered with a thick layer of snow. In the upper half of the print are three poems by Kazentei Tomoyori, Gantantei and Nomimasu respectively. The second reads:

Tobutori no
Asuka no yama ni
chiri kuru wa
gamo ni niitaru
yuki no yūgure

At the hills 'where birds fly': Asukayama,
they spread and come
resembling wild ducks—
snow falling in the evening.

Gantantei.

Some later impressions were spattered with *gofun*, a white pigment, but it has not been used here (a). In later editions (b), which lack Nomimasu's name in the left-hand margin, the two poems on the right are omitted and, later still (c), an entirely new poem by Shōbaitei Takahito, or Takando, appears.

REFERENCES: Uchida, 1932, no. 117 [a]; Suzuki, 1970, no. 18 [a]; Suzuki, 1975, p. 19 [a]; *Ukiyoe taikei*, 11, no. 39 [a]; *Kobijutsu*, 1983, no. 182 [a]; *Ukiyoe hakka*, 1984, no. 37 [a]; Schindler, 1985, no. 179 [b]; Link, 1991, no. IV-10-A [c]; *Meihin soroimono ukiyoe*, 10, no. 12 [a]; Forrer, 1994, G493 [a: this impression]; Sakai, 1996, no. 576 [a]

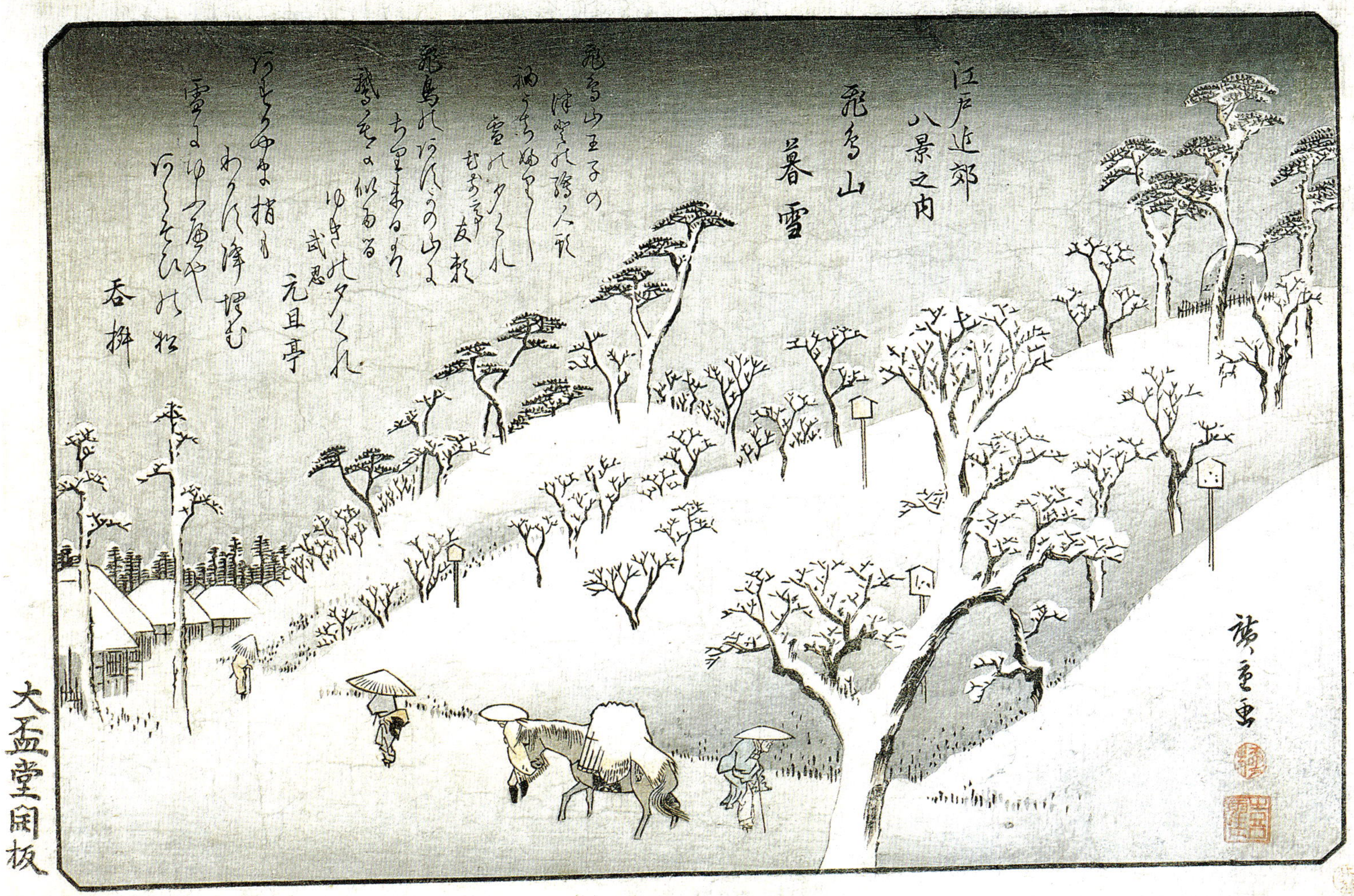
江戸近郊八景之内
飛鳥山暮雪
大盃堂開板

67 WILLOW ON A RIVER-BANK

Autumn Moon over Tama River (Tamagawa no shūgetsu)

from the series *Eight Views in the Environs of Edo (Edo kinkō hakkei no uchi)*
published privately for the Taihaidō poetry club by Sanoya Kihei (Kikakudō), *c.* 1837–8

signed: *Hiroshige ga*
censorship seal: *kiwame*
woodblock, *ōban*, 255 x 372 mm
Baur Collection, Geneva (G499; ex-De Sartiges Collection; ex-Hayashi Tadamasa; ex-Wakai Kenzaburō Collection)

A large willow on the bank of a river, with a few fishermen to the left. There is a fishing boat on the water. Dusk is falling and a full autumn moon is in the sky. The source of the River Tama was in Mount Tanba in Kai Province. It ran through Tama Prefecture and at some point joined the Asa. The river was full of freshwater trout.

In the upper half of the print are three poems by Shōkasai, Yotōtei Katawaza and Yōrōjin Takinari respectively. The first reads:

Itsu made mo
mimu irikata no
yama tsukuru
chiri tani suenu
Tamagawa no tsuki

I have been looking so long
but didn't see it come out of the mountains,
there it is, without any dust:
the moon over the Crystal River

Shōkasai.

A later edition of the print (a) featured a poem by Asayado Manao. This came from a selection of poems that were not used in the prints in the original edition but were printed on two separate sheets, arranged by theme. Sanoya Kihei simply chose the first of the poems on the relevant theme for the new edition (*Meihin soroimono ukiyoe*, 10, p. 143). The sequence of themes is: Evening Rain, Autumn Moon, Evening Bell, Returning Sails, Weather Clearing, Evening Glow, Descending Geese and Lingering Snow.

REFERENCES: Suzuki, 1970, no. 19 [a]; Suzuki, 1975, p. 19 [a]; Narazaki, 1975, no. 13 [a]; *Kobijutsu*, 1983, no. 183 [a]; *Ukiyoe hakka*, 1984, no. 31 [a]; Schindler, 1985, no. 175 [b]; Nagata, 1986, no. 84 [b]; *Meihin soroimono ukiyoe*, 10 no. 5 [a]; Forrer, 1994, G499 [a: this impression]; Sakai, 1996, no. 581 [a]

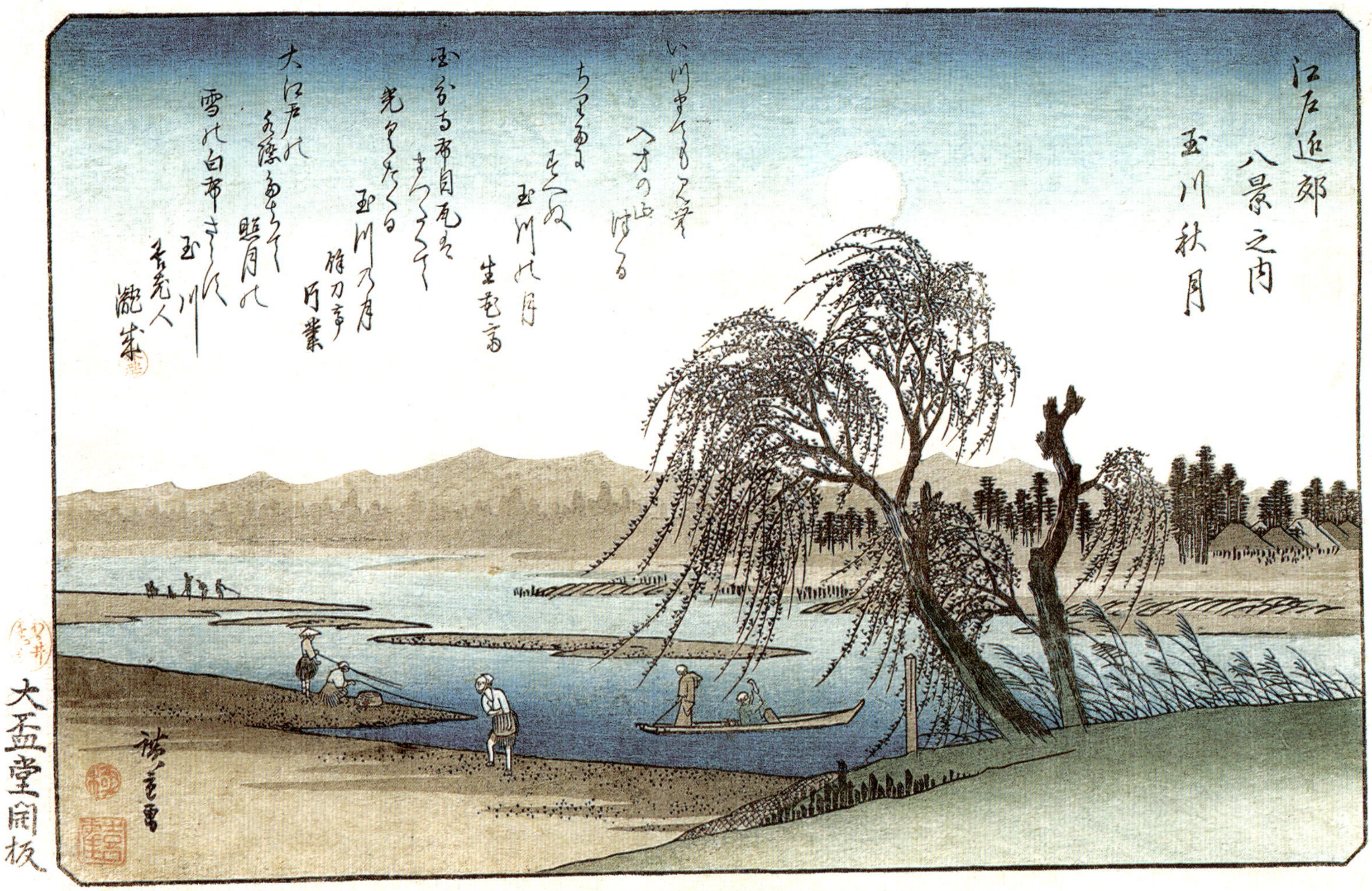

江戸近郊 八景之内
玉川秋月
大盃堂開板

68 EVENING VIEW OF A TEMPLE IN THE HILLS

Evening Bell at Miidera Temple (*Mii no banshō*)

from the series *Eight Views in Ōmi Province* (*Ōmi hakkei no uchi*)
published by Takenouchi Magohachi (Hōeidō), *c.* 1834–5

signed: *Hiroshige ga*
censorship seal: *kiwame*
woodblock, *ōban*, 255 x 384 mm
The Mann Collection, Highland Park, Illinois

Hidden in the hills along the southern side of Lake Biwa is the Miidera Temple. The setting sun reddens the yellow summer sky and the approach of evening is indicated by a dark band along the upper edge of the print. Miidera is the common name for the Onjōji, a temple of the Tendai sect, founded in 858, to the northwest of the city of Ōtsu. In early times the temple played an important political role and was burnt down five or six times. The present building dates from 1690.

The cartouche in the upper right-hand corner contains a *kyōka* poem that reads:

Omou sono
akatsuki chigiru
hajime soto
mazu kiku Mii no
iriai no kane

I think that dawn has made a vow
to wait first outside
until it has heard
the evening bell of Mii Temple.

This print from the series *Eight Views in Ōmi Province*, which was published jointly by Takenouchi Magohachi (Hōeidō) and Yamamoto Heikichi (Eikyūdō), is known in two distinct versions: one exclusively in bluish-grey tints (b) and one, as here (a), in a range of soft greens and browns with a yellow sky. It is noteworthy that the coloured version seems to be earlier than the grey one, even though the text of the advertisement for the series suggests the opposite. This can be deduced, for example, from two areas of apparent damage to the line-block, one on the left-hand side of the frame, just next to the row of trees, and one on the lower side of the cartouche containing the title of the series. This damage can be seen both in the impression in the Honolulu Academy of Art, which is printed in grey tones, and in one of the more colourful impressions—but not the present one. Another difference is that the *kiwame* censorship seal appears in the left-hand margin in some of the colour impressions—as in all other prints of the series—while it seems to have been removed from all the variants printed in grey monochrome. This was no doubt done because the censorship seal occurs in the design itself, in the gourd-shaped cartouche above the abbreviated name of the publisher. Presumably, this was not known when the line-block was cut and the mistake was discovered only later.

The more colourful version is more successful than the grey one in capturing the mood of evening, notably in the atmospheric yellow of the sky and the orange-red streaks of the setting sun. The monochrome variant is dull in comparison.

REFERENCES: Narazaki, 1964, p. 11 [a: lacking censorship seal]; Link, 1991, no. III-4-D [b: lacking censorship seal]; *Meihin soroimono ukiyoe*, 12, no. 15 [a: lacking censorship seal]; Copenhagen, 1993, no. 96 [a: with censorship seal]

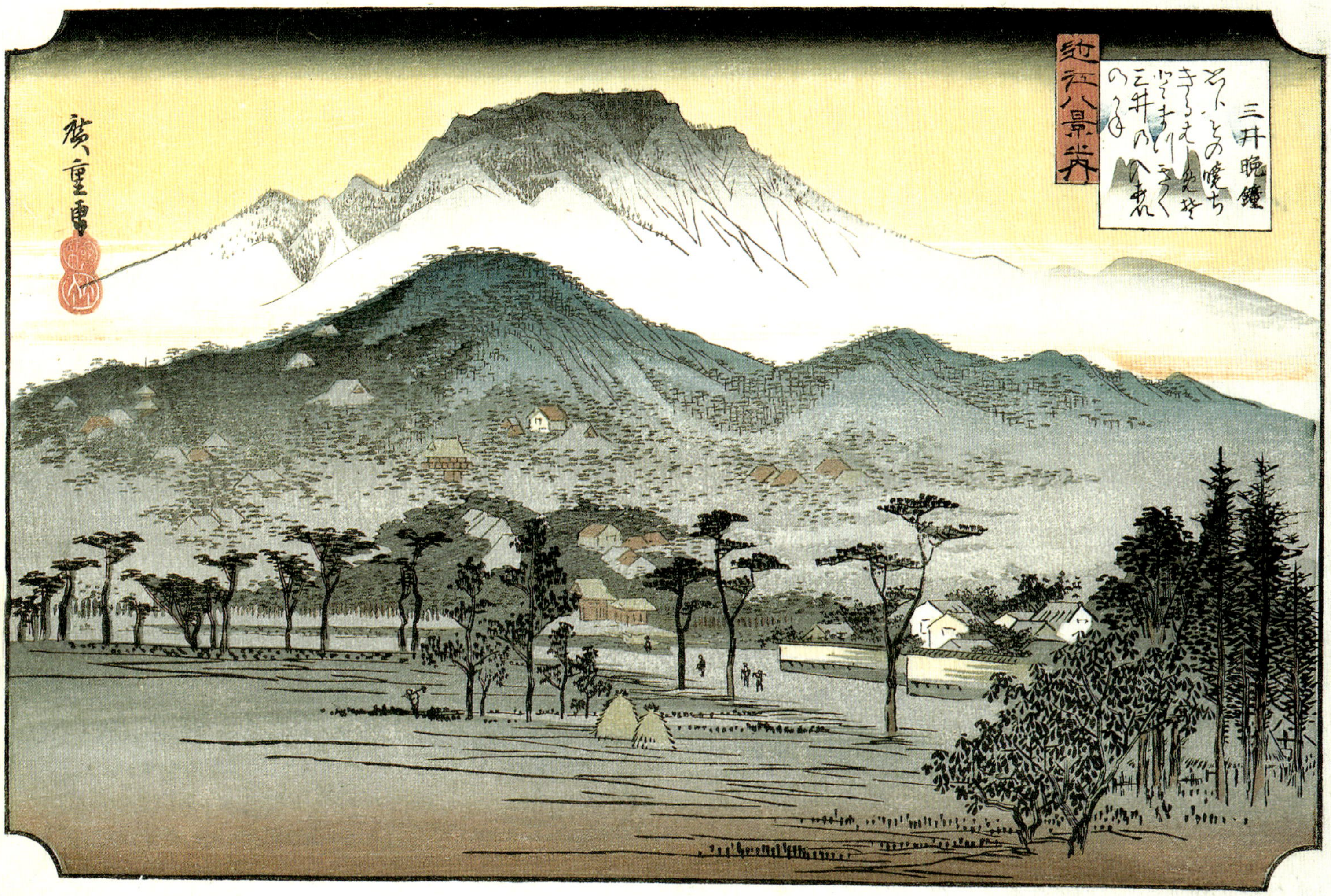
近江八景之内
三井晩鐘
廣重画

69 FULL MOON OVER A MOUNTAIN LANDSCAPE

Autumn Moon at Ishiyama (*Ishiyama no shūgetsu*)

from the series *Eight Views in Ōmi Province* (*Ōmi hakkei no uchi*)
published by Takenouchi Magohachi (Hōeidō), *c.* 1834–5

signed: *Hiroshige ga*
censorship seal: *kiwame*
woodblock, *ōban*, 249 x 380 mm
Private Collection, Denmark

A full autumn moon is in the sky and the whole landscape is transformed into a play of greyish tints. On the left, almost hidden by trees and rocks, is the temple where Murasaki Shikibu (*c.* 978–*c.* 1014) wrote her great novel *Tales of Genji*. Silhouetted in grey against the reflection of the moonlight in Lake Biwa is Seta Bridge, with Mount Hira on the horizon. The cartouche in the upper right-hand corner contains a *kyōka* poem that reads:

> *Ishiyama ya*
> *Niho no umi teru*
> *tsukikage wa*
> *Akashi no Suma mo*
> *hoka naranu kawa*
>
> At Ishiyama, the moon casting light on Lake Niho
> is no less than at Suma and Akashi.

Lake Niho is another name for Lake Biwa, used in classical poetry. The village of Suma is famous for its beautiful setting at the Strait of Akashi in Settsu Province; the comparison in the poem also alludes to the self-inflicted banishment of the protagonist of the *Tales of Genji*, who came to this spot when he was in difficulties after one of his adventures.

It is difficult to tell whether the publisher himself wished to experiment with different colour schemes or whether these were the result of public demand. The variant that comes closest to the text of the advertisement for this series (see cat. 72) seems to be that with the mountains in three shades of grey and with (as here) or without a yellowish tint in the sky (a). Brown was added to the mountains in an early variant (b) in which almost the entire sky is printed blue except for a little grey *bokashi* behind the distant mountain ridge. There is a puzzling variant (c) with brown in the mountains, a clear sky and *bokashi* printing on the peak of the mountain in the distance. This seems to be an early impression with clearly printed white stripes, but it lacks the censorship seal in the left-hand margin. A later variant (d) has more colour: the mountain in the foreground is blue and brown, that in the distance is blue, and the bridge and promontory are brown. The sky has been left white except for a dark purple band along the upper edge of the print and the red behind the hills in the distance.

About a decade later Hiroshige returned to more or less the same landscape, seen from a higher and more distant vantage point, in his series *Famous Views in the Sixty-odd Provinces* (Narazaki, 1964, p. 54). The format is now vertical and only a small part of the mountains on the left is visible; Ishiyama Temple has disappeared entirely. The print offers a good view of Seta Bridge but, even though the moon is full, there is no reflection in the water.

REFERENCES: Narazaki, 1964, p. 16 [b]; Yoshida, 1973, no. 9 [c: with censorship seal]; Narazaki, 1975, no. 10 [a]; *Ukiyoe hakka*, 1984, no. 9 [d]; Nagata, 1986, no. 29 [a: this impression]; Link, 1991, no. III-4-B [c: lacking censorship seal]; *Meihin soroimono ukiyoe*, 12, no. 13 [a]; Copenhagen, 1993, no. 95 [a: this impression]

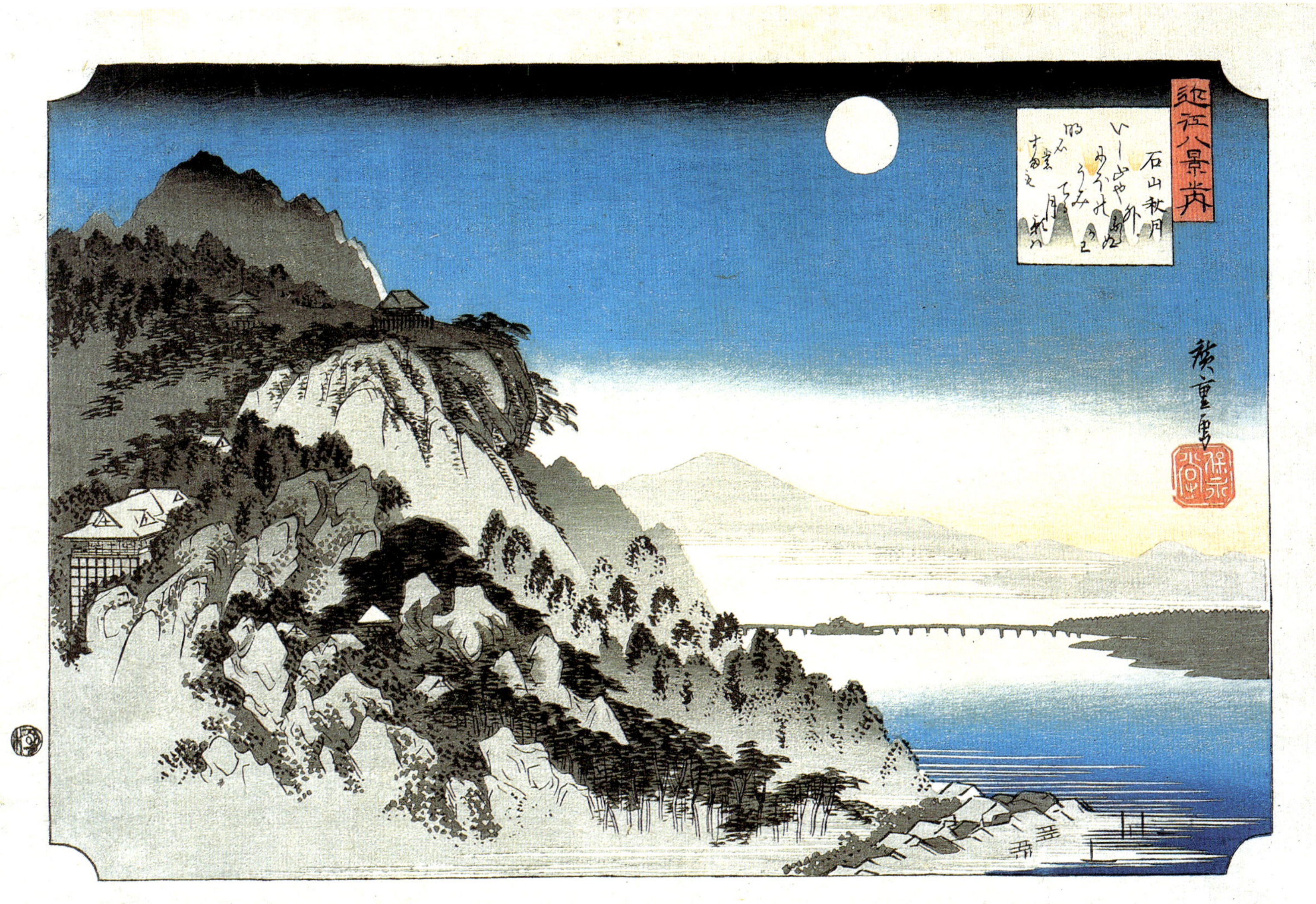
近江八景
石山秋月

70 VIEW OF A LONG BRIDGE ACROSS A LAKE

Evening Glow at Seta Bridge (*Seta no sekishō*)

from the series *Eight Views in Ōmi Province* (*Ōmi hakkei no uchi*)
published by Takenouchi Magohachi (Hōeidō), *c.* 1834–5

signed: *Hiroshige ga*
censorship seal: *kiwame*
woodblock, *ōban*, 250 x 379 mm
Private Collection, Denmark

A view of the two halves of Seta Bridge, which crosses the Seta River at the point where it flows into the south-east end of Lake Biwa. There are a few boats on the lake. Mount Mikami (432 m) can be seen in the distance. The cartouche in the upper left-hand corner contains a *kyōka* poem; it reads:

Tsuyushigure
moru yama tōku
michi sukitsutsu
yūhi no wataru
Seta no nagahashi

Leaking dew and drizzle
it has become thin
on its long journey across the mountains:
the evening sun crossing Seta Bridge.

In early impressions (a) the evening is indicated, as here, not only by a dark strip in the yellow sky along the upper edge of the print, but also by dark areas in the hills on the opposite side and in the town in the foreground. This overprinting in dark grey was omitted in later impressions (b). For the woodblock with which the lines were printed, see cat. 139.

REFERENCES: Narazaki, 1964, p. 14 [b]; Rappard-Boon, 1984, no. 26 [with yellow in sky]; *Meihin soroimono ukiyoe*, 12, no. 18 [a]; Copenhagen, 1993, no. 99 [a: this impression]

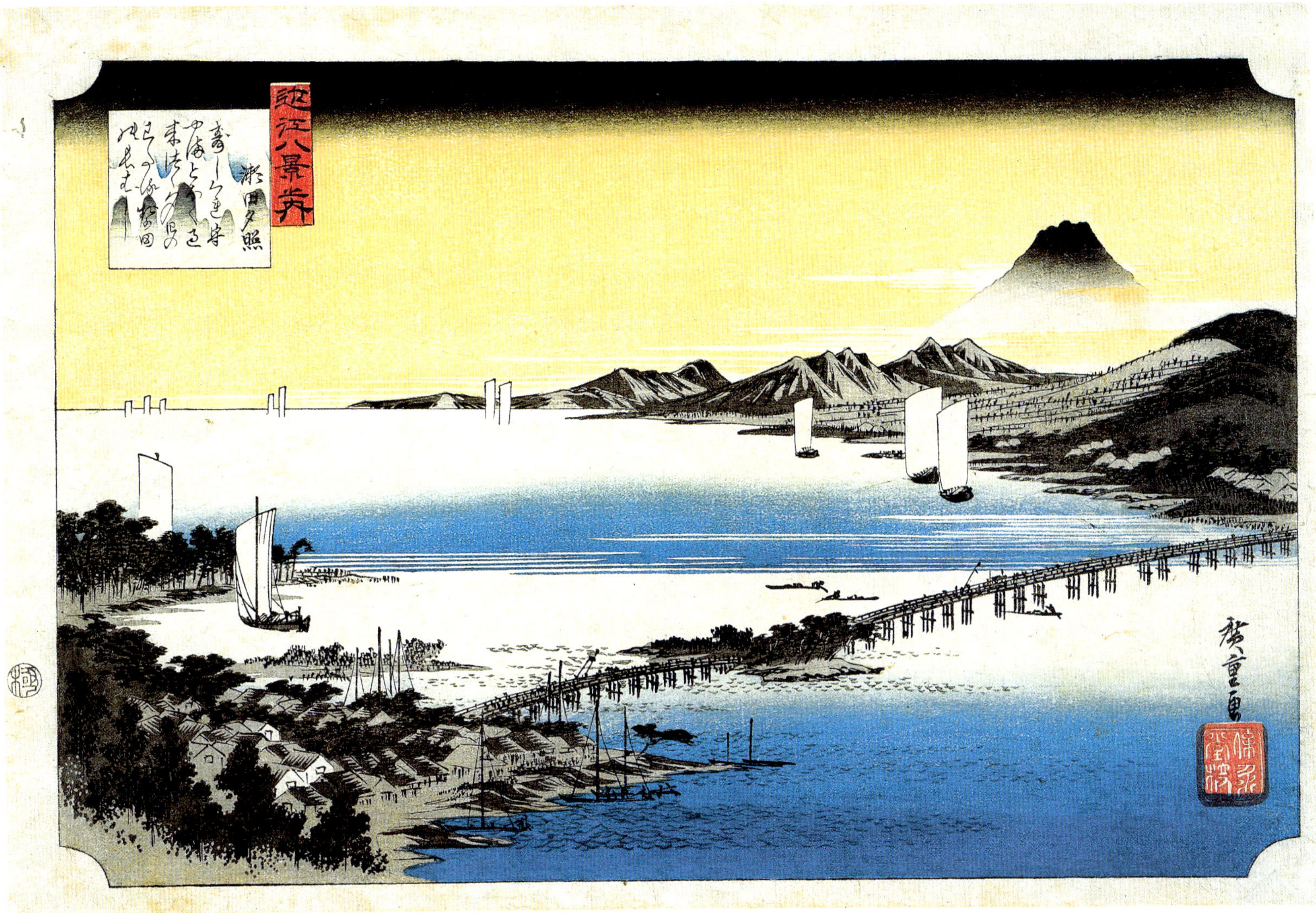
瀬田夕照
廣重画

71 HEAVY RAIN ON A PINE TREE

Evening Rain at Karasaki (*Karasaki no yau*)

from the series *Eight Views in Ōmi Province* (*Ōmi hakkei no uchi*)
published by Yamamoto Heikichi (Eikyūdō), *c.* 1834–5

signed: *Hiroshige ga*
censorship seal: *kiwame*
woodblock, *ōban*, 251 x 374 mm
Private Collection, Denmark

A huge pine tree, its outstretched branches supported by poles, stands near a shrine on a promontory in Lake Biwa, not far north-west of the town of Ōtsu. The masts of a few moored boats can be seen beyond the gate to the shrine. Torrents of rain are pouring from a dark sky. The cartouche at upper left contains a *kyōka* poem that reads:

Yoru no ame ni
oto o yuzurite
yūkaze o
yoru ni natatsuru
Karasaki no matsu

Yielding to the sound in the evening rain
and drawing near to the evening wind,
he grows famous:
the pine tree of Karasaki.

Many variant impressions of this print exist. Apart from a striking difference in the colour of the stone embankment around the shrine complex, which is found in both blue and grey, there are many variations in the inking of the block used to print the tree. Often, as in our impression (a), it is printed in black *bokashi* from the top, extending to the right-hand branches of the pine tree. This emphasises the size of the tree, while retaining a fair amount of detail in the low offshoots of the grey branches. The reverse (e), i.e. when the black *bokashi* extends upwards from the lower part of the tree, probably does more justice to the effect of rain, making the crest of the tree only dimly visible. The stone embankment is usually printed grey in this second variant. There are also variants in which the *bokashi* extends from the crest of the tree to the left (b) or along the contour of the tree on both sides, producing a light-coloured pyramid in the centre (c). This variant is certainly later, as can be seen from the area that has been cut out of the block used for the rain in order to give greater prominence to the publisher's seal. Moreover, there are a number of breaks in the line-block, which can clearly be seen in the poem. A further variant (d) has the tree green.

REFERENCES: Narazaki, 1964, p. 10 [a]; Suzuki, 1970, no. 8 [a]; Suzuki, 1975, p. 118 [a]; *Ukiyoe taikei*, 11, nos. 28 [b], 179 [d]; Yoshida, 1973, no. 2A [a; c: yellow at top, *aizuri*]; Izzard, 1983, no. 28 [c]; *Kobijutsu*, 1983, no. 94 [c]; *Ukiyoe hakka*, 1984, no. 8 [e]; Schindler, 1985, no. 170 [b]; Nagata, 1986, no. 30 [a: this impression]; Link, 1991, no. III-4-A [a]; *Meihin soroimono ukiyoe*, 12, nos. 11 [e], 11A [c]; Copenhagen, 1993, no. 94 [a: this impression]; Forrer, 1994, G513 [e]

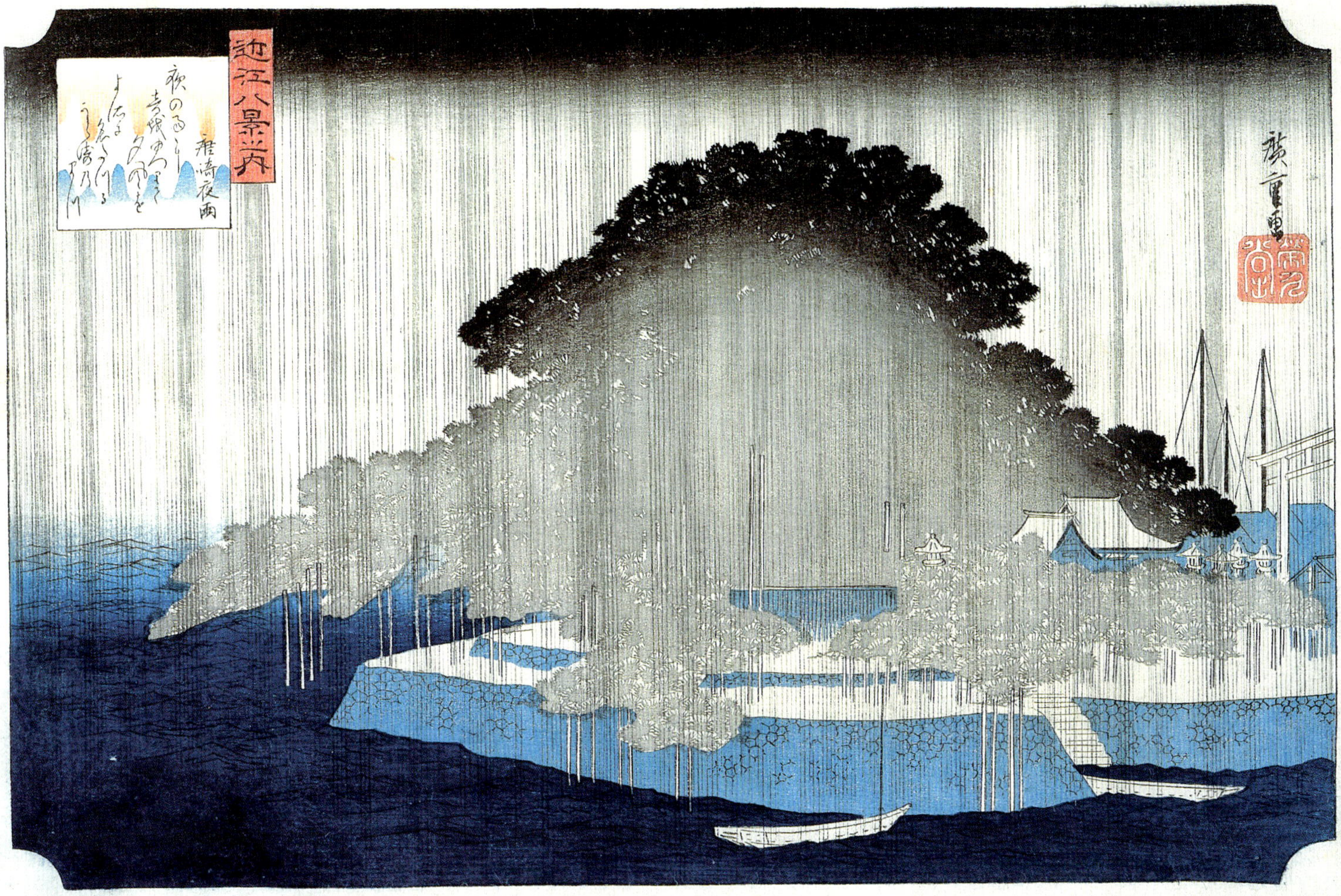
近江八景之内
唐崎夜雨
廣重画

Lingering Snow on Mount Hira (*Hira no bosetsu*)

from the series *Eight Views in Ōmi Province* (*Ōmi hakkei no uchi*)
published by Yamamoto Heikichi (Eikyūdō), *c.* 1834–5

signed: *Hiroshige ga*
censorship seal: *kiwame*
woodblock, *ōban*, 256 x 382 mm
The Mann Collection, Highland Park, Illinois

Mount Hira, on the northern side of Lake Biwa, towers above the valley with a village in the foreground. The cartouche at upper left contains the *kyōka* poem:

Yuki haruru
Hira no takane no
yūgure wa
hana no sakari ni
suguru koro kana

When it clears after snowfall,
the tops of Mount Hira
at dusk surely surpass
the beauty of cherry trees in bloom.

Mount Hira is the name of a chain of mountains, the tallest of which is 1,214 metres, rather than of a single peak.

The series from which this image comes was advertised as 'printed only in subdued tints' and the present print is one of the finest examples of this. An impressive snow landscape is created with nothing but purplish-grey and grey-blue tints. Only the blue water in the foreground breaks the generally grey tone. There are many variants in the impressions of this print, which is constructed entirely from the line-block and a subtle use of gradation printing. There are probably two basic versions of this *bokashi*: either it extends downwards from the peaks of the mountains to indicate that night is falling (b) or, as in this impression, it extends upwards to emphasise the darkness in the valleys (a). The latter accords with Hiroshige's instructions, which have survived on a proof of the line-block (cat. 137). In some impressions Mount Hira disappears in a mist a long way from the border of the print; that in the Pulverer collection has a little green in the foreground to the left. There are apparently also impressions, repeatedly referred to in the Japanese literature, in which the whole mountain is omitted. That this was not Hiroshige's original intention is proved by the line-block proof.

REFERENCES: Narazaki, 1964, p. 12 [b]; Tanba, 1965, no. 64 [a]; *Ukiyoe taikei*, 11, no. 27 [a]; Pulverer, 1990, no. I-78 [a: green in left foreground]; Link, 1991, no. III-4-C [a]; *Meihin soroimono ukiyoe*, 12, no. 12 [a]; Copenhagen, 1993, no. 93 [a]

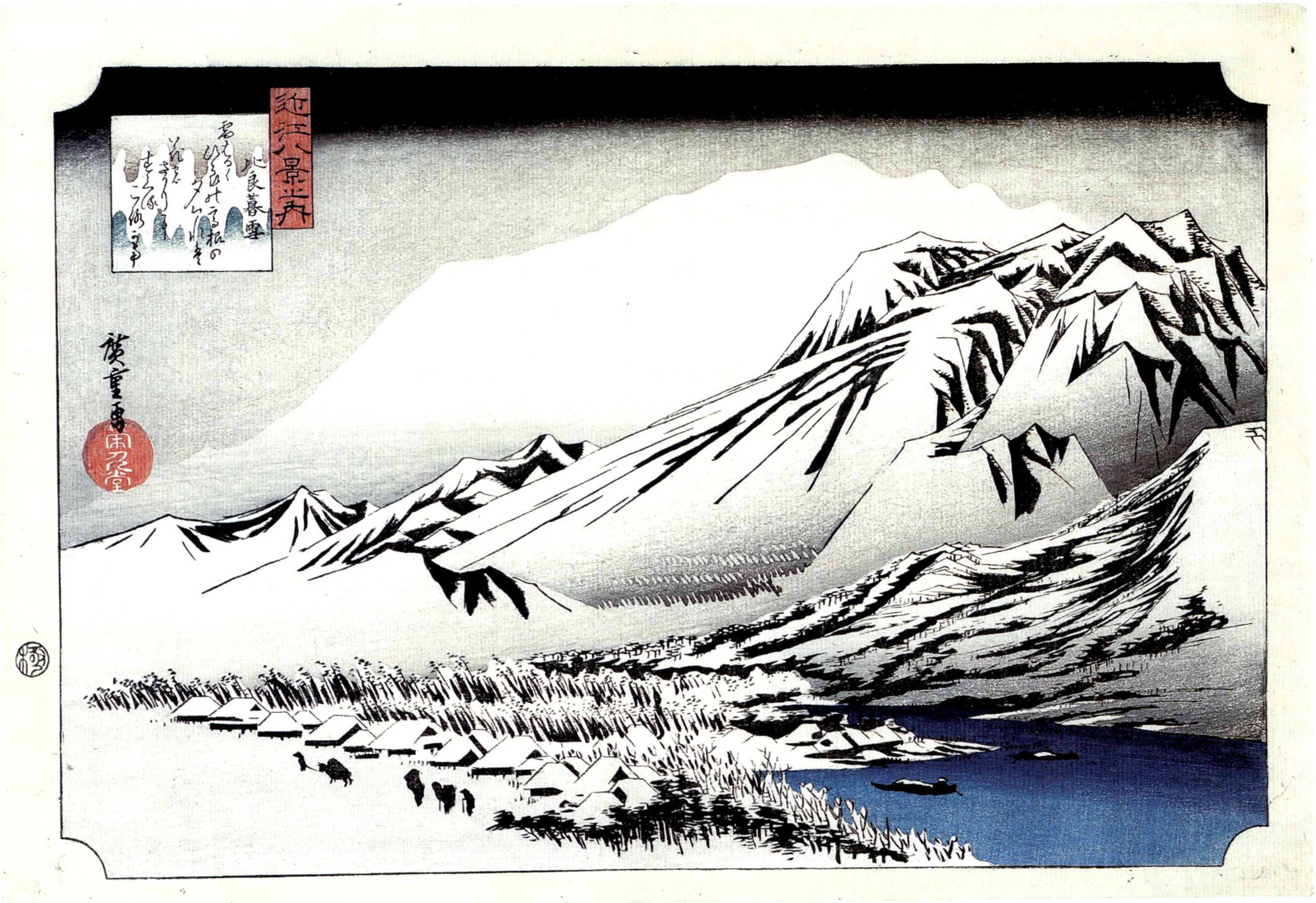
近江八景之内
比良暮雪
廣重画

73 FISHING BOATS ON A LAKE

Descending Geese at Katada (*Katada no rakugan*)

from the series *Eight Views in Ōmi Province* (*Ōmi hakkei no uchi*)
published by Yamamoto Heikichi (Eikyūdō), *c.* 1834–5

signed: *Hiroshige ga*
censorship seal: *kiwame*
woodblock, *ōban*, 229 x 352 mm
Rijksprentenkabinet, Rijksmuseum, Amsterdam (1956–736)

Katada is on the south-west shore of Lake Biwa. In series of prints like this, it is traditionally associated with descending geese. A small auxiliary temple, the Fuondō, belonging to a larger temple dedicated to the god Kannon, was built in the water. It is accessible by a bridge. In the background are the foothills of Mount Hira. The cartouche in the upper left-hand corner contains a *kyōka* poem; it reads:

Mine amata
koete Koshiji ni
yotsu chikaki
Katata ni nabiki
otsuru karigane

Flying across numerous peaks,
and getting really close to Koshiji,
Yet, the wild geese cannot resist
descending at Katada.

Koshiji is a place far away in the north.

Besides the usual differences arising from the inking of blocks of colour that are not clearly demarcated, there are apparently two states of this print: one which displays three distinct peaks on the right-hand side of the mountain in the distance (b) and one with a single peak that extends slightly to the right and then drops and is followed by a smaller peak (a). Minimal differences in the line-block seem to indicate that the latter version, illustrated here, is the earliest, but it is difficult to be certain. It is equally difficult to surmise the reason for the change. Even more puzzling is the fact that in both states the green on the left sometimes stays within the contour and sometimes goes beyond it.

REFERENCES: Narazaki, 1964, p. 15 [b]; Rappard-Boon, 1984, no. 24 [a: this impression]; *Meihin soroimono ukiyoe*, 12, no. 14 [a]; Copenhagen, 1993, no. 98 [a]

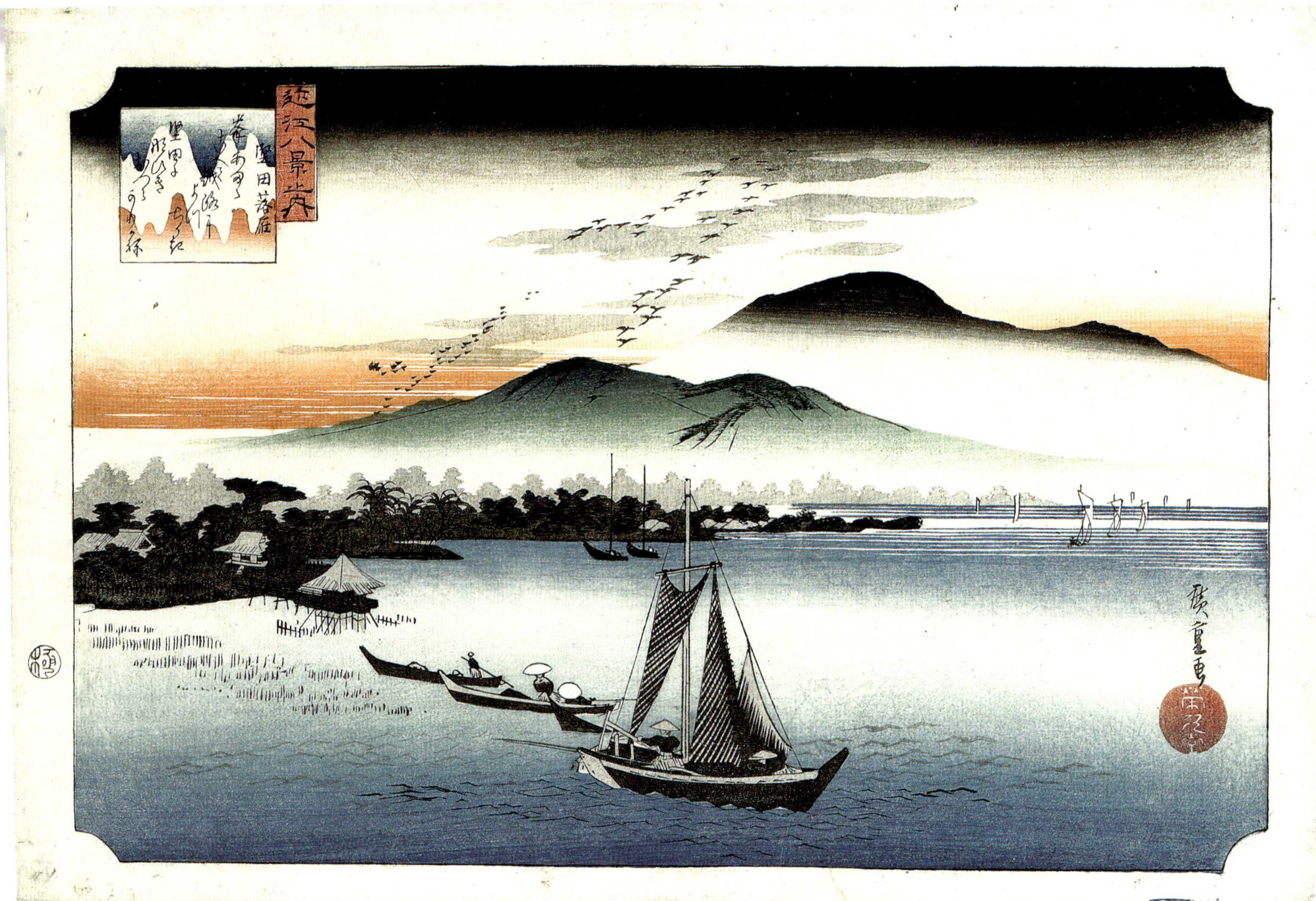
近江八景之内
堅田落雁
廣重画

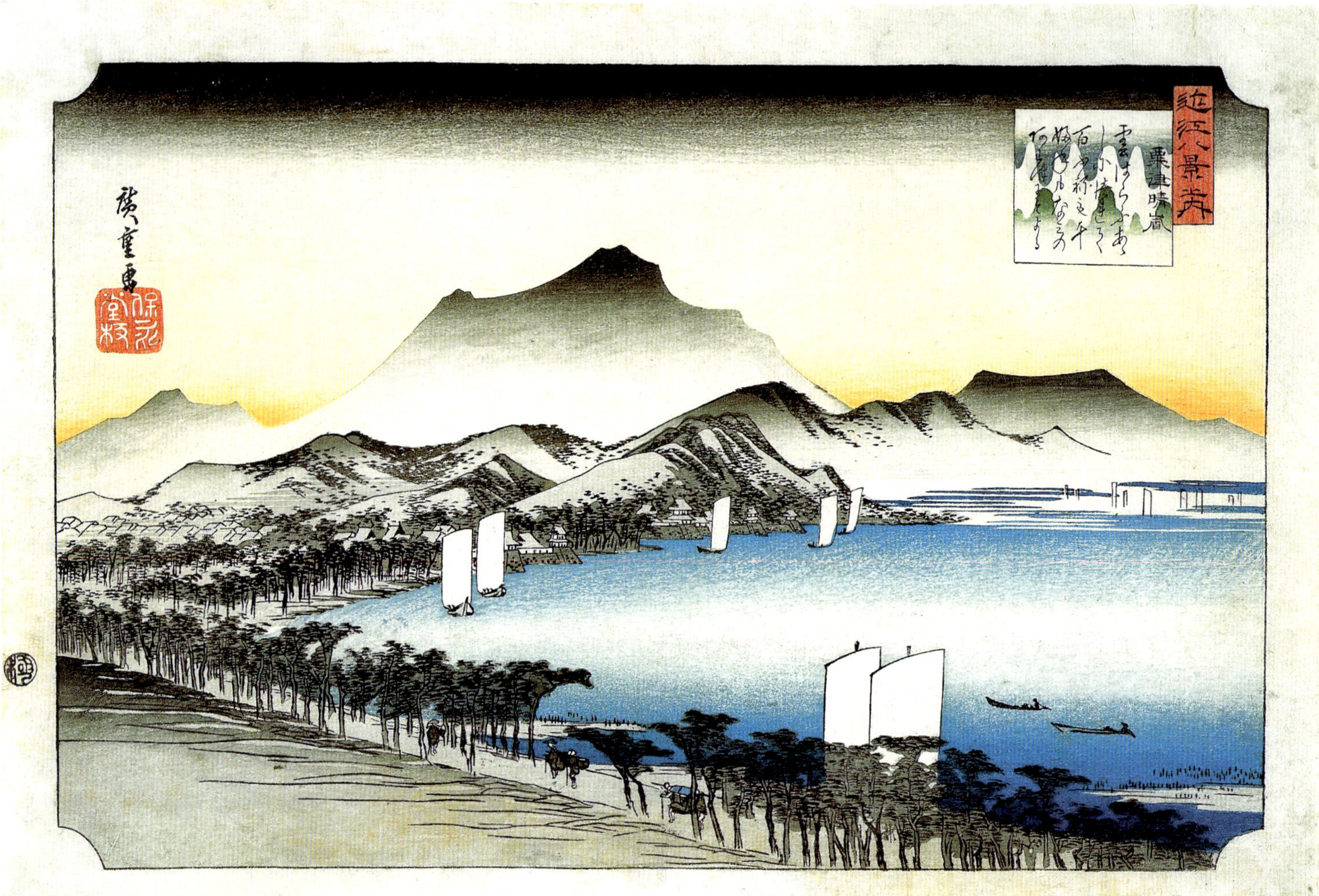

74 A ROAD BESIDE A LAKE WITH SOME BOATS

Weather Clearing at Awazu (*Awazu no seiran*)

from the series *Eight Views in Ōmi Province* (*Ōmi hakkei no uchi*)
published by Takenouchi Magohachi (Hōeidō), *c.* 1834–5

signed: *Hiroshige ga*
censorship seal: *kiwame*
woodblock, *ōban*, 258 x 379 mm
Private Collection, Denmark

Awazu is a village on the southern side of Lake Biwa. From here a road leads along the lake to the town of Ōtsu, which can be seen in the distance, its castle extending into the water. The cartouche in the upper right-hand corner contains a *kyōka* poem that reads:

Kumo harau
arashi ni tsurete
hyakufune mo
senfune mo nami no
Awazu ni zo yoru

When the storm has cleared the sky of clouds,
waves roll to Awazu
like a hundred,
no, like a thousand boats.

Early impressions such as this (a) have a dark strip above the yellow sky, with a red glow behind the mountains in the distance. The strip along the upper edge of the print is blue in later impressions (b), in which most of the sky has been left white. In this case a red glow is added to the mountains in the distance and brown to the foreground. The result is unconvincing.

REFERENCES: Narazaki, 1965, p. 11 [b]; *Meihin soroimono ukiyoe*, 12, no. 17 [a]; Copenhagen, 1993, no. 100 [a: this impression]

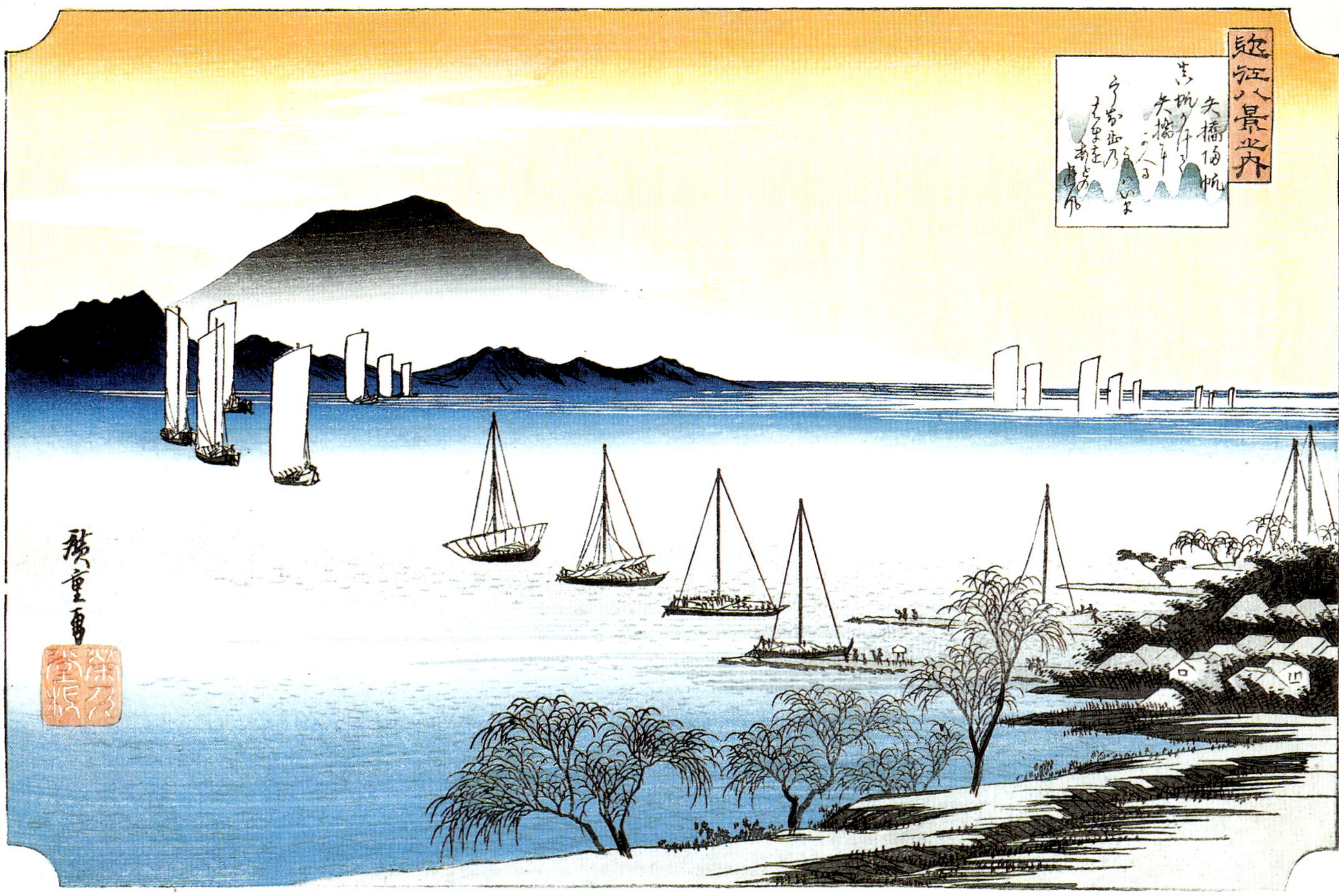

75 BOATS ON A LAKE

Returning Sails at Yabase (Yabase no kihan)

from the series *Eight Views in Ōmi Province (Ōmi hakkei no uchi)*
published by Yamamoto Heikichi (Eikyūdō), *c.* 1834–5

signed: *Hiroshige ga*
censorship seal: *kiwame*
woodblock, *ōban*, 253 x 375 mm
The Board of Trustees of the Victoria and Albert Museum, London (E3696–1886)

A view of Lake Biwa from the town of Yabase to the south-west of Lake Biwa. The *kyōka* poem in the cartouche in the upper right-hand corner reads:

Maho kakete
Yabase ni kaeru
fune wa ima
Uchide-no-hama o
ato no oikaze

The boats running back to Yabase
with full sails
even now leave the shore at Uchide
blown by a fair wind.

Much depends on the printer in the realisation of this design. There are variants, such as this one, with hardly any colour in the water, only some blue in the foreground and on the horizon and a light band of grey in the middle, while in other impressions most of the water is blue, interrupted only to emphasise the grey in it. The mountain in the distance is printed in blue or, as here, in black. The willows naturally form a more marked contrast in impressions in which the water is lighter in colour, especially in the foreground.

REFERENCES: Narazaki, 1964, p. 14; *Meihin soroimono ukiyoe*, 12, no. 16; Copenhagen, 1993, no. 97

76 MOUNT FUJI SEEN ACROSS A LAKE

Misaka Pass in Kai Province (Kai Misakagoe)

from the series *Thirty-six Views of Mount Fuji (Fuji sanjūrokkei)*
published by Tsutaya Kichizō, 1858

signed: *Hiroshige ga*
date seal: Horse 4 (1858/IV)
woodblock, *ōban*, 363 x 242 mm
The Art Institute of Chicago, Chicago,
The Clarence Buckingham Collection (1925.3444)

The many lakes in Kai Province, to the north of Mount Fuji, had inspired Hokusai to draw the mountain with its reflection in the water. Hiroshige here chooses one of his favourite compositions, in which a path in a valley opens out onto a breathtaking view.

77 MOUNT FUJI SEEN ACROSS A BAY

The Pine Beach at Miho in Suruga Province (Suruga Miho no matsubara)

from the series *Thirty-six Views of Mount Fuji (Fuji sanjūrokkei)*
published by Tsutaya Kichizō, 1858

signed: *Hiroshige ga*
date seal: Horse 4 (1858/IV)
woodblock, *ōban*, 379 x 257 mm
Collection of The Newark Museum, New Jersey,
John Cotton Dana Collection (00.123)

A blue-grey silhouette against a yellow sky, Mount Fuji towers over the scene as dusk begins to fall. The famous pine beach at Miho offers one of the most attractive views of the mountain. Hiroshige had already depicted this landscape in the series *Famous Views in the Sixty-odd Provinces* (cat. 57). There he had chosen a high vantage point; the lower viewpoint in the present print seems to bring the mountain nearer.

78 MOUNT FUJI SEEN ACROSS A WILD SEA

The Sea at Satta in Suruga Province (Suruga Satta kaijō)

from the series *Thirty-six Views of Mount Fuji (Fuji sanjūrokkei)*
published by Tsutaya Kichizō, 1858

signed: *Hiroshige ga*
date seal: Horse 4 (1858/IV)
woodblock, *ōban*, 378 x 255 mm
Collection of The Newark Museum, New Jersey,
John Cotton Dana Collection (00.122)

As this print suggests, the sea could be very wild at the point where the Tōkaidō Road followed the coastline. Things improved for travellers with the creation of the Satta Pass in 1655; on the left of the design is the tall cliff on which the pass is situated. Mount Fuji rises majestically in the background. Unaffected by the rough sea, a number of plovers circle above the water. Hiroshige probably hoped that they would initially be taken for specks of foam, as in *Wild Sea Breaking on the Rocks* from the *Sixty-odd Provinces* series (cat. 61). The present print reveals even more clearly that Hiroshige took the idea from Hokusai, who first used it in 1835, in his album *One Hundred Views of Mount Fuji*.

There is a good view of both the journey by water and the route over the pass in the illustration for the station of Yui in Hiroshige's vertical Tōkaidō series (Shiraishi, 1988, p. 48; Tanba, 1965, no. 380).

REFERENCES: Tanba, 1965, no. 385; *Memorial Exhibition*, 1968, no. 428; Izzard, 1983, no. 91

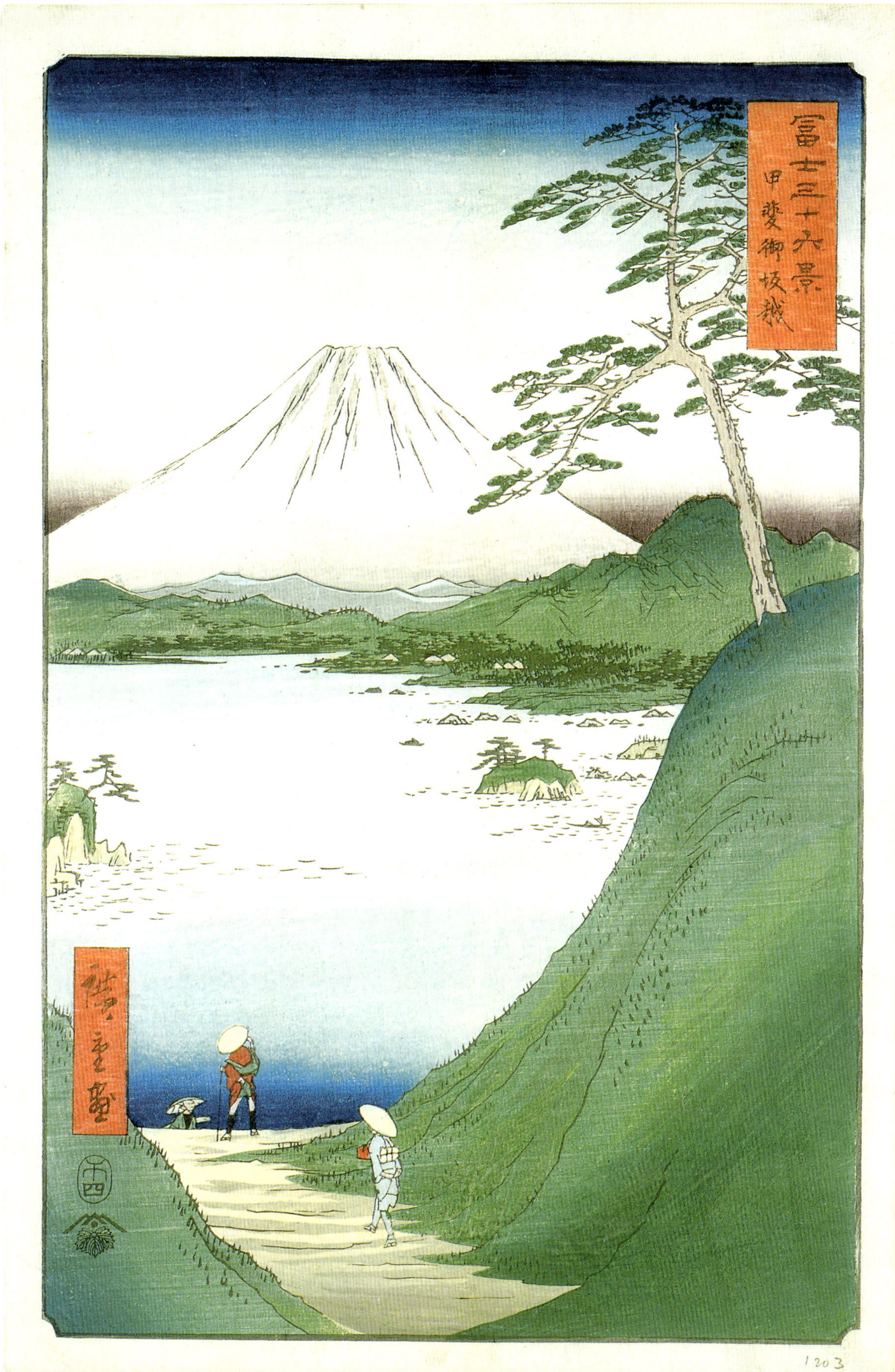
冨士三十六景
甲斐御坂越
廣重画
1203

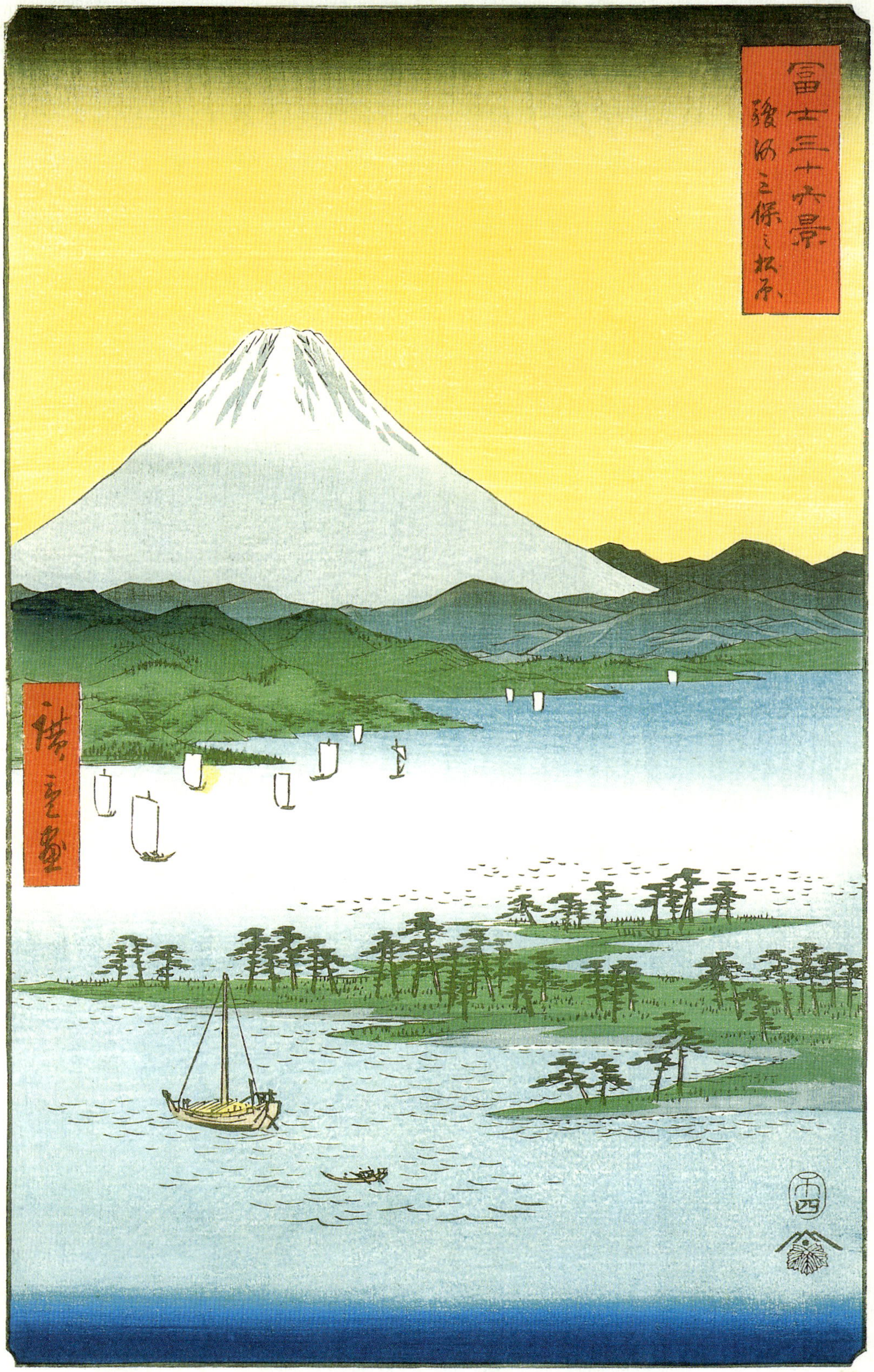
冨士三十六景
駿河三保之松原
廣重畫

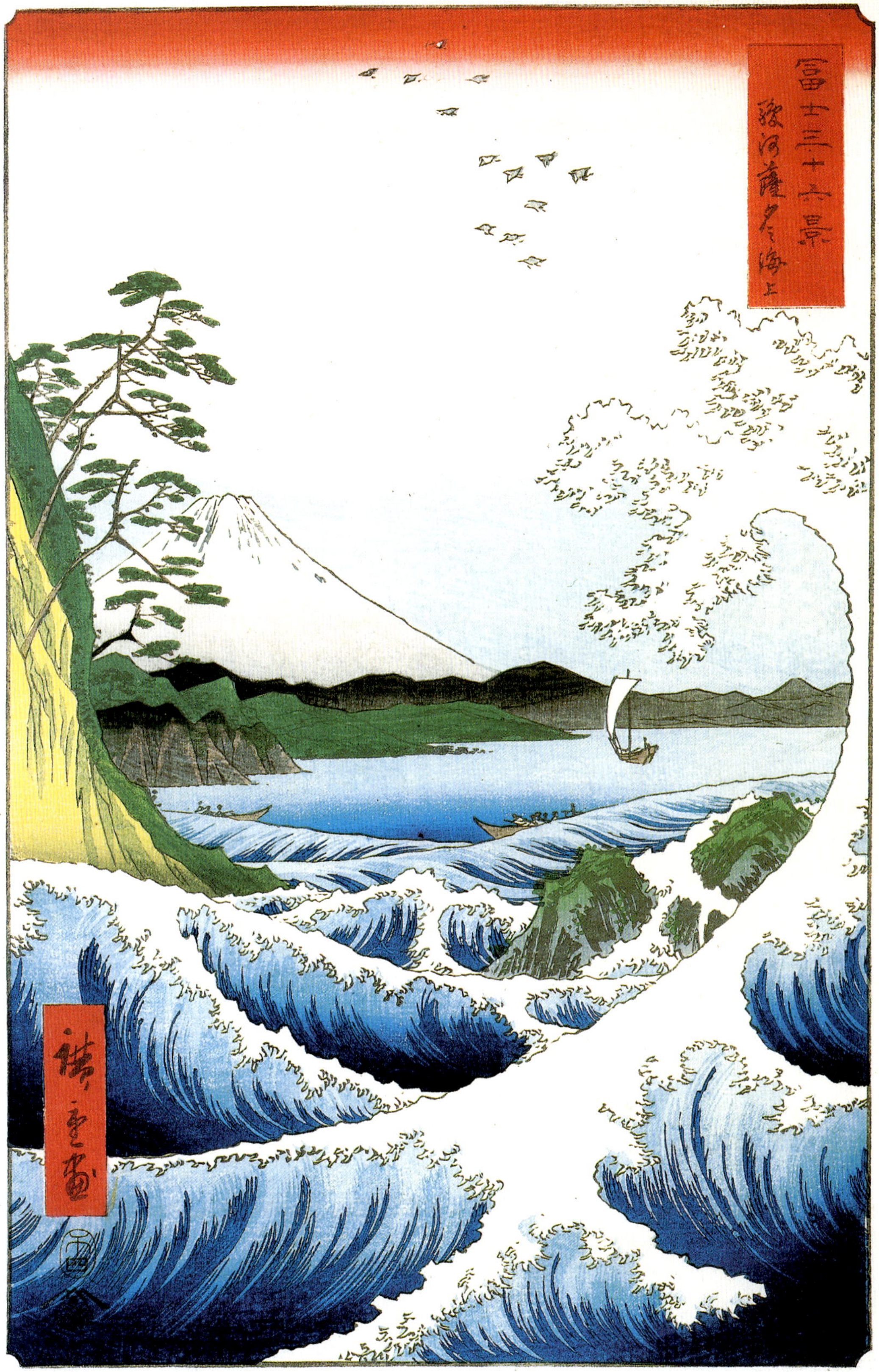
冨士三十六景
駿河薩タ之海上
廣重画

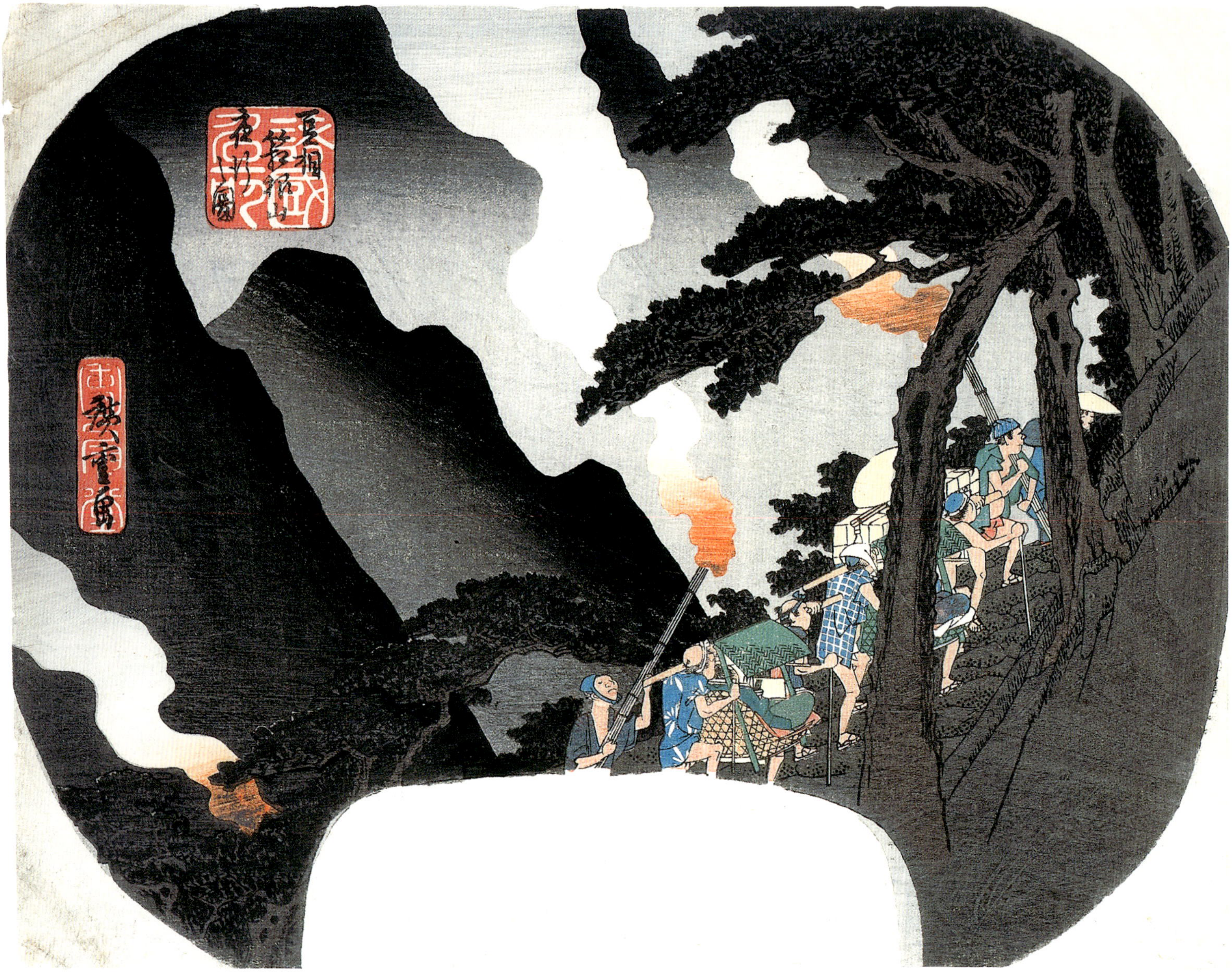

79 TRAVELLERS ON A MOUNTAIN PATH AT NIGHT

Travelling at Night in the Mountains at Hakone on the Border of Izu and Sagami Provinces (*Zusō Hakoneyama yakō no zu*)

from the series *Famous Places in All Provinces* (*Shokoku meisho*)
published by Ibaya Sensaburō (Dansendō), *c.* 1843–5

signed: *Hiroshige ga*
woodblock, fan print, 228 x 296 mm
The Art Institute of Chicago, Chicago,
The Clarence Buckingham Collection (43.691)

Hiroshige returned several times to the theme of travellers with torches crossing the tortuous paths around Hakone. Similar scenes recur in the prints for the station of Hakone in the *Reisho Tōkaidō* (cat. 29) and the *Kyōka Tōkaidō* (cat. 34). The nocturnal aspect and the menace it implies are given great prominence in this fan design.

The publisher Ibaya Sensaburō specialised in fan prints. The only other design from this series to have survived depicts women in a small boat catching fireflies on the banks of the river at Uji, near Kyoto (Suzuki, 1975, p. 128).

REFERENCES: Suzuki, 1970, no. 50; Yoshida, 1973, no. 13

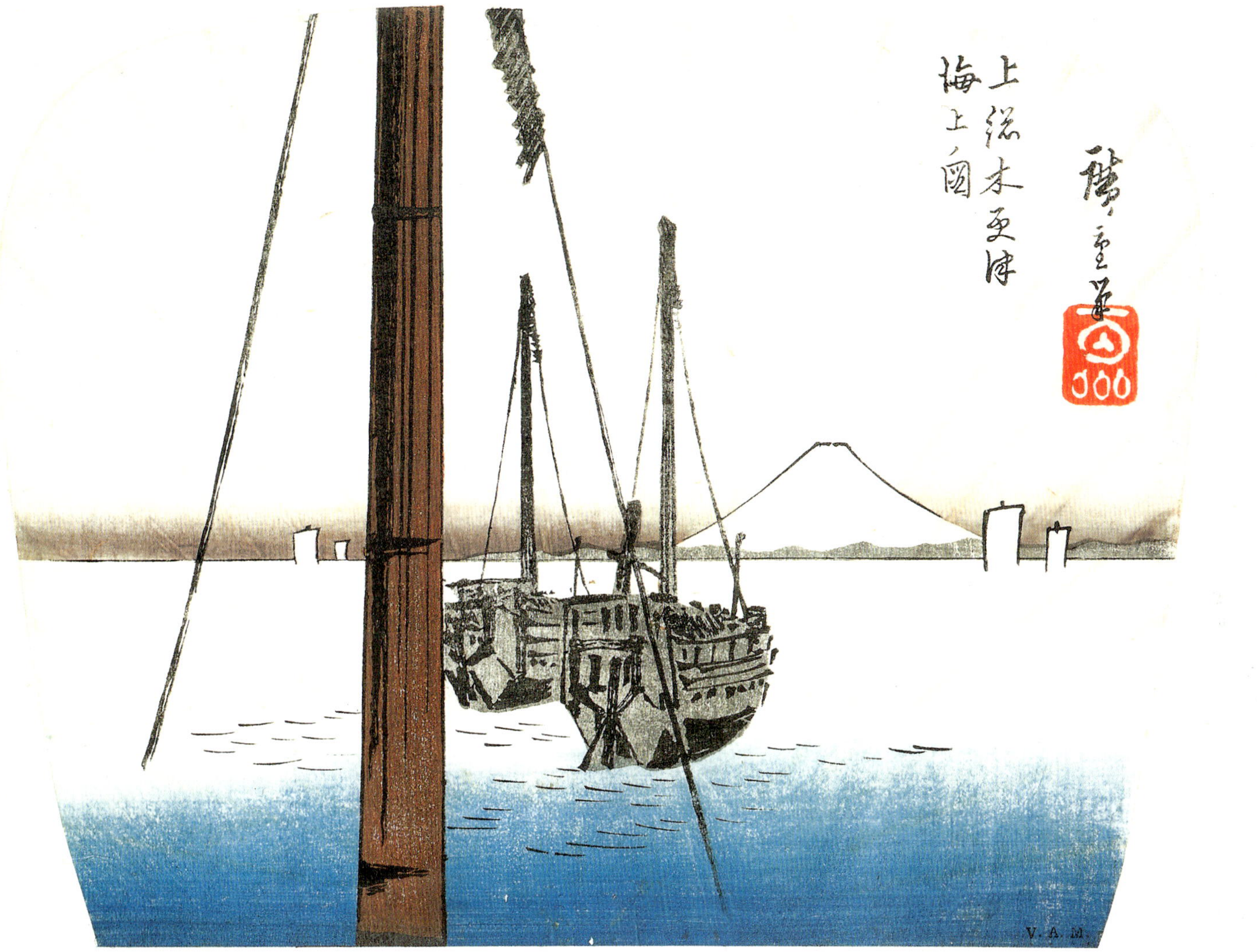

80 MOUNT FUJI SEEN ACROSS THE WATER

A View of the Sea at Kisarazu in Kazusa Province (*Kazusa Kisarazu kaijō no zu*)

published anonymously, *c.* 1842–5

signed: *Hiroshige ga*, with seal: *Ichiryūsai*
woodblock, fan print, 182 x 238 mm
The Board of Trustees of the Victoria and Albert Museum, London (E4894–1919)

Mount Fuji is the sole identifiable topographical feature in this print. The rest of the scene comprises a broad panorama of the sea with two cargo vessels lying at anchor; the mast of a third boat bisects the composition. Only the inscription indicates that this is a view of the port of Kisarazu on what is now the Chiba Peninsula, looking out over the Bay of Edo.

Hiroshige often experimented with masts or bridge struts that bisect a composition—for example in the many views of Tsukudajima—and although it is here applied to a fan, the composition brings to mind the tall, narrow *tanzaku* format. The small format of the fan and the relatively simple execution suggest that this design was made for a minor publisher, which may explain why the print lacks a publisher's trademark. Many fan sellers were not registered as printers with the guild and generally worked anonymously.

REFERENCES: Matsuki, 1925, no. 38; Uchida, 1932, no. 302

STILL-LIFES

CAT. 81–5

81 BOWL OF SUSHI

published anonymously, *c.* 1845

signed: *Hiroshige utsusu*, with seal: *Ichiryūsai*
woodblock, fan print, 224 x 285 mm
Berès Collection, Paris (ex-H. M. Kaempfer Collection)

On a blue and white porcelain dish are a few pieces of *makisushi*: *tamagomaki*, wrapped in omelette; *norimaki*, wrapped in seaweed; and a couple of *nigirisushi*, one with a peeled prawn (*ebi*), the other with a piece of fish (*kohada*). The combination has been garnished with a few bamboo leaves, two of which lie beside the dish.

Pure still-lifes like this are very rare in Hiroshige's oeuvre, otherwise appearing only in a few prints showing a number of different images (*harimazee*). The high degree of naturalism in the print is a form of Western influence that is almost equally rare, though it does occur in the artist's prints of birds and flowers. It receives emphasis here from the 'utsusu' in the signature. Conventional in representations of this kind, this is to be interpreted as an abbreviation for '*shō utsusu*' or '*shasei*', that is, 'drawn from life'.

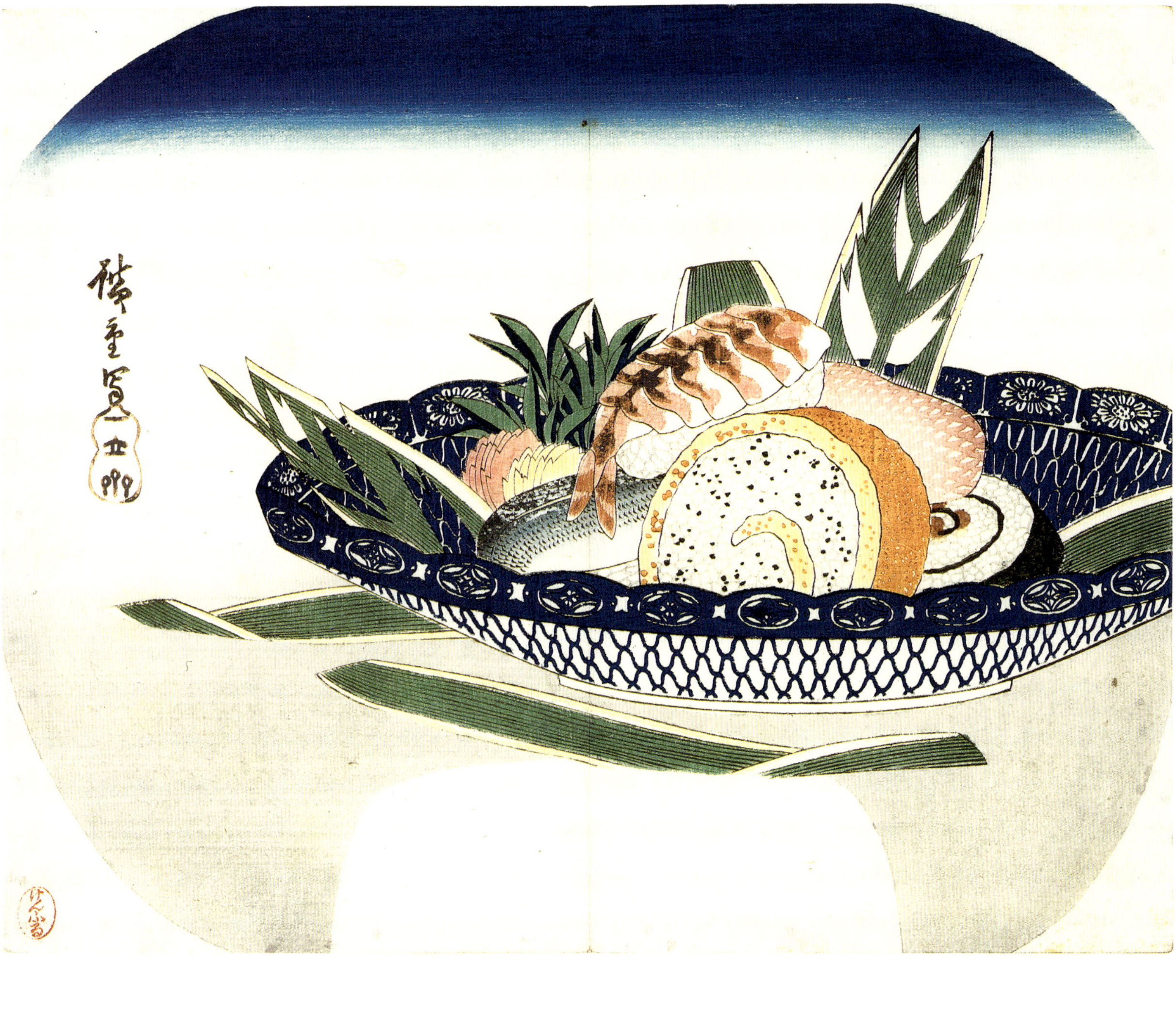

82 GREY MULLET AND CAMELLIA

from an untitled series of large fish
published privately, *c.* 1832–3

signed: *Ichiryūsai Hiroshige ga*
woodblock, *ōban*, 253 x 368 mm
The Mann Collection, Highland Park, Illinois

A still-life consisting of a large grey mullet, a branch of camellia and the Japanese asparagus. In the upper part of the print are two *kyōka* poems by Higaki Kunifune and Toshinomon Haruki respectively. The first relates to the fame of the shore at Tago as a place from which to enjoy a magnificent view of Mount Fuji:

Tago no ura ya
Fuji no utsureru
nami no ue wo
sagaru mo okashi
subashiri no uo

The shore of Tago!
Mount Fuji reflected in the waves
and fish rising and falling.

The second poem reads:

Kaminari no
naruto no bora mo
tsurihari no
inazuma wo mite
heso ya chichimemu

Thunder.
The mullet that sees in a whirl
the lightning flash of a hook
is frightened to death.

This series of ten or eleven prints—it is not certain whether a print of trout belongs to the series or not—was originally commissioned by a poetry club. They were thus first issued as a de luxe *kyōka* folding album and all the prints from the first edition (a) have a centrefold, as here.

Bokashi was added to the upper edge in later impressions (b) of this print. Later still, the subtle *bokashi* on the asparagus disappears (c); it is now simply overprinted as a brown block and the yellow in the lower part is replaced by deep blue.

REFERENCES: Tanba, 1965, no. 93 [c]; *Memorial Exhibition*, 1968, no. 4 [a]; Suzuki, 1970, no. 593 [a]; Izzard, 1983, no. 5 [a]; Nagata, 1986, no. 37 [b]; Copenhagen, 1993, no. 102 [b]; Kruml, 1994, no. 9 [a]

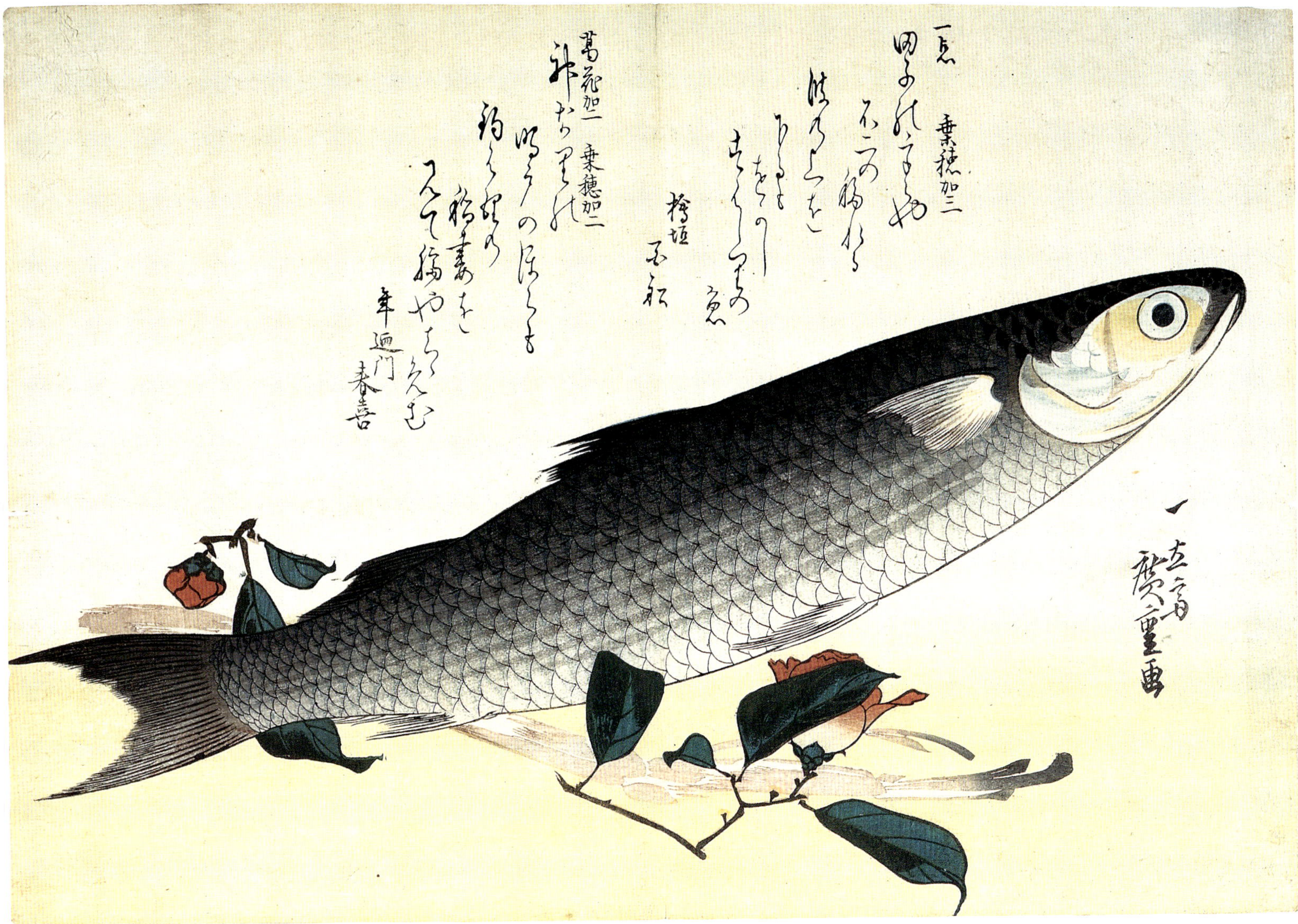
一立斎廣重画

85 CHRYSANTHEMUMS

Autumn (Aki)

from the series *Refined Flower Arrangements for the Four Seasons (Fūryū shiki no ikebana)*
published by Kukiken of Shiba, *c.* 1843–7

signed: *Hiroshige ga*, with seal: *Ichiryūsai*
censor's seal: Fukatsu Ihei
woodblock, fan print, 215 x 288 mm
The Board of Trustees of the Victoria and Albert Museum, London (E4828–1919)

The still-life in this fan print evokes almost an entire landscape. Hiroshige has set a branch of chrysanthemums, traditionally associated with the Ninth Month or autumn in Japan, in a basket against the background of a scroll painting of a full autumn moon. The position of the signature allies it to the scroll painting rather than the print. Nothing is known of the publisher of this print.

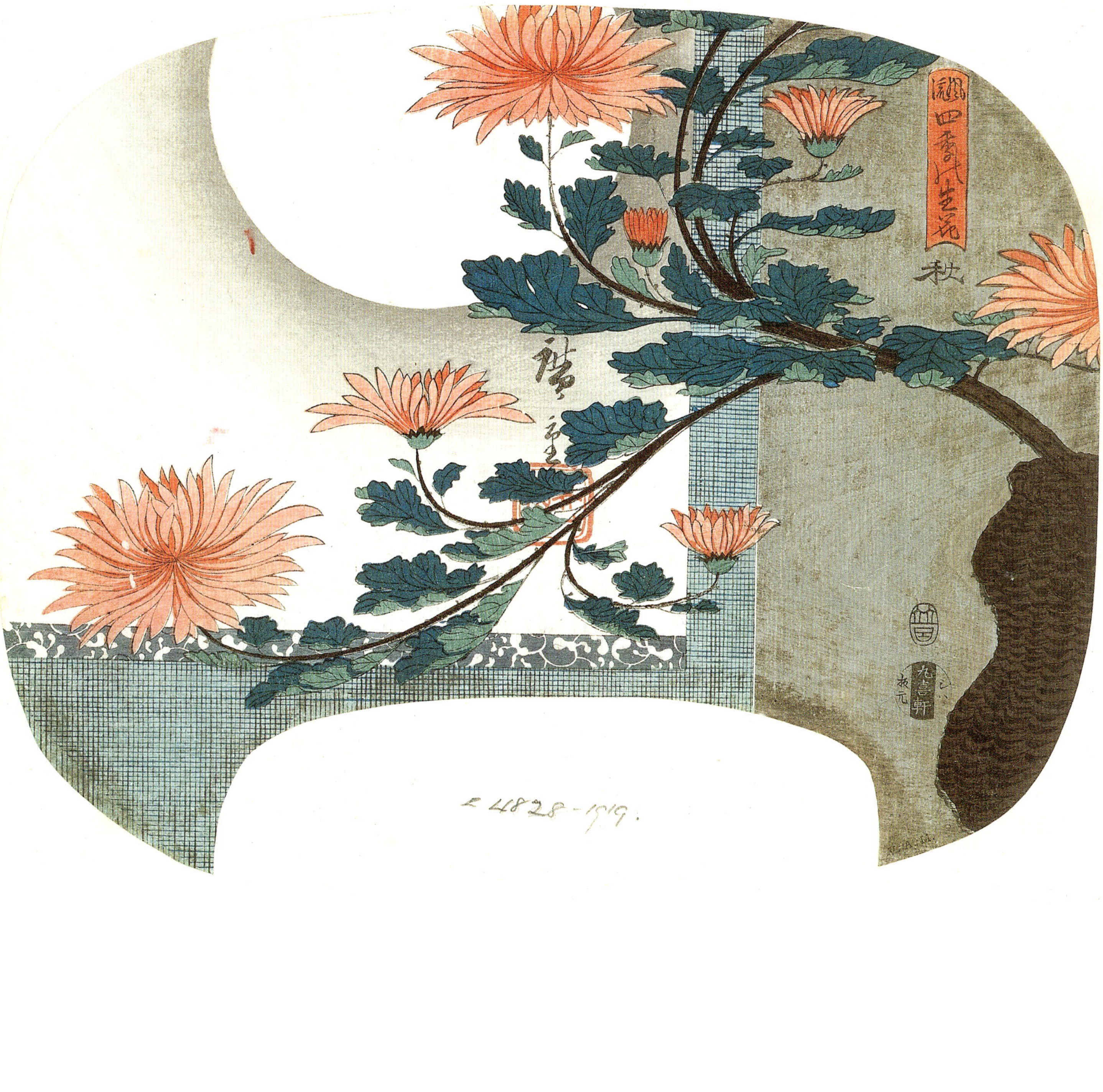

風流四季の生花
秋
E 4828-1919.

VIEWS IN THE PROVINCES II

CAT. 86–92

86 SHRINES IN SNOWY MOUNTAINS

Mount Yugayama in Bizen Province (Bizen Yugayama)

from the series *A Wrestling Match between Mountains and Seas* (*Sankai mitate sumō*)
published by Yamadaya Shōjirō, 1858

signed: *Hiroshige ga*
censorship seal: *aratame*; date seal: Horse 8 (1858/VIII)
woodblock, ōban, 246 x 357 mm
Bibliothèque Nationale de France, Division orientale, Département des Manuscrits, Paris (Fonds japonais 628)

One of Hiroshige's last designs—it was published shortly before his death—this is an impressive landscape in which the falling snow is contrasted with the sky and water and with the darkness falling in the valley. To judge from the gates, there are two Shinto shrines in the valley, in which the roofs of houses are visible too. The right half of the image is dominated by the mountain of the title, with a few solitary trees on the summit.

The idea of this series of twenty prints was to depict mountains that lie directly on the coast and could therefore be engaged in a 'wrestling match' with the sea. This is underscored by the shape of the title cartouche, which is that of the fan used by the referee at a wrestling match—a playful touch of a kind not often encountered in Hiroshige's work.

Early impressions of this print (a) have *bokashi* on the foremost hill to the right, which is printed in a pigment that oxidates easily. This effect is missing from later impressions (b). The colours in this impression have been preserved in excellent condition because the sheet was part of a complete set that was bound in a folding album.

REFERENCES: Tanba, 1965, no. 386 [a]; *Memorial Exhibition*, 1968, no. 429 [b]; Narazaki, 1975, no. 142; *Meihin soroimono ukiyoe*, 12, no. 106 [b]

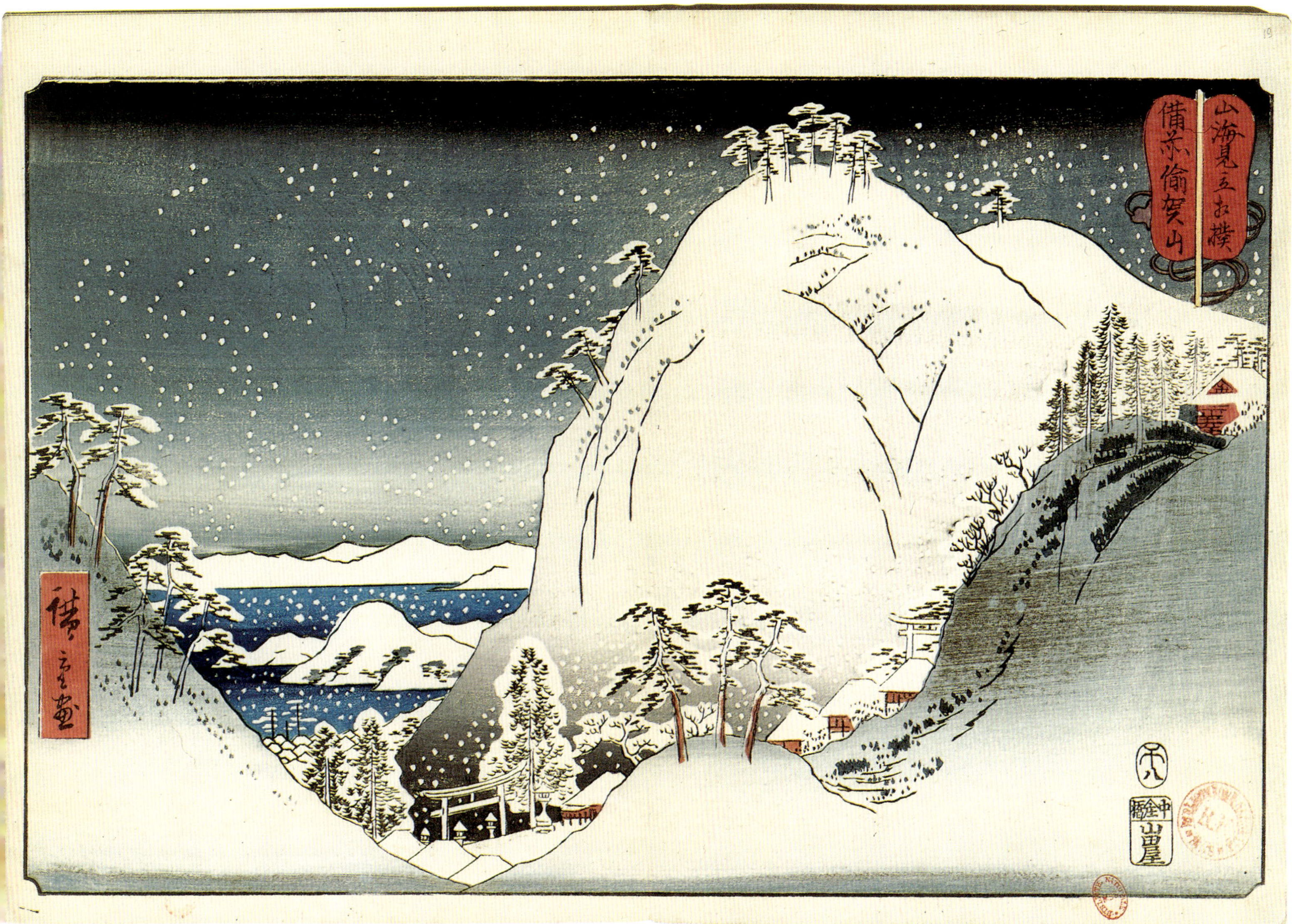
山海見立相撲
備前喩賀山
広重画

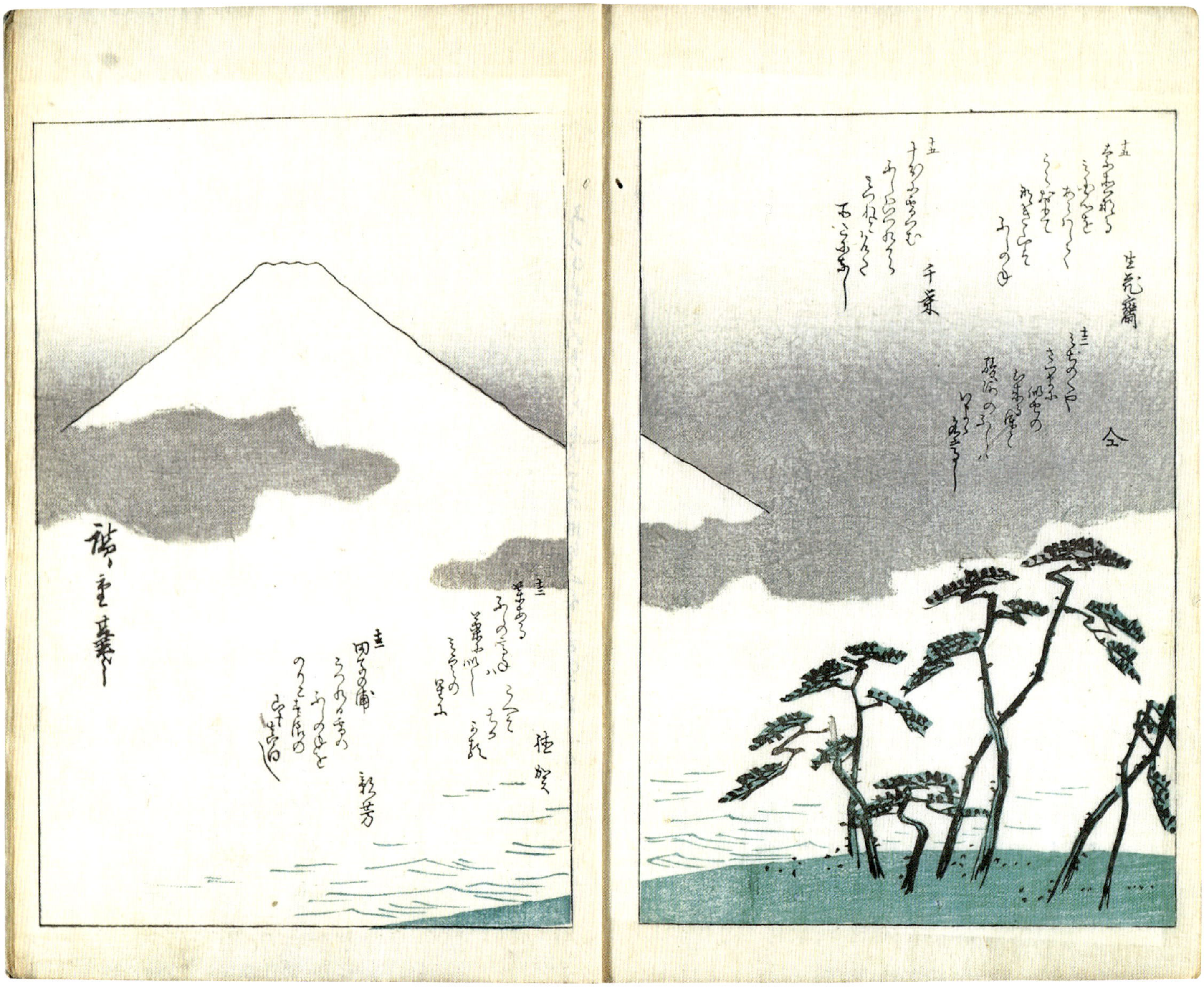

87 MOUNT FUJI SEEN FROM THE BEACH

from the one-volume album *A Second Publication of Haiku Poems* (*Haikaika saihasshū*)
published privately by Midorian, 1840/IX/18

signed: *Hiroshige hitsu*
woodblock, album plate, 226 x 158 mm
Collection Pulverer, Cologne (ex-Ozaki and Matsushita Shimizu collections, and a temple library [Shugyō zōsho])

Mist or cloud partly conceals the towering peak of Mount Fuji. In the foreground are pine trees on the shore at Miho.

This print, its only colours grey and green, is the sole illustration in the album, a private publication by a poetry club. The club apparently wanted simply to issue the collection of poems, selected by Hakukau-ō (Horinouchi Senkaku, 1675–1748), without going to the expense of more illustrations. The first four sheets have a broad decorative border of plants and flowers, also printed in simple colours and probably by Hiroshige. They are followed by eighteen sheets with poems alone; the illustration is on sheets 21b/22a.

REFERENCE: *Kyōka shomoku shūsei*, p. 93

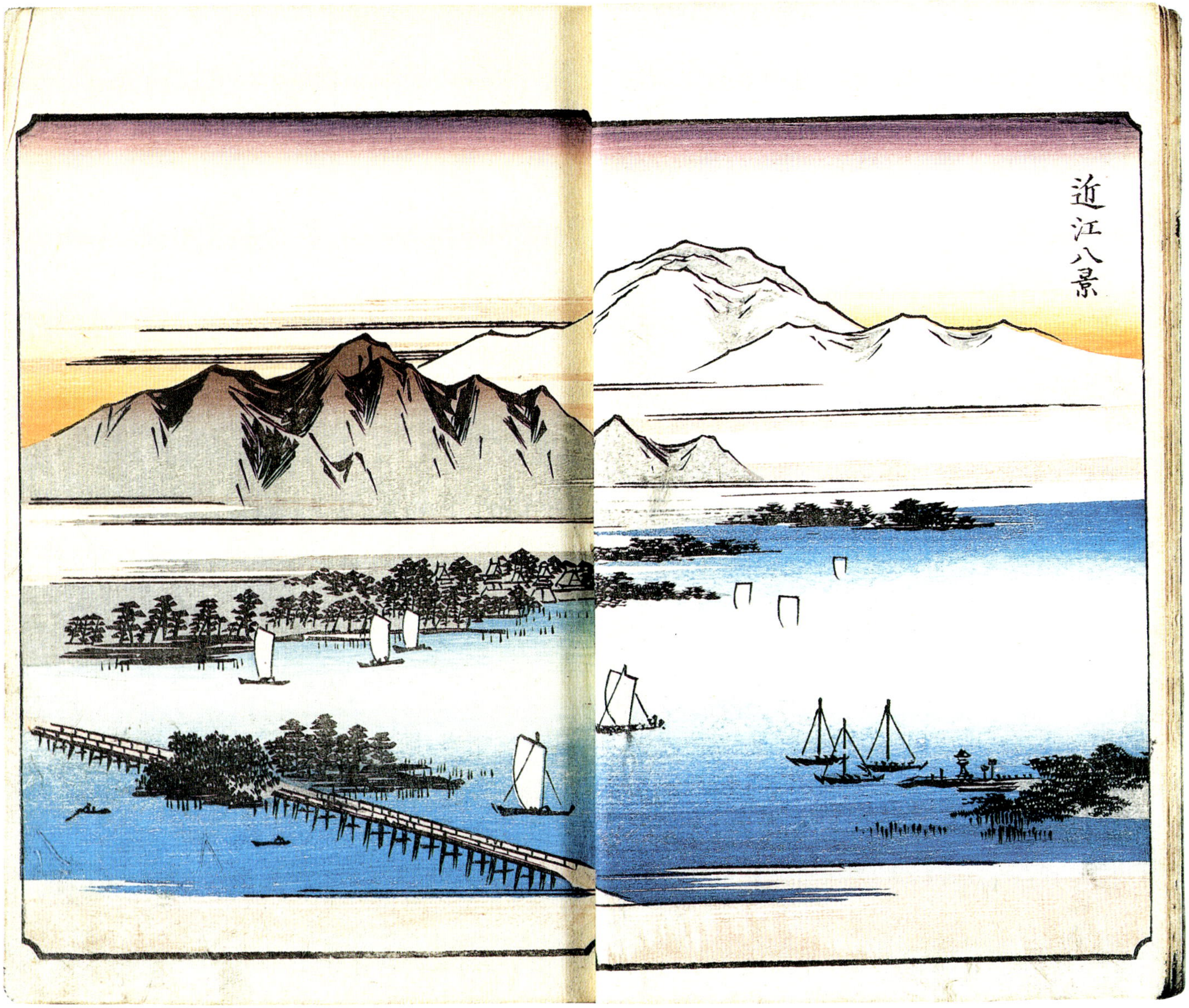

88 VIEW OF A LAKE AND HIGH MOUNTAINS

The Eight Views of Lake Biwa (*Ōmi hakkei*)

from the two-volume *Album of Cursive Drawings of Ryūsai* (*Ryūsai—Sōhitsu gafu*)
published by Ebisuya Shōshichi (Kinshōdō), *c.* 1848 (volume 1) and *c.* 1850 (volume 2)

signed: *Ichiryūsai Hiroshige hitsu*
from volume 2
woodblock, album plate, 181 x 120 mm
Collection Pulverer, Cologne

A view of Lake Biwa from the north-west, with the harbour of Yabase in the right foreground, Seta Bridge on the left and Mount Hira on the far side of the lake.

This small album contains prints of numerous subjects, from landscapes and historical figures to images of various professions and objects. It was apparently aimed at a wide public that wanted to possess an attractive picture book with a variety of designs by Hiroshige. The publication dates are not known; those given here appear underneath the forewords by Ryūkatei Tanekazu (1807–58) and Honchōan Kosanba (1812–53), the latter written 'in a state of inebriation'.

REFERENCES: Toda, 1931, no. 298; *Kokusho sōmokuroku*, 5-280-3

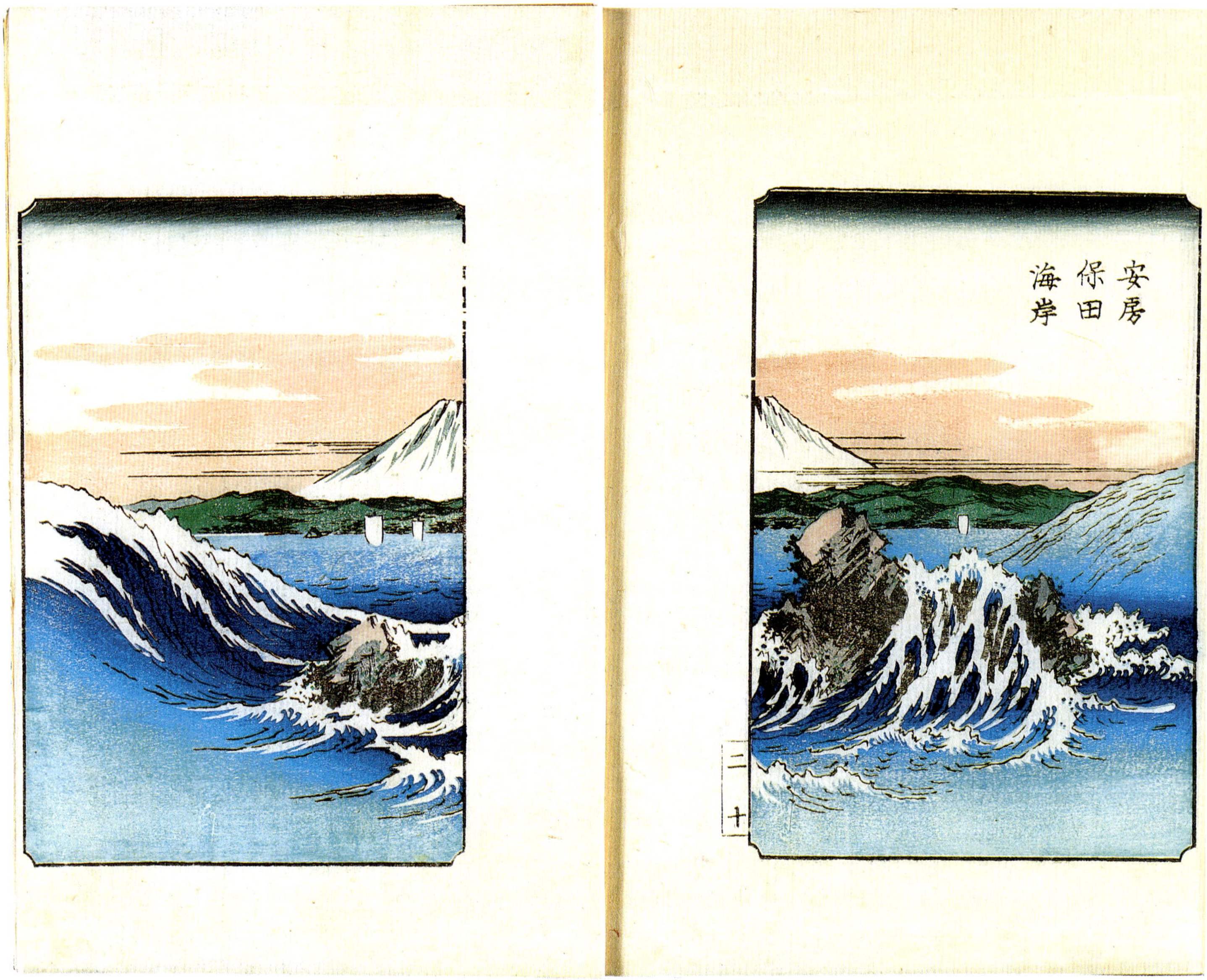

89 MOUNT FUJI AND A WILD SEA

The Coast at Yasuda in Awa Province (*Awa Yasuda no kaigan*)

from the one-volume album *A Hundred Views of Mount Fuji* (*Fujimi hyakuzu*)
published anonymously, *c.* 1859

signed: *Hiroshige hitsu*
woodblock, album plate, 221 x 156 mm
Collection Pulverer, Cologne

A view of Mount Fuji from Yasuda on the south coast of Awa Province, present-day Shikoku Island, with waves crashing against the rocks in the foreground. The *aratame* censorship seal, combined with the date seal 1857/XI on the first page of this album, indicates that the illustrations were ready by the end of 1857 and the blocks cut after that date. It may be deduced from the date of the foreword by Ryūryū Senka (Rittei Senka II, 1837–84), 1859, that the album was not published until after Hiroshige's death. It is not clear why the publisher waited so long before issuing the volume. Perhaps he initially intended to wait until all the illustrations had been finished: a second album, published much later, contains another twenty plates after drawings by Hiroshige, and the complete publication consisted of five volumes.

REFERENCES: Toda, 1931, no. 300; *Kokusho sōmokuroku*, 7-72-4; Hillier, 1987, p. 881

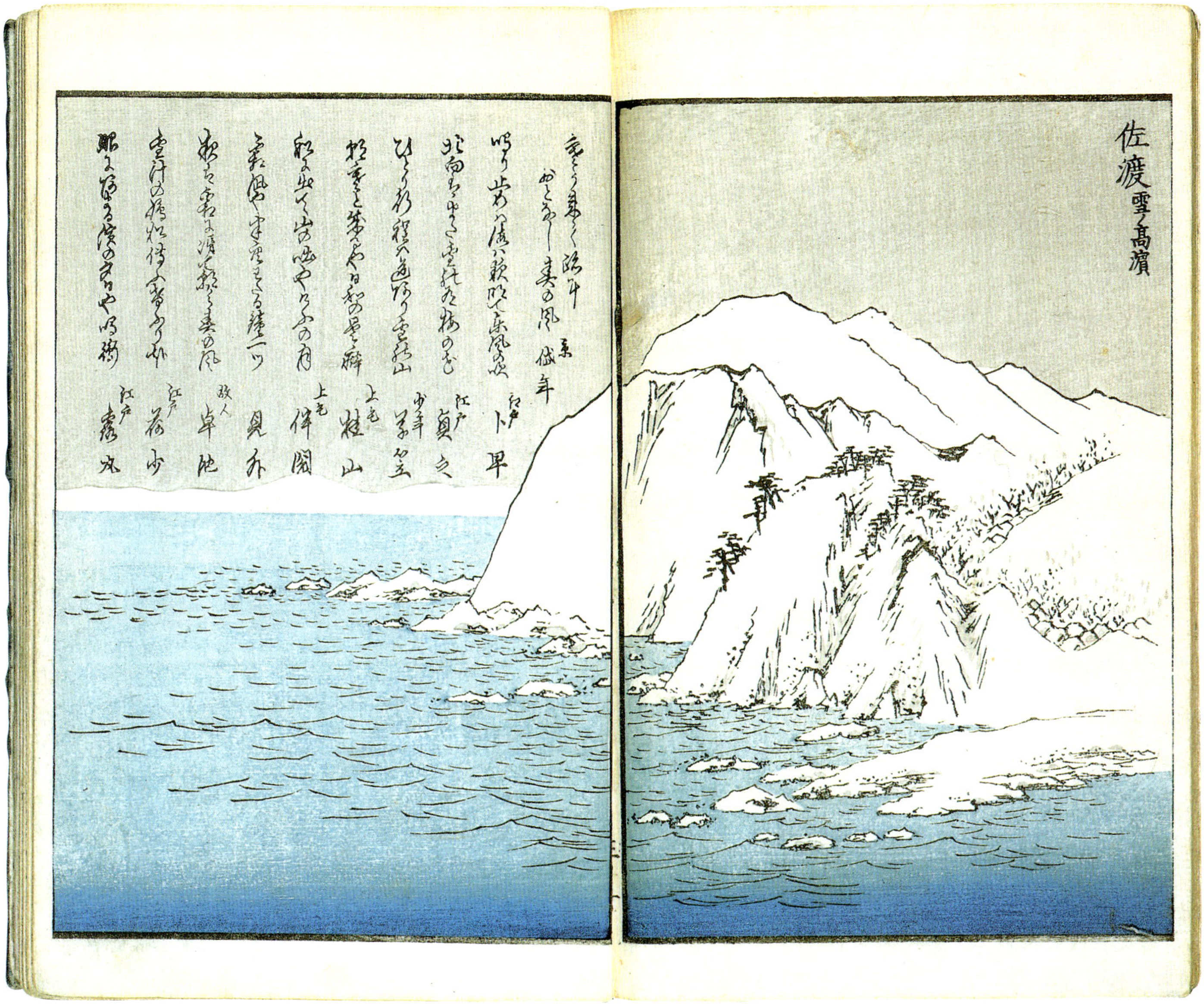

90 MOUNTAINS IN THE SNOW

Snow on the High Valley at Sado Island
(Sado yuki no takasawa)

From the three-volume (?) album *A Collection of Hokku Poems on Famous Places* (*Meisho hokkushū*)
published by Tōkaidō, undated, but volume 3 is probably 1850

signed: *Hiroshige hitsu*, with seal: *Ichiryūsai*
from volume 3, sheets 30b/31a
woodblock, album plate, 220 x 142 mm
The Board of Trustees of the Victoria and Albert Museum, London (E 7030–1916)

A view of Sado Island, desolate in the snow. Sado, an Island in the Sea of Japan off Niigata that consists of two mountainous regions separated by lower land, belonged to the shogun and was a traditional place of banishment—the most severe form of punishment that could be suffered by a living human being. Among those banished to far-off Sado Island were the priests Nichiren and Mongaku—both familiar from prints by Kuniyoshi—and the renowned master of nō theatre, Zeami Motokiyo (1363–1443).

This album was illustrated by a variety of artists, among them Keisai Eisen (1791–1848), who provided the illustrations for volume 2.

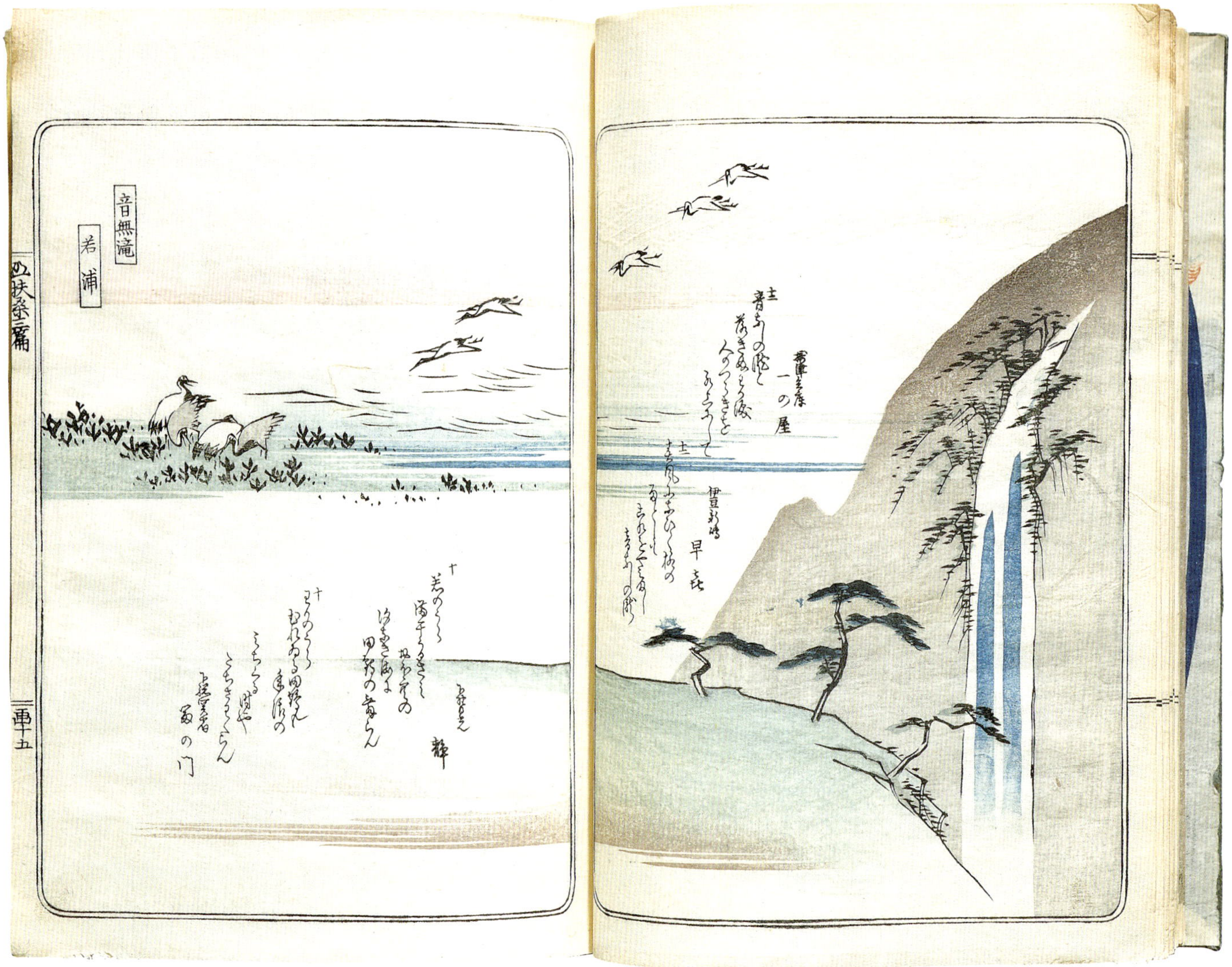

91 VIEW OF A WATERFALL

The Otonashi Fall at Wakanoura (Otonashi no taki/Wakanoura)

from the album *Comic Poems and Famous Views of Japan* (*Kyōka Fusō meisho zue*)
published privately by Shunyūtei Umehiko, 1839
from volume 3, sheets 14b/15a
woodblock, album plate, *hanshibon*, 227 x 165 mm
Mr and Mrs Arthur Vershbow, Newton, Massachusetts

On the right we see a steep mountain from which the Otonashi (literally 'noiseless') waterfall pours. To the left is a view of Lake Wakanoura in Wakayama Prefecture. This lake, especially noted for its birdsong, was a traditional theme of poetry. The composition is accompanied by four *kyōka* poems.

This album of *kyōka* poems is another example of co-operation between Hinokizono Umeaki (1793–1859), head of the Hinokizono poetry club, who selected the poems, the publisher Shunyūtei and Hiroshige. It is not clear how many volumes there were and who illustrated the others. There seems to be no connection with an earlier publication carrying the same title that was illustrated by Totoya Hokkei. Another work with the same title, dating from 1838 and probably one of the earlier volumes of the present publication, was illustrated by Seiyō (*Kyōka shomoku shūsei*, p. 91). However, it is difficult to determine whether two publications with a slightly longer title, *Kyōka Fusō meisho meibutsu zue*, illustrated by Utagawa Yoshitora and dating from 1857 and 1859 respectively (ibid., pp. 107, 108), should be regarded as sequels to our volumes.

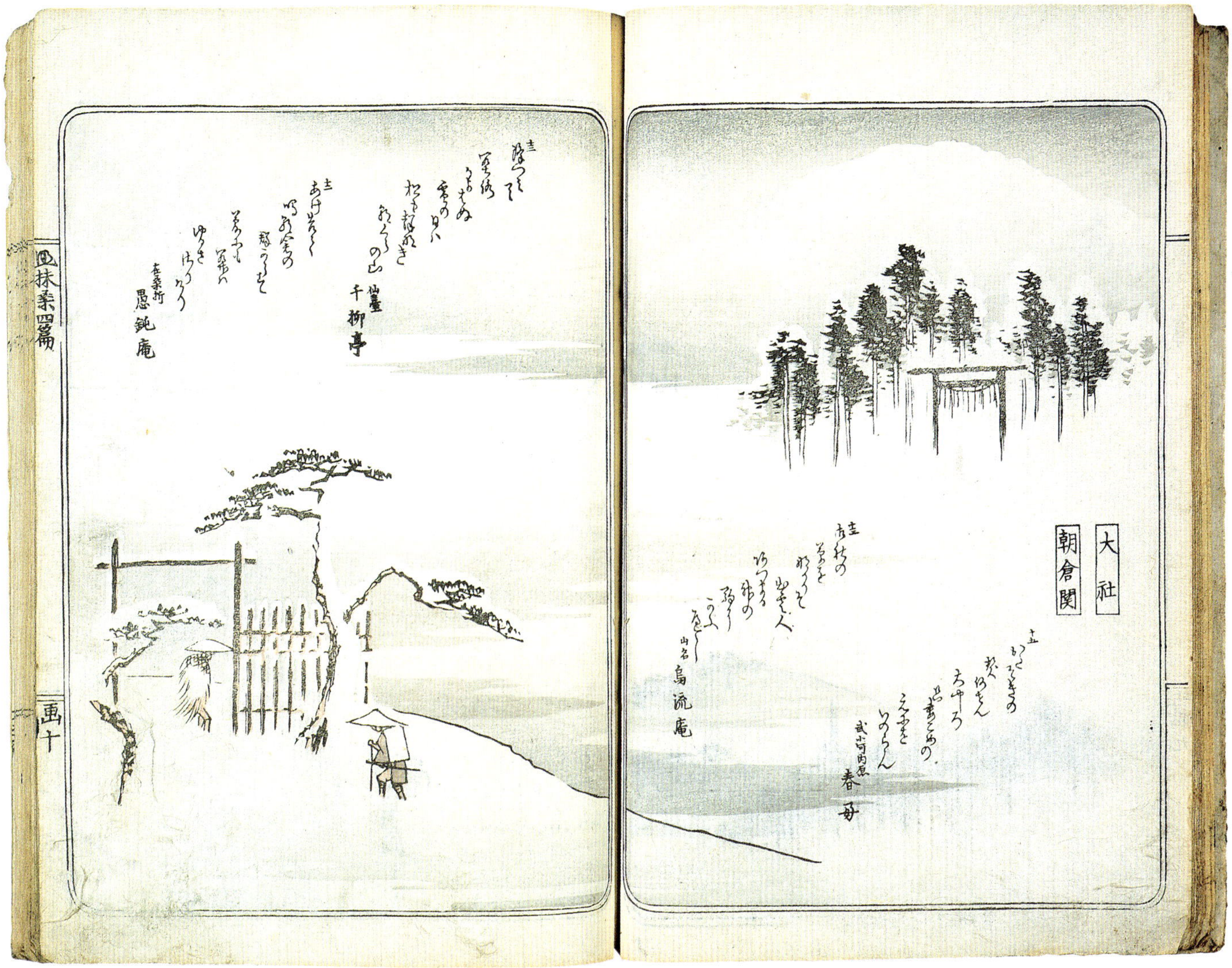

92 TWO MEN BY A GATE IN THE MOUNTAINS

The Great Shrine and the Barrier at Mount Asakura (*Ōyashiro Asakura no seki*)

from the album *Comic Poems and Famous Views of Japan* (*Kyōka Fusō meisho zue*)
published privately by Shunyūtei Umehiko, 1840

from volume 4, sheets 9b/10a
woodblock, album plate, *hanshibon*, 226 x 163 mm
The Trustees of The British Museum, London (267)

The Great Shrine is hidden among the trees on Mount Asakura on the right of this image. On the left is the gate of the barrier at Mount Asakura. A man carrying a load on his back is walking towards the gate, while another man, in a straw cloak, is passing through it towards him. Mount Asakura lies in the present-day Shizuoka Prefecture.

VIEWS OF EDO II

CAT. 93–106

93 ADMIRING THE PLUM TREES IN FLOWER

The Plum Garden at Kameido (Kameido Umeyashiki)

from the series *One Hundred Famous Views in Edo* (*Meisho Edo hyakkei*)
published by Uoya Eikichi, 1856–8

signed: *Hiroshige ga*
censorship seal: *aratame*; date seal: Snake 11 (1857/XI)
woodblock, *ōban*, 377 x 265 mm
Honolulu Academy of Arts, Honolulu,
Gift of James A. Michener, 1991 (24.103)

Umeyashiki is the name of a plum garden on the bank of the Sumida River, just behind the Tenman Shrine at Kameido (see cat. 10). This garden, originally planted by a textile merchant, attracted a large public because of the strong scent of the trees in blossom and undoubtedly also because of its location close to the shrine. Its shape earned the plum tree in the foreground of this print the nickname Resting Dragon Plum (*Garyūbai*), because the branches grew so long that they penetrated the earth and new trees emerged near them. A group of people are admiring the plum blossom from behind a fence. One notes the position of the sign at upper left, receding into the picture and cut off by the borders in order to enhance the feeling of depth.

In early impressions such as this (a) the trunk and broad branches of the plum tree in the foreground acquire extra volume from a subtle *bokashi* along the edges and the grain of the woodblock is clearly visible. Something resembling shadow is indicated beneath the trees. This is absent from later impressions (b), in which a dark grey-blue *bokashi* extends from the upper edge of the print, giving the composition a menacing and gloomy air that accords ill with the general mood of the scene. In an even later impression (c) the *bokashi* on the tree disappears completely.

Van Gogh's 1887 copy of this print bears the curious inscription 'painted by the New Yoshiwara' and seems to have been based on an early impression lacking the *bokashi* along the upper edge. However, the impression now in the Van Gogh Museum in Amsterdam is a very late one and the painter apparently simply omitted the dark strip at the top.

REFERENCES: Yoshida, 1973, no. 10 [c]; Suzuki, 1975, p. 33 [a]; *Ukiyoe taikei*, 11, no. 50, and 16, no. 30 [both a]; *Kobijutsu*, 1983, no. 403 [a]; *Ukiyoe hakka*, 1984, no. 51 [a]; Smith and Poster, 1986, no. 30 [a]; Link, 1991, no. IV-32-B [a]; *Meihin soroimono ukiyoe*, 10, no. 75 [a]; Copenhagen, 1993, no. 109 [c]; Sakai, 1996, nos. 186 and 187 [a], 188 [b]

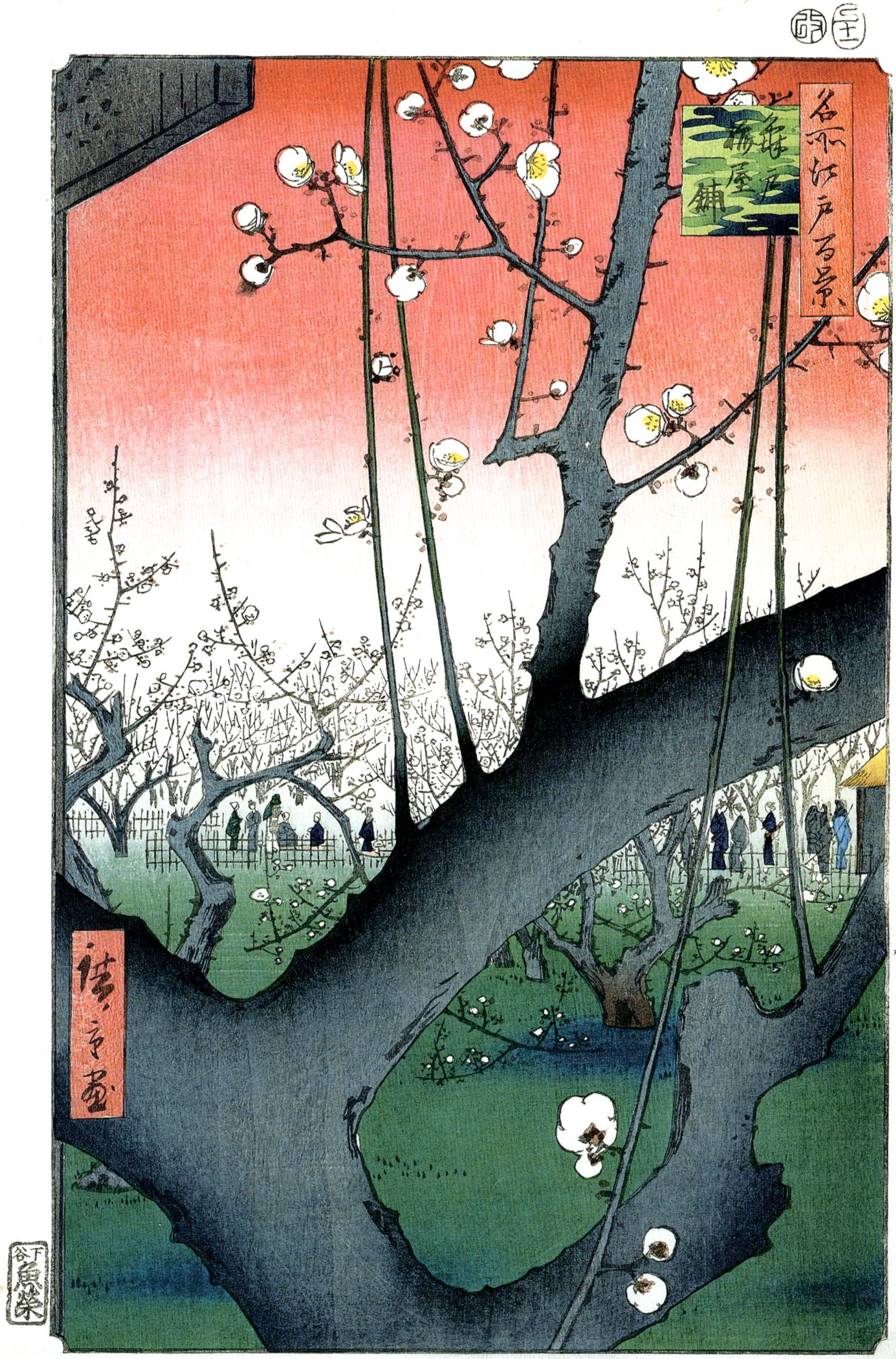
名所江戸百景
亀戸梅屋舗
廣重画
下谷 魚栄

94 PEOPLE ON A BRIDGE SURPRISED BY RAIN

A Sudden Shower over Ōhashi and Atake (Ōhashi Atake no yūdachi)

from the series *One Hundred Famous Views in Edo* (*Meisho Edo hyakkei*)
published by Uoya Eikichi, 1856–8

signed: *Hiroshige ga*
censorship seal: *aratame*; date seal: Snake 9 (1857/IX)
woodblock, *ōban*, 365 x 244 mm
Honolulu Academy of Arts, Honolulu,
Gift of James A. Michener, 1991 (22.746)

People crossing the Ōhashi Bridge are surprised by a sudden shower of rain, which nearly obliterates the contours of the shore. On the left, however, the sheds for the shogun's boats in the Atake neighbourhood and the Honjō district can be made out. The name Ōhashi, literally 'Great Bridge', was applied to both Ryōgoku Bridge and Shin (New) Ōhashi Bridge. The bridge in this print is the latter, which was constructed over the Sumida River to connect Hamachō and the Momi Storage in the Fukagawa district in 1693.

There are considerable differences between the first (a; cat. 94) and the second (b; cat. 95) edition of this print: a mistake was corrected and a number of modifications were made in the second edition. The most striking difference lies in the two small boats near the shore on the other side of the river, which are omitted from the second edition. There seems little reason to have removed them; it is likely that the grey block for the background had to be recut and that the two small boats were simply forgotten in the process. The leaves on the trees are more detailed in the background of cat. 95, while the detail in the houses is even less convincing than in the first edition. A number of other changes were made. For instance, a mistake in the block for the bridge was corrected. The block-cutter had originally cut away a piece of the piles, which was thus left blank during printing. The gap was filled in the second edition. In addition, a deep blue *bokashi* was applied under the bridge to the right and behind it to the left, and a shadow was created on the side of the bridge closest to the viewer. The title cartouche was printed in three colours by adding red to the original yellow and green.

REFERENCES: Suzuki, 1975, p. 31; Link, 1991, no. IV-32-H; *Meihin soroimono ukiyoe*, 10, no. 104a; Copenhagen, 1993, no. 107; Sakai, 1996, no. 171 [all a]

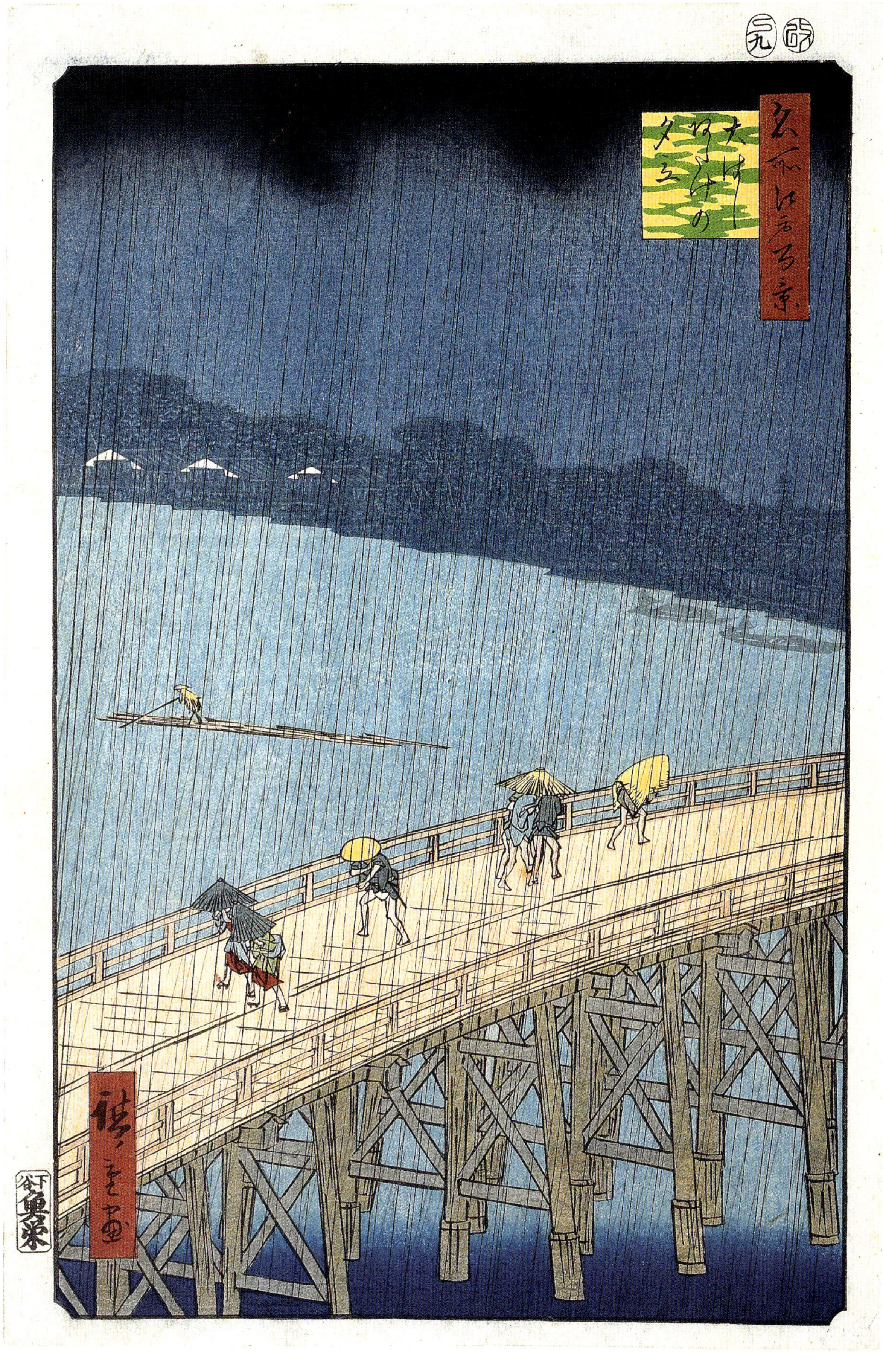
名所江戸百景
大はしあたけの夕立
廣重画

95 PEOPLE ON A BRIDGE SURPRISED BY RAIN

A Sudden Shower over Ōhashi and Atake (Ōhashi Atake no yūdachi)

from the series *One Hundred Famous Views in Edo* (*Meisho Edo hyakkei*)
published by Uoya Eikichi, 1856–8

signed: *Hiroshige ga*
censorship seal: *aratame*; date seal: Snake 9 (1857/IX)
woodblock, *ōban*, 369 x 247 mm
The Mann Collection, Highland Park, Illinois

In addition to the differences already noted between the first edition of this print (cat. 94) and the second (b; cat. 95), it is noteworthy that the distinction in colour between the sky and the water is often less pronounced, particularly in good early impressions. As the background block becomes worn, however, there seems to be an attempt to disguise this by printing the sky in a darker tone. This is almost always the case in very late impressions (c), where the title cartouche is printed in two, not three colours. The shadow on the bridge is also usually absent from these impressions. This view of the sequence of first and second editions—interpreted in exactly the reverse order by Uchida (1932), who was corrected by Suzuki (1970)—is confirmed by the clear break in the left-hand line of the title cartouche, which occurs only in impressions of the second edition (where it is often corrected in ink).

Van Gogh copied this print, too, in 1887 (cf. cat. 93). His version in oils is based on a late impression without the shadow on the bridge and without the deep blue beneath the bridge on the right and behind the bridge on the left. To the left and right of the scene he copied texts from other prints, apparently a series of Eight Views in the Yoshiwara.

REFERENCES: Tanba, 1965, no. 49 [b]; Suzuki, 1970, no. 54 [b]; Narazaki, 1975, no. 19 [b]; Suzuki, 1975, p. 30 [b]; *Ukiyoe taikei*, 11, no. 52, and 16, no. 52 [both b]; Izzard, 1983, no. 83 [b]; *Kobijutsu*, 1983, no. 406 [b]; *Ukiyoe hakka*, 1984, no. 54 [b]; Link, 1991, no. IV-32-G [b]; *Meihin soroimono ukiyoe*, 10, no. 104 [b]; Salamon, 1992, no. 40 [c]; Sakai, 1996, no. 172 [b]

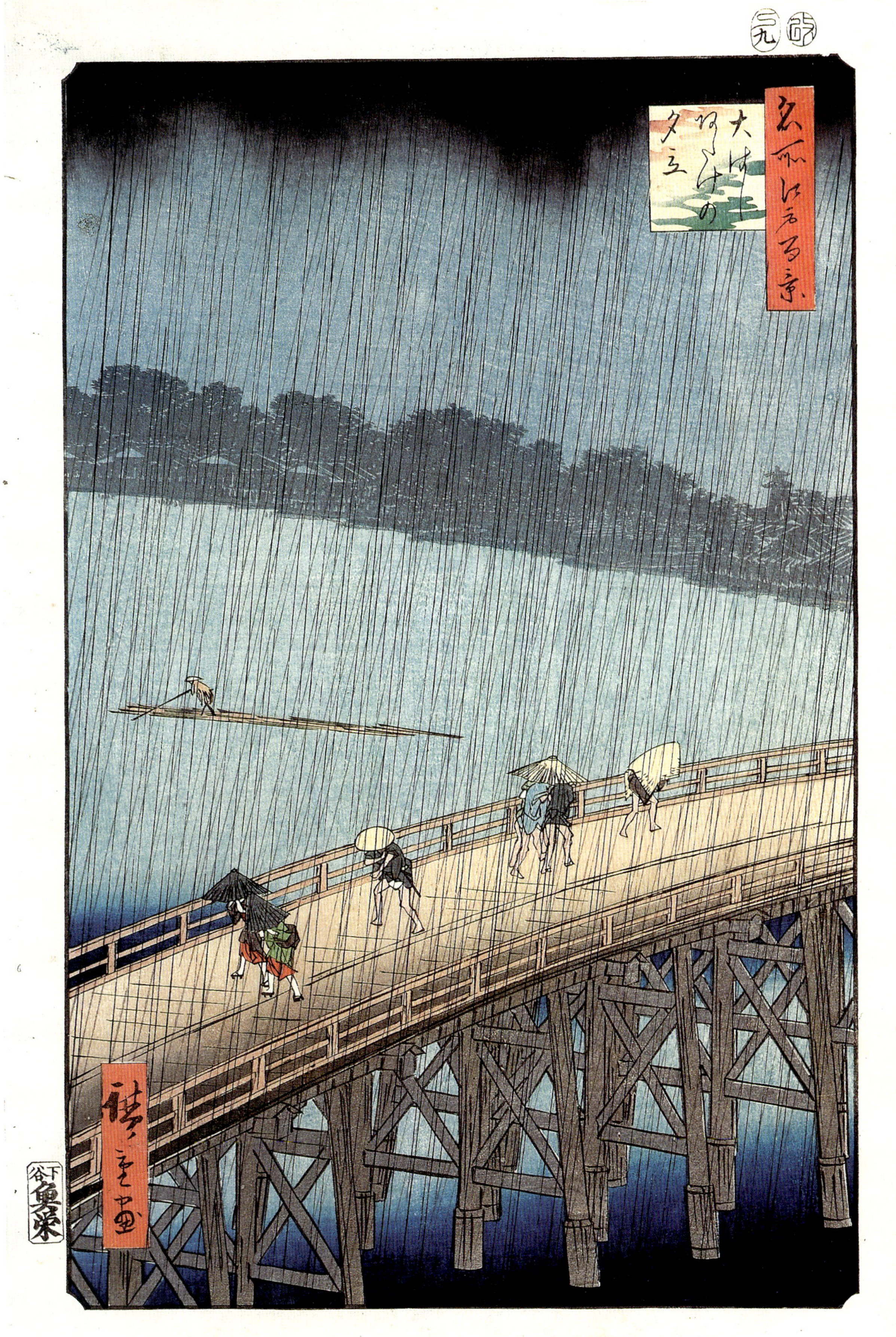
名所江戸百景
大はしあたけの夕立

97 WOMAN ON A RIVER-BANK IN THE EVENING

Evening View of Matsuchiyama and Sanya Canal (Matsuchiyama Sanyabori no yakei)

from the series *One Hundred Famous Views in Edo (Meisho Edo hyakkei)*
published by Uoya Eikichi, 1856–8

signed: *Hiroshige ga*
censorship seal: *aratame*; date seal: Snake 8 (1857/VIII)
woodblock, *ōban*, 358 x 244 mm
The Art Institute of Chicago, Chicago,
The Frederick W. Gookin Collection (39.1393)

Matsuchiyama was a small hill at the point where the Sumida River meets the Sanyabori, a shallow canal about one metre wide, at Imado Bridge. The canal, flanked by restaurants with lights in the windows, and the bridge are visible here on the far side of the river. Behind them is Matsuchiyama Hill. At the end of Sanyabori was the Nihon Dike, which led directly to the gate of the Yoshiwara, Edo's pleasure district. The woman in the foreground is undoubtedly a geisha, following her lantern-bearing escort along the eastern side of the river at Mukōjima in the dusk. On the extreme right is one of the many cherry trees that had been planted beside the river at this point.

There are two variants of this print. One is lighter in colour and clearer as a composition (a): the sky tends more towards blue than grey-blue, so that the grain of the wood is more clearly visible; the water is lighter, and deep blue *bokashi* is applied only at the nearmost river-bank. The other variant (b), illustrated here, has water of a deeper blue, with *bokashi* on both river-banks, and the geisha's over-kimono is blue rather than blue-grey. Another difference is that the title cartouche is blue and salmon pink in the light variant, while in the darker variant it is divided diagonally into areas of red, white and blue.

REFERENCES: *Ukiyoe taikei*, 16, no. 34 [b]; *Kobijutsu*, 1983, no. 404 [b]; Nagata, 1986, no. 126 [b]; Smith and Poster, 1986, no. 34 [b]; Link, 1991, no. IV-32-C [a]; *Meihin soroimono ukiyoe*, 10, no. 79 [b]; Sakai, 1996, nos. 329 [b], 330 [a]

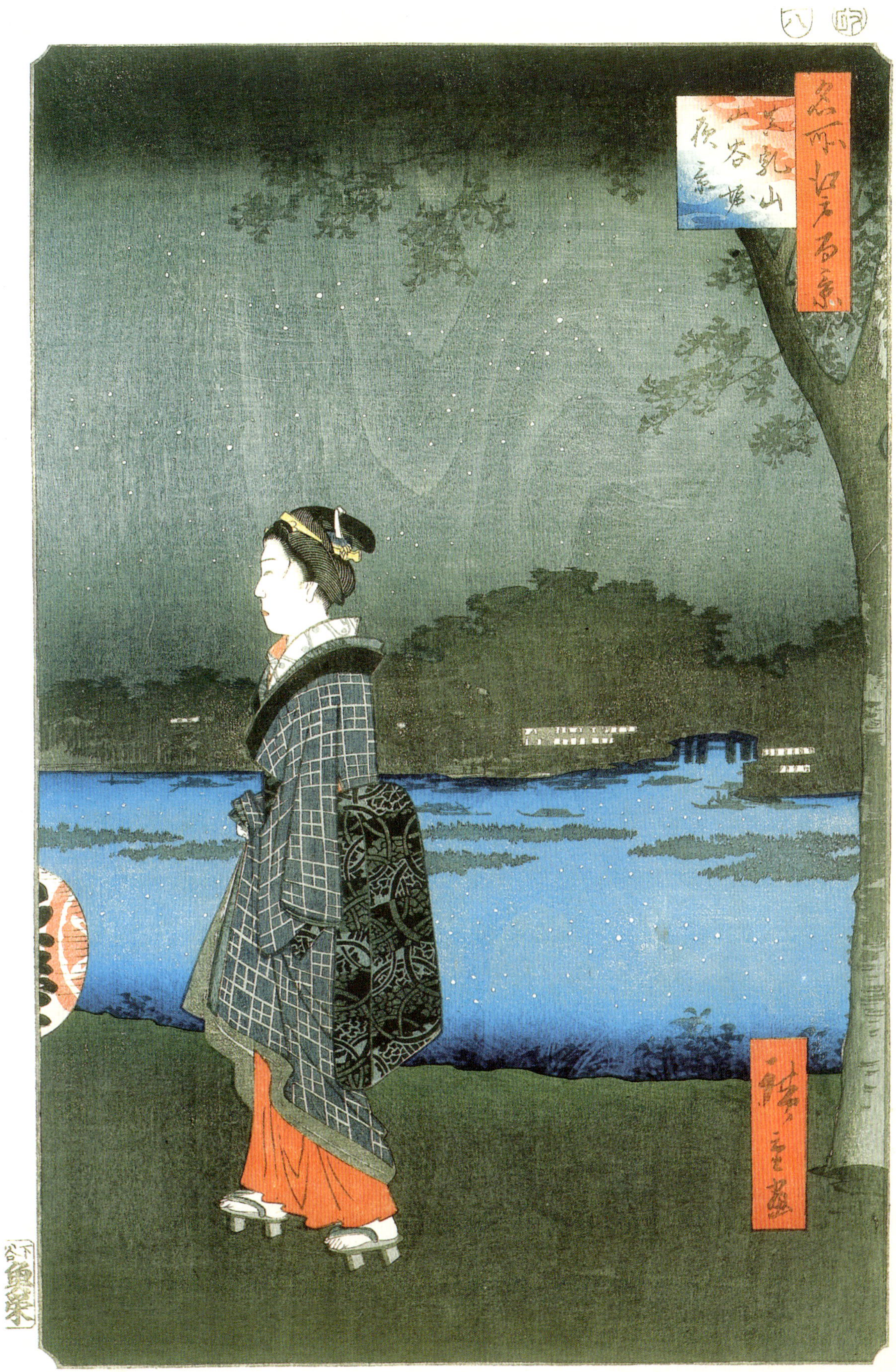
名所江戸百景
真乳山
山谷堀
夜景
廣重画

98 PEOPLE ON A MOONLIT STREET

Evening View of Saruwaka Street
(Saruwakamachi yoru no kei)

from the series *One Hundred Famous Views in Edo*
(*Meisho Edo hyakkei*)
published by Uoya Eikichi, 1856–8

signed: *Hiroshige ga*
censorship seal: *aratame*; date seal: Dragon 9 (1856/IX)
woodblock, *ōban*, 369 x 256 mm
Baur Collection, Geneva (G485)

Saruwakamachi was the street in which the government allowed Edo's kabuki theatres to be rebuilt, in a single block, after a fire in 1841. At first it had refused to have them rebuilt at all, because of the tense political situation at a time of numerous reforms that had been introduced to combat the economic crisis of the 1830s; but permission was later granted. In this print, which is grouped under Autumn in the series list of contents, the theatres, on the right-hand side of the street, are closed: it is the period when the actors retired from the heat of the city or toured the provinces. There is a light only at the Morita Theatre, the first in the street. The tea-houses and restaurants on the left-hand side, however, are open.

The clear depiction of cast shadows on the street indicates Western influence, which accords well with the markedly Western-style perspective of the image, with its single vanishing-point. These devices are seldom used in such a pronounced way in Japanese prints. There are a few instances of bold use of the vanishing-point in Hokusai's series *Thirty-six Views of Mount Fuji* and Kunisada also experimented with it in a night scene. One of the most attractive examples of cast shadows in Japanese prints is to be seen in Kuniyoshi's series of views of Edo.

Early impressions of this print (a) have the façades of the theatres and tea-houses and the street in the same grey tint, with a few *bokashi* accents—below the roof in the foreground and in the green of the blinds, for example. The shadows cast by the figures in the moonlight are in a darker shade of grey. The lanterns are lit and reveal clear patterns in red. On the other hand, the blue of the sky is still rather light, which makes it difficult to account for the shadows and the illuminated lanterns. In this respect, a considerably darker scene (b), is more convincing. In a later impression (c) the lights are on in the houses but the panels on the first floor to the right have become light brown. There are other variants in still later impressions (d), but they seldom achieve a satisfactory balance of the various elements.

REFERENCES: Suzuki, 1975, p. 32 [a]; *Ukiyoe taikei*, 17, no. 90 [a]; *Kobijutsu*, 1983, no. 414 [a]; *Ukiyoe hakka*, 1984, no. 57 [a]; Smith and Poster, 1986, no. 90 [b]; Link, 1991, no. IV-32-J [d]; *Meihin soroimono ukiyoe*, 10, no. 136 [a]; Copenhagen, 1993, no. 118 [c]; Forrer, 1994, G485 [b: this impression]; Sakai, 1996, nos. 214 [a], 215 [b]

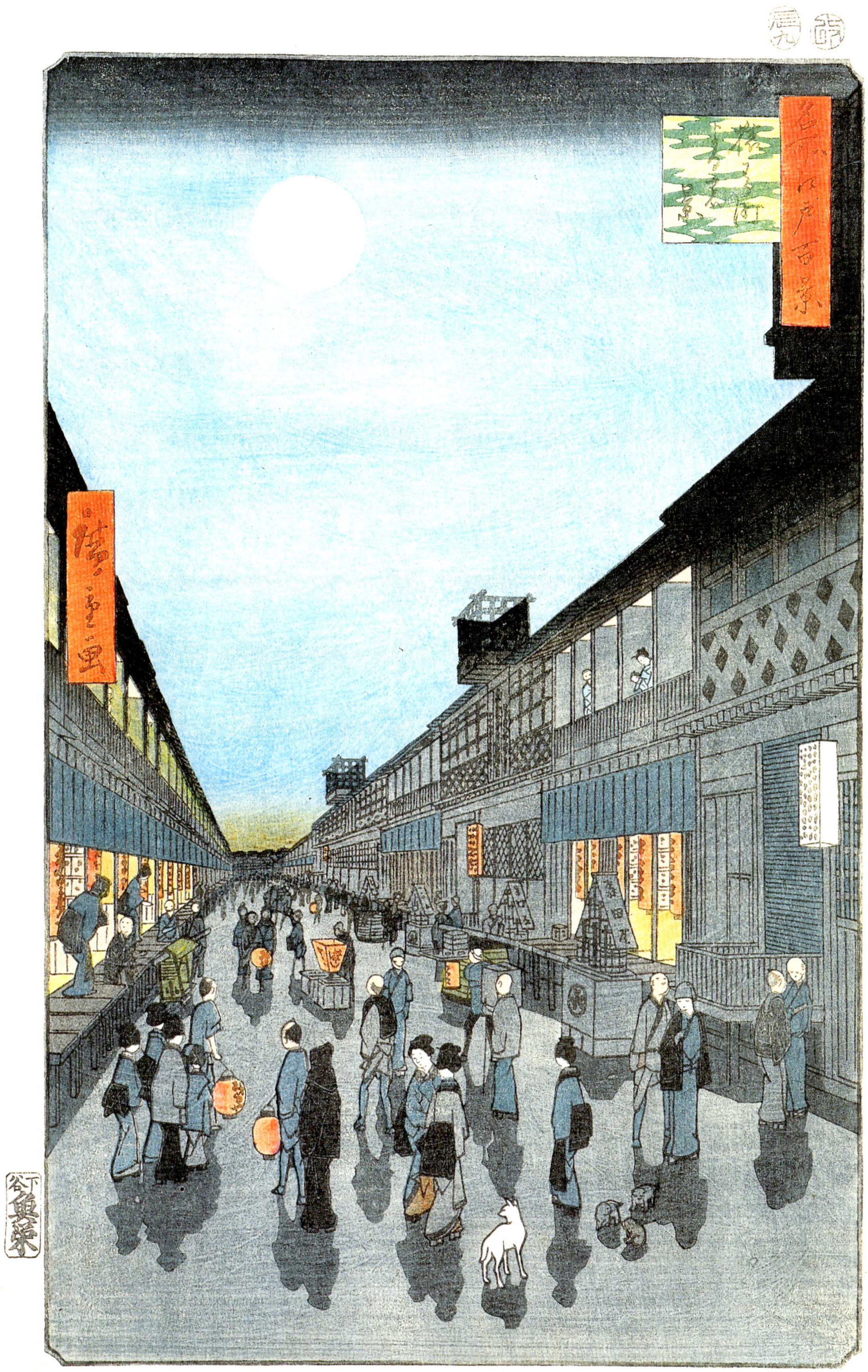
名所江戸百景
猿わか町よるの景
廣重画

99 MOORED BOATS IN THE EVENING

A View of Eitai Bridge and Tsukuda Island (Eitaibashi Tsukudajima)

from the series *One Hundred Famous Views in Edo* (*Meisho Edo hyakkei*)
published by Uoya Eikichi, 1856–8

signed: *Hiroshige ga*
censorship seal: *aratame*; date seal: Snake 2 (1857/II)
woodblock, *ōban*, 357 x 243 mm
Private Collection, Denmark

This view past one of the piles of Eitai Bridge, shored up with extra timbers on the left, looks south towards the island of Tsukudajima in the Bay of Edo. Built in 1698, Eitai Bridge was the last and the widest bridge over the Sumida River. Behind the bridge a few fishermen are trying to attract fish with blazing torches. They are probably fishing for *shirauo*, a small fish that appeared on the shogun's menu every day; the fishermen of Tsukudajima were in his service.

In early impressions (a) the cartouche is in a uniform pinkish colour and the torches of the fishermen are not only reflected in the water but also cast rays. The setting sun gives the horizon a reddish glow. In later impressions, as here (b), the red glow has been replaced, inexplicably, by a blue one and the torches are printed in red, but do not cast rays on the water. In still later impressions (c) the sky is almost black and both the bridge pile and the boat in the foreground are printed in chestnut brown, giving the scene as a whole an even darker appearance. The title cartouche in these impressions is printed in an even yellow.

REFERENCES: *Ukiyoe taikei*, 16, no. 4 [a]; *Kobijutsu*, 1983, no. 399 [a]; Smith and Poster, 1986, no. 4 [a]; Link, 1991, no. IV-32-A [b]; *Meihin soroimono ukiyoe*, 10, no. 49 [a]; Salamon, 1992, no. 38 [c]; Sakai, 1996, nos. 156 [a], 157 [b]

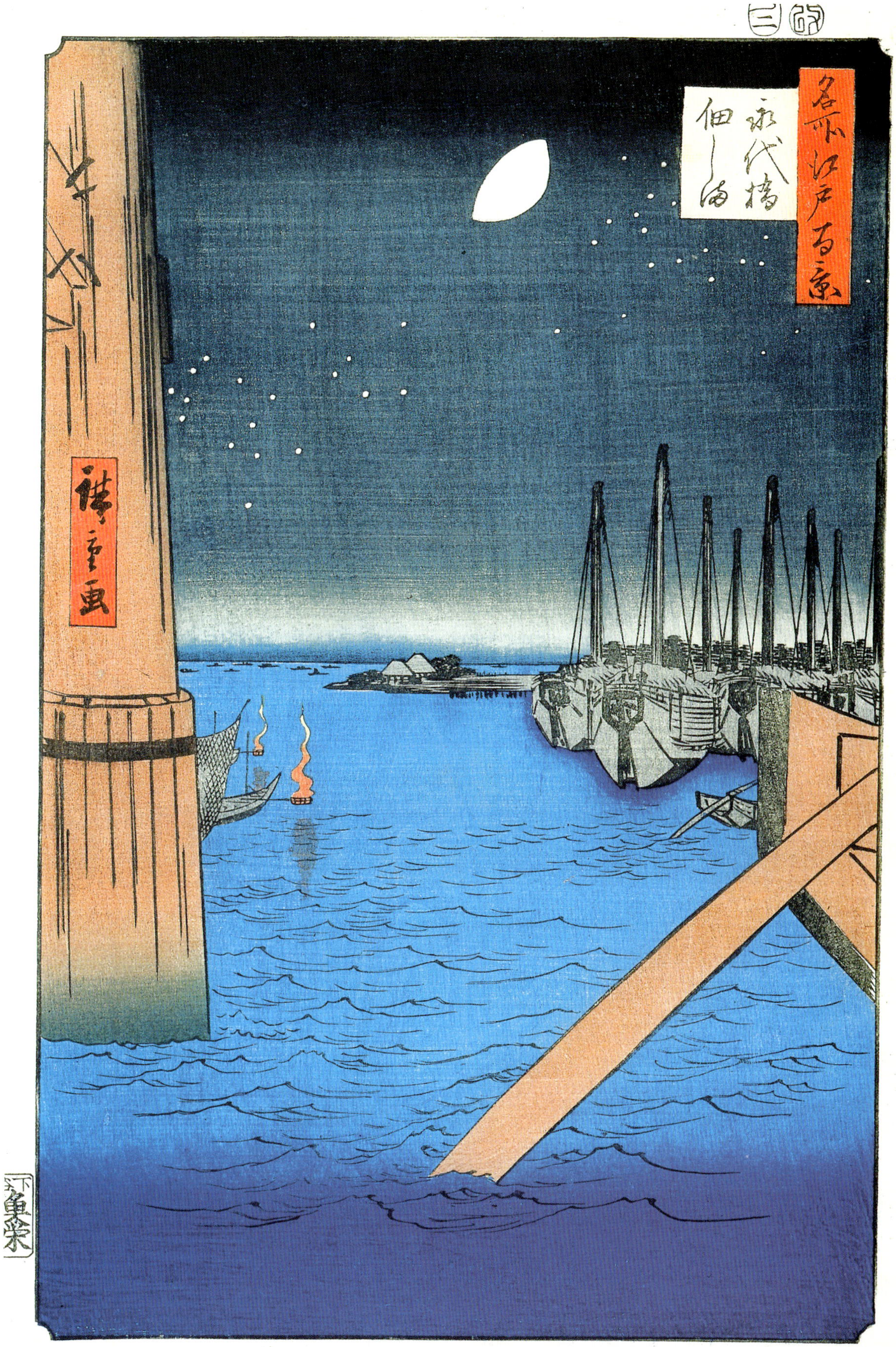
名所江戸百景
永代橋
佃しま
廣重画

100 WINTER VIEW OF A TIMBER-YARD BY A RIVER

The Timber-yard at Fukagawa (Fukagawa kiba)

from the series *One Hundred Famous Views in Edo* (*Meisho Edo hyakkei*)
published by Uoya Eikichi, 1856–8

signed: *Hiroshige hitsu*
censorship seal: *aratame*; date seal: Dragon 8 (1856/VIII)
woodblock, *ōban*, 370 x 251 mm
The Trustees of The British Museum, London (1906.12.20.721)

Honjo Fukagawa was a district on the eastern bank of the Sumida River where, from 1701, some fifteen large timber merchants were assigned a site by the government. At the time this area was only partly cultivated or built up, but rapid supply routes were guaranteed by the Eitai Bridge, constructed over the Sumida in 1698, and by the countless urban waterways. After the major expansion of Edo in the seventeenth century, with the establishment of the government there in 1603 and the first great fire of 1657, wood remained one of the major commodities in the city. Edo was constantly plagued by fires, which often destroyed entire neighbourhoods. The umbrella in the foreground bears the character 'Uo', no doubt an allusion to the publisher of the series, Uoya Eikichi.

The earliest impressions of this snow scene (a) have a light grey to blue sky, with a small cloud just below the birds. The water in the middle of the river is deep blue; the title cartouche is red, white and blue. Such later impressions as that illustrated here (b), in which the sky is still grey, omit the small cloud and the deep blue in the middle of the river. The title cartouche has become red and yellow or red and white. A variant with a somewhat darker sky (c), which emphasises the falling snow, has a title cartouche in red, yellow and green. Once the blocks became worn, the publisher resorted to a familiar ploy: the sky is printed in an even darker shade of grey (d), while the title cartouche is pink / purplish at first, later changing to an even yellow.

REFERENCES: Tanba, 1965, nos. 46–8 [a, c, d]; *Ukiyoe taikei*, 17, no. 106 [a]; Smith and Poster, 1986, no. 106 [a]; *Meihin soroimono ukiyoe*, 10, no. 152 [a]; Copenhagen, 1993, no. 114 [a]; Sakai, 1996, nos. 311–13 [a, c, b]

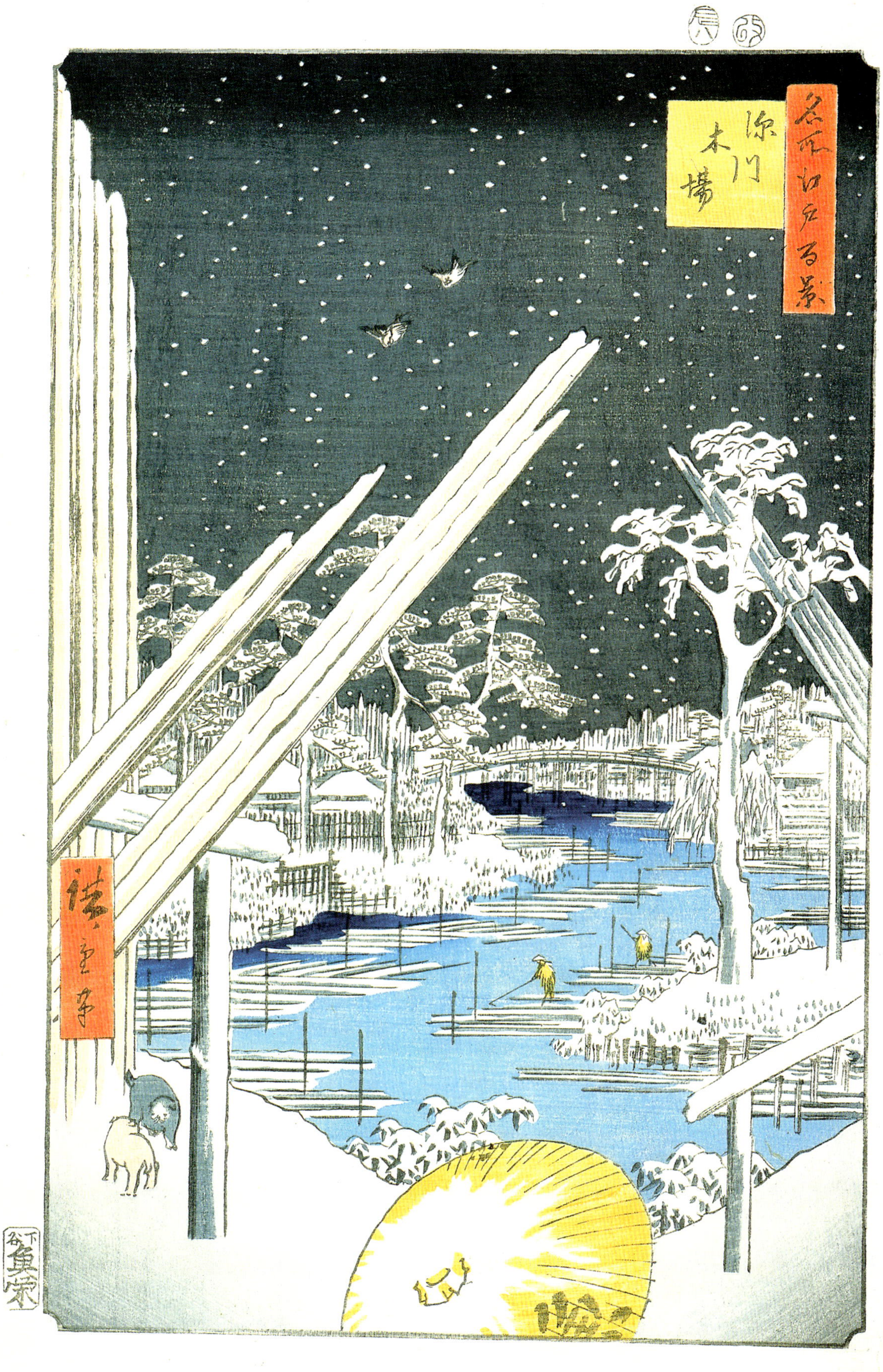
名所江戸百景
深川木場
廣重画

102 VIEW THROUGH A CIRCULAR WINDOW

A View from near Massaki of Suijin Shrine, Uchikawa River and the Village of Sekiya (Massaki atari yori Suijin no mori Uchikawa Sekiya no sato wo miru no zu)

from the series *One Hundred Famous Views in Edo* (*Meisho Edo hyakkei*)
published by Uoya Eikichi, 1856–8

signed: *Hiroshige ga*
censorship seal: *aratame*; date seal: Snake 8 (1857/VIII)
woodblock, *ōban*, 360 x 243 mm
Private Collection, Denmark

North of Asakusa, where the Sumida River bends to the north-east, lies Massaki, famous for its Inari Shrine. This is probably a view from one of the numerous tea-houses and restaurants there. On the far side of the river is the village of Sekiya beside the Uchikawa River, which flows into the Sumida; the gate of the Suijin Shrine can be seen on the right. Hiroshige included a view from Sekiya in this series, with the same Tsukuba Mountains in the background (*Ukiyoe taikei*, 16, no. 35).

The section of round window through which the landscape is seen gives the composition a bold cast; it is almost as if the viewer is a visitor to the restaurant. The plum blossom buds outside show that it is spring. A flowering magnolia can be seen at left in a basket on the inside wall of the restaurant.

In early impressions of this print (a) the title cartouche is in three colours, blue-violet, white and red; later impressions, such as that illustrated here (b), have only two colours, off-white with either red or blue. Otherwise there are only minimal differences between impressions: those with the three-coloured cartouche have a little *bokashi* blue beneath the raft, a detail lacking in the impressions with the cartouche in two colours; and there are variations in the extent to which the deep blue is applied to the river-bank opposite. In very late impressions from heavily worn blocks (c) the title cartouche is green and brown.

REFERENCES: *Ukiyoe taikei*, 16, no. 36 [b]; Smith and Poster, 1986, no. 36 [a]; *Meihin soroimono ukiyoe*, 10, no. 81 [a]; Copenhagen, 1993, no. 123 [b: this impression]; Hori, 1996 [c]; Sakai, 1996, nos. 327 [a], 328 [b]

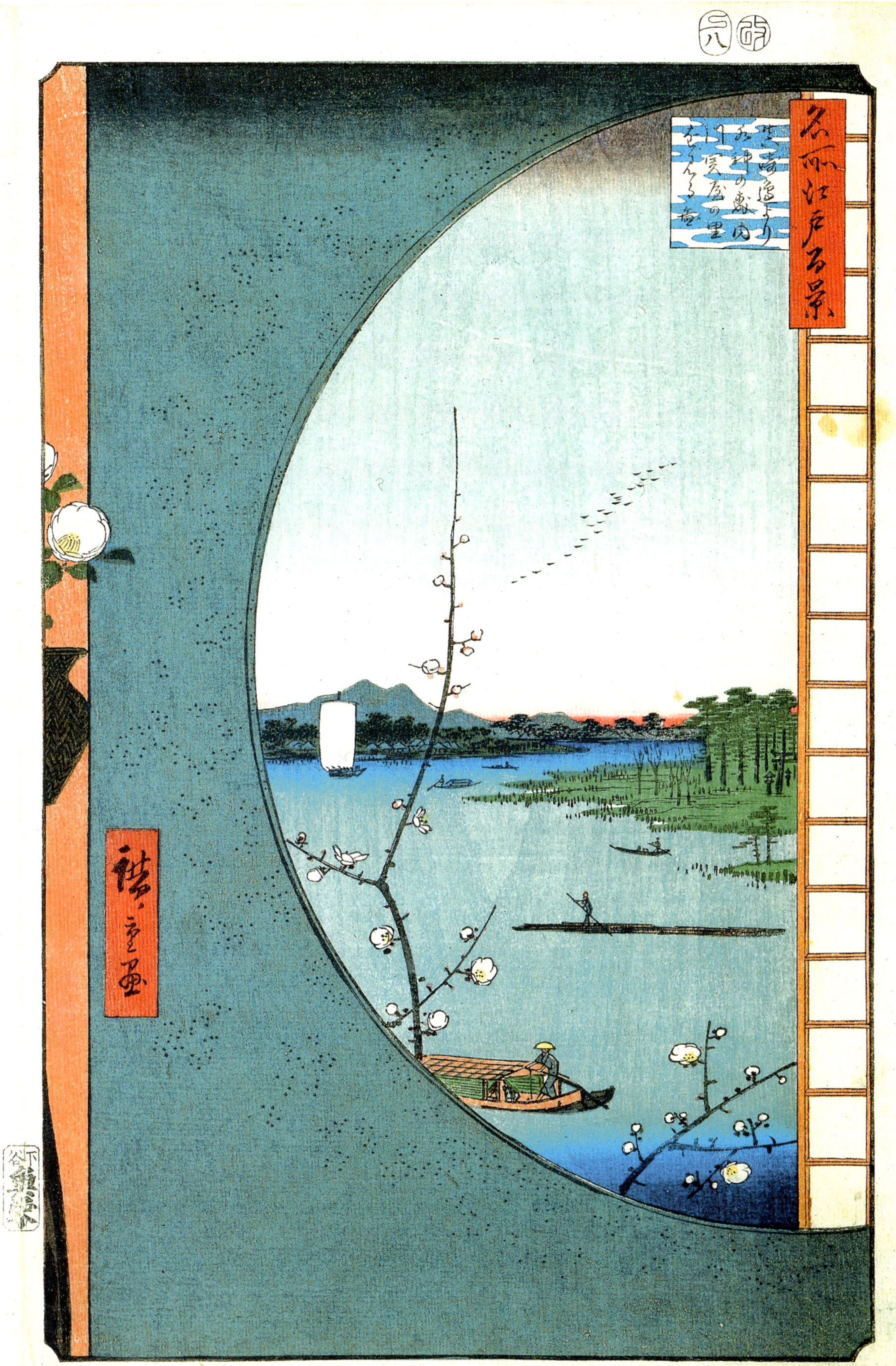

名所江戸百景
廣重画

103 A CUCKOO FLYING OVER THE RIVER

The Komakata Hall and Azuma Bridge (*Komakatadō Azumabashi*)

from the series *One Hundred Famous Views in Edo* (*Meisho Edo hyakkei*)
published by Uoya Eikichi, 1856–8

signed: *Hiroshige ga*
censorship seal: *aratame*; date seal: Snake 1 (1857/I)
woodblock, *ōban*, 363 x 246 mm
The Art Institute of Chicago, Chicago,
The Clarence Buckingham Collection (39.2253)

On the west bank of the Sumida River stood a small temple dedicated to an avatar of the Kannon with the Horse's Head, a god of horses and thus of safe journeys. The building was soon given the name Komakatadō, or Komandō, literally 'Pony Hall'. Its roof is just visible here on the left. A cuckoo, the herald of summer, sweeps through the sky, as at cat. 14 and fig. 4 on p. 22; there are especially close parallels with the latter, an apparently unpublished fan design. The houses of Honjo district can be seen on the far side of the river.

No major changes were made to this image in the course of its printing history. The most notable concern the sky, which is sometimes a summery yellow and shows different patterns of cloud. The most tranquil (a), illustrated here, consists of a very light cloud just below the cuckoo, another below it to the right and a third lower still on the left. A cloud of smoke rises from behind the trees. Occasionally (b), there is a single, somewhat heavy cloud, partly behind or beneath the cuckoo, sometimes even in a sickle-type shape, which looks rather incongruous. Later impressions (c) lack not only the deep blue on the far bank of the river, but also the *bokashi* overprinting on the wood stores in the foreground; the *bokashi* on the roof soon disappears too. In this case the title cartouche is unpatterned, printed in an even yellow or blue. There is also a late variant (d) with a virtually even dark blue sky in which the grain of the wood is heavily, perhaps too heavily, emphasised; the title cartouche is in yellow and green. Peculiar blue clouds suddenly make their appearance on both sides of the sky in still later impressions (e), which show either a yellow and green or a green title cartouche.

REFERENCES: *Ukiyoe taikei*, 16, no. 55 [a]; *Ukiyoe hakka*, 1984, no. 55 [a]; Smith and Poster, 1986, no. 55 [a]; *Meihin soroimono ukiyoe*, 10, nos. 108 [a], 108A [e]; Salamon, 1992, no. 41 [c]; Hori, 1996, no. 62 [d]; Sakai, 1996, nos. 208–11 [a, b, b, e]

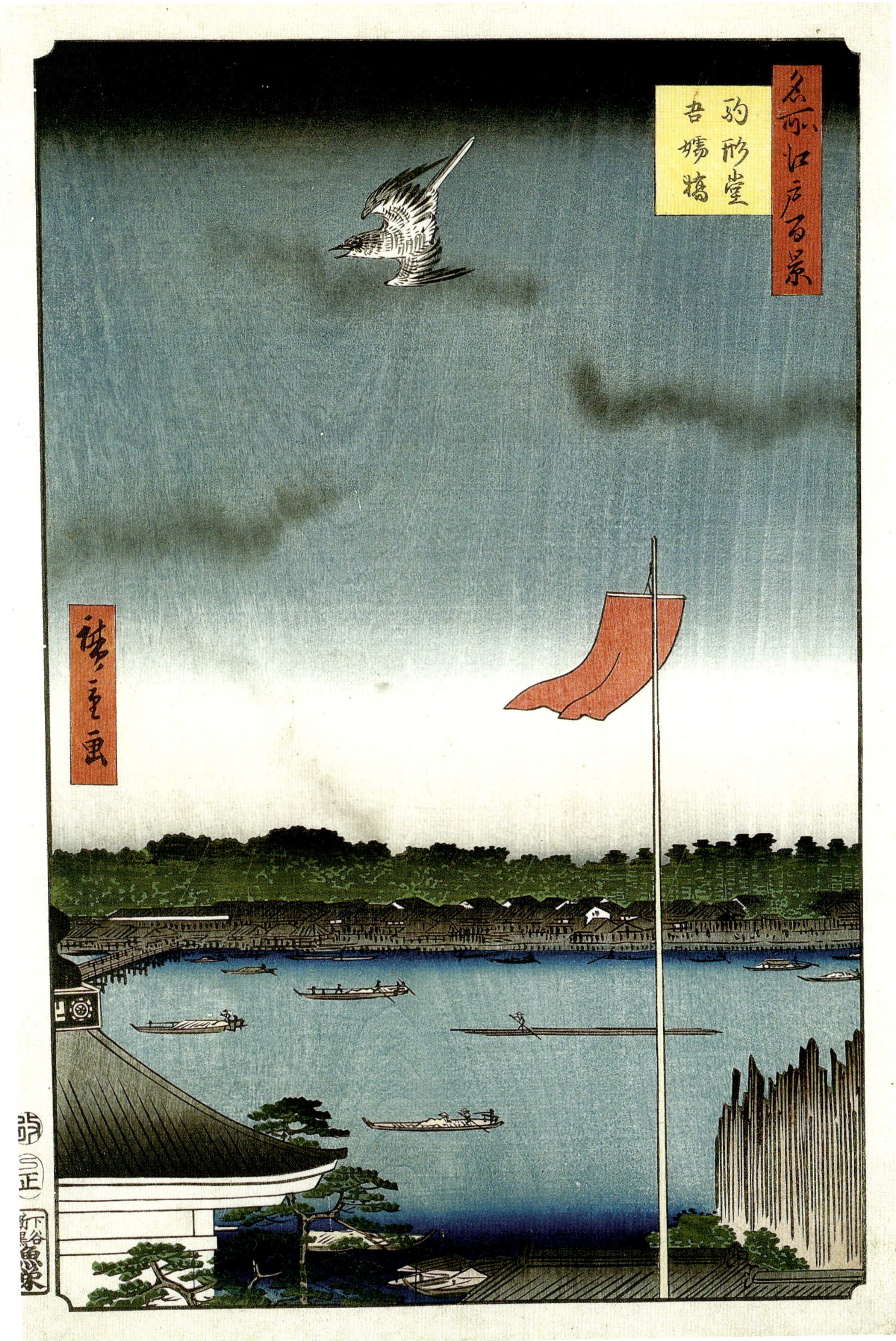
名所江戸百景
駒形堂
吾嬬橋
広重画

104 MOONLIT VIEW OF A RIVER

Kyō Bridge and Bamboo Bank (Kyōbashi Takegashi)

from the series *One Hundred Famous Views in Edo*
(*Meisho Edo hyakkei*)
published by Uoya Eikichi, 1856–8

signed: *Hiroshige ga*
block-cutter: Yokogawa Takejirō (Horitake)
censorship seal: *aratame*; date seal: Snake 12 (1857/XII)
woodblock, *ōban*, 375 x 252 mm
The Metropolitan Museum of Art, New York, The Howard Mansfield Collection, Purchase, Rogers Fund, 1936 (JP2521)

Kyōbashi River flowed from the castle of the shogun to the Sumida River. Travellers taking the Tōkaidō Road from Nihonbashi to Kyoto had to cross it, at Kyō Bridge. This owes its name to its shape, which recalls the large bridge at Sanjō in Kyoto. A large bamboo storage depot can be seen behind the bridge, on the left. This print, with the full moon so typical of Hiroshige, was naturally grouped under Autumn in the list of contents later compiled for the series. The block-cutter Yokogawa Takejirō incorporated his trademark in the red lantern held by the man just left of centre on the bridge.

Early impressions of this print, such as that illustrated here (a), are notable for an extensive, subtle use of *bokashi*: downwards from the upper edge of the print, around the moon, above the bridge, along the top of the wood in storage on the left, at the horizon, along the left bank, on the cargo carried by the boat in the foreground, upwards from the bridge piles and up into the water from the lower edge of the sheet. The only *bokashi* left in later impressions, in which the three-coloured title cartouche is replaced by one in yellow and orange, is that extending upwards from the bridge piles and that either at the level of the boat (b) or extending from the lower edge of the sheet right up to the boat (c).

REFERENCES: Narazaki, 1975, no. 18 [a]; *Ukiyoe taikei*, 17, no. 76 [a]; Smith and Poster, 1986, no. 76 [a]; Link, 1991, no. IV-32-1 [a]; *Meihin soroimono ukiyoe*, 10, no. 122 [a]; Sakai, 1996, nos. 199 [a], 200 [b]

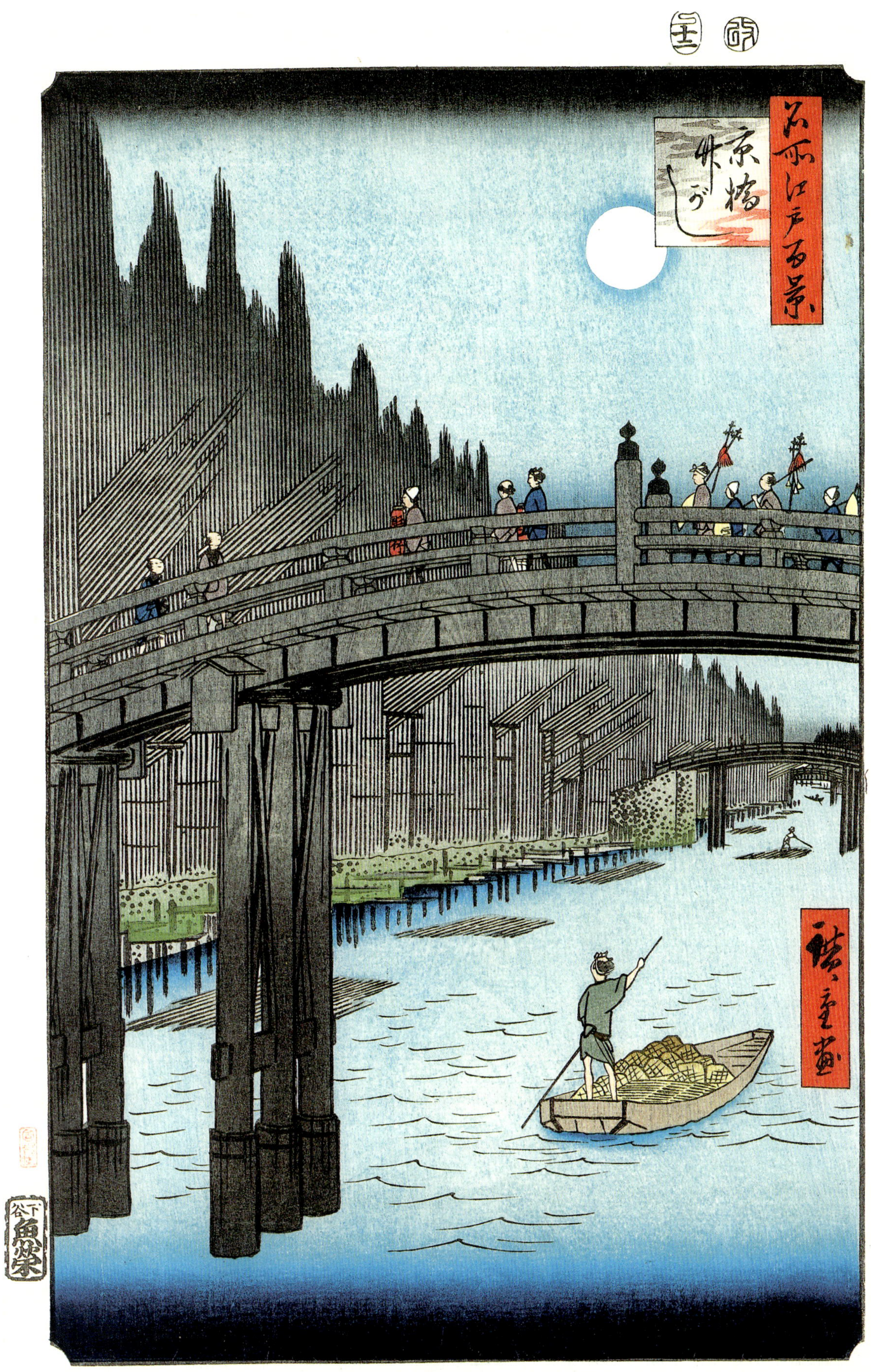
名所江戸百景
京橋
竹がし
廣重画

105 TEMPLE PRECINCT IN THE SNOW

Kinryūzan Temple at Asakusa (*Asakusa Kinryuzan*)

from the series *One Hundred Famous Views in Edo* (*Meisho Edo hyakkei*)
published by Uoya Eikichi, 1856–8

signed: *Hiroshige hitsu*
censorship seal: *aratame*; date seal: Dragon 7 (1856/VII)
woodblock, *ōban*, 368 x 252 mm
Honolulu Academy of Arts, Honolulu,
Gift of James A. Michener, 1991 (22.794)

In the northern part of Edo, not far from the Sumida River, the theatre street (cat. 98) and the Yoshiwara (cat. 8), was a popular temple, the Sensōji, often called Kinryūzan after the hill on which it was situated. The view in this print is from the Kaminarimon gateway, with its large hanging lantern, onto the snow-laden temple precincts. Directly facing the viewer is the Niōmon, a second gateway. The pagoda is on the right (it was rebuilt on the other side after having been destroyed during the Second World War).

There are few striking differences between early and late impressions of this print. Early impressions (a) are preferable because of the clean lines and, if they are well preserved, the fine shading in the grey sky, the brightness of the falling snow and the faint blue tint of the snow on the path leading to the temple. Slightly later impressions (b), such as that illustrated here, sometimes have a blue sky. On some sheets the lantern shows signs of oxidation.

REFERENCES: Suzuki, 1975, p. 29 [a]; *Ukiyoe taikei*, 11, no. 49, and 17, no. 99 [both a]; *Ukiyoe hakka*, 1984, no. 58 [a]; Smith and Poster, 1986, no. 99 [a]; *Meihin soroimono ukiyoe*, 10, no. 145 [a]; Sakai, 1996, nos. 130 [a], 132 [b]

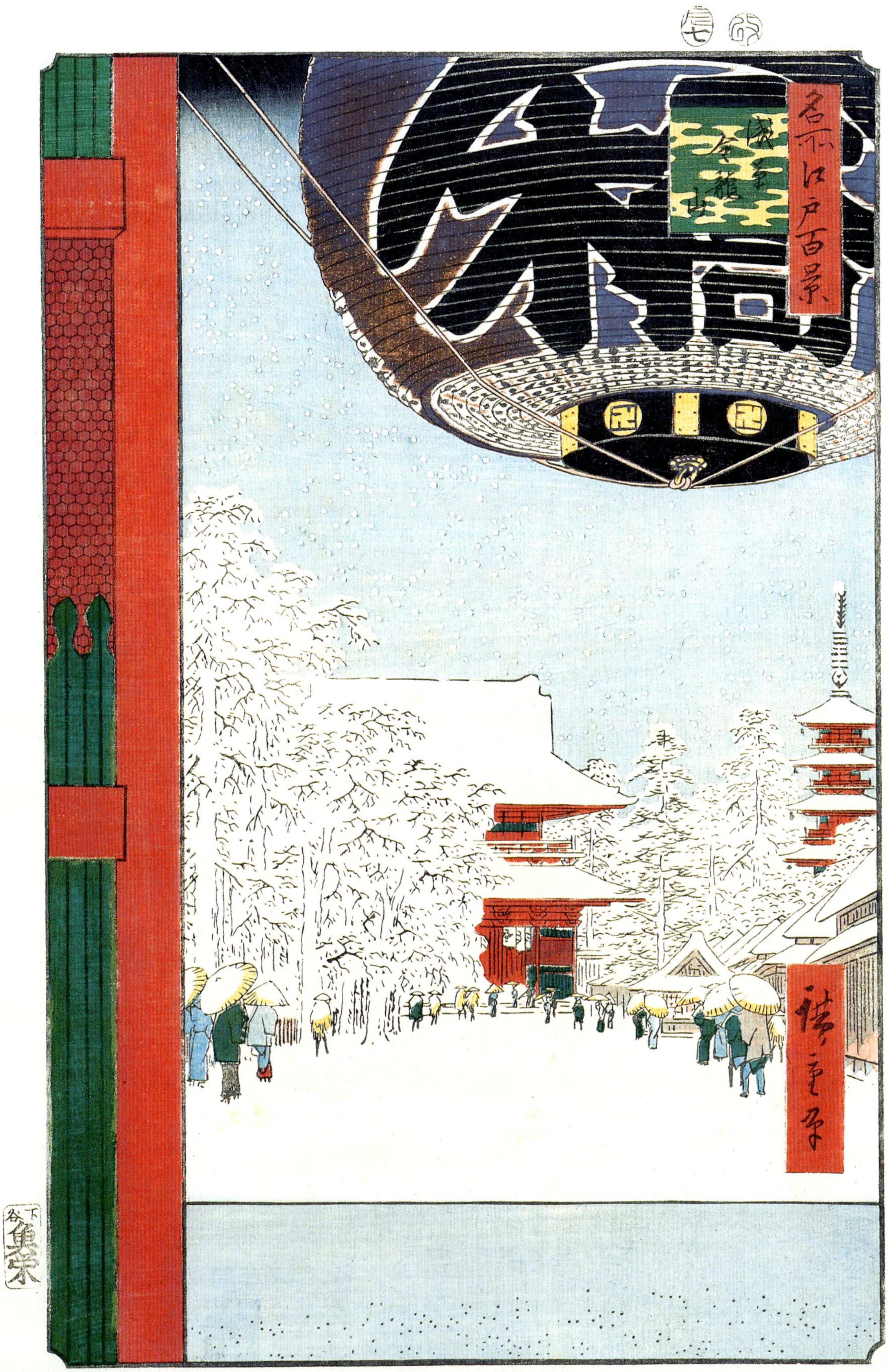
名所江戸百景
浅草金龍山
廣重画

106 DYED CLOTH HANGING TO DRY

Dyers' Street in Kanda (Kanda Konyachō)

from the series *One Hundred Famous Views in Edo (Meisho Edo hyakkei)*
published by Uoya Eikichi, 1856–8

signed: *Hiroshige ga*
censorship seal: *aratame*; date seal: Snake 11 (1857/XI)
woodblock, *ōban*, 354 x 247 mm
Collection Pulverer, Cologne

When Tokugawa Ieyasu established Edo as the seat of his central government in 1603, the various professional groups settled in the surrounding neighbourhoods. The Kanda district was primarily inhabited by artisans who depended on the government and the families of the warrior aristocracy for a portion of their income. It included a street for cloth dyers, Konya Street, depicted here. The strips of dyed cloth are hung to dry in the autumn wind. Behind the castle of the shogun, which is encircled by trees, stands Mount Fuji. Some of the strips of cloth are printed with the *Hiro* seal that Hiroshige used in his later period and with the character '*Uo*', the first sign of the name of the publisher of the series, Uoya Eikichi, as a form of advertisement for both designer and publisher.

The main variations in impressions of this print are in the blue *bokashi* on the strips of cloth. Sometimes, as here (a), the transitions are gradual, while in later impressions (b) the printer used the much simpler method of printing some strips entirely in blue and those that had been brown in light blue.

REFERENCES: *Ukiyoe taikei*, 17, no. 75 [a]; Smith and Poster, 1986, no. 75 [a]; *Meihin soroimono ukiyoe*, 10, no. 121 [a]; Hori, 1996, no. 75 [b]; Sakai, 1996, no. 194 [a]

76.

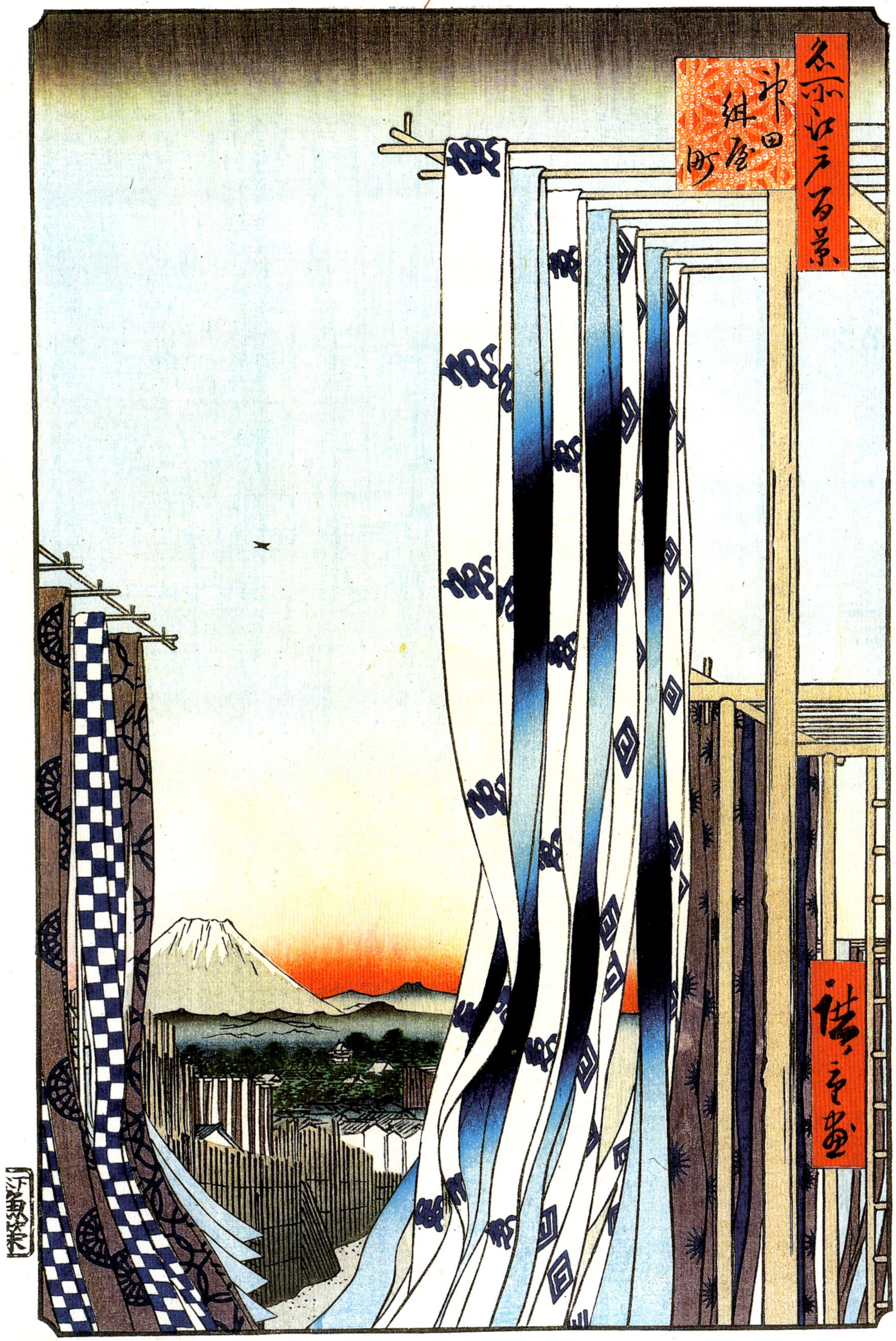

IMAGES OF MIST, RAIN, SNOW AND MOONLIGHT

CAT. 107–26

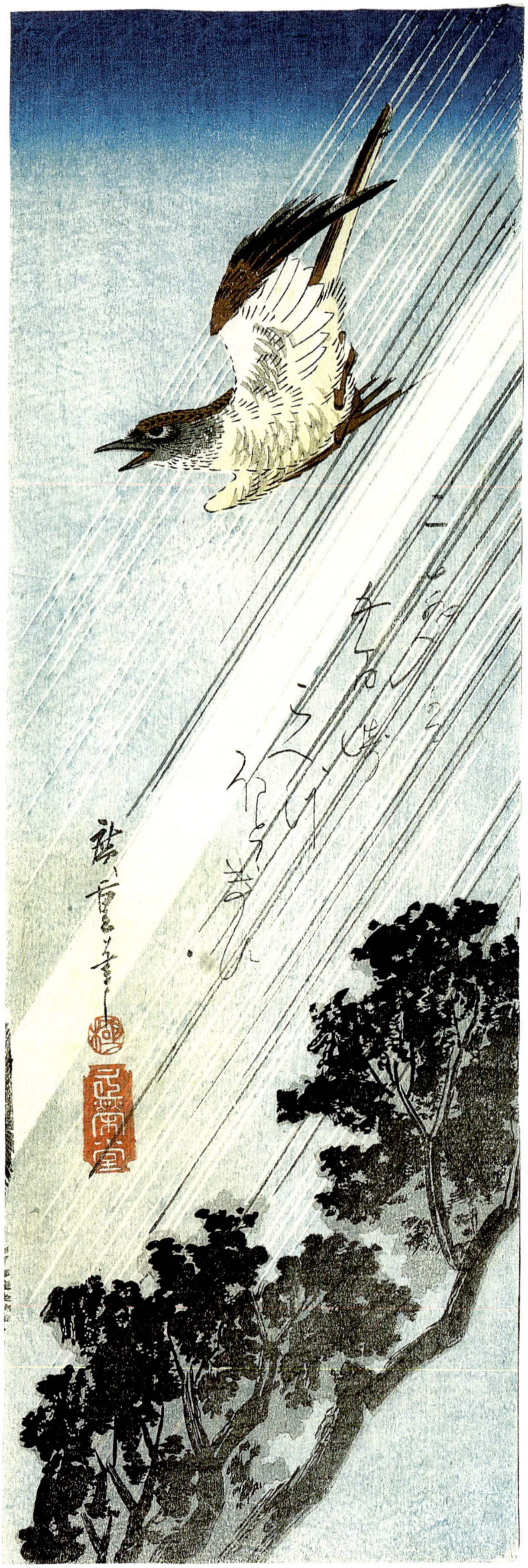

107 CUCKOO IN THE RAIN

from a group of more than forty prints of bird and flower subjects published by Kawaguchiya Shōzō (Shōeidō), *c.* 1832

signed: *Hiroshige hitsu*
censorship seal: *kiwame*
woodblock, *chūtanzakuban*, 376 x 127 mm (margin at top)
The Museum of Art, Rhode Island School of Design, Providence, Gift of Mrs John D. Rockefeller, Jr. (34.247)

A cuckoo flies over a tree during a heavy summer downpour. The sky is blue, printed in *bokashi* from the upper edge of the image. An unsigned *haiku* poem above the leaves of the tree reads:

Futagoe wa
iosaki koetsu
hototogisu

A twofold cry can be heard over five hundred capes—
the cuckoo

The characters that translate literally as 'five hundred' also mean simply 'numerous' or 'a multitude'.

Part of *Owl on a Pine Branch* (cat. 5) is visible at the left-hand edge of *Cuckoo in the Rain*, indicating that both designs were printed from the same block. *Cuckoo in the Rain* bears both the trademark of the publisher, Shōeidō, and the *kiwame* censorship seal. The artist's seal, which he does not appear to have used in this form after 1832, suggests that both prints were issued earlier than most of those published in this format by Kawaguchiya Shōzō.

REFERENCES: Bogel and Goldman, 1988, no. 66 [this impression]; Kobayashi, 1990, no. 95 [this impression]; Ōkubo, 1992, no. 24

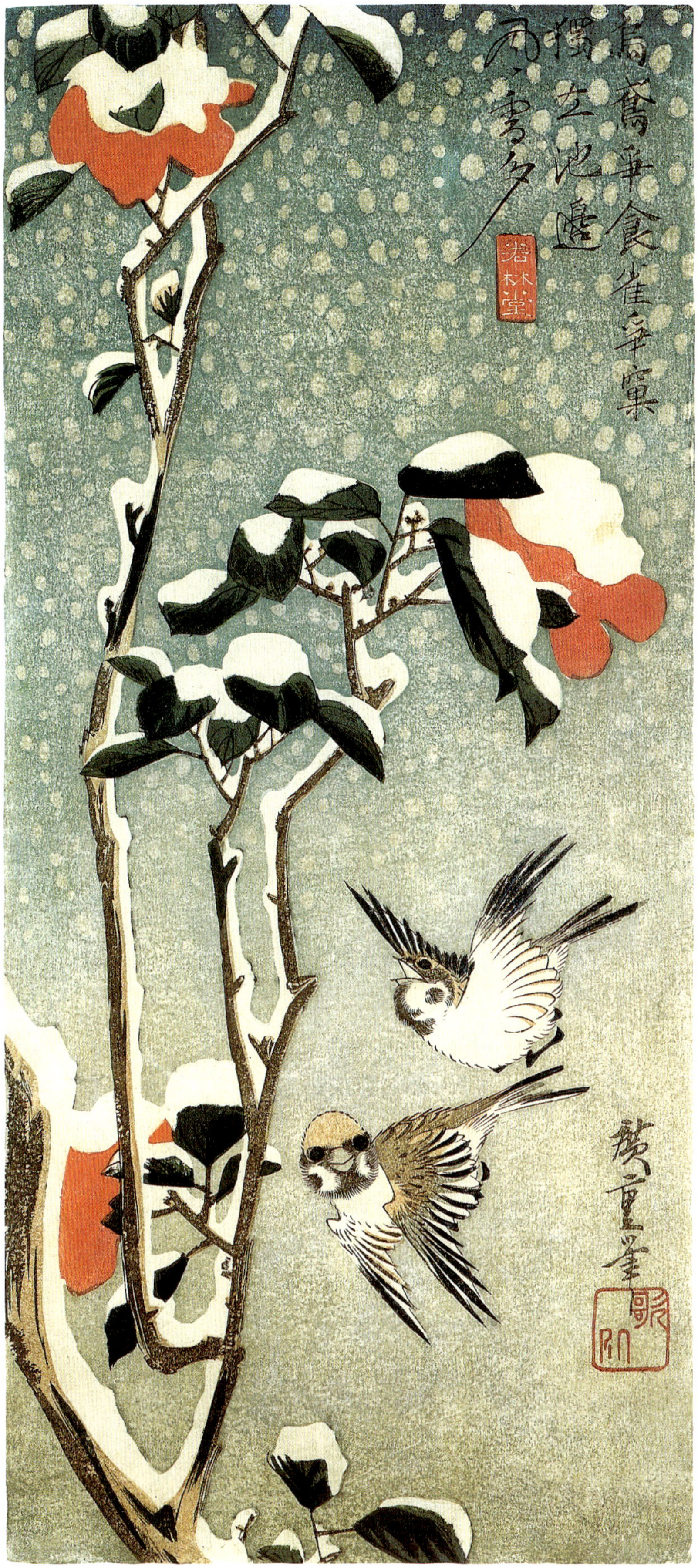

108 SPARROWS AND CAMELLIA IN A SNOWSTORM

from a group of more than twenty prints of bird and flower subjects published by Wakasaya Yoichi (Jakurindō), *c.* 1832–5

signed: *Hiroshige hitsu*, with seal: *Utagawa*
censorship seal: *kiwame*
woodblock, *ōtanzakuban*, 371 x 167 mm
The Mann Collection, Highland Park, Illinois

Two sparrows flutter past a camellia as snow falls, some of it already collected on the flowers and leaves of the camellia. The blue of the sky changes below to dull grey. At upper right is an unsigned Chinese poem, identified by Suzuki (1970) as the opening lines of *Inquiry of a Stork* by Hakurakuten (772–846):

> Crows and storks fight over something to eat
> and sparrows over where to sleep,
> You stand there all alone by the pond
> the wind blows and snow piles up.

A variant (b) of this print exists in which the sky is printed in a uniform grey without snowflakes and the branch of the camellia is printed in grey instead of brown. Otherwise, there are no striking differences and this variant bears the same publisher's trademark. Later, however, the blocks were apparently acquired by Sanoya Kihei, who issued a reprint (c) with a grey sky but with the snowflakes and a slightly different colour scheme. He placed his publisher's trademark in the rectangle that Wakasaya Yoichi had used before him, but surrounded by a large jar-shaped cartouche.

Hiroshige often returned to this theme later in his career, as in two prints in the *chūtanzaku* format, one published by Kawaguchiya Shōzō (Kobayashi, 1990, no. 279) and the other, dating from 1854, by Tsutaya Kichizō (ibid., no. 286), as well as in an anonymously published print in the same format (ibid., no. 273).

REFERENCES: Tanba, 1965, no. 84 [c]; *Ukiyoe taikei*, 11, no. 91 [a]; Narazaki, 1975, no. 162 [b]; Bogel and Goldman, 1988, nos. 10 [b], 11 [a]; Kobayashi, 1990, nos. 70 [b], 71 [a]; Ōkubo, 1992, no. 18; Copenhagen, 1993, no. 53 [c]

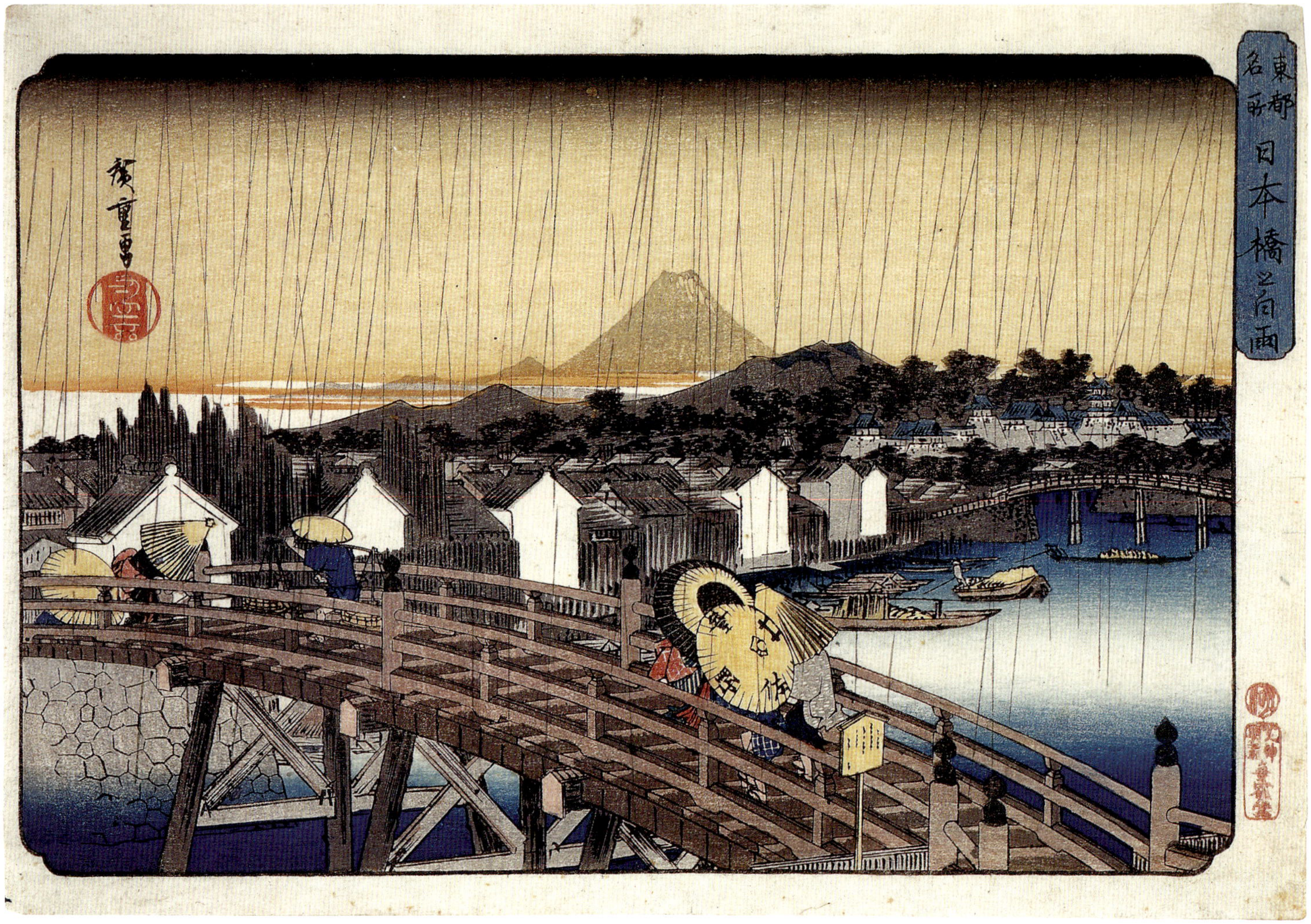

109 A BRIDGE IN THE RAIN

Sudden Rain over Nihon Bridge (*Nihonbashi no hakuu*)

from the series *Famous Views in the Eastern Capital* (*Tōto meisho*)
published by Sanoya Kihei (Kikakudō), *c.* 1832

signed: *Hiroshige ga*, with seal: *Ichiryūsai*
censorship seal: *kiwame*
woodblock, *ōban*, 254 x 365 mm
Honolulu Academy of Arts, Honolulu,
Gift of James A. Michener, 1991 (23.603)

People, some with umbrellas, are crossing Nihon Bridge as a gentle rain falls. The next bridge, Ichikoku, can be seen to the right, with the castle of the shogun behind it and Mount Fuji on the horizon. It is interesting to compare this composition with cat. 15, a view of Nihon Bridge in the snow that offers an almost identical prospect of the castle and Mount Fuji, but from the right bank.

It is a summer shower. The sky is yellowish and the black band along the upper edge of the print indicates the approach of evening. The setting sun has already coloured the horizon red. The title cartouche in this early impression is blue; in later impressions it is yellow.

REFERENCES: Tanba, 1965, no. 26; Suzuki, 1970, no. 10; Sakai, 1996, no. 499

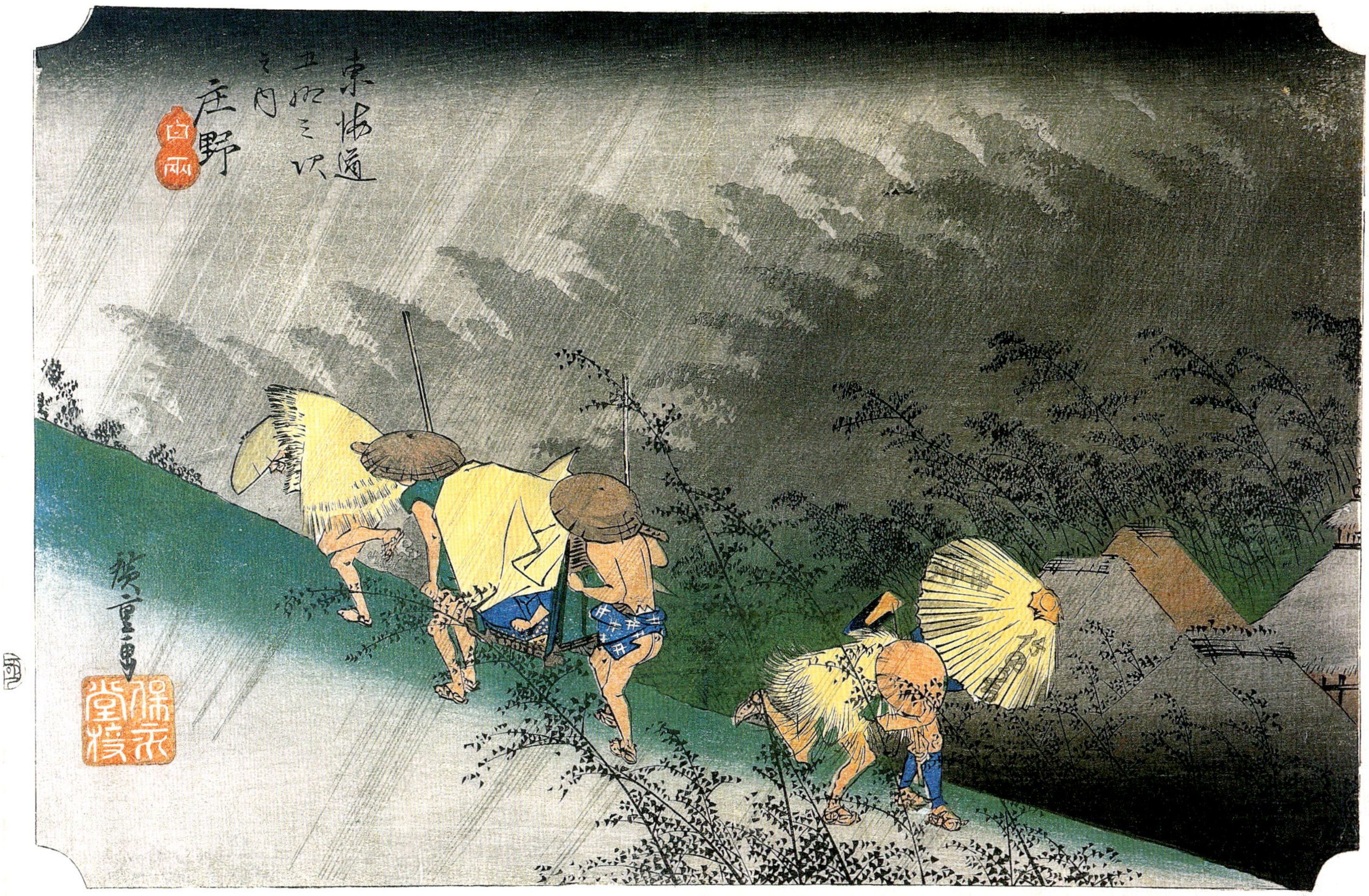

110 TRAVELLERS SURPRISED BY SUDDEN RAIN

Shōno—Sudden Rain (Shōno—Hakuu)

from the series *The Fifty-three Stations of the Tōkaidō Road* (*Tōkaidō gojūsan tsugi no uchi*)
published by Takenouchi Magohachi (Hōeidō), *c.* 1831–4

signed: *Hiroshige ga*
censorship seal: *kiwame*
woodblock, *ōban*, 241 x 363 mm
Collection Pulverer, Cologne

The same print as at cat. 25, but a later impression, in which the rain and the late hour receive more emphasis. This print underwent various transformations. While the rows of bamboo are printed uniformly in three different shades of grey in the earliest impressions, the rain is much more to the fore here and it falls in dark, distinct squalls. This usually required the crests of the two rows of bamboo to be printed in heavy black *bokashi* if they were to stand out properly. In our impression (a), however, the printer has managed to avoid this and has even included black *bokashi* in front of the houses and green *bokashi* behind them. Often (b) these refinements are lacking in impressions that place more emphasis on the rain.

REFERENCES: Tanba, 1965, no. 56 [a]; Izzard, 1983, nos. 17b, c [b], 17d, e [a]; Link, 1991, no. I-1-Ab [b]; Copenhagen, 1993, no. 77 [b]; Forrer, 1994, G450 [a]

113 DAIMYŌ PROCESSION CROSSING A BRIDGE

Tsuchiyama—Spring Rain (*Tsuchiyama—Haru no ame*)

from the series *The Fifty-three Stations of the Tōkaidō Road* (*Tōkaidō gojūsan tsugi no uchi*)
published by Takenouchi Magohachi (Hōeidō), *c.* 1831–4

signed: *Hiroshige ga*
censorship seal: *kiwame*
woodblock, *ōban*, 243 x 359 mm
The Metropolitan Museum of Art, New York,
Rogers Fund (JP520)

The procession of a *daimyō* crosses a wooden bridge over a raging torrent during a heavy downpour. The bridge is probably the Tamura; the shrine that can be seen through the trees would then be the Tamura Daimyōjin.

In early impressions of this print (a) the trees on the left are printed, as here, in six different shades, ranging from pinkish-brown at the front to grey at the rear. In slightly later impressions (b) three of the trees are printed in grey, two in ochre and one still with a pinkish tinge. The rain in subsequent impressions is printed in far darker tones. Later still (c), the palette changes considerably: most of the trees are predominantly brown, as are the river-banks, and the man at the head of the procession is dressed in blue instead of green.

REFERENCES: Narazaki, 1960, no. 36 [a]; *Ukiyoe taikei*, 14, no. 50 [a]; *Kobijutsu*, 1983, no. 79 [b]; Shiraishi, 1988, p. 123 [b]; *Meihin soroimono ukiyoe*, 11, no. 50 [a]

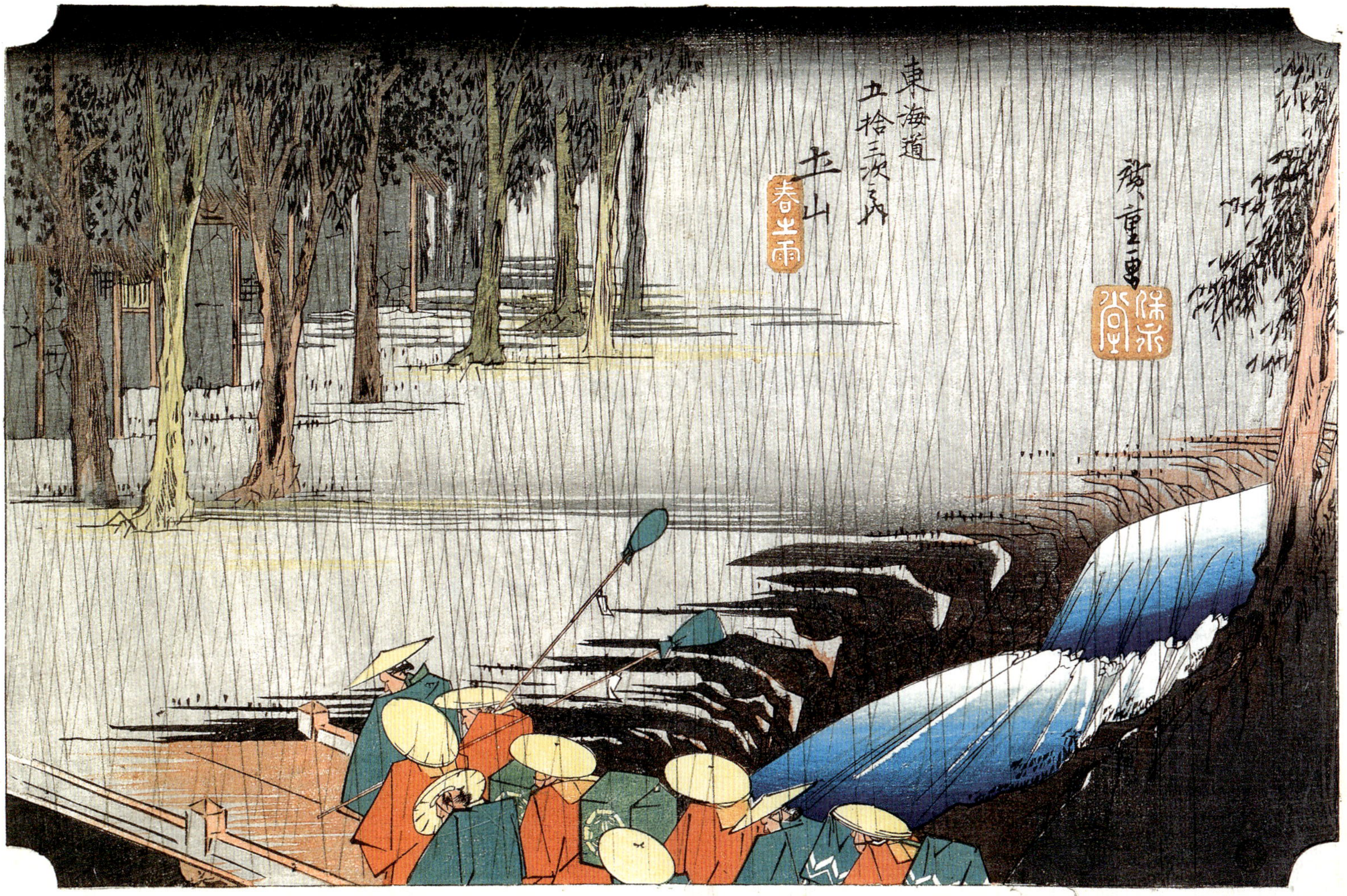
東海道
五拾三次之内
土山
春之雨
廣重画
保永堂

114 A MAN ON HORSEBACK IN THE SNOW

Fujikawa

from the series *The Fifty-three Stations of the Tōkaidō Road* (*Tōkaidō gojūsan tsugi*), the so-called *Kyōka Tōkaidō*
published by Sanoya Kihei (Kikakudō), *c.* 1839–40

signed: *Hiroshige ga*
censorship seal: *kiwame*
woodblock, *chūban*, 167 x 229 mm
Honolulu Academy of Arts, Honolulu,
Gift of James A. Michener, 1992 (22.430)

The village depicted here lies between the stations of Akasaka and Fujikawa on the Tōkaidō Road, where the thoroughfare follows a valley flanked by mountains. The *kyōka* poem on the print reads:

Yukisugiru
tabibito tomete
yadohiki no
sode ni matsu haru
Fujikawa no eki

The traveller has gone too far
but halts when the hotel runner
grasps him by the sleeve
at Fujikawa station

Tokiwaen Shigekyō.

Hiroshige's illustration for the station of Fujikawa in the vertical Tōkaidō series of 1855 (Shiraishi, 1988, p. 96) has a very similar view—a path through a valley in the snow, a row of houses in the distance and a man on horseback in the foreground—but with a river on the left. Hiroshige chose almost the same spot, although seen from a different angle, for Fujikawa in the album *Tōkaidō fūkei zue*. The illustration for the station of Ishiyakushi in the so-called *Gyōsho Tōkaidō* of *c.* 1841–2 (Shiraishi, 1988, p. 111) and that for the station of Ōi in the Kisokaidō series (cat. 117) both feature a close-up of the man on horseback in the snow.

REFERENCE: Shiraishi, 1988, p. 97

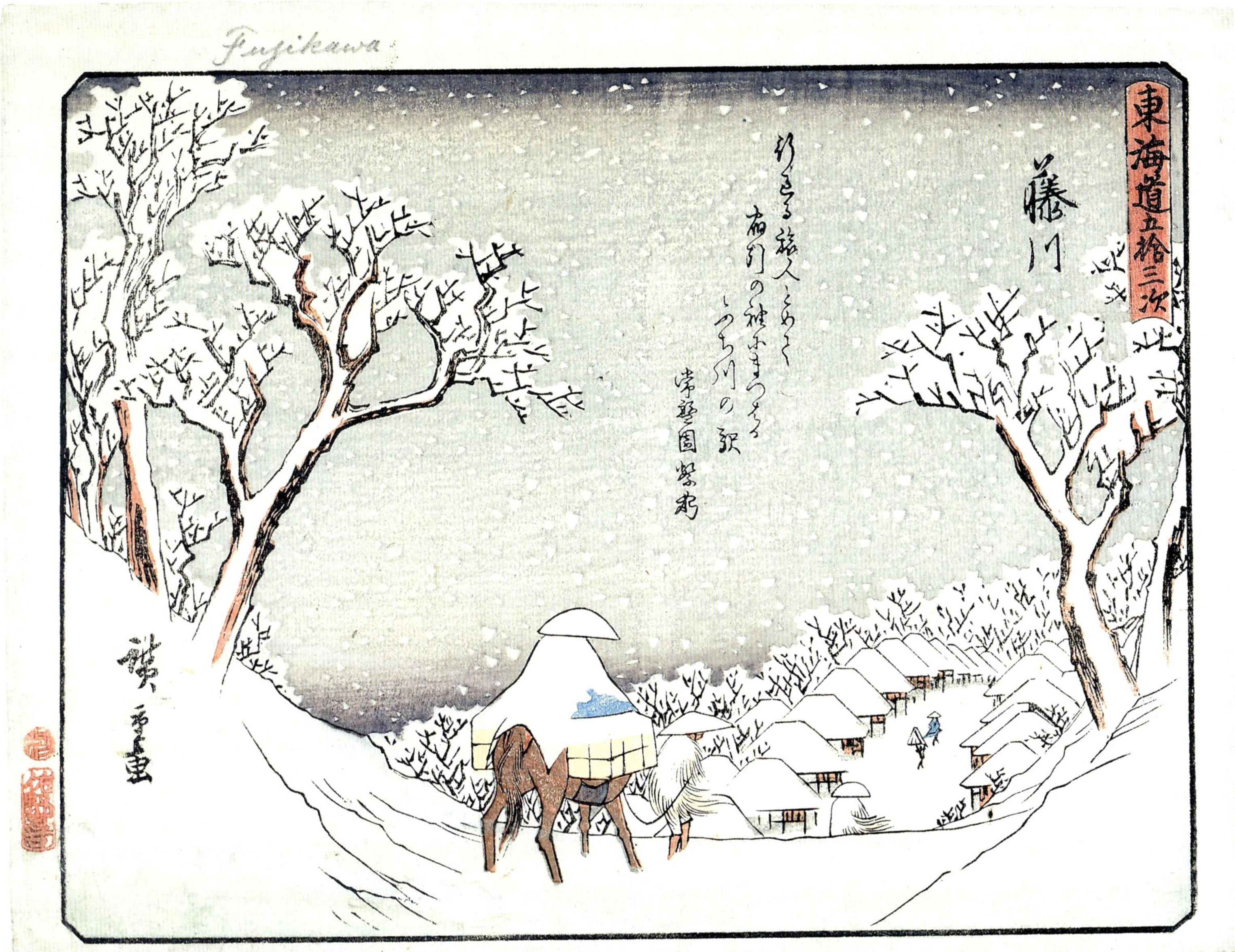
Fujikawa
東海道五拾三次
藤川
廣重

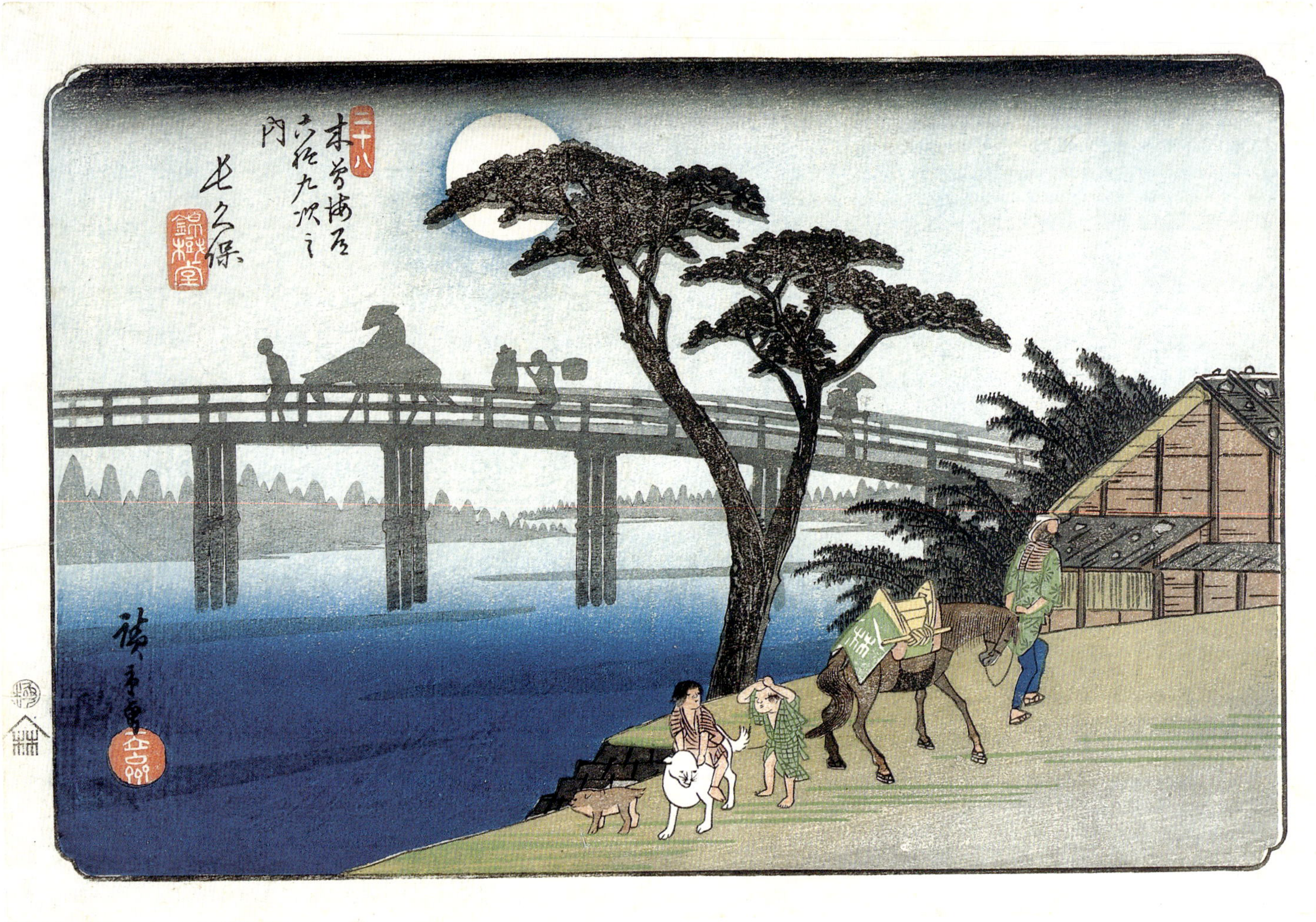

115 MAN ON HORSEBACK CROSSING A BRIDGE

Nagakubo—No. 28

from the series *The Sixty-nine Stations of the Kisokaidō Road* (*Kisokaidō rokujūkyūtsugi no uchi*)
published by Iseya Rihei (Kinjudō), *c.* 1834–42

signed: *Hiroshige ga*
censorship seal: *kiwame*
woodblock, *ōban*, 255 x 378 mm
Honolulu Academy of Arts, Honolulu,
Gift of Mrs Charles Montague Cooke, 1934 (10.143)

The same print as at cat. 37, in what appears to be the earliest state (a), without the mountains in the distance and with an appreciably lighter sky. The only *bokashi* is in the blue around the moon. The red seals in this, as in all impressions that lack the mountains, are still very sharply printed. This state is more convincing than the later ones, since the addition of the mountain, which appears to be floating in the sky, upsets the balance of the composition. In what may be an intermediate state (b), the mountains have been added, but the railing on the other side of the bridge has been omitted. Here the red seals are still relatively sharp. The dominant tone is blue.

REFERENCES: Izzard, 1983, no. 39 [b]; Link, 1991, no. II-1-E [a]; Forrer, 1994, G462 [a]

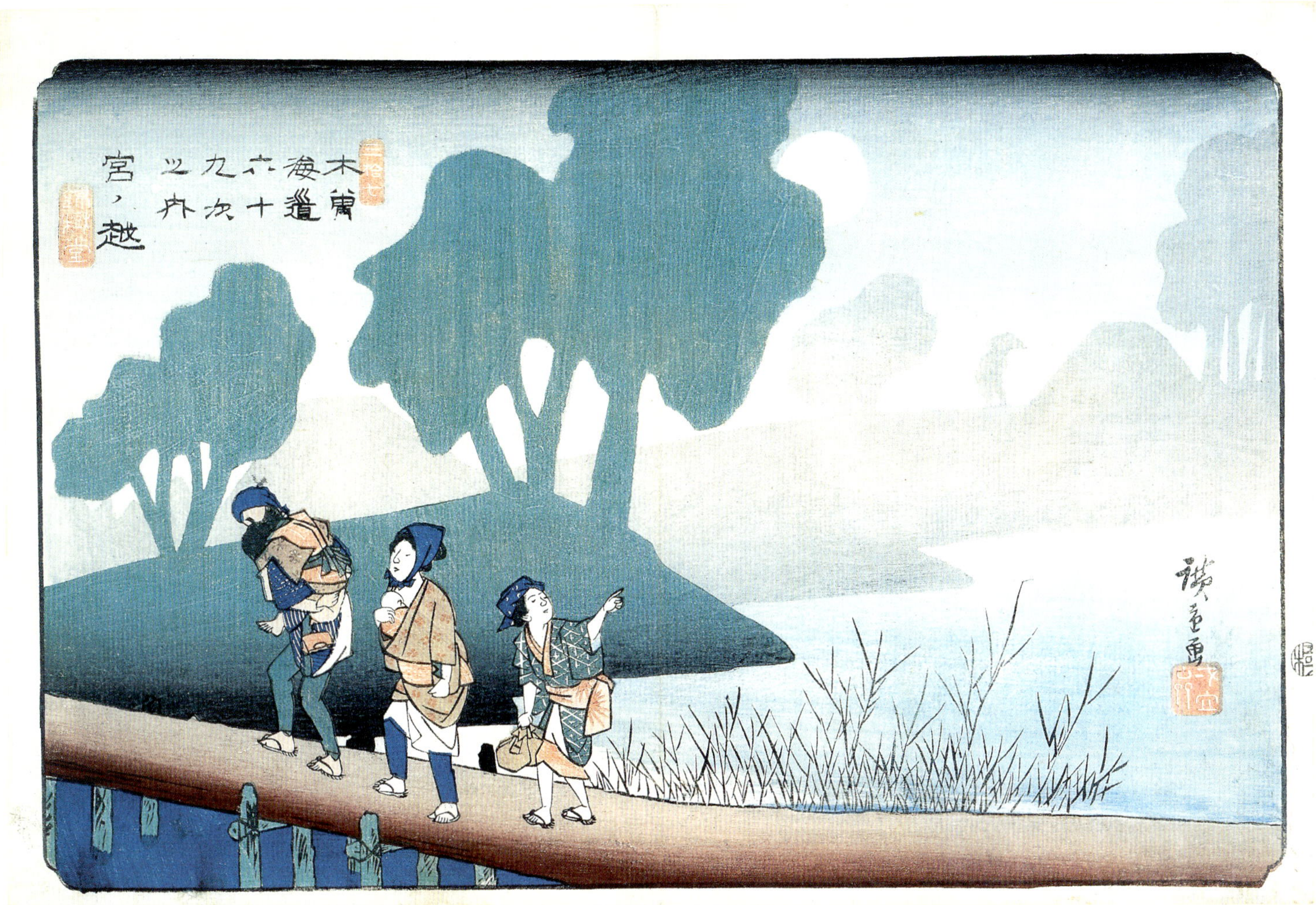

116 A FAMILY IN A MISTY LANDSCAPE

Miyanokoshi—No. 37

from the series *The Sixty-nine Stations of the Kisokaidō Road* (*Kisokaidō rokujūkyūtsugi no uchi*)
published by Iseya Rihei (Kinjudō), *c.* 1834–42

signed: *Hiroshige ga*
censorship seal: *kiwame*
woodblock, *ōban*, 244 x 368 mm
Honolulu Academy of Arts, Honolulu,
Gift of James A. Michener, 1970 (15.632)

A man crosses a small bridge carrying a child on his back. He is followed by a woman with a baby and, behind them, is a girl with a bundle in her hand. Reeds are clearly visible beside the bridge, but the heavy mist has already rendered some of the trees beside the river-bank no more than silhouettes, completely lacking in detail, as are the roof and the walking man.

This print was probably originally intended as a misty scene at dusk, the time of day indicated by the band of dark *bokashi* extending down from the upper edge of the print. If this supposition is correct, the man would have been silhouetted against a blue sky. The trees in this impression (a) are still green, the water is blue and the family in the foreground is clearly defined. In later impressions (b) the mist thickens, the trees are printed in grey and the brown *bokashi* on the bridge is omitted.

REFERENCES: Suzuki, 1970, no. 26 [a]; Yoshida, 1973, no. 6 [a]; Narazaki, 1975, no. 8 [a]; *Ukiyoe taikei*, 11, no. 23 [a], and 15, no. 37 [a]; *Kobijutsu*, 1983, no. 231 [a]; Nagata, 1986, no. 178 [a]; Link, 1991, nos. II-1-H [a: this impression], II-1-I [b]; *Meihin soroimono ukiyoe*, 11, no. 90 [a]; Forrer, 1994, G464 [b]

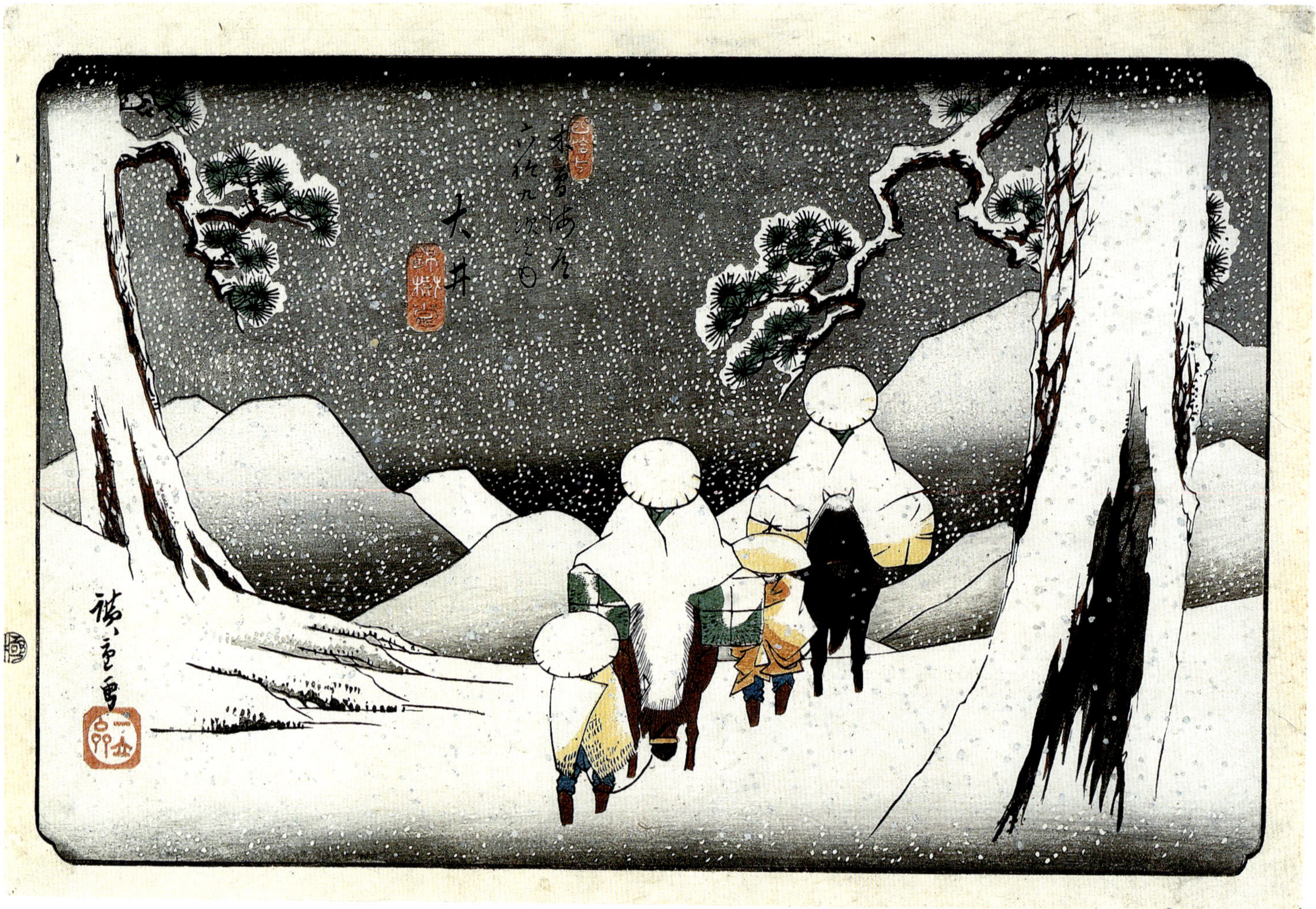

117 TRAVELLERS ON HORSEBACK IN THE SNOW

Ōi—No. 47

from the series *The Sixty-nine Stations of the Kisokaidō Road* (*Kisokaidō rokujūkyūtsugi no uchi*)
published by Iseya Rihei (Kinjudō), *c.* 1834–42

signed: *Hiroshige ga*, with seal: *Ichiryūsai*
woodblock, *ōban*, 248 x 376 mm
The Mann Collection, Highland Park, Illinois

Travellers pass through the mountains in a desolate, snow-covered landscape. The only other sign of life are the emerging pine needles. The feet of the footmen and horses are completely buried in the snow.

This print is found in a variety of tones. The sky may be lighter (a) or darker (b). The *bokashi*, however, is always applied from the upper edge of the print and from the horizon behind the mountains, as well as on the mountains themselves from the bottom upwards. The grey block appears to have been damaged early on: a small white line has usually remained unprinted along the lower edge beneath the border of the path on the left.

REFERENCES: Narazaki, 1964, no. 72 [a]; Tanba, 1965, no. 67 [a]; Yoshida, 1973, no. 7 [a]; *Ukiyoe taikei*, 15, no. 47 [b]; *Meihin soroimono ukiyoe*, 11, no. 102 [a]; Copenhagen, 1993, no. 90 [a]; Forrer, 1994, G466 [a]

118 A SNOWY GORGE

untitled print published by Sanoya Kihei, *c.* 1843–4

signed: *Hiroshige hitsu*, with seal: *Ichiryūsai*
woodblock, double *ōban*, 736 x 251 mm
Baur Collection, Geneva (G530)

Although this print looks like part of a panel from the snow triptych (cat. 120), it is in fact the Fuji River, not the Kiso River, that here winds its way between tall mountains. This river arises from the confluence of the Fuefuki and Kamanashi to the west of Mount Fuji and eventually flows into Suruga Bay. Hiroshige travelled to the provinces to the north and north-west of Edo in 1842/IV and he is bound to have crossed the Fuji as he followed the Kōshūkaidō Road to Kōfu in Kai Province. Given the month of his trip, he must have added the snow from his own imagination.

Both the perspective and the format of this print give the composition something of the appearance of a scroll painting: what the viewer sees as he or she peruses the print from top to bottom corresponds to increasing degrees of proximity. Moreover, some of the shapes of the rocks recall Chinese and Japanese paintings on literary subjects. On the other hand, the *bokashi* extending from the upper edge of the image and the depiction of the river belong exclusively to the world of the print.

In early impressions of this print, such as that illustrated here (a), a few lines in the blue of the waterfall have been left white. Later (b) they seem to have filled up. The two small peaks below the tall mountain to the left are always printed without outlines.

REFERENCES: Narazaki, 1964, p. 129 [a]; Tanba, 1965, no. 71 [b]; Suzuki, 1975, p. 132 [b]; *Kobijutsu*, 1983, no. 216 [a]; Copenhagen, 1993, no. 126 [b]; Forrer, 1994, G530 [a: this impression]

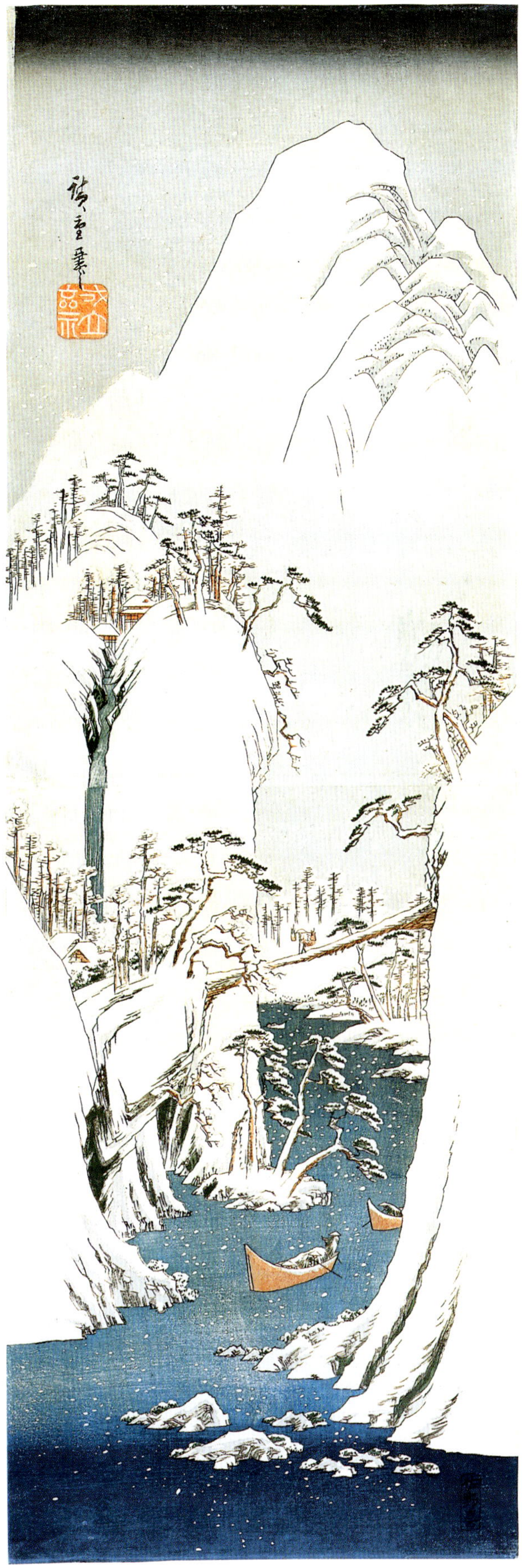

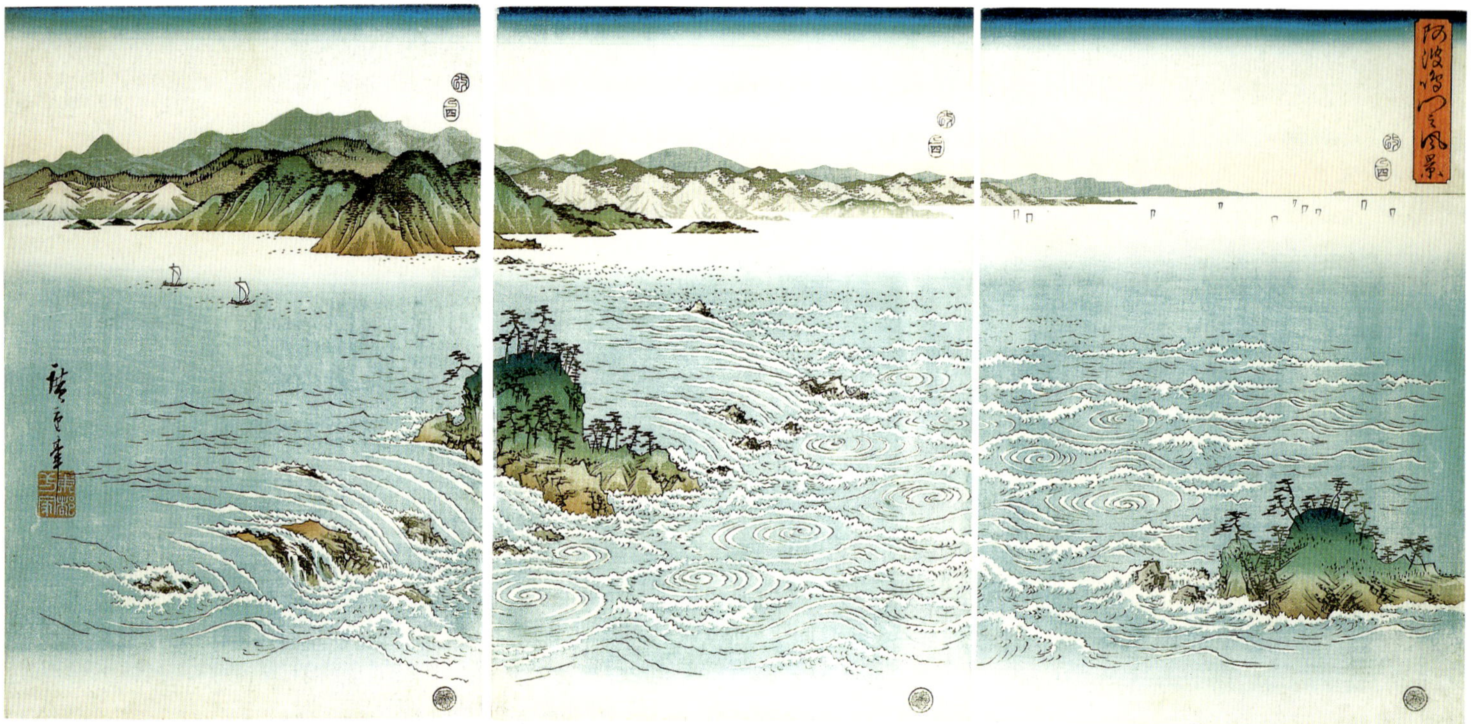

119 WHIRLPOOLS ON A ROCKY COAST

Landscape with the Whirlpools at Awa (*Awa no naruto no fūkei*)

from an untitled series of triptychs
published by Okasawaya Taheiji, 1857

signed: *Hiroshige hitsu*, with seal: *Tōto Ikka*
censorship seal: *aratame*; date seal: Snake 4 (1857/IV)
woodblock, *ōban* triptych, 359 x 251, 360 x 250 and 359 x 251 mm
The Art Institute of Chicago, Chicago,
The Clarence Buckingham Collection (1925.2303)

The whirlpools at Awa, between the province of Awa on the island Shikoku and Awaji island, had already featured as the theme of a print in the series *Famous Views in the Sixty-odd Provinces* (cat. 61). Here the composition is horizontal, panoramic, while the vertical image was more in the nature of a close-up. The mass of whirlpools here are often regarded as flowers, in accordance with an interpretation of this series of triptychs as variations on the theme of Snow, Moon and Flowers (see cat. 120).

In early impressions, as here (a), the horizon is indicated at right by a thin line; this is missing from later impressions (b). It is impossible to determine whether this was the result of accidental damage to the block or whether the horizon line was deliberately cut out of the block.

REFERENCES: Narazaki, 1964, p. 140 [b]; Suzuki, 1975, p. 130 [b]; *Ukiyoe taikei*, 11, nos. 31–3 [b]; *Kobijutsu*, 1983, no. 417 [b]; *Ukiyoe hakka*, 1984, no. 42 [b]; Link, 1991, no. VII-A-2 [a]; Forrer, 1994, G533 [b]

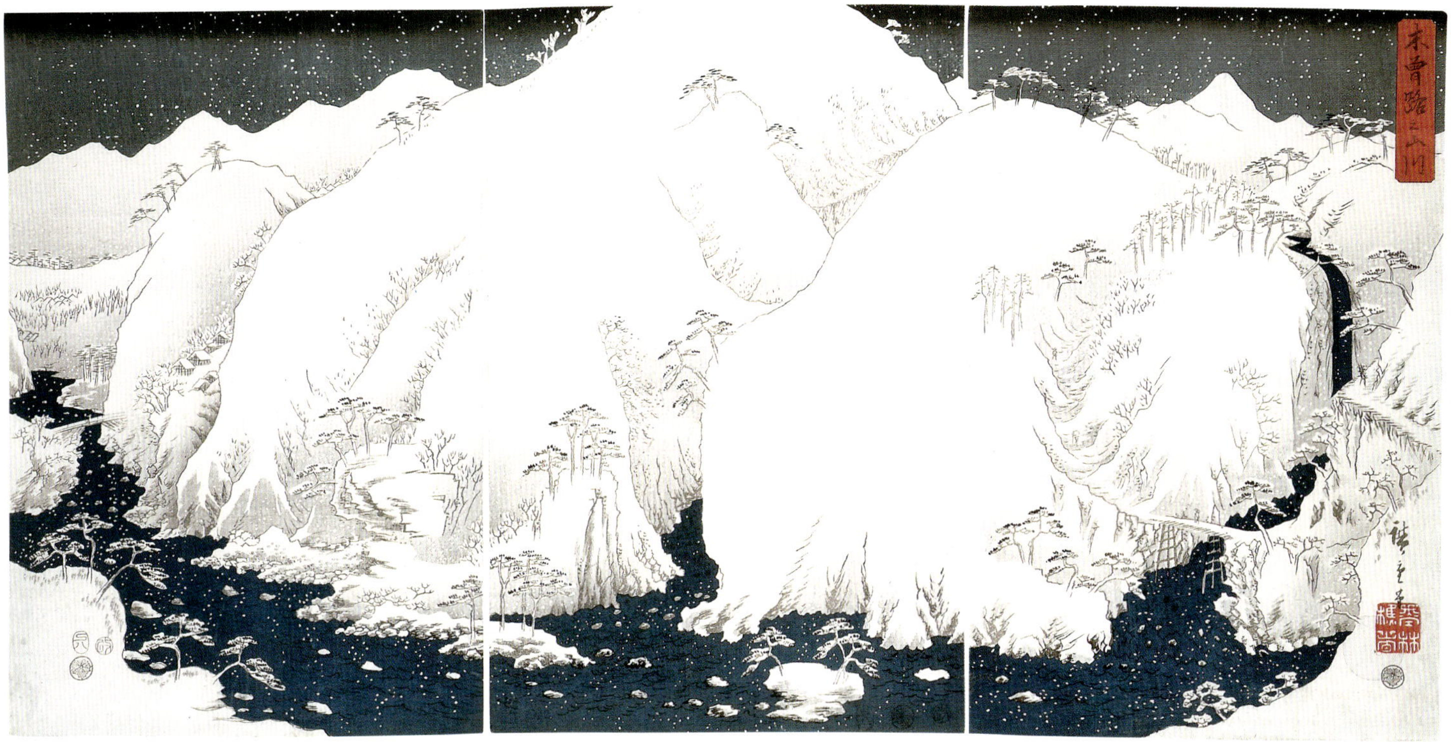

120 A RIVER AMONG SNOWY MOUNTAINS

Mountains and Rivers on the Kiso Road
(Kisoji no yamakawa)

from an untitled series of triptychs
published by Okasawaya Taheiji, 1857

signed: *Hiroshige hitsu*, with seal: *Bokurin Shokoku*
censorship seal: *aratame*; date seal: Snake 8 (1857/VIII)
woodblock, *ōban* triptych, 370 x 246, 369 x 247 and 370 x 246 mm
The Art Institute of Chicago, Chicago (RX21419)

An impressive landscape with the mountains beside the Kiso River encased in a thick layer of snow. This is among the most rugged parts of the Kisokaidō Road, one of the oldest in Japan, formerly known as Tōsandō or Nakasendō. However, it became less important after the construction of the Tōkaidō Road at the beginning of the seventeenth century, which was both an easier and a faster route. For centuries the attractive landscape had been praised in poems and recorded in paintings. Among Hiroshige's predecessors in the woodcut medium were Kaibara Ekken, Shiba Kōkan and Katsushika Hokusai, and they are also featured in popular travel guides. It is difficult to determine exactly which spot is depicted here.

This composition is generally, though conjecturally, regarded as one of a series of three triptychs on the theme of Snow, Moon and Flowers, the others being cat. 119 and 121. The theme was certainly a common one in Japanese prints of the time, but the sequence of publication—'Flowers' in 1857/IV, 'Moon' in 1857/VII, and 'Snow' in 1857/VIII—lends support to the suggestion made by Suzuki Jūzō in conversation with the present author that the series was, in fact, devoted to the Four Seasons, with 'Spring' still to come. Yet, if this really was the intention, it is difficult to explain why Hiroshige did not design the fourth print before his death in 1858/IX.

A striking feature of the early impression reproduced here is the soft tone of the ink, which is greyish rather than black. This variant, which is not mentioned in the literature, is distinguishable by two small, but clearly recognisable features: the omission of the censorship seal to the left of the title cartouche, an error that was later rectified by inserting a plug into the woodblock; and a peculiarity in the writing of the second character of the title, which was also corrected.

REFERENCES: Narazaki, 1964, p. 132; Yoshida, 1973, no. 8; *Kobijutsu*, 1983, no. 415; *Ukiyoe hakka*, 1984, no. 44; Link, 1991, no. VII-A-4; Forrer, 1994, G531

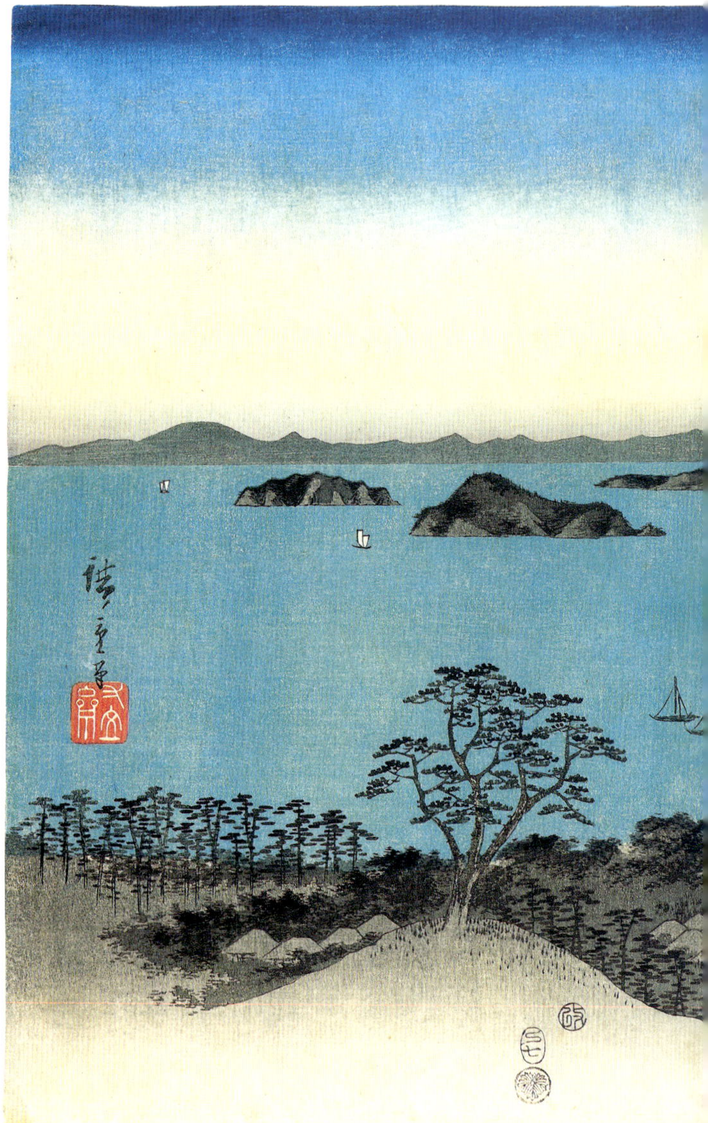

121 COASTAL LANDSCAPE IN MOONLIGHT

Evening View of the Eight Famous Sites at Kanazawa in Musashi Province (Buyō Kanazawa hasshō yakei)

from an untitled series of triptychs
published by Okasawaya Taheiji, 1857

signed: *Hiroshige hitsu*, with seal: *Ichiryūsai*
censorship seal: *aratame*; date seal: Snake 7 (1857/VII)
woodblock, *ōban* triptych, 376 x 253, 377 x 255 and 378 x 254 mm
Collection Pulverer, Cologne

Hiroshige had devoted a series of prints to eight famous sites at Kanazawa in Kaga Province in the mid-1830s (see cat. 126). He seems to have wanted to depict all eight places in this one triptych, or so the title suggests. Only a few are identifiable, but this in no way detracts from the power of this broad coastal panorama, seen beneath a beautiful autumn moon that casts a grey sheen over the whole landscape.

REFERENCES: Narazaki, 1964, p. 136; Tanba, 1965, no. 81; *Ukiyoe taikei*, 11, nos. 34–6; *Kobijutsu*, 1983, no. 416; *Ukiyoe hakka*, 1984, no. 43; Link, 1991, no. VII-A-3; Forrer, 1994, G532

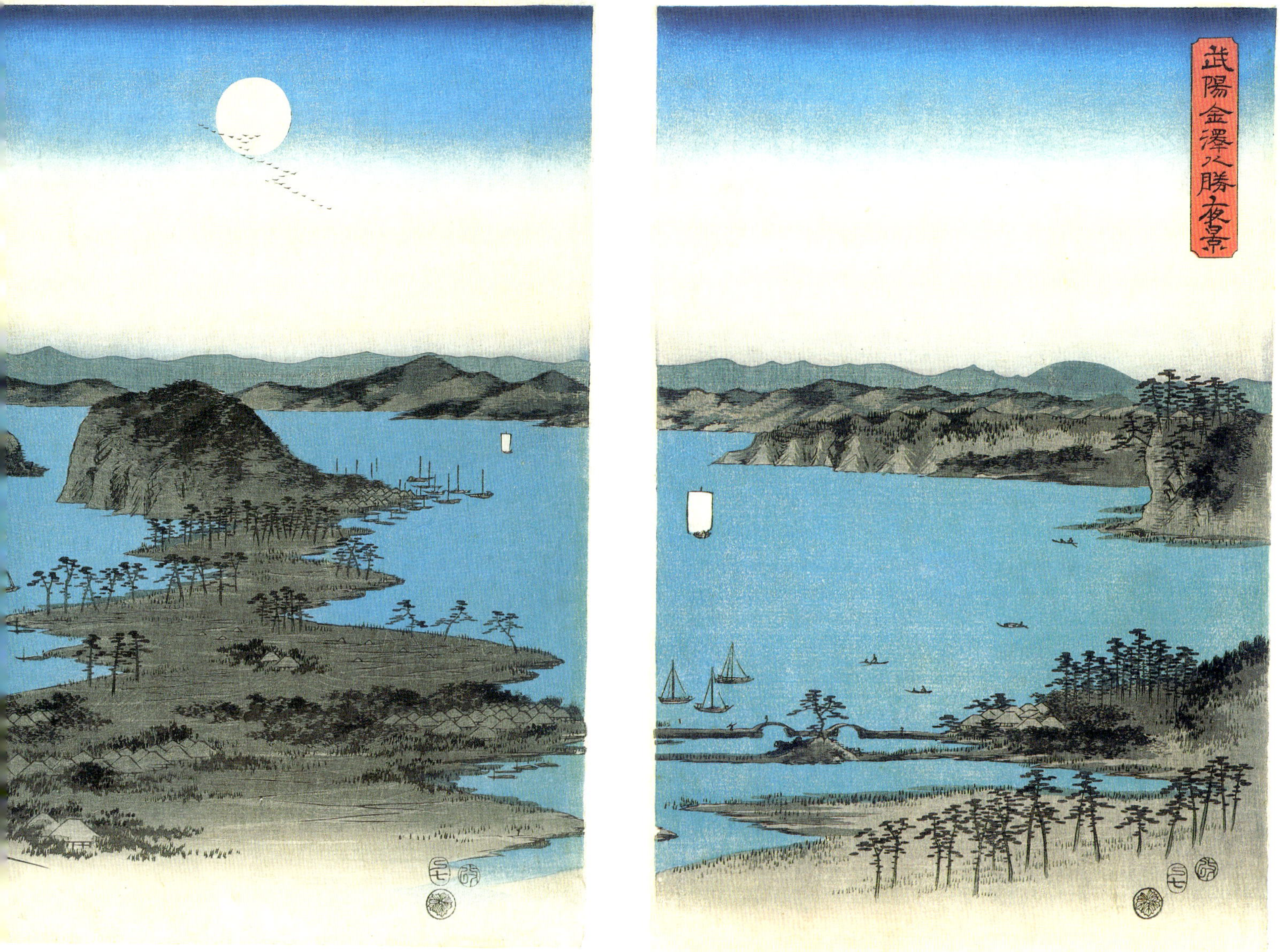
武陽金澤八勝夜景

122 THE MOON OVER A WATERFALL

The Moon Seen through the Leaves (Hagoshi no tsuki)

from the series *Twenty-eight Views of the Moon*
(*Tsuki nijūhakkei no uchi*)
published by Wakasaya Yoichi (Jakurindō), *c.* 1832

signed: *Hiroshige hitsu*
censorship seal: *kiwame*
woodblock, *ōtanzakuban*, 380 x 172 mm
The Trustees of The British Museum, London (1924.3.27.021)

A full autumn moon illuminates a waterfall and casts into sharp silhouette a tree on the cliff. The upper part of the sky is deep blue. Leaves fall, set off against the sky or against the water; it is autumn. The Chinese poem by Hakurakuten (772–846), from the anthology *Wakan rōeishū*, reads:

> It is not so sad that maple leaves fall,
> scattered on the moss-covered ground—
> it is only sad when the wind gets chilly and rough,
> and rain clouds darken the sky.

According to its title, this series was to consist of twenty-eight designs, yet only two are extant (cat. 122, 123). The first edition was published by Wakasaya Yoichi and is known in two variants: one, as here (a), with a partly light-coloured sky, and one (b) with an entirely deep blue sky. A later reprint (c) bears the trademark of the publisher Sanoya Kihei.

REFERENCES: *Kobijutsu*, 1983, no. 74 [a]; *Ukiyoe hakka*, 1984, no. 85 [a]; Link, 1991, no. VI-1-A [b]

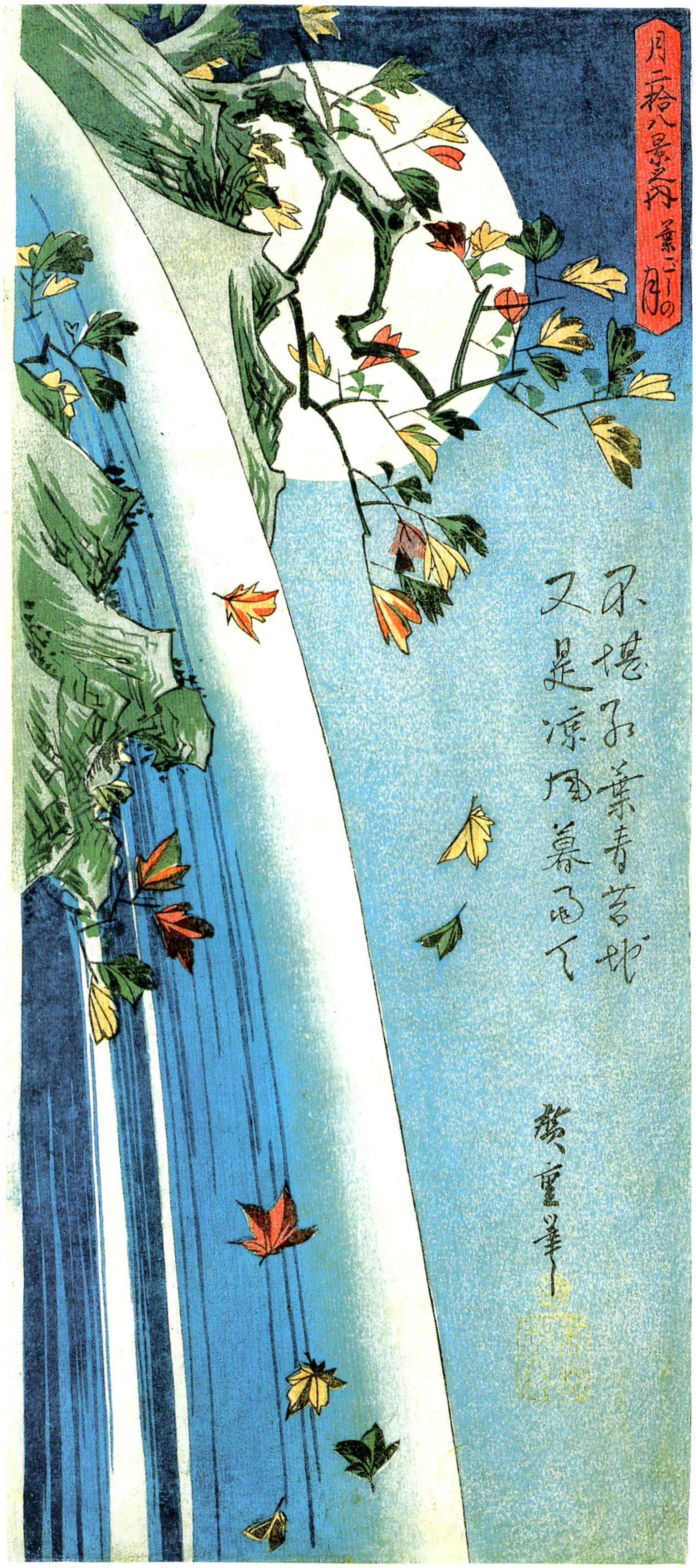
月二拾八景之内 葉ごしの月
不堪紅葉青苔地
又是涼風暮雨天
廣重筆

124 A BRIDGE IN A SNOWY LANDSCAPE

from the series *A Collection of Japanese and Chinese Poems* (*Wakan rōeishū*)
published by Jōshūya Kinzō, *c.* 1842–3

signed: *Hiroshige hitsu*, with seal: *Ichiryūsai*
censorship seal: *kiwame*
woodblock, *ōban*, 375 x 257 mm
The Mann Collection, Highland Park, Illinois

Two men, both wrapped in straw cloaks, cross a bridge over a river in a snow-covered landscape. The roofs of a few houses are visible and the snowflakes continue to fall. In the upper part of the print is a Chinese poem by Hakurakuten (772–846) that, in translation, reads:

> The falling snow resembles goose feathers
> blown in disorder;
> bathing in it, the people seem to walk around
> dressed in cranes' wings.

Eight designs are known from this series. They illustrate a number of poems from the *Wakan rōeishū*, a popular Japanese anthology of Chinese poetry.

REFERENCE: Link, 1991, no. III-10-A

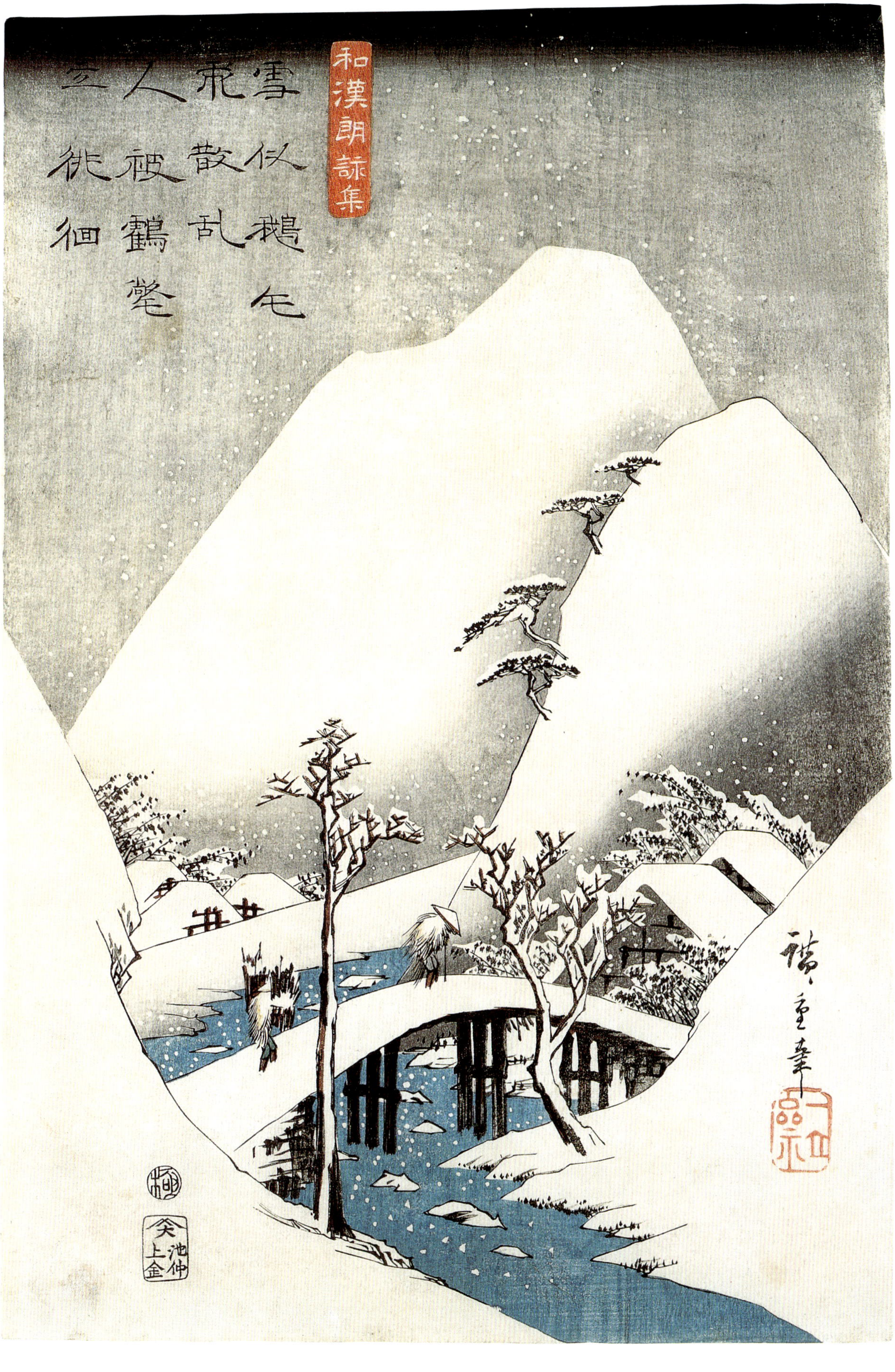

和漢朗詠集
雪似鵝毛
飛散乱
人被鶴氅
立徘徊
廣重筆

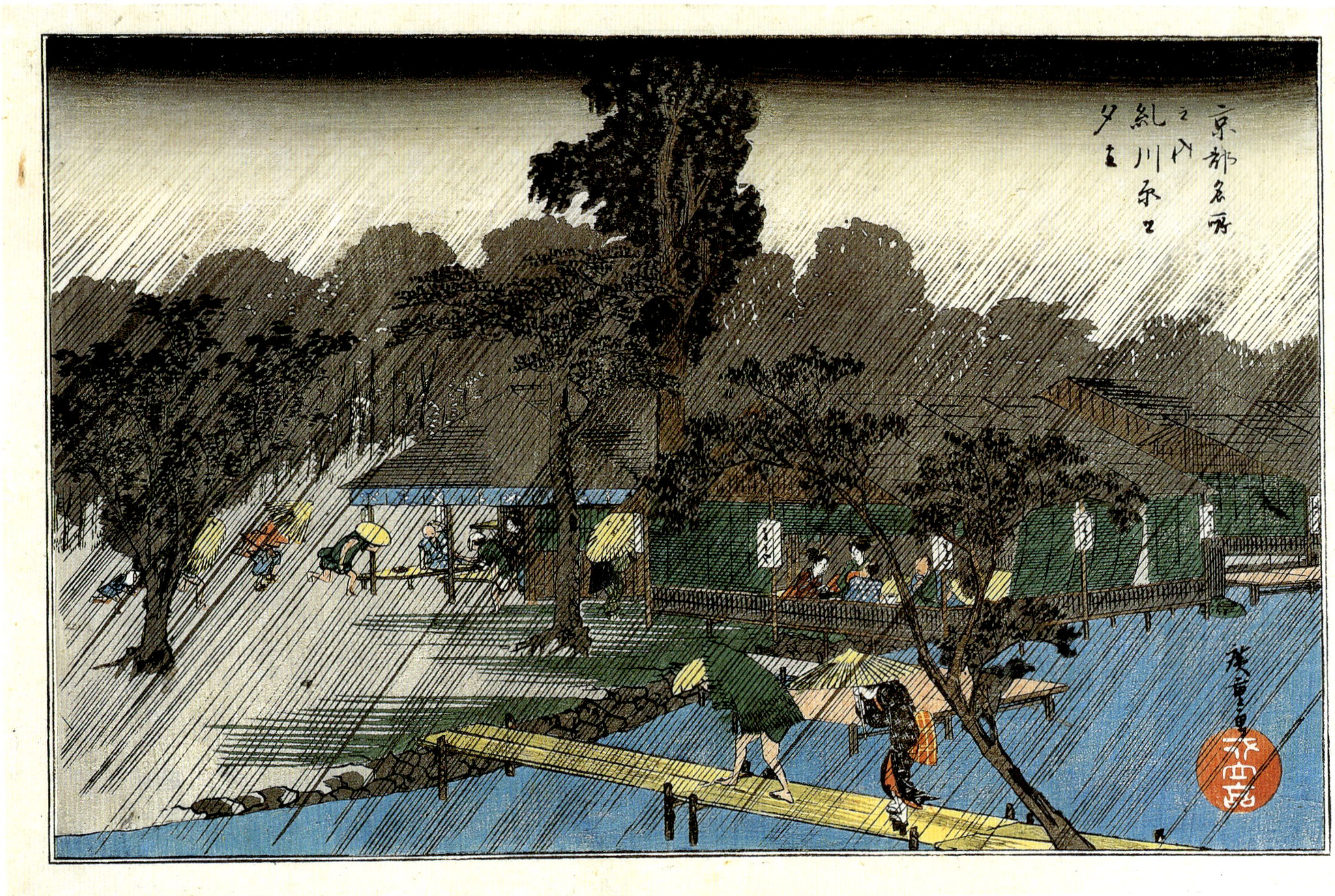

125 PEOPLE SHELTERING FROM THE RAIN

Sudden Rain at Tadasugawara
(*Tadasugawara no yūdachi*)

from the series *Famous Views of Kyoto* (*Kyōto meisho no uchi*)
published by Kawaguchiya Shōzō (Eisendō), *c.* 1834

signed: *Hiroshige ga*
censorship seal: *kiwame*
woodblock, *ōban*, 240 x 372 mm
The Mann Collection, Highland Park, Illinois

South of Kyoto, at the confluence of the Kamo and Kōya rivers, was a wood called Tadasunomori, where the Shimogamo Shrine was a popular place to enjoy the cool evening air. Visitors to it are here caught in a sudden shower of rain. The sky is menacingly dark and the rain falls in torrents. It seems to have come as no great surprise, however, since the visitors brought their umbrellas and cloaks.

REFERENCES: Narazaki, 1964, p. 26; Link, 1991, no. III-5-B; *Meihin soroimono ukiyoe*, 12, no. 3; Forrer, 1994, G508; Satō, 1994, no. 3

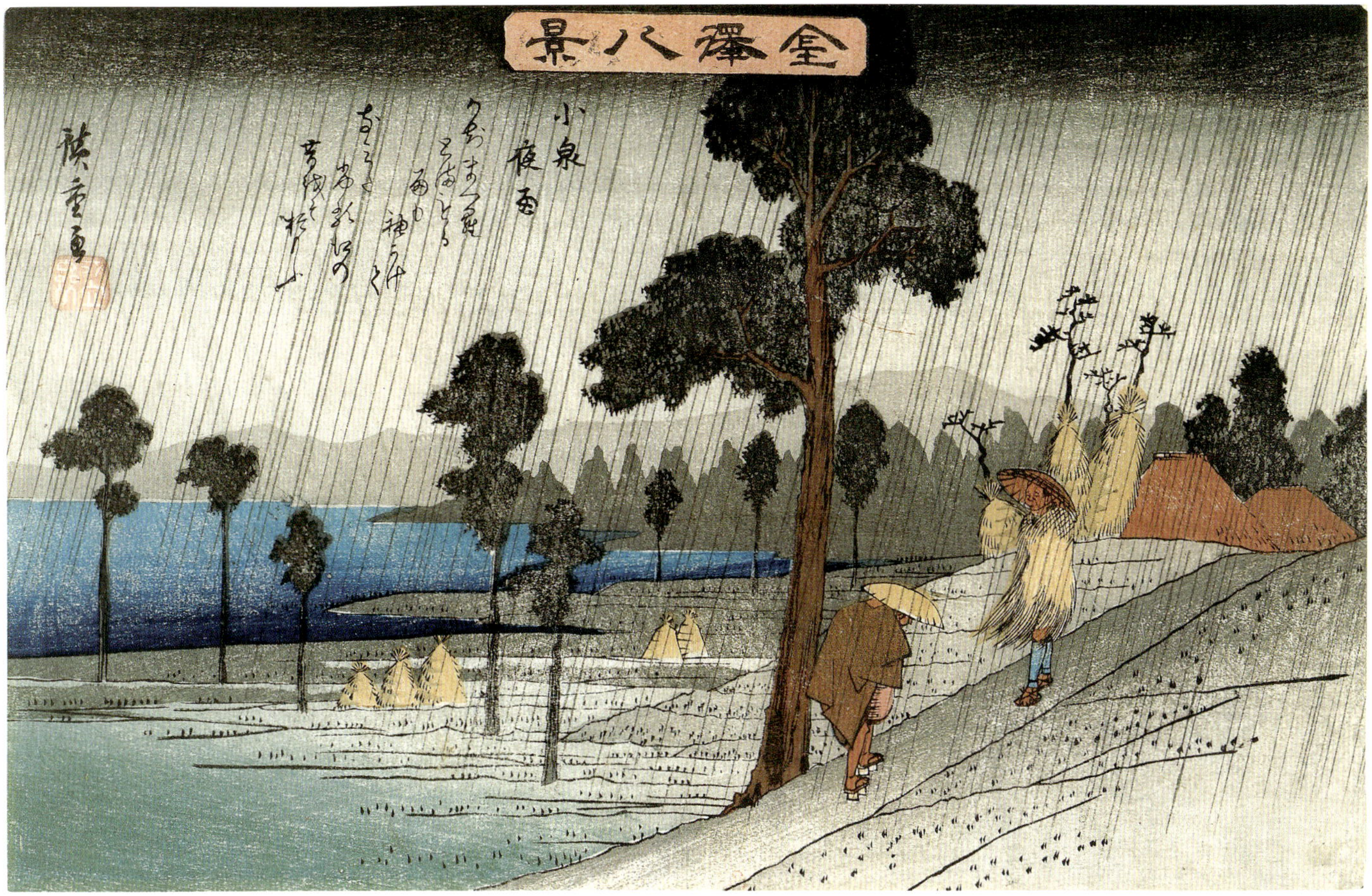

126 TWO MEN ON A SLOPING ROAD IN THE RAIN

Evening Rain at Kozumi (Kozumi no yau)

from the series *Eight Views in Kanazawa* (*Kanazawa hakkei*)
published by Koshimuraya Heisuke, *c.* 1835–6

signed: *Hiroshige ga*
censorship seal: *kiwame*
woodblock, *ōban*, 216 x 341 mm
Bibliothèque Nationale de France, Département des Estampes, Paris (JB119BIS)

Two men wearing cloaks are walking down a sloping road between rice-fields. The roofs of a cluster of houses can be seen in the background on the right. The pouring rain reduces the trees in the foreground to little more than abstract contours, while those in the background and the hills in the distance are only vaguely discernible. In the upper part of the print is a *kyōka* poem.

This series of eight prints, rather unusually depicting Kanazawa in the province of Musashi near Edo, is relatively rare. It is difficult to determine whether this is because the series was commissioned by a poetry club and therefore issued as a limited edition or because it was only moderately successful.

DRAWINGS, ETC.

CAT. 127–42

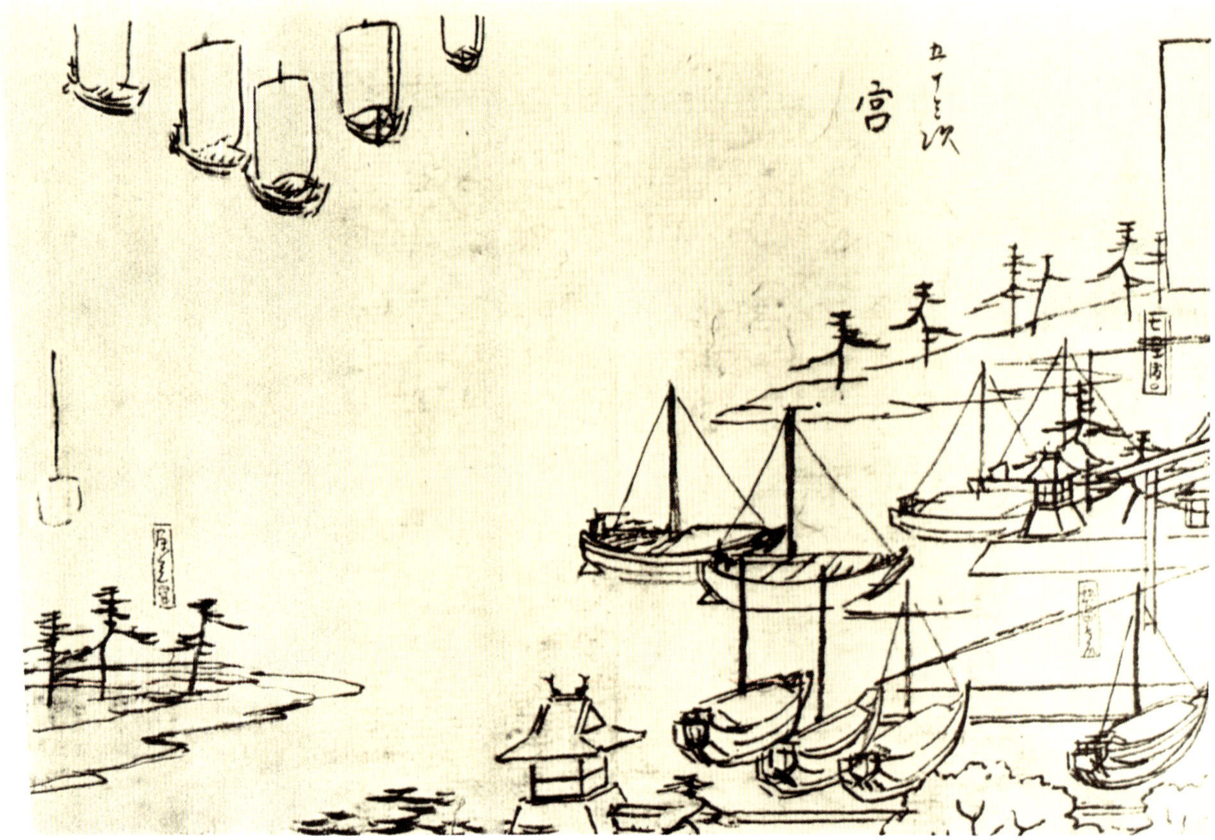

127 VIEW OF A HARBOUR

Miya

design for the series *The Fifty-three Stations of the Tōkaidō* (*Tōkaidō gojūsan tsugi*), the so-called *Reisho Tōkaidō*
c. 1847–52

unsigned
ink on paper, 150 x 220 mm
Berès Collection, Paris

Hiroshige's design for the print at cat. 128. This drawing is noticeably less schematic than cat. 131-4; it is easy to imagine that the copyist found it sufficiently detailed to work from. Apparently, he was left to fill in the stones in the embankment, the details of the roof and tower of the foreground building and such like.

A fairly large number of designs for this series have survived, for example for the stations of Tsuchiyama and Goyū (Hillier, 1965, nos. 56, 82), Fuchū and Kawasaki (Hillier, 1980, nos. 124, 125).

REFERENCE: Hillier, 1965, no. 70

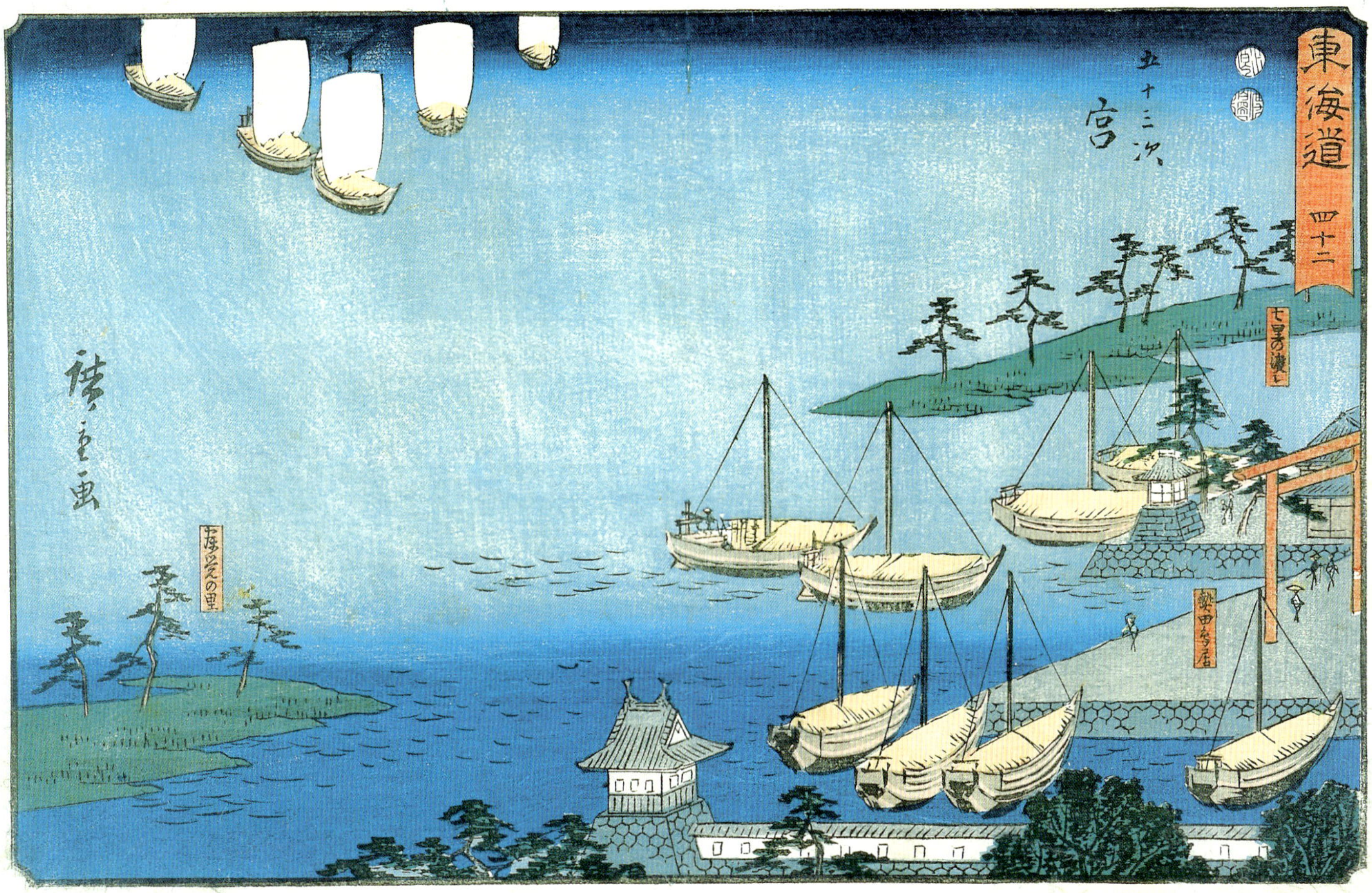

128 VIEW OF A HARBOUR

Miya—No. 42

from the series *The Fifty-three Stations of the Tōkaidō* (*Tōkaidō gojūsan tsugi*), the so-called *Reisho Tōkaidō*
published by Maruya Seijirō, *c.* 1847–52

signed: *Hiroshige ga*
censors' seals: Mera and Watanabe
woodblock, *ōban*, 236 x 359 mm
The Trustees of The British Museum, London (1906.12.20.848)

A bird's-eye view of the harbour of Miya, with the gateway of the Seta Shrine, the point of departure for those who travelled by sea to the next station, Kuwana.

REFERENCE: Shiraishi, 1988, p. 105

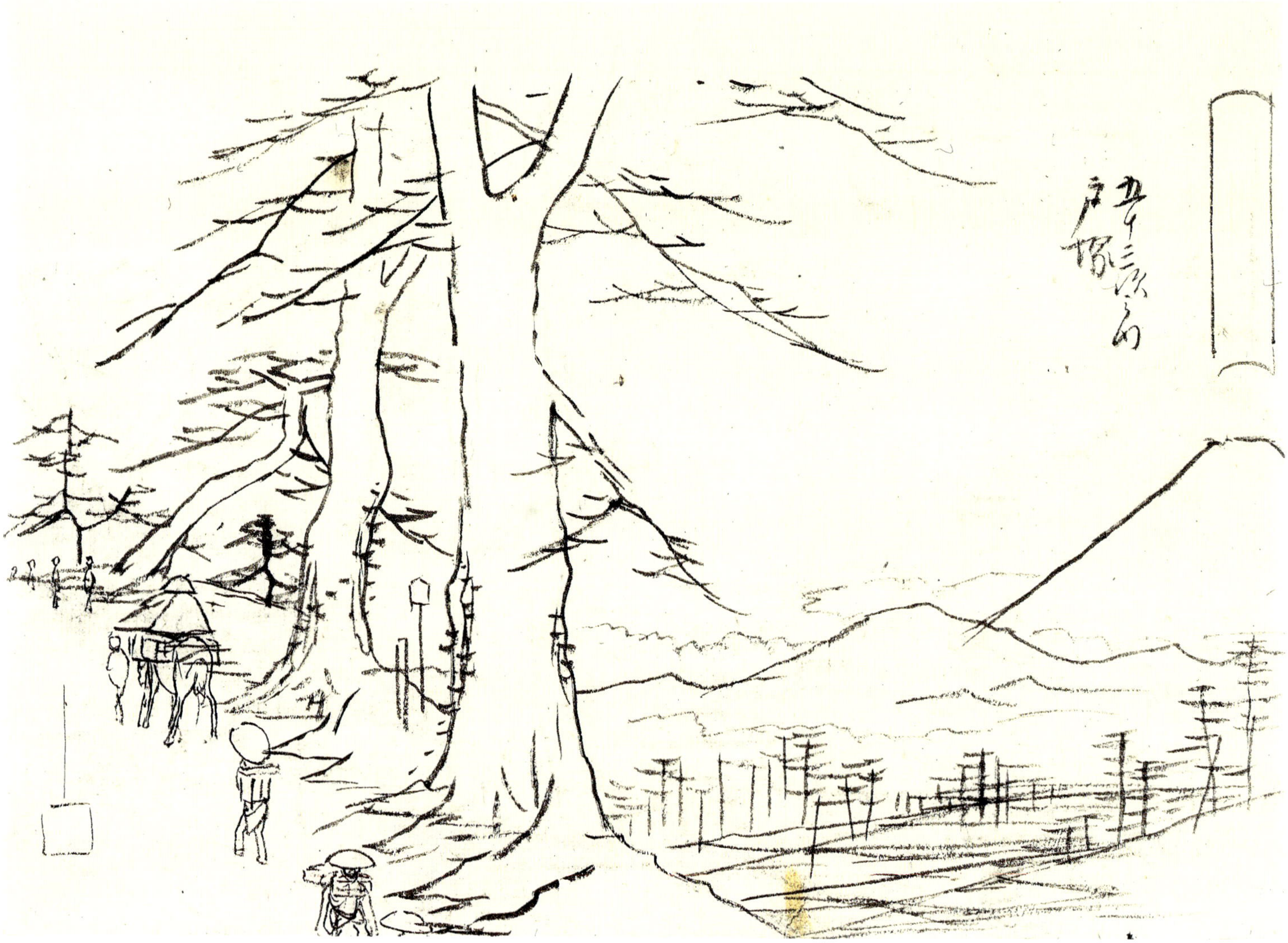

129 TRAVELLERS ON A SLOPING ROAD

Totsuka

design for the series *The Fifty-three Stations of the Tōkaidō* (*Tōkaidō gojūsan tsugi*), the so-called *Reisho Tōkaidō*
c. 1847–52

unsigned
ink on paper, 241 x 337 mm
Berès Collection, Paris

Several travellers, one of them on horseback, are climbing a road with large pine trees on one side. They pass a wide plain with hills in the distance. Mount Fuji is visible on the right.

This drawing, despite the sketchiness of the trees on the plain, contains the essence of the final print (Shiraishi, 1988, p. 23) to a striking degree. Judging by the drawing, Hiroshige originally intended to have fully formed clouds in the sky, but in the print this has become the conventional blue type with a few white lines.

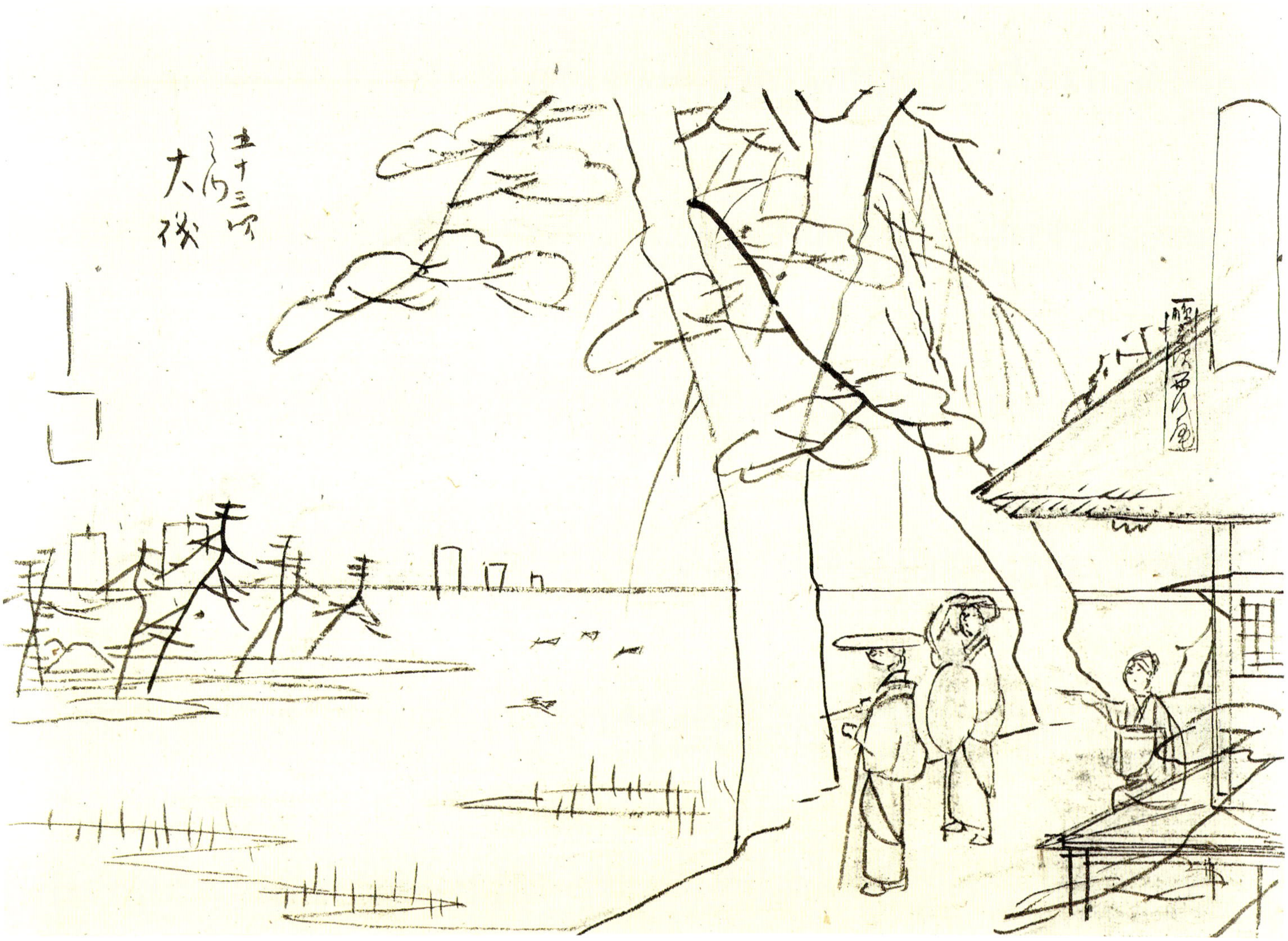

130 PEOPLE OVERLOOKING THE WATER

Ōiso

design for the series *The Fifty-three Stations of the Tōkaidō* (*Tōkaidō gojūsan tsugi*), the so-called *Reisho Tōkaidō*, *c.* 1847–52

unsigned
ink on paper, 240 x 338 mm
Berès Collection, Paris

Just past the station of Ōiso was a small cottage known as the 'cottage where the storks ascend', Shigitatsuan or Saigyōan, where the poet and priest Saigyō (1118–90) wrote one of his most famous poems. In this drawing a few people have gathered outside the cottage to enjoy the view and several storks are indeed flying over the water.

In the final print (Shiraishi, 1988, p. 29) the seated figure is slightly turned, resulting in a profile view, and the rear tree has become a willow whose branches can also be seen below the roof of the cottage. The number of boats on the water has been reduced from the five in the drawing to three.

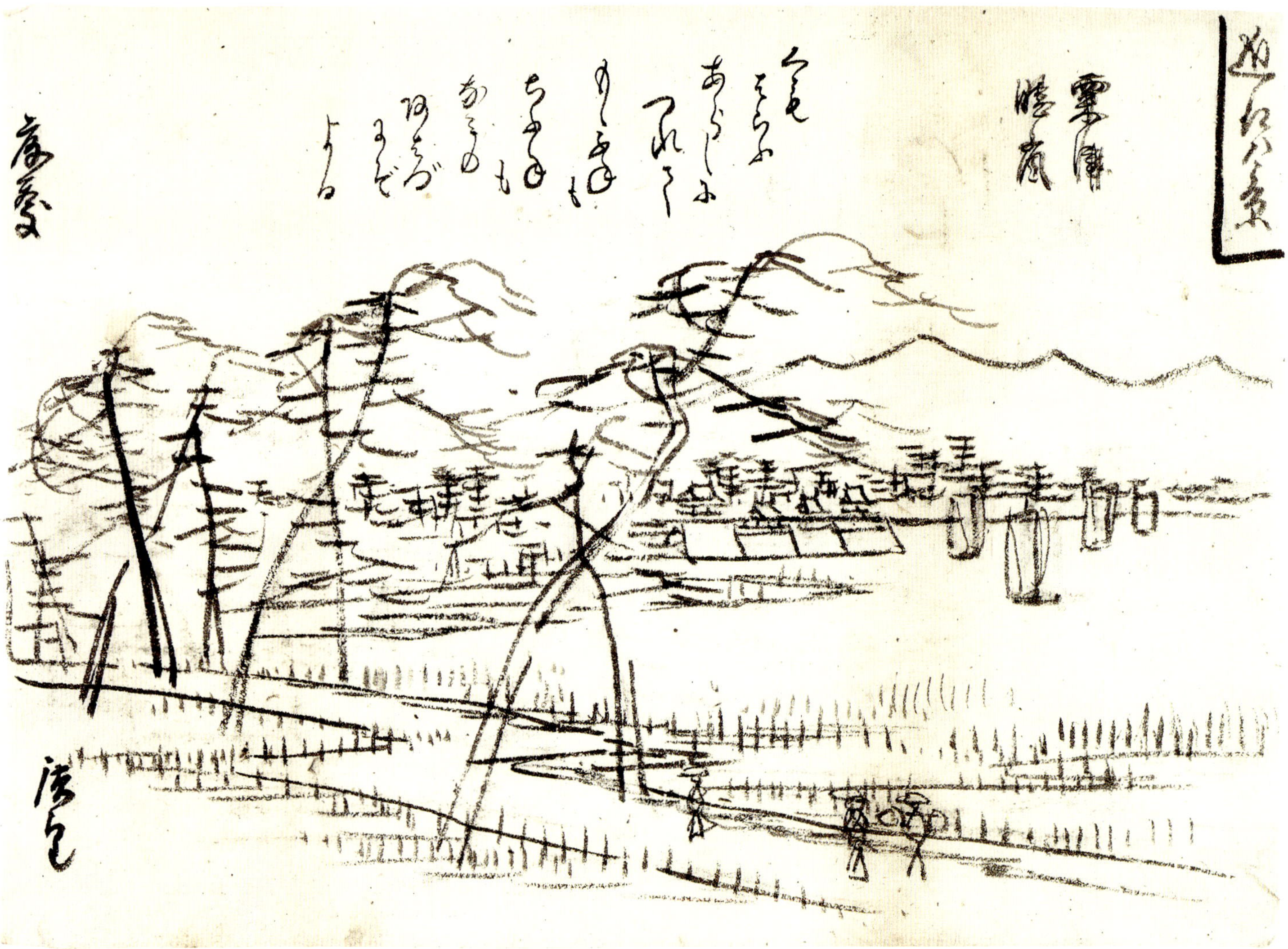

131 VIEW OF A ROAD BESIDE A LAKE

Weather Clearing at Awazu (*Awazu no seiran*)

design for a series *Eight Views in Ōmi Province* (*Ōmi hakkei no uchi*), *c.* 1837–40

signed: *Hiroshige*
ink on paper, 246 x 346 mm
Berès Collection, Paris

A few people walk along a winding road beside the lake. To the left of the boats is Ōtsu Castle, behind which the mountains tower above the horizon. The trees beside the path are rendered with rapid strokes. For a translation of the poem above them, see cat. 74.

Apart from that illustrated at cat. 68–75, we know of no horizontal *Eight Views in Ōmi Province* by Hiroshige in the standard *ōban* format. This suggests that the sketch was never elaborated for publication, which deprives us of the possibility of seeing how this highly schematic drawing was interpreted by the copyist and then the block-cutter. The sketches at cat. 132–4 would seem to belong to the same group, as would that for *Lingering Snow on Mount Hira* in the Tikotin Museum of Japanese Art, Haifa (Hillier, 1980, no. 123).

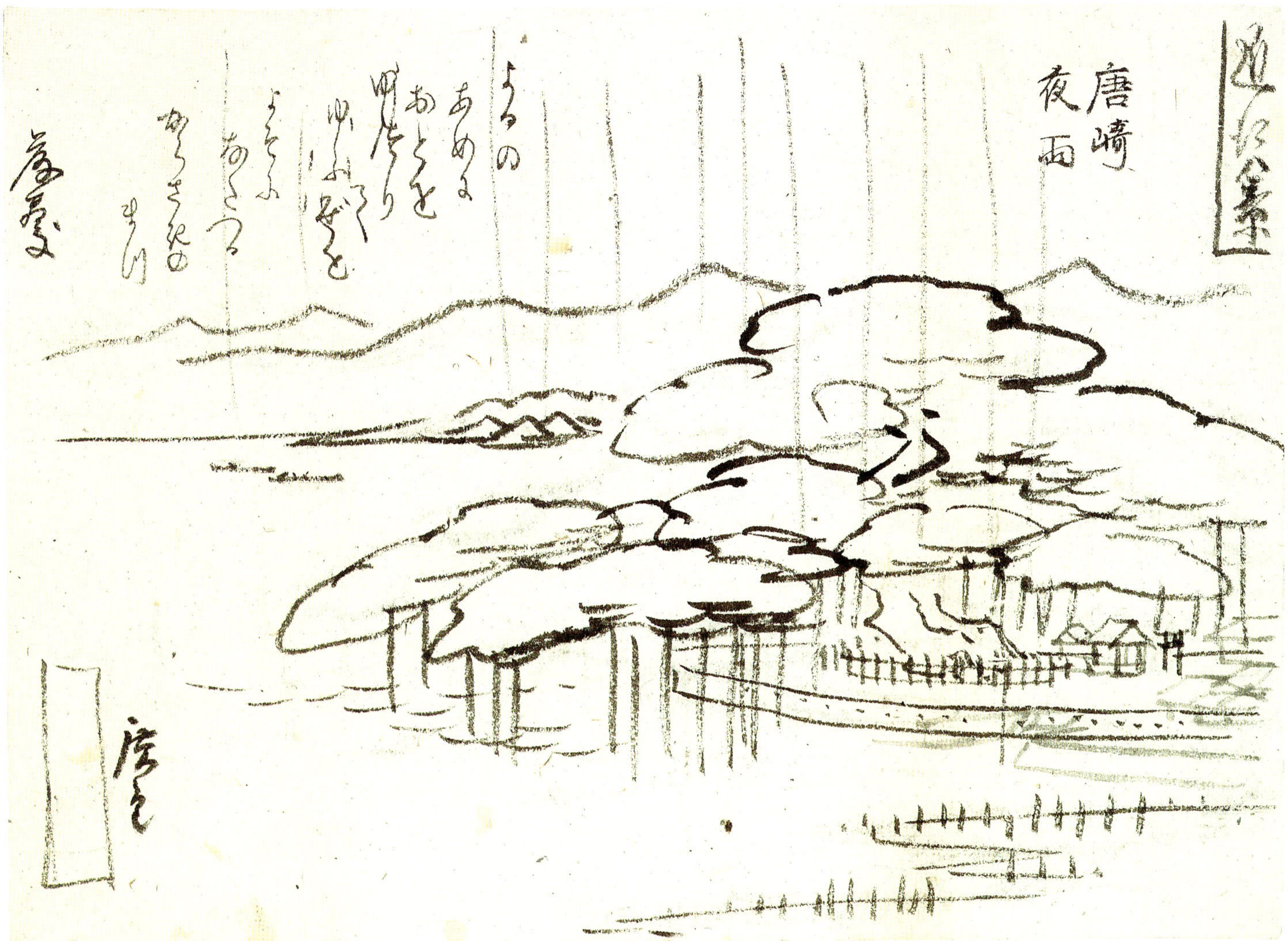

132 HEAVY RAIN ON A PINE TREE

Evening Rain at Karasaki (Karasaki no yau)

design for a series *Eight Views in Ōmi Province (Ōmi hakkei no uchi)*, *c.* 1837–40

signed: *Hiroshige*
ink on paper, 246 x 345 mm
Rijksprentenkabinet, Rijksmuseum, Amsterdam (1956:192)

The huge pine tree of Karasaki stands on a small platform in the water. To the left is a view of Lake Biwa and the mountains that surround it. The rain is indicated by lines. For a translation of the poem at upper left, see cat. 71. By comparison with that print, the drawing focuses less exclusively on the pine tree.

The sheet bears clear traces of underdrawing, sketchy, preliminary indications of the positions of various elements, probably executed in a very light ink (the medium could not be determined with the aid of a microscope). Also visible is a study, in a very light grey, for the stone embankment and the shrine; these were later assigned a different position in heavier ink.

REFERENCE: Rappard-Boon, 1984, p. 7

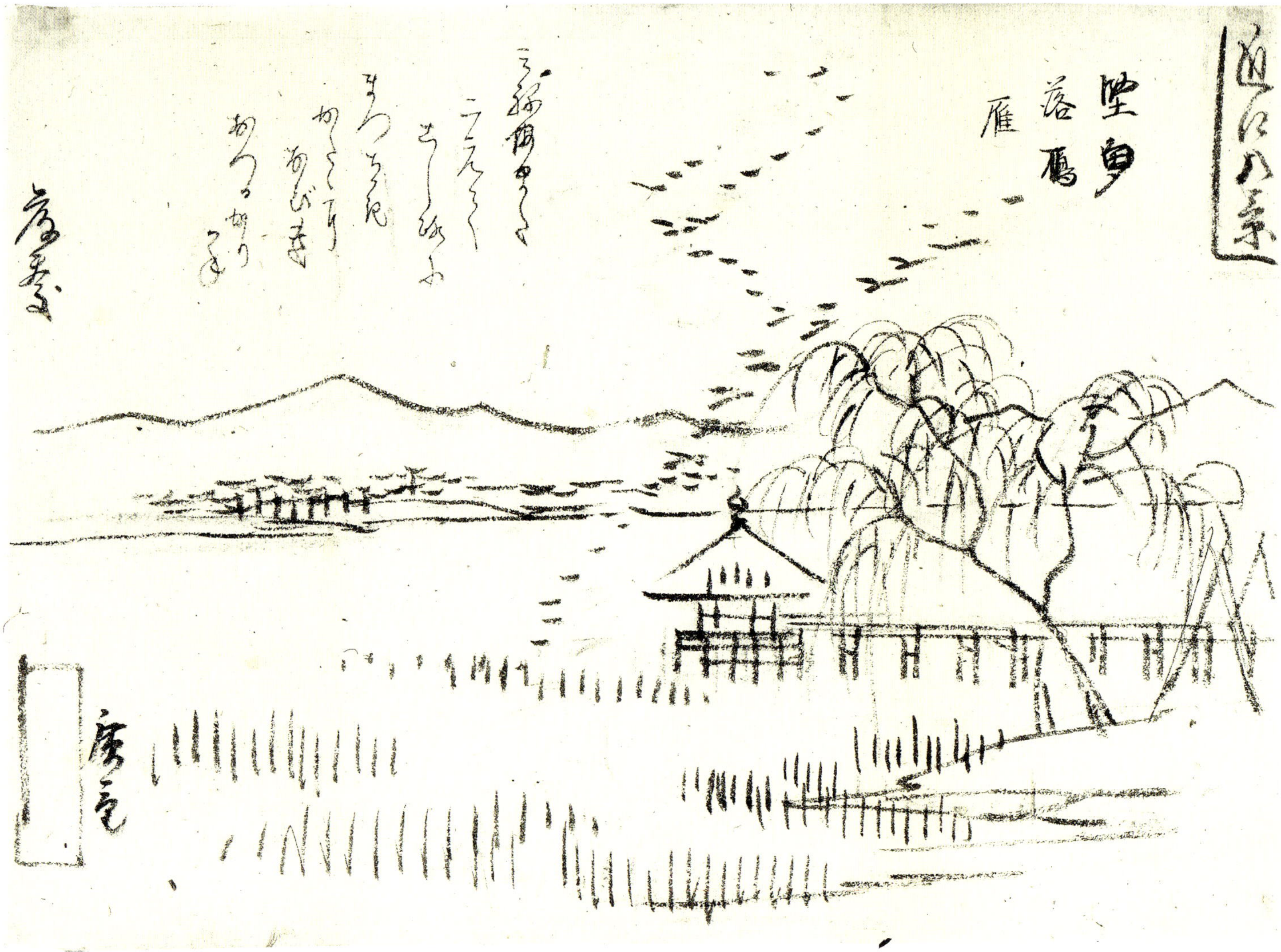

133 A WIDE VIEW OVER A LAKE WITH A FLIGHT OF GEESE

Descending Geese at Katada (Katada no rakugan)

design for a series *Eight Views in Ōmi Province (Ōmi hakkei no uchi)*, *c.* 1837–40

signed: *Hiroshige*
ink on paper, 245 x 344 mm
Berès Collection, Paris

A view over Lake Biwa from the south-west, showing the small shrine built out into the water. There are a few willows in front of it. A flight of geese descends above the building. For a translation of the poem, see cat. 73. It is striking that Hiroshige originally made a mistake in writing the character for 'goose'; the corrected version can be seen to the left.

REFERENCE: Hillier, 1965, no. 67

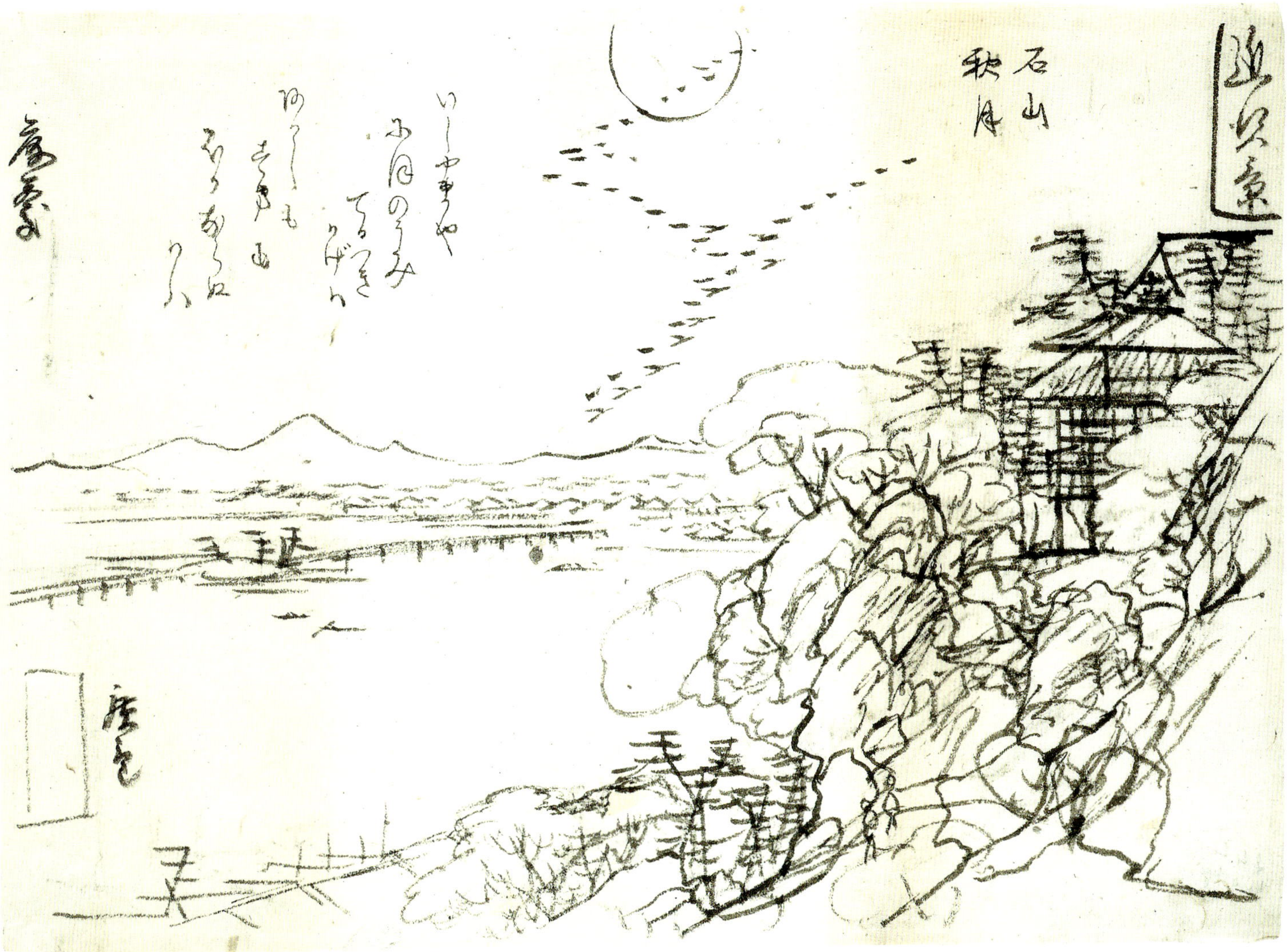

134 VIEW OF A LAKE WITH A TEMPLE ON THE RIGHT

Autumn Moon at Ishiyama (*Ishiyama no shūgetsu*)

design for a series *Eight Views in Ōmi Province* (*Ōmi hakkei no uchi*), *c.* 1837–40

signed: *Hiroshige*
ink on paper, 246 x 344 mm
The Art Institute of Chicago, Chicago,
Japanese Print Purchase Fund (58.190)

A view of Lake Biwa, with Ishiyama Temple on the right and Seta Bridge on the left. A flock of birds, probably ducks or geese, flies down from in front of the moon. For a translation of the poem on the left, see cat. 69. The print from the published *Eight Views in Ōmi Province*, where the temple is almost hidden among the trees and rocks on the left and Seta Bridge appears on the right (cat. 69), is a mirror image of this composition. The mountains on the far side of the lake do not appear in the print and Bowie's hypothesis that it was based on this sketch is thus without foundation.

REFERENCE: Bowie, 1975, no. 84

135 TEMPLE COMPLEX ON AN ISLAND AND FERRIES ON A RIVER

design for the subjects *A Morning View of Shinobazu Pond* and *Ferry Boats in Late Autumn Rain at Sumida River* (*Shinobazu no ike asa no kei* and *Sumidagawa watashibune shigure no zu*) from a series of *Famous Views in the Eastern Capital* (*Tōto meisho*) in the *kotanzaku* format, *c.* 1840–3

signed: *Hiroshige ga*
ink on paper, 382 x 204 mm
Honolulu Academy of Arts, Honolulu,
Gift of James A. Michener, 1992 (22.156)

Hiroshige designed at least three different series of *Famous Views in the Eastern Capital* in the *tanzakuban* format featuring both the Shinobazu pond with the Benten Shrine on the island and the equally traditional ferries on the Sumida River. These two drawings, however, were apparently never realised in print form.

In view of the relatively detailed execution, including the neat writing of the series and print titles and the full signature, these sheets seem to represent an intermediate stage between the initial rough sketch and the very precise drawing from which the block was cut. A correction to the trees was made on a separate piece of paper, which was then pasted on the original drawing. It is noteworthy, however, that the publisher is not named, perhaps because his trademark would have appeared as a red seal on the final print.

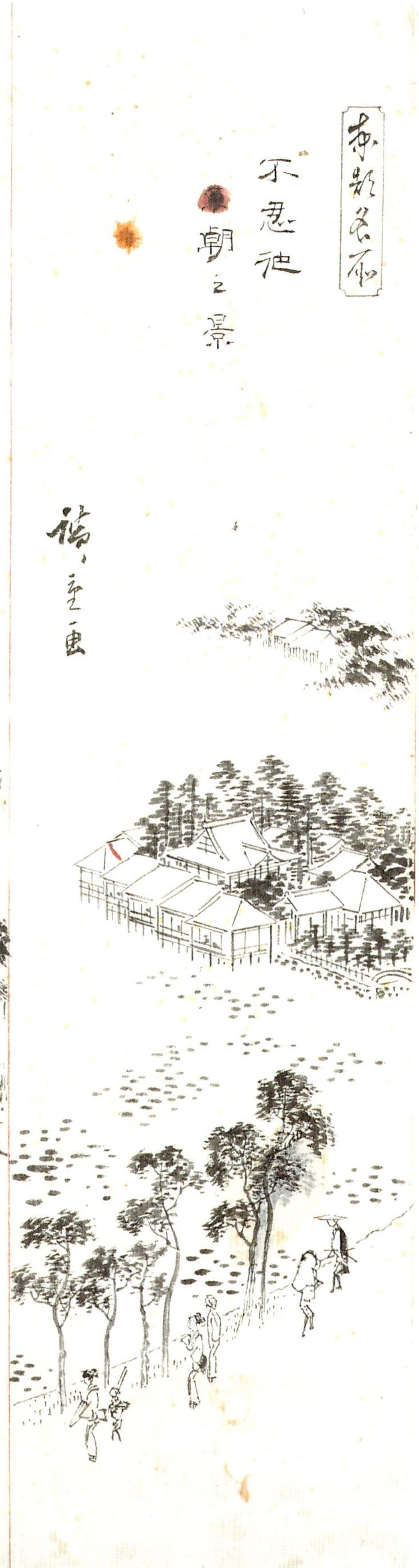
東都名所
不忍池
朝之景
廣重画

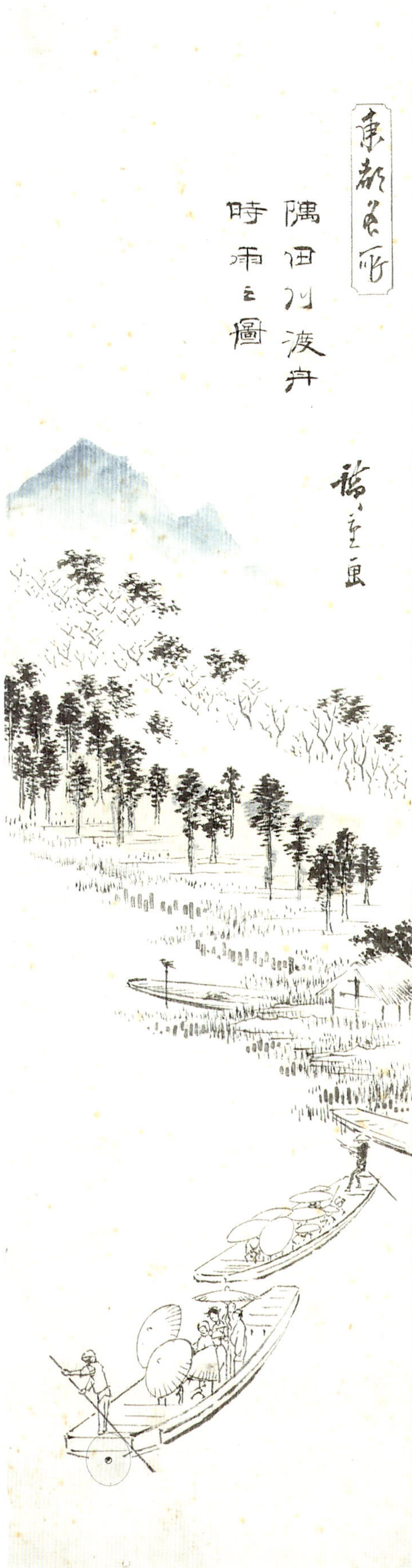
東都名所
隅田川渡舟
時雨之圖
廣重画

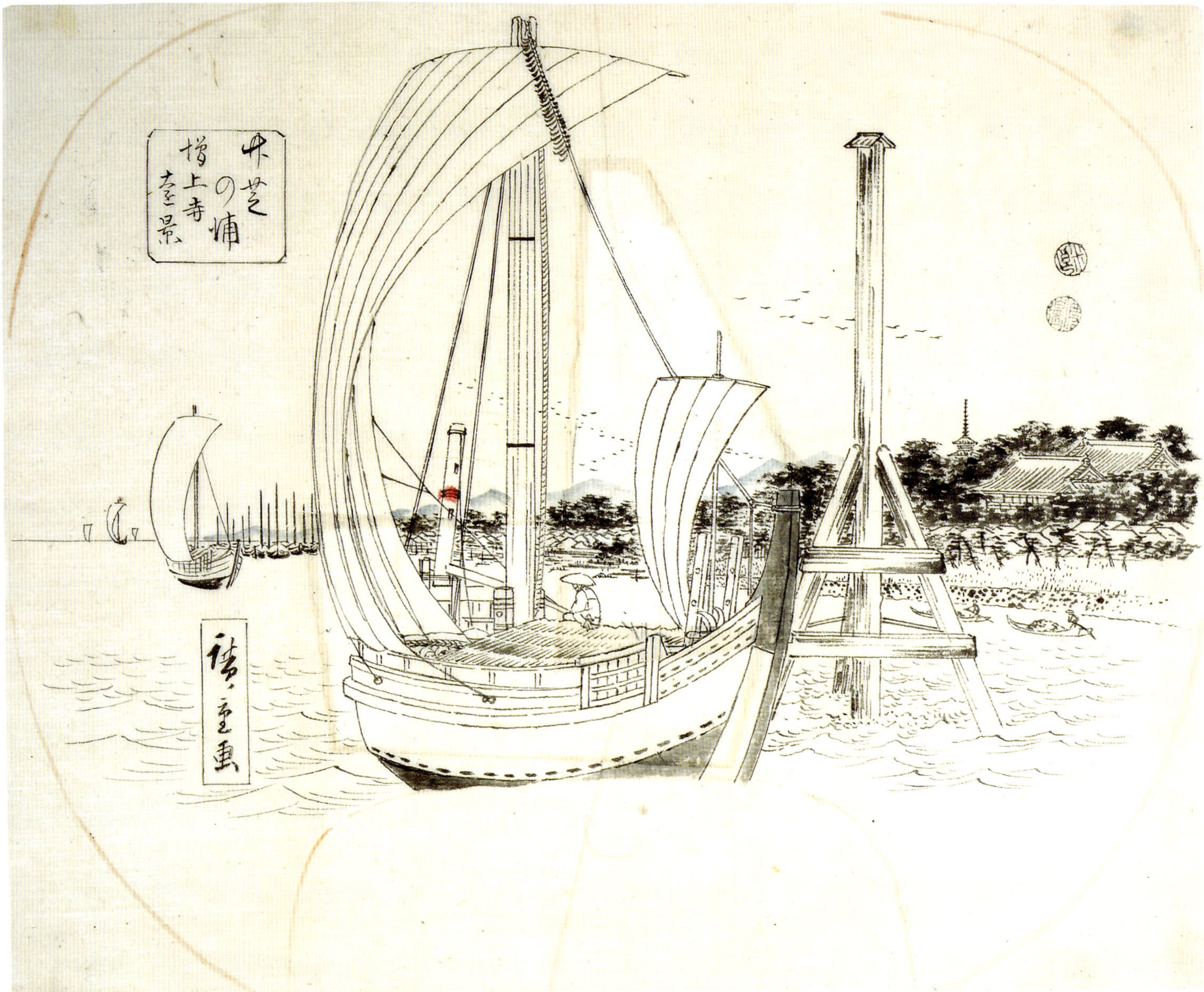

136 SAILING BOATS BY THE COAST

finished design for a fan print on the subject *The Coast at Shiba and Zōjōji Temple* (*Soto Shibaura Zōjōji*), *c.* 1851

signed: *Hiroshige ga*
censors' seals: Mera and Watanabe
ink on paper, 241 x 343 mm
Honolulu Academy of Arts, Honolulu,
Gift of James A. Michener, 1991 (21.691)

A design for a fan print showing some boats near Shiba in the Bay of Edo. The large Zōjōji Temple complex can be seen between the trees at right. This finished drawing, which will have been worked up from a Hiroshige sketch either by one of the artist's pupils or, more likely, by a copyist employed by the publisher, has already been submitted to the censors for permission to cut the blocks and publish the print. The existence of the drawing, however, is evidence that the print was never issued, as it would have been destroyed during the cutting of the line-block.

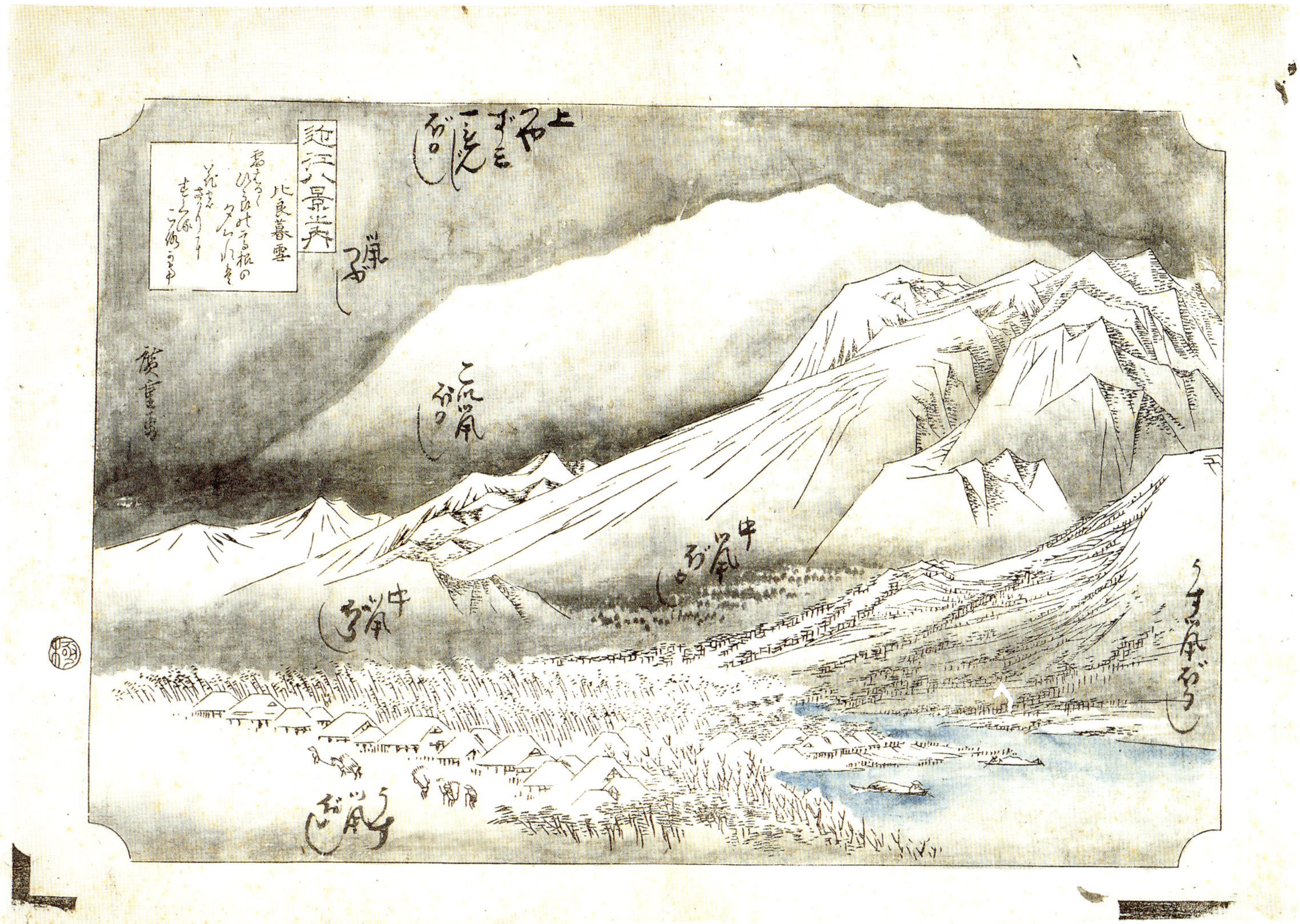

137 A MOUNTAIN IN THE SNOW

Lingering Snow on Mount Hira (Hira no bosetsu)

line-block proof, *c.* 1834

signed: *Hiroshige ga*
censorship seal: *kiwame*
woodblock, *ōban*, 256 x 382 mm
Honolulu Academy of Arts, Honolulu,
Gift of James A. Michener, 1958 (14.241)

A proof of the line-block for the print at cat. 72. The clarity of the lines is remarkable, and the proof shows that the minor blemish on the lower side of the rectangular cartouche containing the poem was present from the outset.

The usual procedure was to make a number of impressions from the line-block. On these proofs the designer indicated which areas were to be printed in which colours, usually taking one proof for each colour. The proofs were then pasted to woodblocks and everything but the coloured parts was cut away. In this way a separate block was produced for each colour. The cutting of these colour blocks thus entailed the destruction of the proofs. The marks necessary to ensure an accurate register were part of the line-block and thus appeared on all proofs; they can be seen here at lower right—a line—and lower left—a right-angle.

The present line-block proof was used by the artist to indicate how he wanted the printer to apply the *bokashi*. The more detailed instructions, which are not in Hiroshige's hand, were apparently added by the printer. These instructions read: '*tsuyazumi itten bokashi*' ('dark black gradation') at the upper edge; '*nezumi bokashi*' ('mouse-grey') in the middle and '*usu nezumi bokashi*' ('light mouse-grey') on the mountain farthest to the right and on the road below. It should be noted that, according to a written communication from Suzuki to the present author, some of the terms used here may not yet have been current in the 1830s.

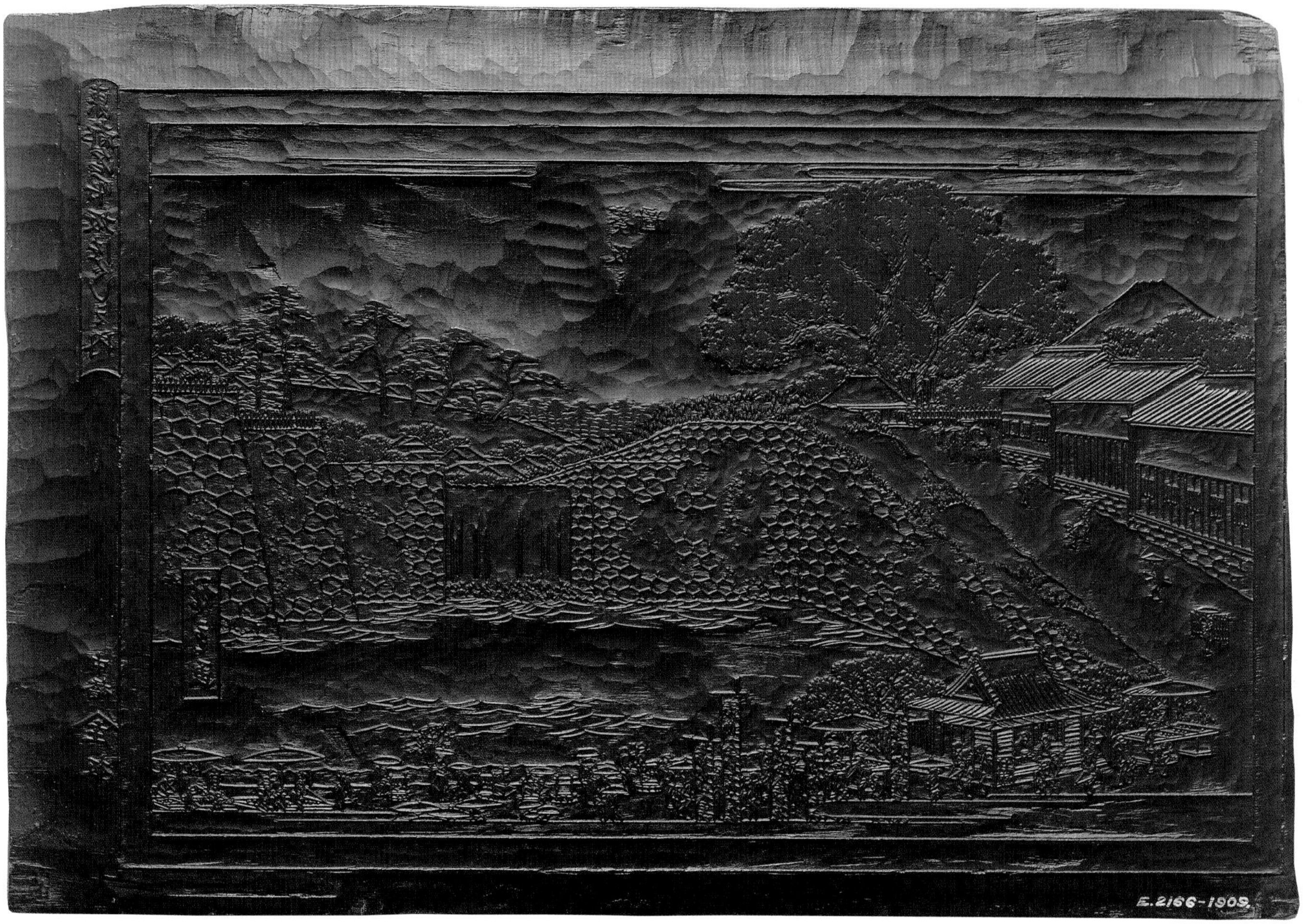

138 A SLOPING ROAD BESIDE THE WATER

A View of Aoisaka (*Aoisaka no zu*)

line-block

signed: *Hiroshige ga*
ōban, 241 x 343 mm
The Board of Trustees of the Victoria and Albert Museum, London (E2166–1909)

This is the line-block for a print from one of Hiroshige's relatively uncommon series devoted to places in Edo, *Famous Views of the Hills and Slopes in the Eastern Capital* (*Tōto meisho sakatsukushi no uchi*), published by Yamadaya Shōjirō *c.* 1842–4. The series consists of ten prints. The Kinpira Shrine in the foreground here affords a prospect of Aoisaka, the road climbing up on the right, and of the water that falls into the canal surrounding the shogun's castle. The scene is enclosed by a decorative border with a repeated gourd motif.

For illustrations of the print, see Sakai, 1996, nos. 659, 660.

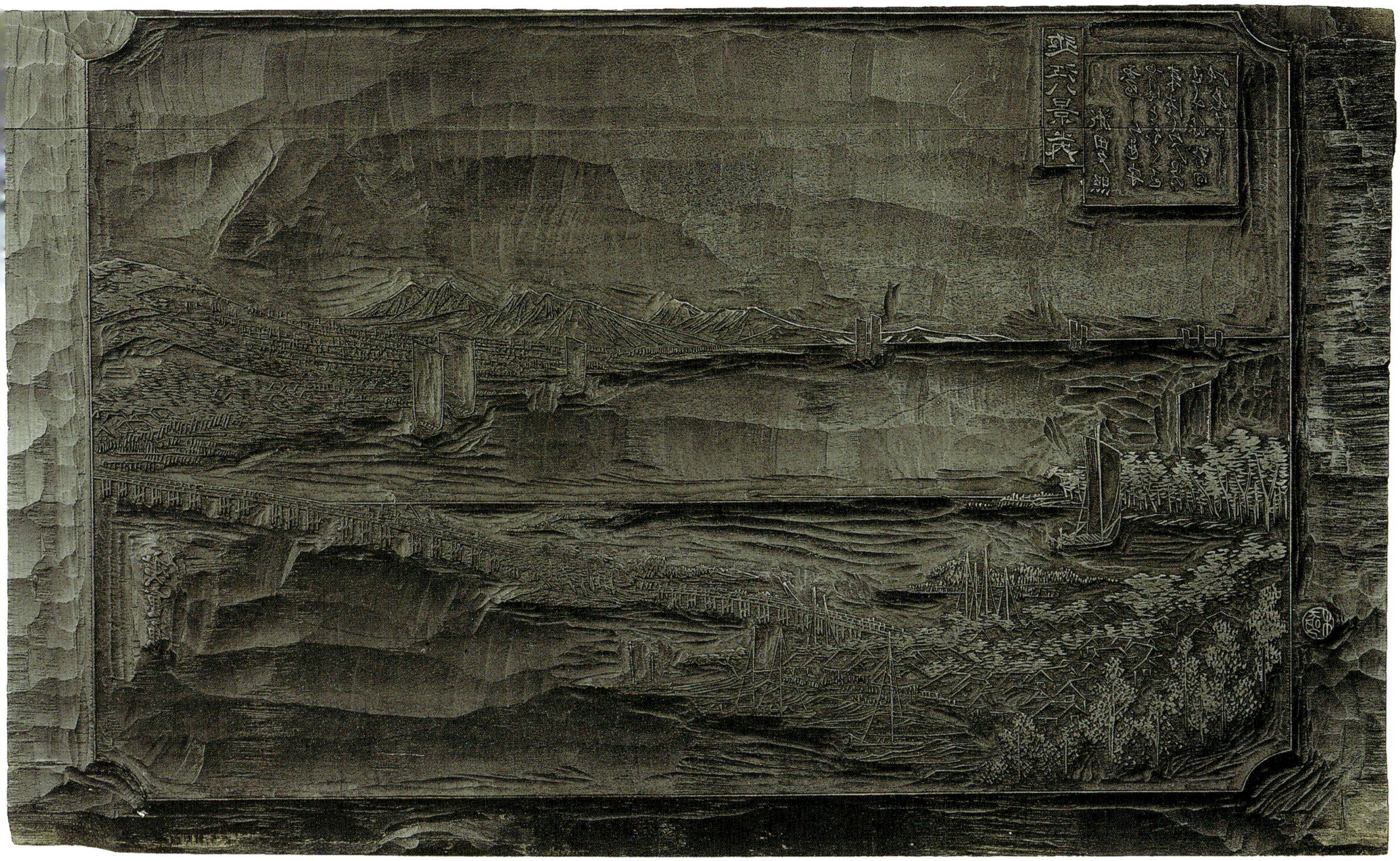

139 VIEW OF A LONG BRIDGE ACROSS A LAKE

Evening Glow at Seta Bridge (Seta no sekishō)

line-block

signed: *Hiroshige ga*
censorship seal: *kiwame*
ōban, 245 x 410 mm
Honolulu Academy of Arts, Honolulu,
Gift of James A. Michener, 1957 (14.108)

The line-block for the print at cat. 70.

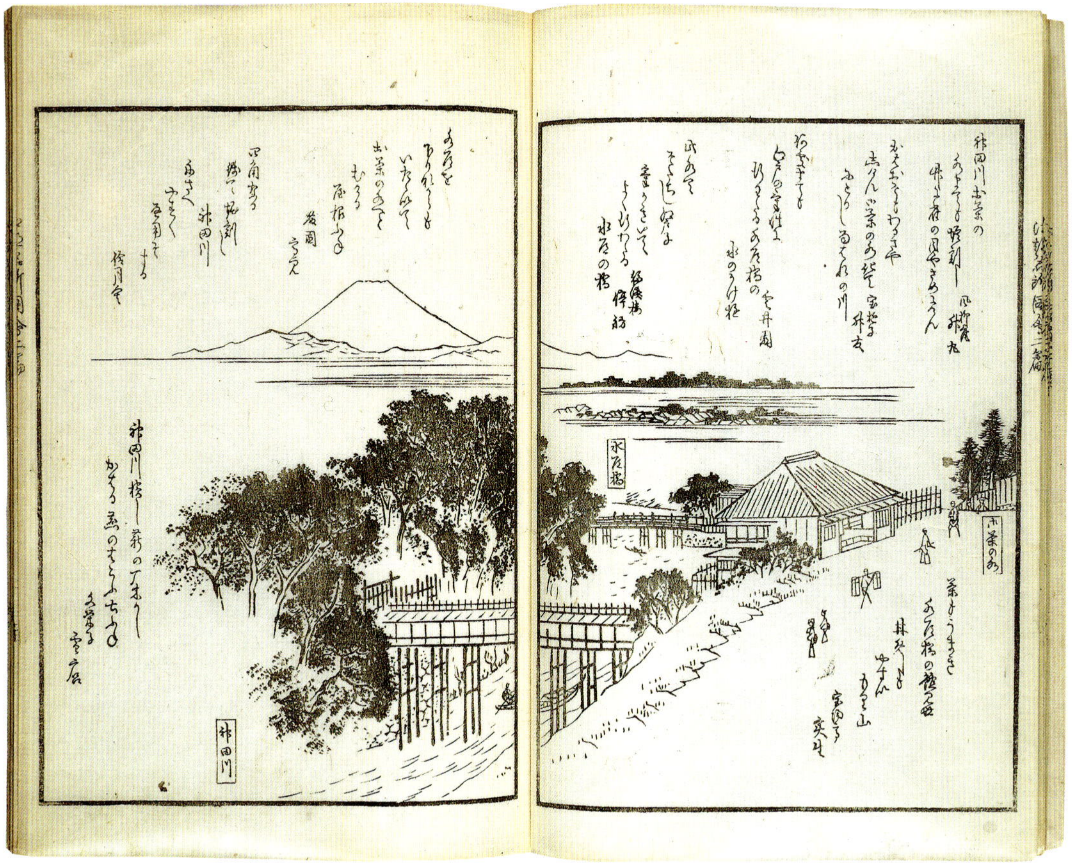

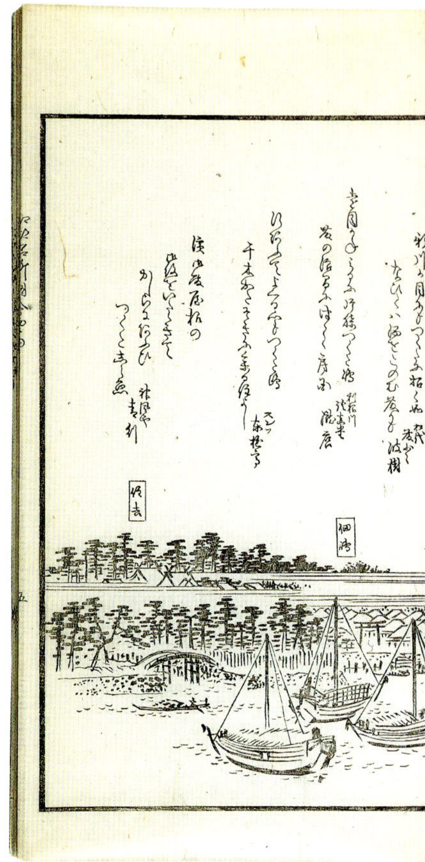

140 A SLOPE BESIDE A RIVER

Ochanomizu, Suidōbashi and Kandagawa

from the sixteen-volume album *Comic Poems and Famous Views of Edo* (*Kyōka Edo meisho zue*)
published privately by Tenmei Rōjin, 1854–6

volume 2, sheets 8b/9a
woodblock, album plate, *hanshibon*, 267 x 178 mm
The Art Institute of Chicago, Chicago,
The Martin A. Ryerson Collection (V-3.8)

A view of the Kanda River with the hill known as Ochanomizu (cf. cat. 11) on the right. The river is spanned in the foreground by an aqueduct and, further up, by Suidō Bridge. Mount Fuji is in the distance.

This album consists of a total of sixteen slender volumes in a large format, all with *kyōka* poems on the famous places of Edo. The first fourteen volumes were illustrated by Hiroshige, the last two by his pupil Hiroshige II.

REFERENCES: Toda, 1931, no. 299 (14 vols.); *Kyōka shomoku shūsei*, p. 104 (6 vols., 1854); *Kokusho sōmokuroku*, 2-487-1

141 BOATS AT ANCHOR OFF AN ISLAND

Tsukudajima and Sumiyoshi

from the sixteen-volume album Comic Poems and Famous Views of Edo (*Kyōka Edo meisho zue*)
published privately by Tenmei Rōjin, 1854–6

volume 4, sheets 4b/5a
woodblock, album plate, *hanshibon*, 259 x 178 mm
The Art Institute of Chicago, Chicago,
The Martin A. Ryerson Collection (V-3.8)

The island of Tsukudajima in the Bay of Edo (cf. cat. 6, 16) with fishing boats lying at anchor. The roofs of the large Sumiyoshi Shrine can be seen above the mist.

REFERENCES: Toda, 1931, no. 299 (14 vols.); *Kyōka shomoku shūsei*, p. 104 (6 vols., 1854); *Kokusho sōmokuroku*, 2-487-1

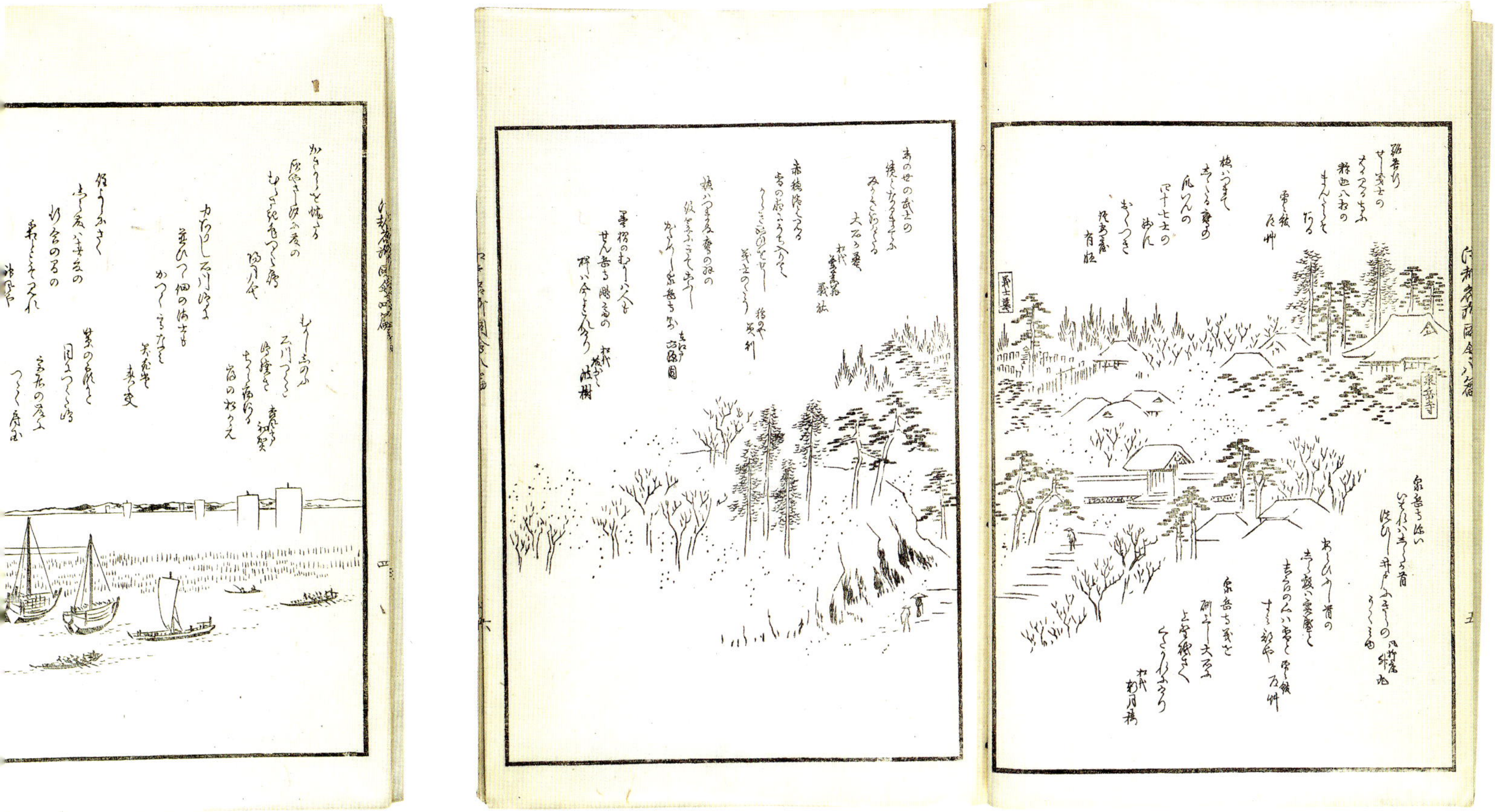

142 A TEMPLE IN THE SNOW

Sengakuji and the Graves of the Loyal Retainers (Sengakuji/gishi no haka)

from the sixteen-volume album *Comic Poems and Famous Views of Edo (Kyōka Edo meisho zue)*
published privately by Tenmei Rōjin, 1854–6

volume 8, sheets 5b/6a
woodblock, album plate, *hanshibon*, 258 x 178 mm
The Art Institute of Chicago, Chicago,
The Martin A. Ryerson Collection (V-3.8)

A view of the large Sengakuji temple complex in the snow. The choice of season probably relates to the fact that forty-seven loyal retainers of Kira Kōzukenosuke committed ritual suicide here on the 14th day of the Twelfth Month in 1703, after avenging the death of their master. Their burial site is the enclosed area in the centre.

The thick layer of snow is depicted with extreme skill in this illustration, which was printed only from the line-block.

REFERENCES: Toda, 1931, no. 299 (14 vols.); *Kyōka shomoku shūsei*, p. 104 (6 vols., 1854); *Kokusho sōmokuroku*, 2-487-1

GLOSSARY

aiban

literally 'medium-large block', a size of paper used for prints that measures approximately 235 x 330 mm

aizurie

a type of print that is restricted to shades of non-fugitive blue

aratame

literally 'examined', the censorship seal that appears on nearly all prints issued from 1853/II to 1871

bokashi

the effect produced by gradation printing. To achieve it, the pigment on the woodblock is partly removed with a moist plug of fabric, resulting in a gradated intensity of the colour as it appears on the print (see cat. 139). If not done meticulously—for example, if a damp cloth is used simply to wipe away some of the pigment—it results in a crude, streaked effect

Buddhism

a doctrine of salvation preached by Buddha in northern India in the fifth century BC. It was introduced to Japan from Korea in the mid-sixth century AD and became a major religion there

censor's seal

a seal applied to prints by publishers appointed by the authorities to enforce censorship regulations. They appear on almost all prints issued from 1843 to 1852/I

chūban

literally 'medium block', a size of paper used for prints that measures approximately 195 x 265 mm

chūtanzaku

literally 'medium narrow block', a size of paper used for prints that measures approximately 390 x 132 mm

colour block

a block used for printing one shade of colour. Colour blocks were cut from the line-block proofs, on each of which the artist marked the areas to be printed in a particular colour

daimyō

a lord in charge of a province, of which there were sixty-eight in pre-1868 Japan. All *daimyō* were answerable to the shogun

date seal

a censor's seal consisting of the zodiacal sign for the year and the number of the month. Date seals appear on almost all prints issued from 1852/II to 1875

geisha

a woman trained in singing, dancing and playing the shamisen (a banjo-like instrument) who, as a 'hostess', earned a living in tea-houses and brothels

gradation printing

see *bokashi*

hanshibon

literally 'half-paper book', a size of book that measures approximately 240 x 165 before, and about 230 x 158 mm after, trimming

haiku

a genre of poems, consisting of seventeen syllables, generally on subjects linked to the seasons

impression

strictly, each sheet printed from the same blocks constitutes an impression. The term is often used loosely to denote each print run from the same blocks; changes to the blocks are then said to result in a different impression, though this is more properly referred to as a different 'state'

kabuki

a popular form of theatre in which the actors do not wear masks; the plays are either contemporary love-stories or heroic historical dramas

kamuro

a courtesan's young servant girl, who herself is trained for a possible future career as a courtesan

kimetsubushi

a technique in which the surface of the woodblock is rubbed down or treated with stiff brushes so that the pattern of the grain is faintly impressed on the print

kiwame

literally 'approved', the censorship seal that appears on almost all prints issued from 1790 to 1842

koban

literally 'small block', a size of paper used for prints that measures approximately 165 x 235 mm

kotanzaku

literally 'small narrow block', a size of paper used for prints that measures approximately 390 x 106 mm

kyōka

a genre of poems, consisting of thirty-one syllables, on diverse subjects, often parodying classical poems

line-block

the block that is cut from the final drawing and used for printing the outlines of a design (cat. 140, 141). The line-block also prints the marks that are transferred from the proofs to the colour blocks to ensure an accurate register of all blocks during printing

nō

the classical form of Japanese theatre, in which the actors wear masks and fine clothing *ōban*

literally 'large block', a size of paper used for prints that measures approximately 265 x 390 mm

ōtanzaku

literally 'large narrow block', a size of paper used for prints that measures approximately 390 x 176 mm

oxidation

a chemical process that takes place when agents in some pigments, especially red and pink, but sometimes also grey, react with oxygen. The resulting change in the printed colour was sometimes deliberately sought after by designers, even though the process was difficult to control

samurai

members of the aristocratic military class serving their *daimyō* and, by extension, the shogun

Shinto

literally 'The Way of the Gods', the pantheistic and partly animistic native religion of Japan

shogun

the military leader of Japan, whose castle was at Edo. Only nominally subservient to the emperor, he was responsible for running the country

surimono

a privately issued presentation print, often of exceptional quality. *Surimono* were usually commissioned by wealthy merchants or poetry clubs to celebrate special events—especially New Year—serving as invitations to dance, theatre or other types of performance; for these reasons they were invariably inscribed with *kyōka* poems or with details of the performance.

tanzakuban

literally 'narrow block', a term denoting various sizes of paper used for prints that measure approximately 390 x 106-176 mm

uchiwa

literally 'fan', a size of paper used for prints that measures approximately 230 x 330 mm

ukiyoe

literally 'pictures of the floating [i.e. fleeting] world', often used as a generic term for Japanese woodblock prints. The fashionable, predominantly urban culture of the 'floating world' was governed by the precept '*carpe diem*' and encompassed paintings, prints and picture albums, its own literature and use of language, and rapidly changing fashions in dress

SELECT BIBLIOGRAPHY

ASANO, 1988

Asano Shūgō, '"Kisokaidō rokujūkyū tsugi" ni tsuite', in *Utagawa Hiroshige botsugo 130-nen Kisokaidō rokujkyū tsugiten*, exhibition catalogue, Tokyo, Riccar Art Museum, 1988

BOGEL AND GOLDMAN, 1988

C.J. Bogel and I. Goldman, *Hiroshige: Birds and Flowers*, New York, 1988

BOWIE, 1975

T. Bowie, *Japanese Drawing*, Bloomington, 1975

COPENHAGEN, 1993

Ukiyo-e: Japanske farvetræsnit bloktrykte bøger og album surimono fra Danske samlinger, exhibition catalogue, Copenhagen, Ny Carlsberg Glyptotek, 1993

EDMUNDS, 1922

W.H. Edmunds, 'The Identification of Japanese Colour Prints I-IV', *Burlington Magazine*, 40-41 (1922)

EDOGAKU JITEN, 1984

Edogaku jiten (Encyclopaedia of Edology), Tokyo, 1984

ENDŌ, 1960

Endō Kintarō, *Hiroshige enikki, 1* (Hiroshige's Illustrated Accounts of his Travels), Tokyo, 1960

FENOLLOSA, 1901

M.M. Fenollosa, *Hiroshige: The Artist of Mist, Snow and Rain*, San Francisco, 1901

FORRER, 1994

M. Forrer, *The Baur Collection: Japanese Prints*, 2 vols., Geneva, 1994

HAMADA, 1973

Hamada Giichirō, *Edo bungaku chimei jiten* (Encyclopaedia of Edo Place Names in Literature), Tokyo, 1973

HAPPER, 1909

J.S. Happer, *Catalogue of the Happer Collection of Japanese Prints*, auction catalogue, London, Sotheby's, 14–18 June 1909

HILLIER, 1965

J. Hillier, *Japanese Drawings from the 17th through the 19th Century*, Boston and Toronto, 1965

HILLIER, 1980

J. Hillier, *Japanese Drawings of the 18th and 19th Centuries*, exhibition catalogue, Washington, D.C., 1980

HILLIER, 1987

J. Hillier, *The Art of the Japanese Book*, 2 vols., London, 1987

HORI, 1996

Hori Kōmei, *Edo kiriezu de aruku: Hiroshige no ō Edo meisho hyakkei sanpō* (Walking the One Hundred Famous Views in Edo on Detail Maps), Tokyo, 1996

IIJIMA, 1941

Iijima Kyōshin (Hanjirō), *Ukiyoeshi Utagawa retsuden* (Biographies of the Utagawa School *Ukiyoe* Designers) (1894), Tokyo, 1941; reprinted 1993

IMAHASHI, 1995

Imahashi Riko, *Edo no kachōga: Hakubutsugaku o meguru bunka to sono hyōshō* (Prints of Flowers and Birds from Edo: The Culture of Natural Sciences and their Representation), Tokyo, 1995

IMAI, 1969

Imai Kingo, *Shōsetsu Edo meishoki* (A Detailed Explanation of the Guide to Famous Places in Edo), Tokyo, 1969

IZZARD, 1983

S. Izzard, *Hiroshige: An Exhibition of Selected Prints and Illustrated Books*, exhibition catalogue, New York, Ukiyo-e Society of America, 1983

KEYES, 1984

R.S. Keyes, *Japanese Woodblock Prints: A Catalogue of the Mary A. Ainsworth Collection*, Oberlin, Ohio, 1984

KOBAYASHI, 1990

Kobayashi Tadashi, *Yomigaeru bi: Hana to tori to — Rokkufueraa ukiyoe korekushonten* (Revived Beauty: Flowers and Birds — Exhibition of the Rockefeller *Ukiyoe* Collection), exhibition catalogue, Tokyo, 1990

KOBIJUTSU, 1983

Jojo gashi Hiroshige gagyoten (Exhibition of Hiroshige), Tokyo, 1983, special issue no. 3 of *Kobijutsu*

KOKUSHO SŌMOKUROKU

Kokusho sōmokuroku (A Comprehensive Bibliography of Japanese Books), 8 vols., Tokyo, 1963–77

KRUML, 1994

R. Kruml, 'Hiroshige: A Shoal of Red Herrings', *Andon*, 49 (1994), pp. 5–41

KYŌKA SHOMOKU SHŪSEI

Suga Chikuhō, *Kyōka shomoku shūsei* (Bibliography of Kyōka Anthologies), Kyoto, 1936

LINK, 1991

H.A. Link, *Prints by Utagawa Hiroshige in the James A. Michener Collection*, 2 vols., exhibition catalogue, Honolulu, Honolulu Academy of Arts, 1991

MATSUKI, 1925

Matsuki Kihachirō, *Ichiryūsai Hiroshige uchiwae tenrankai roku* (Catalogue of an Exhibition of Fan Prints by Hiroshige), Kyoto, 1925

MEIHIN SOROIMONO UKIYOE

Suzuki Jūzō, *Hiroshige I*, Tokyo, 1991, vol. 10 of *Meihin soroimono ukiyoe*
Yamaguchi Keisaburō, *Hiroshige II*, Tokyo, 1991, vol. 11 of *Meihin soroimono ukiyoe*
Yamaguchi Keisaburō, *Hiroshige III*, Tokyo, 1992, vol. 12 of *Meihin soroimono ukiyoe*

MEMORIAL EXHIBITION

Memorial Exhibition of Hiroshige, Tokyo, 1968, vol. 18 of *Ukiyoe geijutsu/Ukiyoe Art*

NAGATA, 1986

Nagata Seiji, *Ukiyoe Yan Buuru korekushon: Hiroshige to kihin* (*Ukiyoe* from the Jan Buhl Collection), exhibition catalogue, Tokyo, 1986

NARAZAKI, 1960

Narazaki Muneshige, *Ukiyoe IV: Hokusai, Hiroshige*, Nihon hanga bijutsu zenshū 5, Tokyo, 1960

NARAZAKI, 1964

Narazaki Muneshige, *Shokoku meisho* (Famous Views in the Provinces), Hokusai to Hiroshige 6, Tokyo, 1964

NARAZAKI, 1975

Narazaki Muneshige, ed., *Hiroshige*, Nihon no bijutsu 104, Tokyo, 1975

NOGUCHI, 1932

Noguchi Yonejirō, *Ichiryūsai Hiroshige*, Tokyo, 1932

ŌKUBO, 1992

Ōkubo Junichi, 'Utagawa Hiroshige no kachōga ni tsuite' (On Hiroshige's Prints of Flowers and Birds), *Museum*, 494/5 (1992), pp. 23-36

POLSTER, 1983

E. Polster, *Hiroshige*, exhibition catalogue, Albuquerque, Albuquerque Museum, 1983

PULVERER, 1990

Doitsu Puruberaa korekushon ukiyoe hanga meihinten (Masterpieces of *Ukiyoe* from the Pulverer Collection), exhibition catalogue, Tokyo, 1990

RAPPARD-BOON, 1984

C. van Rappard-Boon, *Hiroshige and the Utagawa School: Japanese Prints, c. 1810-1860*, Catalogue of the Collection of Japanese Prints [in the Rijksprentenkabinet, Amsterdam] 4, Amsterdam, 1984

SAKAI, 1996

Sakai Gankō, *Hiroshige: Edo fūkei hanga daishūsei* (Great Collection of Hiroshige's Prints of Edo Scenes), Tokyo, 1996

SALAMON, 1992

S. Salamon, *Hiroshige: Notturni*, Turin, 1992

SATŌ, 1994

Satō Hironobu, *Santō meishoeten: Hiroshige egaku Kyō, Naniwa, Edo* (Famous Views of the Three Cities Kyoto, Osaka and Edo), Yokohama, 1994

SCHINDLER, 1985

Shindoraa korekushon ukiyoe meihinten (Masterpieces of *Ukiyoe* Prints from the Schindler Collection), exhibition catalogue, Tokyo, 1985

SHIRAISHI, 1988

Shiraishi Tsutomu, *Hiroshige: Tōkaidō gojūsantsugi* (The Fifty-three Stations of the Tokaido), Tokyo, 1988

SHIRAISHI, 1993

Shiraishi Tsutomu, *Edo kiriezu to Tōkyō meishoe* (Detail Maps of Edo and Famous Places of Tokyo), Tokyo, 1993

SHIRAISHI, 1995

Shiraishi Tsutomu, *Yūyū shōyō Edo meisho* (A Leisure Walk through the Famous Places of Edo), Tokyo, 1995

SMITH AND POSTER, 1986

H. D. Smith and A.G. Poster, *Hiroshige: One Hundred Famous Views of Edo*, New York, 1986

STRANGE, 1925

E. F. Strange, *The Colour Prints of Hiroshige*, London and New York, 1925; reprinted 1973

SUZUKI, 1970

Suzuki Jūzō, *Hiroshige*, Tokyo, 1970

SUZUKI, 1975

Suzuki Jūzō, *Hiroshige*, Taiyō ukiyoe shiriizu 3, Tokyo, 1975

SUZUKI AND ŌKUBO, 1996

Suzuki Jūzō and Ōkubo Junichi, *Hiroshige Rokujūyoshū meisho zue: Puruberaa korekushon* (Hiroshige's Sixty-odd Provinces: From the Pulverer Collection), Tokyo, 1996

TANBA, 1965

Tanba Tsuneo, *Hiroshige ichidai* (The Great Hiroshige), Tokyo, 1965

TODA, 1931

K. Toda, Descriptive Catalogue of Japanese and Chinese Illustrated Books in the Ryerson Library of the Art Institute, Chicago, Chicago, 1931

UCHIDA, 1932

Uchida Minoru, *Hiroshige*, rev. edn., Tokyo, 1932; reprinted 1978

UKIYOE HAKKA, 1984

Hiroshige, Tokyo, 1984, vol. 8 of *Ukiyoe hakka*

UKIYOE TAIKEI

Yamaguchi Keizaburō, *Hiroshige*, Tokyo, 1975, vol. 11 of *Ukiyoe taikei*
Yoshida Susugu, *Tōkaidō gojūsan tsugi*, Tokyo, 1976, vol. 14 of *Ukiyoe taikei*
Kikuchi Sadao, *Kisokaidō rokujūkyū tsugi*, Tokyo, 1976, vol. 15 of *Ukiyoe taikei*
Miyao Shigeo, *Meisho Edo hyakkei*, Tokyo, 1976, vols. 16, 17 of *Ukiyoe taikei*

VIGNIER AND INADA

C. Vignier and H. Inada, *Toyokuni Hiroshigé*, vol. 6 of *Estampes japonaises...*, exhibition catalogue, Paris, Musée des Arts Décoratifs, 1914

WATANABE, 1918

Watanabe Shōzaburō, *Catalogue of the Memorial Exhibition of Hiroshige's Works on the 60th Anniversary of his Death*, Tokyo, 1918

YAMAGUCHI, 1995

Yamaguchi Keizaburō, 'Hiroshige Eisen ga "Kisoji(kai)dō rokujūkyū tsugi no uchi"' (The Kiso Road by Hiroshige and Eisen), in *Hiroshige Eisen shugyoku no meihin ni yoru Nakasendō rokujūkyū tsugi no tabi*, exhibition catalogue, Ōmiya, 1995

YOSHIDA, 1967

Yoshida Susugu, 'Hiroshige to kachōga' (Hiroshige and Prints of Flowers and Birds), *Ukiyoe: A Journal of the Floating World*, 29 (1967), pp. 48-53

YOSHIDA, 1973

Yoshida Susugu, 'Ihan no kōzō' (The Structure of Variant Blocks), *Ukiyoe: A Journal of the Floating World*, 55 (1973), pp. 81-107

YOSHIDA, 1971

Yoshida Teruji, *Ukiyoe jiten* (*Ukiyoe* Encyclopaedia), 3 vols., Tokyo, 1971

LENDERS TO THE EXHIBITION

EIRE

Trustees of The Chester Beatty Library and Gallery of Oriental Art, Dublin

FRANCE

Berès Collection, Paris
Bibliothèque Nationale de France, Département des Estampes et
la Division orientale, Département des Manuscrits, Paris

GERMANY

Collection Pulverer, Cologne

GREAT BRITAIN

The Trustees of The British Museum, London
The Board of Trustees of the Victoria and Albert Museum, London
The British Library, Oriental and India Office Collections, London

THE NETHERLANDS

Rijksmuseum, Rijksprentenkabinet, Amsterdam

SWITZERLAND

Baur Collection, Geneva

UNITED STATES OF AMERICA

The Art Institute of Chicago, Chicago
The Mann Collection, Highland Park, Illinois
Honolulu Academy of Arts, Honolulu
The Newark Museum, Newark
Mr and Mrs Arthur Vershbow, Newton, Massachusetts
The Metropolitan Museum of Art, New York
The Museum of Art, Rhode Island School of Design, Providence

and those lenders who wish to remain anonymous

PHOTOGRAPHIC CREDITS

All works of art are reproduced by kind permission of the owners.

Specific acknowledgements are as follows:

Amsterdam, © Rijksmuseum, Amsterdam, cat. 73, 132

Del Bogart, cat. 19

Chicago, photo © 1997 The Art Institute of Chicago, All Rights Reserved. cat. 9, 18, 23, 27, 28, 40, 50, 76, 79, 98, 103, 119, 120, 134, 140, 141, 142

Copenhagen, © Peter Schandorf, cat. 51, 54, 62

Geneva, © Baur Collection photographs by Marian Gerard, cat. 31, 63, 64, 65, 66, 67, 98, 118

Hawaii, © Honolulu Academy of Arts, photographs by Shuzo Uemoto, cat. 8, 11, 12, 15, 20, 21, 22, 29, 30, 33, 34, 36, 37, 38, 39, 56, 93, 94, 101, 105, 109, 114, 115, 116, 135, 136, 137, 139

London, © The British Museum, cat. 16, 92, 100, 111, 112, 122, 128

London, Courtesy of The Trustees of the Victoria and Albert Museum / photographer Ian Thomas, cat. 75, 80, 85, 90, 138

Newark, The Newark Museum/Art Resource, NY, cat. 77, 78

New York, © 1997 The Metropolitan Museum of Art, cat. 13, 26, 32, 35, 55, 104, 113